AN INTRODUCTION TO THE STUDY OF ORGANIZED LABOR IN AMERICA

THE MACMILLAN COMPANY
NEW YORK · BOSTON · CHICAGO · DALLAS
ATLANTA · SAN FRANCISCO

MACMILLAN & CO., LIMITED
LONDON · BOMBAY · CALCUTTA
MELBOURNE

THE MACMILLAN CO. OF CANADA, LTD.
TORONTO

AN INTRODUCTION TO

THE STUDY OF ORGANIZED LABOR IN AMERICA

BY

GEORGE GORHAM GROAT, Ph.D.

PROFESSOR OF ECONOMICS, UNIVERSITY OF VERMONT; AUTHOR OF
"TRADE UNIONS AND THE LAW IN NEW YORK," AND
"ATTITUDE OF AMERICAN COURTS IN LABOR CASES"

New York
THE MACMILLAN COMPANY
1922

Norwood Press:
Berwick & Smith Co., Norwood, Mass., U.S.A.

PREFACE

The study of labor organization here presented is offered in the hope that it will encourage a more general interest in the subject. That the problems of labor constitute one of the most serious issues of our industrial and social life is a contention that needs no arguing. It is perhaps less generally recognized that these problems center in labor organizations. It is assumed that the American labor problem is the problem of organized labor; that American unions are the embodiment of the aggressiveness, the restlessness, the hopes, the fears and the ideals of American laborers. In accordance with this assumption the accompanying study has been limited to organizations of laborers.

That there is need of a more thorough understanding of these associations is quite evident. The multiplication of courses in colleges and universities, the increase of books, the abundance of discussion in periodical literature all attest a growing interest. The confusion of essentials and the emphasis of non-essentials in much of the writings and public discussion show a need for more systematic study. It is to meet such a need and to encourage such a study that this book is offered.

It is an Introduction to such a study. It does not aim to say the last word on any topic. Any finality would be fatal to the purpose. It hopes to start and not to conclude such study.

It is a Study of these associations. Its aim is to promote discussion — to promote difference of opinion if need be; for there are issues about which intelligent differences of opinion must and should exist.

With this end in view representative opinions have been introduced on various sides of the questions. The desire has been to present these conflicting opinions as frankly and fully as space would allow. Of course the author accepts no responsibility for the views thus presented. Nor does he ask the reader to accept his own views unless they appear reasonable. Since it has not been the author's purpose primarily to present his own views, they have not been given any special prominence. They must come into prominence only as they are borne up by reason and fact.

Much difficulty has been encountered in selecting material. The supply has been so overwhelming and the space so relatively limited that heroic measures were necessary. The selection may or may not appear as the best. Doubtless many will think of things that might have been introduced in place of some that do appear. The choice has involved standards, and as no generally accepted standards exist, the basis has had to be personal choice. While much of the material that has been used is transient and might not have been used a year later, it none the less illustrates the principle involved and so serves its purpose. It will be for the student to substitute new material for himself as new situations develop. By the time these pages reach the public, some of the facts stated may not be true. That is of course inevitable in dealing with such a subject. It is believed, however, that the facts were substantially true at the time of writing.

It may appear to some that undue emphasis has been placed upon a side favorable to the unions, that not enough has been said in criticism of them and in favor of the employers. The author must not be understood as urging a thick-and-thin support of unions, regardless of what they do. He believes that they have a heavy responsibility and shares with many a doubt as to the fullness with which they meet such obligation. He further believes, however, that in public discussion generally the unions do not get a fair and understanding hearing. There is no danger at present of their cause being presented too favorably or of readers being too much prejudiced in their favor. Were this not so, this study might be open to the charge of laying too much emphasis on the favorable side of unionism. Under the circumstances, with the sources of information that are most easily accessible to students and readers, it is not believed that any favorable emphasis made in these pages will pass entirely unchallenged by ideas and impressions with which the reader will already be abundantly supplied.

The main divisions into which the study falls appear to be quite natural. The first part should not be understood to be in any sense a history of the organized labor movement. The struggles of the past, however, have left so deep an impression upon the unionists of to-day that it is quite impossible to understand their spirit apart from the trials of earlier days. The union man may not be an historian, but he knows the important experiences of the past so far as his class is concerned.

It is believed that there is a lack of clear understanding as to the extent to which organization has been carried. Many are surprised upon first learning of so complete and so intensely practical an organization and interrelation of the parts of the movement. For this reason a description has been attempted that will cover the essential points and bring into prominence the elements that reveal the character and working of the structure of the associations.

The field from which supplementary material may be gathered is so wide, the material itself is so varied in value and much of it is so transient that no attempt has been made to include any comprehensive list of references. In a separate section will be found suggestions for further readings along the lines treated in the several chapters.

It may seem to some that more references should have been given in the text and that footnotes should have been used more extensively. The author has thought best to keep the pages of an Introductory Study free from the interruptions of such references. In all cases where authorities could be definitely stated, they are named in the body of the text. It is not assumed that the material is so new or unusual that critics will wish to verify it. Moreover, the sources are so widely scattered and many of them so transient that they are not ordinarily available.

The author's incentive for getting together the material has come from a variety of sources — college instructors, employers, labor leaders, warm friends and warmer enemies of the labor movement. To the active-minded students in his classes who have tried to get at the truth and the right of things and to form a habit of open and fair mindedness the author is more indebted than he can tell.

GEORGE GORHAM GROAT.

BURLINGTON, VERMONT,
  April, 1916.

TABLE OF CONTENTS

PART I

THE BACKGROUND

PART II

THE STRUCTURE

PART III

COLLECTIVE BARGAINING

INTRODUCTION

"This that they call the organization of labor is the universal vital problem of the world." — *Carlyle*.

"Do not let anyone mislead you into the belief that the day of the union is over. It is not over. It is the very foundation upon which the whole superstructure of individual liberty will one day be reared." — *Kier Hardy*.

"The labor movement is the labor question, and the labor question, concretely stated, is the effort of wage-workers to secure a higher standard of living. It is their struggle upward. How to secure the ends for which the struggle is instituted is probably the great question of the day." — *Carroll D. Wright*.

"A long study of the history of labor has convinced me that trade unions are not only the best friends of the workmen, but the best agency for the employer and the public, and that to the extension of these associations political economists and statesmen must look for the solution of some among the most pressing and the most difficult problems of our own time." — *Thorold Rogers*.

Motto: "I am not defending; much less denying; I am explaining."

Any study of organized labor must recognize at the outset two serious difficulties. The first grows out of the very large number of activities to be taken into account and the necessary limitation of space that is imposed by a written description. This necessitates selection and rejection. To make these choices some standards must be adopted and standards are very largely matters of personal judgment. What to include and what to omit is quite as difficult to decide as it is to determine how to deal with the topics selected.

The second difficulty grows out of the fact that these organizations are living, acting and therefore changing. This fact greatly increases the burden of an undertaking that would, even otherwise, be far from easy. Changes at times are rapid as well as unexpected. Many are trivial, of secondary importance only;

xi

while some are of prime significance. Because of this, any description must soon become out of date as far as details are concerned. It is believed, however, that there are some principles that are relatively abiding; that there are some elements that are permanent enough as well as significant enough to warrant an effort to reduce them to a more concrete expression through detailed description. The details will change, possibly before these pages find their way to the reader; yet the principles cannot change quite so soon. The details, believed to be accurate at the time of writing, may serve to give life and reality to the more fundamental elements.

To those who follow through the pages of this book some introductory explanation may be helpful. It has been the writer's purpose to assist the reader in gaining a comprehension of what the organized labor movement is. It is with this aim in mind that the material has been arranged.

The movement should first be seen against its background, giving at the same time a sense of historical perspective and an industrial setting in current business organization. Both of these are essential to enable one to catch the spirit that animates this movement.

That the spirit must be embodied in some concrete form is of course evident. Yet these forms of organization are not so well understood as they should be. The perfection and detail of organization is often overlooked or given but slight attention. For this reason a description of current forms of association as types has been given somewhat in detail. It is hoped that the description is sufficiently concrete, and no more than sufficiently so, to present a picture of the organs through which union purposes are sought to be realized.

By far the most important phases are the activities themselves. Here the process of selection and rejection has of necessity been most extensively applied. Of the many lines of interest that have engaged the attention of the unions and led to action, those that have seemed most important in themselves and best illustrative of the spirit and purposes of unionism have been included. It is a matter of regret that others could not be added to the list here chosen. The division of these activities, as it will appear, seems to fall quite naturally into two parts: industrial and political. If more space had been allowed for describing the benefit and insurance features it would have been quite justifiable to put this description into a third separate division. As the topic has been treated with relative brevity, it has been thought best to include it as a part of industrial activity, or a phase of collective bargaining.

By no means would any discussion be in the least adequate that did not take account of transitional movements. That these are present no one will doubt. Toward what they may be leading cannot with any certainty be predicted.

Doubtless the study will appear to some as all too limited in its scope. Of such an objection the author has already expressed in part his view. Many other topics might have been included. But it is held that the labor movement today in all of its essential elements is the movement of *organized* labor. The power of combination is today so great that nothing of the proportions of a movement can develop among the unorganized, large though these are in numbers. The interests of these dissociated groups or masses are intimately connected with what associations are doing. Individual laborers may be counted, described, classified and tabulated (and all would be both interesting and profitable), but as individuals they do not and cannot constitute the labor movement. It is safe to say that the American labor movement of today is an organized movement and the labor organizations are its embodiment. For these reasons many topics have been omitted that otherwise might have been included.

Even the most enthusiastic admirer of these unions will not escape without finding something to criticize or to disapprove. It is expected that the most positive opponent will find something of which he must approve. Trade unions would not be human organizations if they did not have that usual mixture of good and bad that characterizes all human activities. The day has passed when either blind admiration or blind condemnation can be tolerated. From the present temper of public opinion it appears that there is rather less danger from the former than from the latter in many quarters so far as labor unions are concerned. Let no one adopt the attitude of setting out to see what labor unions are doing and proving that they are wrong.

Finally it may be said that the author's purpose has been to start the study of the organized labor movement, not to conclude it. Nothing in these pages is to be regarded as final. Opinions on questions of such vital importance are always stimulating. Many opinions have been stated; opinions of those entitled to speak with some authority on both sides of disputed issues. To these have been added the author's views scattered throughout the discussion. The author does not accept responsibility for the views of others. Nor does he ask the reader to accept his own as necessarily final. Of the value of them all the reader will judge for himself after giving all sides a hearing.

Opinions will change. Conditions will not remain the same. The issues to be fought out will be altered from time to time. The one abiding fact is the human struggle upward. This generation and the next must witness this conflict centered around the struggle of the laboring classes, those who work with their hands. The organized effort among these laborers is today the labor problem of America.

SUGGESTIONS FOR FURTHER READINGS

Parts I and II. For the historical part of the work a supplementary knowledge may be secured from any or all of the many standard industrial histories of England and America.

Among the English works are particularly Webb, The History of Trade Unionism; Rogers, Six Centuries of Work and Wages; Unwin, Industrial Organization in the Sixteenth and Seventeenth Centuries.

Among those for the United States are: Documentary History of American Industrial Society (Commons and others, Editors); Powderly, Thirty Years of Labor (1859–1889); Trant, Trade Unions — Their Origin and Objects, Influence and Efficiency; Wright, Industrial Evolution of the United States.

For Wage Theories: Haney, History of Economic Thought; Gide and Rist, History of Economic Doctrines.

For Modern Industrialism, it is a matter of reading current descriptive industrial literature together with observation.

For specific studies in the historical and descriptive field there are valuable detailed sources. Johns Hopkins University Studies in Historical and Political Science; Columbia University Studies in History, Economics and Public Law; University of California Publications in Economics; Publications of the American Economic Association, and other learned societies in the field of the social sciences; Bulletins of the United States Bureau of Labor Statistics; bulletins of some of the state departments of labor, particularly of New York and Massachusetts; many interesting historical and descriptive articles in the various economic and other periodicals.

For the structure of unions the material is more widely scattered. Hollander and Barnett, Studies in American Trade Unionism, is the one large collection. Other important detailed studies may also be found in the several series named above and in the economic periodicals. Both the Massachusetts and the New York departments publish at intervals directories of the trade unions of the country. The constitutions of the various unions furnish descriptions of their organization.

Parts III, IV and V. In this field the literature is still more widely scattered. Government publications and periodical literature furnish the main sources. Much may be taken from trade union literature, a wide field of variable value. Trade union journals, employers' publications, proceedings of conventions, legislative enactments, commissions of investigation, discussions before learned bodies, and — most important of all — the things that are being done, a part of the news of the day, are the sources to which the reader must go to secure the information desired. These are not anywhere very fully indexed and so they are not very easily available. There are, however, the helpful Pool's Index and the Readers' Guide, aids to the finding of material that may be found in any library. These open up the periodical literature better than any other single aid. Other sources of information are matters of observation and interpretation and these are open to all.

In general it may be said that aside from the historical parts, the sources that are of real significance are very transient. Topics of to-day give way to others of to-morrow. To know the movement the student must keep abreast of the changes, and this cannot be done by tying up to any fixed and unchanging list of references.

PART I

THE BACKGROUND

AN INTRODUCTION TO

THE STUDY OF ORGANIZED LABOR IN AMERICA

CHAPTER I

BEGINNINGS IN ENGLAND

A Wage-Earning Class. — The problems of organized labor did not originate in modern times. While current conditions determine largely their specific nature, the beginnings are to be found only by tracing the lines of development far back into industrial history. The movement toward organization followed inevitably upon the difficulties connected with wages and these in turn arose with the beginnings of a wage-earning class. The rise of this class was slow and irregular extending over more than a century of changing industrial conditions.

In Agriculture. — The division of function came first in agriculture and was connected with the passing of the serfs and villeins into a free tenant class. Payment of rent in money rather than in labor arose out of the conditions of manorial lords who were so generally in need of cash. Within the free tenant class a subdivision began to appear; the more industrious and frugal becoming small farmers and those less able to adjust themselves to the demands of the newer situation became agricultural laborers, having small patches of land of their own in some cases but not enough to support themselves nor to occupy their entire time in labor. These cottars and poorer villeins hired out their services to their more successful neighbors, thus beginning the development of a class who lived more and more upon wages paid them for labor performed for and under the direction of others.

The changes here so briefly stated took place in England very gradually and were closely associated with the many other modifications of feudalism during the thirteenth and fourteenth centuries. The manorial lords and greater barons were commuting the primitive forms of feudal dues in the form of payment in services into money payments such as rents and taxes. This finally led to the more complex relations of the later mediæval and early modern periods.

Customary Wage. — That troubles early arose over the amounts offered and those demanded as wages there is plenty of evidence. Yet it is altogether probable that so far as possible custom and precedent were relied upon to determine what sums should be paid. But the new situation was not to be met entirely with the aid of established custom and therein were the beginnings of difficulty. A readjustment to the new phases probably would have been made in course of time without much disturbance had it not been for the series of famines and plagues that came during the early years of the fourteenth century. These disasters created a scarcity of labor under the new conditions and thus gave those who survived a real advantage in demanding an increase in compensation. The matter reached a climax with the Great Plague of 1348 when scarcity of numbers gave the laborers such an advantage that they demanded greatly increased pay for their labor. The difficulties arising out of demands for increase over the customary wage resulted in a new public policy. The Great Plague marked the beginning of the attempt to define and regulate the income of the laboring class throughout the realm as a whole.

Money Wage. — With the use of money in payment for services it became easier for the wage earner to leave his "customary" place of work; and by payment of the small fine imposed as an ancient feudal right he could go out into a wider market to seek work. These changes resulted in great advantage to the laborers, increasing their wages probably from twenty to fifty or sixty per cent and the increase stood for a long period. It did not come without resistance, however. Prior to the Great Plague wages had been subject to local regulation through manorial or guild authority. The situation was now such as to be entirely beyond the control of these local officials. Edward III in 1349 issued a proclamation ordering that no laborer should demand and no person should pay wages higher than the rate customary before the plague. Parliament in the following year enacted the requirements of this proclamation as the Statute of Laborers, the first of a series of laws in which matters of wages and hours of labor were dealt with. Thus the segregation of a class of wage earners had become so real and so important by the middle of the fourteenth century that it first became, what it continued for centuries to be, the subject of regulation and control by King and Parliament.

Other Industries. — This movement in agriculture was accompanied by one in many respects similar in other lines of industry and which overlapped the former one in time. Artisans, such as shoemakers, copper and iron smiths, carpenters, weavers, workers in glass and pottery, must have been necessary from a much earlier period. These were not in the earlier stages wage earners. They worked in guilds where the relations were quite unlike those of laborers and their employers. The guilds had become influential organizations and their regulations were often oppressive to the expansion of industry and its development along new lines. For several reasons, among which was the tyranny of the guilds, the manufacturers removed their establishments from the larger guild towns to smaller villages where such organizations did not exist. Liberated thus from their control the master was free to organize as he might choose and as a result a combination and division of labor was effected along new lines. This new system was not that of the earlier days but as Gibbons describes it "the germs of the modern system were there; . . . a system of congregated labor organized upon a capitalist basis by one man — the organizer, head and owner of the industrial village — the master clothier." The effect of the Great Plague on wages was marked in this line of labor also. Carpenters, masons and others secured increases in about the same rate while their masters joined with the agricultural employers in the protest that led King Edward to issue his proclamation of 1349.

Proclamation and Laws. — Just how well the provisions of this regulatory act were enforced seems not entirely clear. Differences of opinion indicate that the problem existed and that it grew directly out of the conditions and the difficulties of the labor market. There is satisfactory evidence that the laboring classes were generally in good condition during the fourteenth and fifteenth centuries. With small plats of land of their own to till they were able to supplement the returns of their vocations, and such avocations doubtless enabled them to live very comfortably. By the time of Elizabeth's reign conditions were changing. Enclosures and other methods of adding small parcels of land to the larger estates took away from the wage laborer his means for supplementing his income. Sheep raising required a less number of laborers than the raising of agricultural crops. This threw many out of employment and at the same time took from them their only means of self-support. Unemployment became a real difficulty. Wages naturally fell. At the same time prices of necessities were rising. Poverty and distress challenged attention. This it received, leading to two laws of unusual importance. The Elizabethan Poor Law was an attempt to deal in a national way with the conditions of distress. The Statute of Laborers of 1563 was aimed at the wage problem. By this latter measure public control was again exercised over wages, but this time not directly by Parliament. The justices of the peace for each locality were empowered to fix the amounts that should be paid. As these officials were generally either employers themselves or of the same class it was natural that those employing labor should exercise undue influence over wages. The extent to which this statute was effective is a subject of some dispute. Gibbons sums up the controversy by asserting that "it certainly seems to be the case that, in spite of the continued increase in the price of the necessaries of life, the wages of labor did conform to the justices' assessments and that these assessments were too low to give the laborer an opportunity of really comfortable subsistance." To this he adds that "there can be no dispute that, whether owing to the assessment or not, wages steadily declined in the sixteenth and seventeenth centuries, taken as a whole." This statute remained in force for more than two hundred years and the laborers' wages were thus subject to control during that period. By the beginning of the eighteenth century the laborers' condition had become one of poverty and distress to no small degree.

This policy of control of wages had its natural outcome in the necessity for some form of relief work as a supplement to the wages thus arbitrarily fixed. In 1722 the relief thus made necessary was limited by law to those only who would enter the workhouses. This provision remained in force for about three-quarters of a century, a period in which at least two if not three generations lived their lives as working men. In 1795 the law was repealed and the older plan was revived. Any poor person could receive aid at his house. During the period of high corn prices and heavy taxation wages were not increased proportionately and the justices of the peace were of necessity very generous in their allowances from the rates. Relief of this character was very general from the beginning of the nineteenth century to well beyond the quarter-century mark. Often the amounts thus granted in relief exceeded the sums paid as wages.

Such were in brief the antecedents and such the conditions of the wage-earning classes in England at the time of the Industrial Revolution. Out of the events of that period came a new relation, a new view and a new activity. There began the struggle for organization of a type that would more effectively meet the new demands.

BEGINNINGS OF ORGANIZATION

Three facts may be named as accountable for the organization of laborers. One is the sweeping changes in all branches of industry that constituted the Industrial Revolution. Another is the opposition that laborers met in their efforts to improve the conditions of living during the period of a century prior to this time. A third is the effects of the wars for colonial expansion in which England was engaged. The changes of the Industrial Revolution were too numerous for discussion here. Suffice it to say that the living of wage earners was deeply affected, so much so as to change quite entirely their mode of life and their outlook for the future. The efforts to improve conditions had been attended by disturbances often of a serious nature and had been opposed by the superior influence of employers, by the power of Parliament and by the force of long years of precedent during which it had come to be held that combination to affect wages was illegal. The wars had been desperately fought, drawing heavily upon the resources of the kingdom. They were followed with heavy debt, consequent high taxation with a tax system not adapted to the conditions, disbanded armies of men who had lost the habit of industry while in the service, a large amount of unemployment, deep poverty and distress among the poorer classes, abnormally high prices for the necessaries of life. In domestic relations England had paid heavily for her successes in foreign fields. Thorold Rogers rates the latter part of the eighteenth century and the first of the nineteenth as a time in which the conditions of the working classes sank to as low an ebb as at any time during the six hundred years included within his study.

The Guilds. — Some confusion as to the origin of permanent labor organizations has prevailed owing to a suggested connection between them and the guilds of the earlier period. In fact there has been prevalent a popular impression, assumed rather than reasoned, that the former were the direct outgrowth of the latter. This view may seem at first hand a natural one as there are so many points in common in the two organizations. The first authoritative statement on this subject was by Brentano in 1870 when he suggested that the guild was the predecessor of the union, though not tracing a direct connection between them. Howell reproduced Brentano's account and gave general credence to the opinion that trade unions originated in some manner, not clearly described, from craft guilds. The subject has been more recently and more thoroughly examined by the Webbs in their History of Trade Unionism and also by Unwin. The Webbs especially undertake at some length to show that Brentano's account is misleading. Prior to the beginning of the eighteenth century, they claim, there was in England nothing that partook sufficiently of the nature of a permanent organization to be characterized as a union in the sense in which that term is used by them. Such organizations as are recorded in the annals of mediæval town life seem to have been occasional and only for the purpose of securing some specific end. As the occasion for the association passed it was broken up, not to be brought together again until some new occasion arose. They were transient, and while they may have served to teach important lessons in the value of such activity the movement of the present day could never have become what it is had only such methods continued. The craft guilds were so unlike modern trade organizations, as the Webbs insist, that it would be as reasonable to call labor unions the successors of craft guilds as it would to claim such a relation for capitalist syndicates, employers' associations, boards of factory inspection or school visitors. In the guild system the master craftman was the practical administrator and dominant influence. The typical guild member was not wholly, or even chiefly, a manual worker. He performed many of the functions of an entrepreneur, such as supplying capital, knowledge of markets, both of raw material and finished products. One will at once recognize, as the Webbs insist, that these are not characteristics of modern unionism. The conclusion of the Webbs after their exhaustive study of all available material is that, while a more complete examination of unpublished material might possibly disclose a series of fraternities among journeymen, yet there has been brought to light no evidence of any permanency of association among the wage earners against their employers during the middle ages. Such associations as did continue an existence for any considerable period were so closely connected with masters or employers as to lack the essential elements that so prominently characterize the unions of to-day. Finally the Webbs assert "with some confidence that in no case did any trade union in the United Kingdom arise, either directly or indirectly, from a craft guild." They have not "been able to trace the slightest connection between the slowly dying guilds and the upstarting trade unions." Unwin asserts that the attempts to bring these two different forms of association into historical relation "have a sound instinct behind them." Yet the guild, he says, is to be regarded not as the parent of the trade union but the ancestor, as it was the ancestor of other industrial forms. The two "were separated by centuries of development and the earlier was dead before the latter were born." In summing up the evolution from the one to the other the stages through which the development passed are journeymen, rise of small masters, beginning of industrial capitalism, emergence of organized wage earners.

The Causes. — As has already been stated, the Industrial Revolution furnishes the background for the development of the movement. Changing relations between all parts of industry characterized this period. Yet it is manifestly too broad to state that the Revolution was the cause of the formation of labor unions and leave the matter there. More specific causes must be found and stated, as they are essential to the understanding of union activity in modern times. As stated above the craft guilds may be accepted as "sociological antecedents" and journeymen's fraternities as more immediate "prototypes." Accepting these as true relations, and coming more closely to consideration of real causes, the first to note is the increasing division of function and the separation of the more skilled, more energetic, more daring into groups that divided the industrial operations between them. Each became more proficient in the branch of work in which experience showed him to be best qualified, whether in manual labor, superintendence, buying material, selling the product, assembling the factors, or opening newer opportunities. This soon developed a situation very unlike the old régime in which the apprentice as a matter of course became the journeyman, and he in turn equally as a matter of course became a master having under his direction and intimately associated with him other apprentices and journeymen, who in turn would make the same progress in their station. In the older order the way was open to practically all workingmen to move up to the higher stations as age and experience counted in their favor. Specialization and subdivision of function closed the door to this series of changes. Added to this there was the growing need for capital in larger sums. As the industries were expanding with the increasing activities of this remarkable period, more and better machinery and tools were necessary, a larger supply of raw material, a greater stock of finished goods. All of this required money in far larger quantities than the ordinary small master could supply from his own store or secure with his limited credit. Those who failed at this point had but one way open to them. That was to drop back into the ranks of the skilled workmen who hired their services to their more energetic or more fortunately situated companions. The one fact that stands out in greatest prominence from these developments was that those who were workingmen or artisans must in large numbers remain such while only a few could take advantage of the chances for betterment through the developing opportunities of capitalism. With the slow recognition of this new limitation, this closing of the door of larger opportunity to so many, came a feeling of restlessness, of dissatisfaction with the conditions themselves. They were tolerable so long as they were stepping stones to better things. Without this prospect, the outlook was not so encouraging. Shut off from the ways that had been opened to their ancestors for generations, and thrown back upon themselves, a feeling of common disappointment soon came to be a binding tie that brought them together in groups for discussion and commiseration. This stage in the development marks the most important crisis in the slow formation of the new order. The bulk of the workers had ceased to be independent producers controlling their own material, processes and activities. Not alone had they become wage earners and wage earners only; they must remain such.

With every opportunity for meeting, the members of this new class came into a fuller consciousness of the inevitableness of the changes and of the consequences that must follow to themselves and their families. These meetings form secondary causes that must be added to the list. They were frequent. Many of them were merely incidental. Others may be looked upon as having a purposefulness connected with them. Groups often came together for reasons purely social. The "social pint" was the incentive for many a gathering and it was not long before conversation quickened by the cheer of the occasion turned upon the topic that must have been uppermost in the minds of all. The prospects; the new employers; the new regulations and systems of control; these certainly did not fail to receive attention. Parliament had for a long time been the protector of this class. Petitions had often been submitted and had led to relief. This new situation was certainly one of sufficient importance to form the subject of a petition. Such petitions must be drawn up and signed, and in the doing of this the assembly was again brought into a realization of the importance of common action. Petitions once presented must often be followed up by some form of agitation. The adoption of certain public houses by particular trades as headquarters where members of the trade would gather for purposes of society and also for information as to places for work became exchanges for information and discussion. The adoption of plans for sick and funeral benefits and for the relief of tramping workmen still further contributed to the common consciousness. When trouble was acute the strike was an old weapon and it was used. It could not be brought into effect without further realization of the common interests. Thus every opportunity for assembly became in a sense a cause of organization in that it quickened and deepened the feeling that resistance to the reduction of wages and dependence upon the employer must be offered through some organized activity if it was to be effective. It has been stated that many of the small masters not being able to command the increased capital necessary for continuing in that capacity were forced to drop back to the dependent class. This small master was a man of vigor and initiative or he would not have been a master at all. To him the lost opportunity came hardest and doubtless it was under his leadership that the new associations were formed and guided. He possessed considerable independence and strength of character. He possessed much skill and had known a high standard of life. He was of the new class, the one who had been the most prosperous and the one to whom the new régime came as the hardest blow. From such came the leadership necessary for the new movement. If anything was lacking to force this consolidation it appeared in due time in the attitude that was taken by Parliament. More and more this body had come under the influence of the new trading class. It was exercising its influence in a nation-wide manner. It now saw fit to adopt a general political policy that would bring all trades into line and protect the new industrialism that had accompanied capitalist expansion. This change of attitude completed the movement. Organizations of laborers were formed in the various trades. The special purpose of these organizations was to oppose the employer in his efforts to secure a cheap labor market and to set up the standard for the long fight for better conditions of labor.

Influence of Inventions. — It is sometimes said that labor organizations came as a result of the inventions of machinery and the development of the factory system. This is not exactly accurate. Machinery and factory were parts of the great change that was taking place and came in common with labor associations but they were not the cause. Organizations of hand labor in some crafts came fully a half century before the factory and its machinery. By the beginning of the eighteenth century the typical journeyman tailor in London had become a lifelong wage earner. One of the earliest permanent unions was among the tailors. There was no association of laborers where the divorce from opportunity had not taken place. The factory system hastened the formation of unions but did not cause it.

PERIOD OF ILLEGAL ORGANIZATION

If the date fixed by the Webbs is accepted, unions of any considerable permanency can be traced no farther back than 1700. From that time forward for over a century the development was very irregular. Troubles arose in various trades at different times and from a variety of causes. These led to controversy, appeals to Parliament, strikes and the formation of an organization that assumed some degree of permanency. Slowly they increased in number. The members came more fully into a realization of a community of interest among the several groups. Loose forms of federation were made and the organizations began to assume the characteristics that determine the modern trade union movement. During the years of the eighteenth century they took different names, showing no comprehensive idea of what the movement was eventually to become. They were known among their members as "institutions," "associations," "trade clubs," "trade societies," "unions," "union societies." None of these names shows any comprehension of the scope of the movement that was to develop in the latter part of the nineteenth century.

Secrecy. — There are in the events of this eighteenth century some facts that are essential to an understanding of the spirit of present day unionism. The most important is the legal status. The history is full of traditions, as the Webbs tell us, of "the midnight meeting of patriots in the corner of the field, the buried box of records, the secret oath, the long terms of imprisonment of the leading officials," all legendary references not without a basis in fact. To understand this situation one must recall the long established precedents for the regulation of wages through government agency. This control extended to all the important relations between the wage earner and his employer, and so far as the letter of the law was concerned they were binding upon both parties. In practice, however, the law was enforced very irregularly. The matter was not regarded seriously when relations were peaceful. The police authority of the government was but poorly developed and there were no public prosecutors who made it their business to enforce the law. Consequently associations of laboring men existed and in many cases no action was taken against them. If, however, they became troublesome to an employer by asking wages above those currently paid in the trade or demanding any other conditions legally under government control, it was an easy matter for him to proceed against them. An appeal to Parliament quite generally led to an act directed against the trade. One must not think that regulation of laborers only was the intention of the law at this early period. It was possible to appeal to this same principle to restrain the employer as well. Cases are recorded where Parliament on petition interfered to prevent an employer from reducing wages below the current rate. Thus not only was the employer checked but the hearing of the petition was a virtual recognition of the existence of a union which in other circumstances might have been proceeded against by parliamentary authority. Of course it may be said that this was not really a recognition of the organization since Parliament received petitions from groups of signers without recognition of any definite organization among them of a permanent character. Yet it does seem clear that though unintentionally this recognition of petition from men generally known to be associated in a peculiar way was virtually a tacit recognition of the existence of that union. So that while in point of law these associations were during the whole century unlawful, in fact they were prosecuted only when their activity led them into some overt illegal act that was particularly troublesome to an employer.

Advantage of Employer. — Even while Parliament seems to have been somewhat lenient with these organizations, the fact must be noted that the employer always had the advantage, even if the law was impartially applied. Industrial conditions during the century were slowly changing so as to give the single employer an advantage over his employees. He employed them in larger numbers as he increased his capital and expanded his business. Thus the employer single-handed was more than a match for his employees single-handed. If one laborer attempted to deal with him unaccompanied by his fellows he could scarce hope to gain his ends, but the employer could without acting in association with anyone discharge his entire force. Besides this there was present that subtle recognition of common interests which early began to effect a tacit understanding among the members of this class. Combinations, even this early, were easier to prove against workmen than against employers. Again, the political atmosphere was not favorable to the growth of these associations. Conditions had been so disturbed during the strife of kings, upper classes and parliaments, that associations of any kind were looked upon with suspicion. It was a political offense that received the name of illegal combination or conspiracy. Employers, so important in the development of England's foreign trade, could carry public confidence. Their employees, however, whose demands would mean a handicap in favor of foreign rivals, could not inspire such confidence. They might be conspirators in disguise. Conditions and experiences at home supplemented by the examples of the Revolution in France, tended to a high degree of caution which easily led to the characterization of all associated activity of journeymen as conspiracy.

General Act of Restriction. — This situation continued until 1799. Prior to that date the legislation referred to was regarded as a part of the general policy of individual regulation applicable alike, in theory, to both employers and their journeymen. The several statutes dealt with particular groups of workmen wherever and whenever the occasion required. In the closing period of the century all these several acts were gathered into one general statute in which all combinations whatsoever were declared illegal. This law was reënacted in an amended form in the following year, and from 1800 for a quarter of a century it stood not simply as a codification of previous acts but as a radical departure from former lines of legislation. Prior to this date it was generally the case that only when there was disagreement between employer and workmen did either party resort to Parliament for the exercise of old-established methods of regulation and intervention. The part played by justices of the peace had grown steadily less, leaving wage agreements to be adjusted practically by bargaining agreements between the two interested parties. With this method becoming general it will be clear that the enactment of a law rigidly prohibiting combinations of journeymen worked a real hardship to this class. A single journeyman could not do more than accept such terms as an employer, eager for profits, pushed by competitors, shrewd and possibly unscrupulous, chose to offer. If such a master offered lower wages than were acceptable, the law made it an offense for all to refuse together. There appears some doubt as to just how rigidly this act of 1800 was enforced. Probably in many instances it was not vigorously administered, as there was no corresponding strengthening of the administrative arm of the government during that period. Even in such a case the associations could scarcely expect to push their activities beyond the point of the "social pint of porter," the provision for sick members, and such as were "tramping" in search of work. Such activities would call forth no serious opposition. But it may readily be believed, as there is evidence in so many cases to show, that the employer would be quick to invoke the law at the slightest appearance of combined resistance to his plans before such opposition became serious. The numerous arrests and imprisonments indicate the revived vigor with which the law was enforced. The feeling of journeymen is echoed by Francis Place who writes of the time: "The cruel persecutions of the Journeymen Printers employed on the Times newspaper in 1810 were carried to an almost incredible extent. . . . No judge took more pains than did this judge on the unfortunate printers, to make it appear that their offence was one of great enormity, to beat down and alarm the really respectable men who had fallen into his clutches and on whom he inflicted scandalously severe sentences." This act of 1800 is described again as "a tremendous millstone round the neck of the local artisan which has depressed and debased him to the earth: every act which he has attempted, every measure that he has devised to keep up or raise his wages, he has been told was illegal: the whole force of the civil power and influence of his district has been exerted against him because he was acting illegally: the magistrates, acting, as they believed, in unison with the views of the legislature, to check and keep down wages and combination, regarded, in almost every instance, every attempt on the part of the artisan to ameliorate his situation or support his station in society as a species of sedition and resistance of the government: every committee or active man among them was regarded as a turbulent, dangerous instigator, whom it was necessary to watch and crush if possible."

LEGALITY ESTABLISHED

Such conditions existed until the noteworthy acts of 1824 and 1825. After the quarter century of such conditions, regarded more and more as intolerable by England's working classes, relief came through the skillful efforts of a small group of active and determined men. Among these the leaders were Francis Place, a master tailor, J. R. McCulloch, at that time editor of a provincial newspaper, the Scotsman, and Joseph Hume, a member of Parliament and a leader in the radical party. The legislation that came as the result of this agitation took permanent form in the act of 1825 and for the first time established for workingmen the right to bargain collectively and withhold their labor by collective action for the purpose of securing better wages and conditions of labor.

It will not be necessary to trace farther the events in England. Up to this point the influence upon the labor movement in America was very direct. In fact, it may be regarded as a part of American development. The legal right to free and open association did not come in England until conditions in the United States became more unlike those across the water. Prior to that time and especially during the long colonial period the law, the precedents, the traditions and the spirit, if not the conditions, were essentially the same in the two countries. These traditions of English law determined the legal attitude in the colonies and later in the commonwealths. The traditions in the minds of laborers, established in generations of experience, determined also the attitude of working classes in the same way. The spirit of organized labor in America to-day is very deeply colored by the knowledge of these past experiences in which leaders are very well versed and upon which they continually draw for material to influence their followers. While one need not look behind the present to find conditions that account very naturally for the existence of antagonism between employer and employee, these do not explain it fully. To the legal opposition of former centuries one must look to explain the extent to which rigid discipline is maintained within the organization and upon all the members, and the arbitrary manner in which laborers are treated who either refuse or are not allowed to become members. To the necessity for a vigorous fighting organization, a present day need, must be added the lessons deeply inculcated through the need for secrecy and all that it implied in rigorous discipline, arbitrary leadership and unquestioning submission to its dictation.

From this brief description it will appear evident that to comprehend the movement of organized labor it is necessary to know something of its beginnings. Despair figured largely in its inception. A fight against the inevitable with the dogged spirit that such a fight engenders marks the beginnings of this struggle and has left its impression upon the spirit of the organization even to the present.

CHAPTER II

BEGINNINGS IN AMERICA

English Influence. — In the first chapter the account related quite entirely to conditions in England. These events are of value in explaining the development of the movement in America as well. It must be remembered that so far as legal precedents and political principles are concerned their effects were practically the same. Experiences of workingmen, stored away and preserved as traditions, were potent in shaping mental attitude. The period of early colonization ran parallel with the economic conditions in England with but little division of labor and less division of industrial functions. There were the guild control, or at least, distinct traces of it; developing commercial activity, both encouraged and controlled by English colonial policy; and the century-old methods of agriculture. Settlers came with habits formed by these activities and views shaped by tradition. Industrial motives, as compared with religious and political, were of greater importance in colonization than has yet been generally recognized. These motives induced large numbers of settlers to come to the new world. During the succeeding century when communication with England was closer and new colonists were continually arriving, the policy of suppression was in vogue in the mother country, culminating in the sweeping legislation of 1799 and 1800 condemning all combinations to affect wages as being "in restraint of trade."

Effects in America. — Here in America the conflict was repeated. Statutes were enacted regulating rates of wages, providing punishment for those who refused to work for the customary wage, and fixing prices of staples. These enactments came just at the breaking up of the period to which they were adapted and were of little if any practical importance in effective regulation. It is doubtful if they were enforced very generally. Their passage, however, indicates that the theory of

government supervision and regulation was still accepted while
in practice there was lax enforcement and a growing tendency
toward more open bargaining. The development in the colonies is an epitome extending over a comparatively brief period
but including all the essential stages of the slower development
in England. In 1648 two guild charters were granted by the
Massachusetts Bay Colony, one to the shoemakers and the other
to the coopers of Boston. These guilds were composed of both
masters and journeymen. Passing through the several stages
that marked the final breaking up of the guilds there evolved
later the subdivision of functions culminating in the different
groups as separate classes organized by themselves: the Society
of Master Cordwainers, the Federal Society of Journeymen
Cordwainers, the United Beneficial Society of Journeymen
Cordwainers, — all within the shoe industry. These stages of
development were determined, as has already been said, by
traditions brought from the home land and were modified in
their detail by the newness of environing conditions in colonial
life, the absence of cumulative precedent with its powerful
binding force as it prevailed in England, the spirit of independence and self-assurance that dominated the settlers, and
the near approach to a feeling of equality that tended to obliterate lines of class distinction. The events of this development,
so far as they are known, have been pieced together by Professor
Commons into a very complete story of the origin and development of the shoe industry in America from 1648 to 1895, in
the first part of which appears the account of the beginnings
of capital activity through the accumulation of stock, the going
out after trade, the organization of the business so as to provide shoes of different grades of workmanship, booking orders
that could not be filled without a differentiation of the labor
in respect of skill and wages, all of which opened the way for
the most aggressive to become entrepreneurs and leaving those
who lacked initiative to become workmen. Closing the account,
the author adds: "Thus have American shoemakers epitomized
American industrial history. Common to all industries is the
historical extension of markets. Variation of form, factors and
rates of progress change the picture but not the vital force.
The shoemakers have pioneered and left legible records. Their
career is 'interpretative' if not typical." Here is repeated the

story of the closing of the door of opportunity to the less efficient, or those least able to keep up with the developments in the expanding industry, and the increasing necessity for them to remain wage earners. The development of the common interests, the meetings at which such interests were discussed, and the beginnings of permanency in associations thus formed are familiar after the events related in the first chapter.

FIRST PERIOD

To sketch in brief the history of organized labor in America is a difficult task. The time has not yet come when the story may be told in its final form. Some further agreement in definition of terms is necessary. There must also be a clearer limitation of periods. New material is being brought to light that reveals new facts or modifies the truth of what formerly has been regarded as settled. The progress of labor's development, however, lies along a path the high points of which may be indicated though the intervening portions may remain for the present in part unrevealed.

Taking the first period of our industrial history as coming to a close with the war of 1812, there were present in the field of labor most of the colonial influences that shaped all phases of industry. Remnants of guild organization, influences from England through the close political ties with the mother country (until the Revolution severed them) and the effects of England's trade policy that continued until the second war, the newness of the settlements, the free public land, the dominating influence of agriculture, the sparse population scattered on the land because of the absence of capital,—all these conditions were instrumental in keeping the population homogeneous and their interests harmonious. In all this situation the differentiation of function had not proceeded to the point where the master and journeyman were of two separate classes. The door of opportunity was still open to the journeyman. By skill, application and initiative he could become a master in his turn. This condition made the journeyman stage an apprenticeship, in fact a stepping stone to a higher economic plane.

Organizations. — In this period there were organizations among laborers, just as there were organizations in other groups.

They had trade interests to protect and the purpose of the association was to protect them. A reduction in rate of wages would not infrequently cause such an association to be formed. Constitutions and by laws were adopted and put into operation. The effort was quite generally turned in the direction of securing what now would be called the "closed shop." At least those societies that have left any trace have done so through this sort of struggle. One of the rules was that members of the society should not work for any master who employed a journeyman not a member of the organization. This policy on the part of these early societies was of course resisted and denounced with vigor, as the records abundantly show.

In this period, then, is to be found a laboring population, with some degree of organization. The laborers had not yet become a class with class-conscious motives. The organization was transient and local. There was no labor movement. Traces of what was later to develop into a movement may, perhaps, be found, and it is the discovery of these traces that probably leads some writers erroneously to speak of this period as "The Inception of the Labor Movement." "Little or nothing was heard of labor organizations in America one hundred years ago," writes Professor Ely, in 1886 in The Labor Movement. "I find no traces of anything like a modern trades-union in the colonial period of American history, and it is evident on reflection that there was little need, if any, of organization on the part of labor at that time."

Early Societies. — Among these early societies, most were formed toward the close of the period. The society of ship calkers, known as the Calkers' Club, existed as early as 1724. Its name would indicate that it was a trade society, but its purpose was in fact largely to control the selection of political officers. It was a political society. Not until the opening years of the nineteenth century did trade societies appear in any number. In 1803 the New York Society of Journeymen Shipwrights was incorporated. In the same city three years later the house carpenters were organized. The same year witnessed the formation of a society of tailors. While the close of this period has been arbitrarily fixed with the war of 1812, the influences continued a few years after the war. In 1819 an association of hatters was organized, and in 1822 the shipwrights organized under the formidable name of Columbian Charitable Society of Shipwrights and Calkers of Boston and Charlestown. This society was chartered by the state legislature in the following year. The compositors of New York were organized in the early years of the century as the New York Typographical Society. The exact date is not known, though Thurlow Weed was elected to membership in 1817.

SECOND PERIOD

The second period of our industrial growth extends from the war of 1812 to the Civil War. In industry its characteristics were the growth of the factory system and the beginnings of the aggregation of capital. This development was influenced on the financial and political side by important developments that have left their permanent impress upon the period, such as the irregularity in banking laws and practices, variation in prices, the differing policies in controlling the public lands, the tariff changes, the extension of the suffrage, and finally the growing importance of the slavery controversy. It was, especially in the first half, an era of active political discussion with great issues of moral reform that touched very intimately the lives of all classes. In this agitation the workers were directly interested and took a very active part.

Moral Awakening. — Efforts to assign definite causes for this period of general moral awakening have met with but partial success. Doubtless many agencies worked together to bring about one of those eras that every people experiences at intervals, a period of awakening moral sense and a more searching examination into existing conditions.

Communism. — The forces of the period were cumulative and did not begin to assert themselves in a noticeable way until about 1825. The situation was favorable to the visit in 1824 of Robert Owen, the manufacturer, philanthropist, reformer and social experimenter, who had already made his influence felt in England and whose fame preceded him to America. He was received with enthusiasm and listened to with thoughtful attention. His plans were adopted by some of his most ardent admirers and American life had its experiences in Communistic settlements. Owen brought a message of universal brotherhood and preached it with great earnestness. Fourierism added to the strength of the current of the movement and led to the two notable experiments; New Harmony, established under the immediate direction of Owen, and Brook Farm, an experiment more directly connected with the teachings of Fourier. In addition to these two there were during the years that immediately followed probably no less than two hundred other settlements in different parts of the country. None of them proved to be long lived. Their influence, however, was more enduring, continuing for a quarter of a century or more. Owen directed attention particularly to the lives of the laboring classes. His experiments were made in their behalf. It was they whom he interested particularly.

The Suffrage. — Another fact of immediate importance in this connection was the general extension of the suffrage at the beginning of the period. The laborer profited most by the change. A new door of opportunity was opened to him.

Thus were brought together the three factors that determined the course of the labor development for the period. The general moral awakening afforded the nourishing atmosphere for the movement. Owen's agitation directed attention to the needs of the workers in particular and to some plans for satisfying these needs. Finally the ballot appeared as the instrument by which these advantages were to be secured.

Various Reforms Advocated. — By no means must it be concluded that the agitation of the period centered about the organization of labor. This was but one of the issues and at first hardly heard of. No period of our history has surpassed this in the number of issues and the amount of discussion called forth. The period, says Professor Commons, "far outran the other periods in its unbounded loquacity," in which "a medley of movements" were topics for discussion. "It was the golden age of the talk-fest, the lyceum, the brotherhood of man—the 'hot air' period of American history," with Robert Owen the inspirer and Horace Greeley its "prophet," the "Tribune of the People."

This is not the place to enter upon a discussion of the reforms inaugurated during this interesting period of American history. Yet a brief recital of some of them shows the scope of the agitation. In addition to slavery there were woman's suffrage, mechanics' lien, reform of the militia system, shorter hours of work, abolition of imprisonment for debt, exemption laws, land reforms, a general bankrupt law, free schools, abolition of lotteries and the auction system.

Prices. — It was with this background of development that labor organizations were supported in this period of their history. A situation more immediately affecting their progress was the change in prices and the variable prosperity of the period. The editors of the Documentary History of American Industrial Society attach such importance to these that the periods are divided with reference to them. "Each upward turn of the curve of prices points to a period of business prosperity, each pinnacle is a commercial crisis, and each downward bend is an index of industrial depression. During the time when the level of prices is rising, employers generally are making profits, are multiplying sales, are enlarging their capital, are running full time and overtime, are calling for more labor, and are able to pay higher wages. On the other hand, the cost of living and the hours of labor are increased, and workmen, first as individuals, then as organizations, are impelled to demand both higher wages and reduced hours. Consequently, after prices are well on the way upward the 'labor movement' emerges in the form of unions and strikes, and these are at first successful. Then the employers begin their counter-organization, and the courts are appealed to. The unions are sooner or later defeated, and when the period of depression ensues, with its widespread unemployment, the labor movement either subsides or changes its form to political or socialistic agitation, to ventures in coöperation or communism, or to other panaceas. This cycle has been so consistently repeated, although with varying shades and details, that it has compelled recognition in the selection and editing of the documents of this series."

Characteristics of the Period. — Although this middle period is the period of the beginning of labor problems and labor organization, it must not be inferred that either problems or organizations were the same as to-day. The problems were those of a new country. The organizations were of quite a different type, combining, especially in the earlier part of the period, much more of the political than those of the later time. The new country made the United States a "land of promise" for laborers. They were so much aware of their position that their attitude impressed visitors from Europe as striking. These men formed associations, as did all other men, for a great variety of purposes. DeTocqueville was impressed with our genius for association. "Americans of all ages, all conditions and all dispositions constantly form associations. They have not only commercial and manufacturing companies, in which all take part, but associations of a thousand other kinds, — religious, moral, serious, futile, general or restricted, enormous or diminutive. . . . Wherever, at the head of some new undertaking, you see the Government in France, or a man of rank in England, in the United States you will be sure to find an association. . . . The English often perform great things single, whereas the Americans form associations for the smallest undertakings." The unusual degree of independence of the workingmen impressed those who were more accustomed to the conditions in Europe. Martineau notes that "There are troubles between employers and their workmen in the United States, as elsewhere; but the case of the men is so much more in their own hands there than where labor superabounds, that strikes are of a very short duration. . . . All the strikes I heard of were on the question of hours, not of wages." The same idea is found again in the following description written in 1823, "It must not be dissembled that there are circumstances which render it disagreeable to carry on manufactures in America. The workmen are under very little subjection: sometimes they are absent from their work for several days, to the great detriment of the employer; but should they be reprimanded, it might cause the proprietor to be insulted; and the indignation of the working people in this land of equality is really to be dreaded. Those workmen who are attentive and of economical habits soon acquire a little property, and with this they buy land and quit their former employers, for all species of servitude is disliked in the United States."

Workers and Non-Workers. — In order to understand further the nature of the problems of this period, it must be understood that the movement was not so much one of the workingmen against their employers. It was rather a demonstration by the workers against the non-workers. Industry had not developed to the point where it was no longer within the expectation of the journeyman to become a master, or of the workman to become a small employer. The free or cheap land contributed much to this feeling of independence and helped to continue a feeling of common interest between all those who worked. Improved methods of transportation, the wider use of credit through the increasing number of banks and other agencies that widened the market had resulted in the differentiation of the "merchant-capitalist" who was in position to dictate conditions to both the journeyman and the master. The evidence gathered in the Documentary History shows that the journeymen were reluctant to break away from the masters and at the same time the masters were inclined to choose the side of the journeymen against the capitalist. "We would not be too severe on our employers; they are the slaves to the capitalists as we are to them." "The boss is often brought back to journeywork by hard luck, and the journeyman may expect in his turn to become an employer, while both of them are invariably imposed upon and treated as if belonging to an inferior grade of society by those who live without labor."

Taking up the thread of association it is found that in a sense it was continuous from the former period into the one under present discussion. These earlier associations were essentially transitory and local. Some of them have been aggressive, as the printers (1786) and the cordwainers (1794). These associations were limited to a particular trade. Their activity led to charges against them at court and to trials for conspiracy. Yet the whole difference lies in the statement that "an isolated society might create a disturbance — not until it united with others could it create a 'movement.'"

Labor Literature. — During this period appeared the beginnings of a distinctly labor literature. The first American labor paper, The Mechanics' Free Press, was established in 1828. In the following year the two brothers, George and Frederick Evans, who had come to America five years before, began the publication of the Working Man's Advocate. Later these same men edited two other papers, the Daily Sentinel and Young America.

Organizations. — It is not possible to describe in detail the various organizations that were formed in this awakening period. Brief mention of the more important ones will suffice to show how the spirit of the day expressed itself. The first labor movement that involved more than a single trade was the Mechanics' Union of Trade Associations. The carpenters of Philadelphia had struck for a ten-hour day in 1827 and had not succeeded in carrying their point. Other trades came to the support of the carpenters and an organization was effected. It formed, perhaps, the first city central union. It is probable that at one time it embraced as many as fifteen societies. This union went into politics to gain its ends. It undertook the organization of a Workingmen's Party and named candidates for offices at elections. This it continued to do for four years until after the election of 1831. After this date it disappeared. The withdrawal is said "not to have been due to defeat but to two other causes: first, discouragement over inability to increase the voting strength of the party beyond a certain fixed point (a maximum of from 800 to 1,000); and, second, the overshadowing importance during the next year of questions of national politics upon which the working men had from the beginning declared themselves neutral."

The First Trades' Union. — A further interest attaches to this particular organization. It can lay a valid claim to being the first trades' union; not alone the first in America, but the first of its kind in any country. Inasmuch as this origin has been commonly associated with England, the contention of Professor Commons is important. "England is considered the home of trade-unionism, but the distinction belongs to Philadelphia. The first trades' union in England was that of Manchester, organized in 1829, although there seems to have been an attempt to organize one in 1824. But the first one in America was the 'Mechanics' Union of Trade Associations,' organized in Philadelphia in 1827, two years earlier. The name came from Manchester, but the thing from Philadelphia. Neither union lasted long. The Manchester union lived two years and the Philadelphia union one year. But the Manchester union died and the Philadelphia union metamorphosed into politics. Here again Philadelphia was the pioneer, for it called into being the first labor party. Not only this, but through the Mechanics' Union Philadelphia started probably the first wage-earners' paper ever published, — The Mechanics' Free Press, — antedating, in January, 1828, the first similar journal in England by two years."

Workingmen's Parties. — In 1829 began the existence of the Working Men's Party of New York. This organization extended rapidly and in the next year it was found throughout the state generally. Its struggle was essentially to retain the ten-hour day already generally secured in some of the trades. It put in nomination candidates for political office including a nomination for governor of the state. Its success was not great as it polled less than 3,000 votes. It ran upon the rocks of factionalism and was split into three different organizations, which later were absorbed by the larger regular parties. In New England the movement took on a more general form as is indicated in the name of the organization: The New England Association of Farmers, Mechanics and Other Working Men. This association spread to all of the New England states except New Hampshire. It even went so far as to discuss the plan of calling a national convention. The movement yielded to the tendency toward trade unions with the more definite demands of trade policy. The conventions of this association entered upon the discussion of the general program of reform embracing all of its main features. It included such topics as the relation of employer and employee, the ten-hour day, the right of laborers to organize to protect their interests and the probability of trades unions as a factor in diminishing strikes and lockouts.

In New York, in 1833, was repeated the experience of Philadelphia a few years before. The carpenters struck. Several other trades came to their support. The printers, taking the lead, called a convention of all trades and nine societies responded by sending delegates. Thus was formed the General Trades' Union of New York and Vicinity. The activities of this association were not so generally political. Conventions were held annually. The second year of its existence twenty-one societies were represented. The next year the numbers were swelled by representation from Newark and a monster procession was organized "a mile and a half long." The association was particularly active in supporting strikes, sending aid and encouragement as far away as Boston and Philadelphia. So aggressive was it that a case was made in court charging the leaders with conspiracy. Twenty of them were arrested and convicted. The outcome of this trial was the convening of a mass meeting of protest with 27,000 in attendance, and the formation of a party, the Equal Rights Party, demanding especially the repeal of the conspiracy laws and the reform of the judicial system. Thus again the movement ended in politics.

A companion to this organization was the one in Philadelphia, the General Trades' Union of the City and County of Philadelphia, formed in 1833. This began with the factory operatives and was taken up by the mechanics. It began with the union of twelve societies and by 1836 it numbered fifty societies with 10,000 members. It was aggressive in the support of strikes and generally successful. Its existence continued until 1839. The minutes show it to have been "a very active and very powerful force in the industrial life of Philadelphia." These may be taken as typical of trades unions formed in other cities during the decade prior to 1837.

National Organizations. — The natural outcome of these various trades unions was the formation of one on a national scale. In 1834 an invitation was sent out from the General Trades' Union of the City of New York and Vicinity for a delegate convention to meet in New York. The first response was a meeting with thirty delegates. Its purpose was purely discussion. The constitution that it adopted created merely a national medium of agitation with no administrative or disciplinary control over locals. Finding that its suggestions were not acted upon, the third convention revised the constitution making an organic change in the nature of the organization. The national union was strengthened. Its acts were no longer merely advisory; they were binding upon the locals. It also instituted a stronger financial control. Thus in a smaller way was repeated the experiences of the nation under its Articles of Confederation and the "critical period" resulting in the new constitution. The new strength of the union was almost immediately turned in the direction of the support of strikes. The extent of this union was not national in much more than name. It was, according to the Documentary History, "merely an union of what would now be called 'city central bodies' and of local trade unions. No provision was made for the representation of national trade unions." The organization disappeared in the panic of 1837.

An outgrowth of the National Trades' Union was the formation of national trade unions. Following a meeting of the
convention of the former in 1835 the cordwainers who were
in attendance remained and began organizing their trade on a
national scale. Their first convention was held in the following
year. Its constitution made special provision for the support
of strikes that were undertaken by any of the associations in
the union. Forty-five delegates were in attendance representing five states. It is known that calls were issued for subsequent conventions but no record is found to show that the conventions met. In the next two years at least five national trade
unions were formed by uniting local trade societies within each
trade. The panic of 1837 checked this movement.

Two Classes. — It will be noticed that the nature of these
associations makes it possible to divide them into two quite
distinct classes. The earlier ones looked more directly to political action as the best means of accomplishing the purposes.
Later the political nature yielded to the more limited policy
of union activity through methods such as the strike and the
attendant activities of collective bargaining. The fate of the
earlier associations was a lesson, and guided by this experience
they refrained from entering upon political or party contests.
The democratic spirit and the optimistic attitude toward the
possibilities of the ballot were followed by the sobering effects
of experience and the newer policies were turned to quite uniformly. The material gathered in the Documentary History
leads its editors to name the year 1832 as the dividing line in
these activities. The more distinct trade union activities appeared in 1833. Out of the agitation of this period came the
more vigorous action of the new trades unions. "Although
the trades unions existed prior to 1835, it was not until that
year, with its rise in prices, that they awoke to vigorous action."

Number of Members. — It is quite impossible to give an accurate idea of the number of the membership of societies in this
period. Some facts are doubtless interpretative, however. In
some cities the ratio of members to non-members among workingmen was as high as it is at present. In 1836 the trades unions of
Philadelphia consisted of forty-eight separate and independent
societies. Two of these claimed to have 900 members each and
four more claimed 700 each. At the time of the formation of

the National Trades' Union, in 1834, it was estimated that there were 26,250 members of societies, distributed as follows: New York and Brooklyn, 11,500; Philadelphia, 6,000; Boston, 4,000; Baltimore, 3,500; Newark, 750; Washington, 500.

A Complex Period. — During the latter years of this period the forces that were struggling for expression were numerous and complex. Owen's return to America in 1840 was marked by a revival of the coöperative and associationist philosophy. Eleemosynary plans in considerable variety were preached and practiced. Several leaders voiced the hopes of the masses in speech and writing and urged that steps be taken toward the realization of these hopes. The detailed analysis of these forces can find no space in this brief sketch. The various plans and theories led to the formation of numerous organizations, conventions, programs and settlements. The laborers were alive to the movement. They were susceptible to every new thing and among them were found followers of every program. "The whole trade-union movement (of 1850)," according to the Documentary History, "in New York, Boston and Pittsburgh was permeated with the idea that coöperation offered the best mode of protection to workmen and the ultimate means of solution for the problems of labor."

Accompanying these newer movements the older currents continued. Newer elements came in to reinforce them. At the close of the period they had acquired added force through the formation of women's organizations, resulting from their introduction into industry with the factory and its machinery; of organizations of unskilled workmen who also entered the field with the increasing use of machinery; and of organization among foreigners as their number increased through the immigration of the period. The tendency toward national trade associations was quickened, too, through the widening of the market and the area of competition as a result of the expansion of the growing railway systems.

In the beginning of the fifties the situation changed again in the direction of clearing up the atmosphere. The confusion attendant upon the large number of reforms and the conflicting claims urged in their favor was passing. The movement of the forties combined the necessary and immediate relief measures such as the strike with the more far-reaching remedies such as coöperation. This combination disappeared with the beginning of the fifties. Rising prices forced the necessity for immediate results. In response to its demands the workingmen "broke away from the beneficial and coöperative sideshows of the preceding ten years."

THIRD PERIOD

But for the interruption of the Civil War the beginnings of the present period might have been dated earlier. Already, in 1855, the change was becoming evident. Trade unionism was taking on its modern form and policies. The wave of general reform was passing and the undercurrent beginning again to assert its force. Joined with the forces that had been slowly gathering momentum during the period of confusion it appeared as a new type, a "pure and simple" unionism. Shorter hours and higher pay, formerly the leading issues, now were joined to issues of the minimum wage, the closed shop, the restriction of apprentices, and the secrecy of proceedings. As characterized by the editors of the Documentary History: "It steered clear of all programs of social and political reform, and confined its activities to improving the conditions of the trade. Its main weapon was the strike; its aim to establish a minimum wage for the trade and to maintain it by means of a closed shop. This new and limited program made possible trade agreements between unions and employers, which fixed for a stated period the wages, hours, and other conditions of employment."

The close of the Civil War ushered in a new period in industry. Since that day organization has been the magic word throughout the entire field. Accompanying the centralization of industry into large units there has been a rapid concentration of labor organizations. Locals have been gathered into central bodies; these, in turn, into state federations and finally into great national organizations. Along trade lines also the locals have been gathered up into great national and international unions with a jurisdiction covering the United States and Canada. The lines of these numerous associations, amalgamations and federations run out into a network of great complexity.

The Beginnings. — The beginnings of the movement extend back into the years just preceding the war. It was about the year 1853 that trade unionism took on its modern form and policies. The oldest union now in existence is the International Typographical Union. It is directly connected with the National Convention of Journeymen Printers that met in 1850. At a third annual meeting, in 1852, a permanent organization was effected under the name of the National Typographical Union. In 1869 some locals from Canada were admitted and the name changed to the International Typographical Union of North America. In the early years of this period the combination into nationals progressed rapidly for so early a date. In 1853 was formed the Journeymen Stonecutters Association of North America. Perhaps the next oldest society is among the hatters. In 1854 the National Trade Association of Hat Finishers of the United States of America was organized. This union continued until 1868 when a part withdrew, following the division of labor in the trade, and formed the Silk and Fur Hat Finishers Trade Association of the United States of America. One year later the United States Wool Hat Finishers Association was formed. This last named association still maintains its separate existence. The other societies have disappeared as distinct associations and have reappeared in the United Hatters of North America. This union claims direct lineage with the earlier organizations and in its official documents gives the date of its birth as 1854.

In 1859 first appeared the Iron Molders Union of North America. The Brotherhood of Locomotive Engineers was organized in 1863. For the first year of its existence it was known as the Brotherhood of the Footboard. Other unions of the earlier years that have maintained an existence to the present are the Cigar Makers International Union (1864); Bricklayers, Masons and Plasterers International Union (1865); Order of Railway Conductors of America, first taking the name of Conductors Brotherhood (1868); Brotherhood of Locomotive Firemen and Enginemen (1873); Amalgamated Association of Iron and Steel Workers (1876); Granite Cutters International Association of America (1877); United Brotherhood of Carpenters and Joiners (1881); Glass Bottle Blowers Association of the United States and Canada (1876); Operative Plasterers International Association (1864); Lake Seamens Union (1863); International Spinners Union (1878); Machine Printers (Textile) Beneficial Association of the United States (1873). By 1860, as

Coman says, "more than a score" of unions had been formed and by 1866 "some thirty or forty national trade organizations" had come into existence.

An examination of seventy-four of the leading unions of the present day shows that four were formed prior to 1860. Six were organized during the decade 1860–1869. In the seventies six more were founded. Prior to 1880, sixteen were permanently established.

Though there were many instances of associations of laboring men in the earlier periods that have been reviewed, these must be regarded as the forerunners of the present movement, not as a direct part of it. Whether or not the earlier forms be regarded as belonging to the present order depends upon interpretation. That there were associations resembling in form those of the present, there can be no doubt. If the situation be regarded as a definite "movement," however, it cannot be so readily shown that it was characteristic of the earlier forms of association. It is true that the former societies served as precedents for the later ones. The spirit, however, was different, as was the scope of the organization both in territorial area and in objects to be attained.

Causes. — "The immediate cause of the organization of wage-labor," writes Professor Commons, "was the rise of prices and cost of living which began with the disappearance of gold and the appearance of greenbacks in 1862. There was in that and the preceding years practically no organization of labor in the United States. Four national unions had a nominal existence but the panic and depression of 1857 had nearly eliminated the local unions that existed before." To this may be added Professor Callender's testimony. "The modern labor problem can hardly be said to have existed in America until after the middle of the nineteenth century. Before that time the American people had indeed their labor problem as most new countries have, but it was something quite different from what now passes under that name."

Decreasing Opportunity. — Following the same development as in England, the opportunities for advancement were growing less. This did not take place all at once, and so it is not easy to fix the time on the calendar when the movement of organized labor began. As the situation became more and more evident to the workingmen in larger groups the development of the movement became more and more evident also. The situation in England is described at length by the Webbs.

"The explanation of the tardy growth of stable combination among hired journeymen is, we believe, to be found in the prospects of economic advancement which the skilled handicraftsman still possessed. We do not wish to suggest the existence of any Golden Age in which each skilled workman was his own master, and the wage system was unknown. The earliest records of English town history imply the presence of hired journeymen who were not always contented with their wages. But the apprenticed journeyman in the skilled handicrafts belonged, until comparatively modern times, to the same social grade as his employer, and was, indeed, usually the son of a master in the same or an analogous trade. So long as industry was carried on mainly by small masters, each employing but one or two journeymen, the period of any energetic man's service as a hired wage earner cannot normally have exceeded a few years, and the industrious apprentice might reasonably hope, if not always to marry his master's daughter, at any rate to set up in business for himself. Any incipient organization would always be losing its oldest and most capable members, and would of necessity be confined . . . to 'the young people' or . . . to a 'race at once youthful and unstable' from whose inexperienced ranks it would be hard to draw a supply of good Trade Union leaders. We are therefore able to understand how it is that, while industrial oppression belongs to all ages, it is not until the changing conditions of industry had reduced to an infinitesimal chance the journeyman's prospect of becoming himself a master, that we find the passage of ephemeral combinations into permanent trade societies."

The greater industrial advantages together with the changed economic organization in America made the development of this movement unlike that of England in many important particulars. The essential elements, however, did not change nor did they lose their effectiveness. As the door of opportunity for industrial independence slowly closed to the individual in the United States, the more or less loose and vague associations of laborers slowly began to merge into positive organizations with a definite common purpose and an increasing unity.

Professor Carlton, reviewing the labor literature of the sixties, finds an editor emphasizing the fact that the workingmen were slowly abandoning the hope of becoming capitalists. "The hope that the workingman may enter this circle (of capitalists or employers) is a glittering delusion held up before him to distract his attention from the real object of his interest." And, finally, only about ten years ago, John Mitchell began his book on Organized Labor with this sentence: "The average wage earner has made up his mind that he must remain a wage earner. He has given up the hope of a kingdom to come, where he himself will be a capitalist, and he asks that the reward for his work be given to him as a workingman. Singly, he has been too weak to enforce his just demands and he has sought strength in union and has associated himself into labor organizations."

CONSPIRACY

The full effects of early events upon the spirit of modern unionism cannot be rightly understood without reference to early conspiracy laws. These laws were applied to associations of laborers in such a way as to cause them to be more than ever conscious of restrictions upon what they regarded as their liberties.

Early Developments. — Though the early labor associations were not formed for any length of time, their activities attracted attention at once and they became subject to legal consideration. On this point the traditions of England were important. Several trials were held during the first quarter of the nineteenth century in which English law figured prominently. They usually involved the local associations that were most active, such as boot and shoe workers, hat makers, tailors, spinners and weavers. The cases were tried in the courts of Philadelphia, Pittsburgh, Baltimore, New York, Buffalo and other smaller towns in the same states. Eight cases were against cordwainers alone. The circumstances of these cases were in general the same. An association of workingmen had been formed. They had refused to work except for the wages demanded by them and for any master who employed any workman who was not a member of their society. In one instance a case was brought against a group of masters who had joined in reducing wages to a point at which they had fixed them before they had been compelled by a strike to raise them.

In these trials the English law was cited to show that the acts charged came within the English common law of conspiracy and that this law was binding within the jurisdiction of the American court. The defense generally sought to establish the claim that the English law was not applicable to the states, as the political separation had severed the connection. Arguments over the applicability of the English common law were elaborate and figured prominently especially in the earlier cases. In the outcome the legal training and the traditions counted heavily. The English law of conspiracy was held to be in force.

In the charge to the jury in the earliest of these cases (Philadelphia Cordwainers' case, 1806) the Recorder stated that "a combination of workmen to raise their wages may be considered in a twofold point of view: one is to benefit themselves; the other is to injure those who do not join their society. The rule of law condemns both." In the New York Cordwainers' case (1809) the Mayor in his charge to the jury declared: "There were two points of view in which the offence of a conspiracy might be considered; the one where there existed a combination to do an act unlawful in itself to the prejudice of other persons; the other where the act done or the object of it was not unlawful, but unlawful means were used to accomplish it. As to the first, there could be no doubt that a combination to do an unlawful act was a conspiracy. The second depended on the common principle that the goodness of the end would not justify improper means to obtain it." This view reached its extreme form in the New York Hatters' case, in 1823. "Journeymen confederating and refusing to work, unless for certain wages, may be indicted for a conspiracy, . . . for this offence consists in the conspiracy and not in the refusal; and all conspiracies are illegal though the subject-matter of them may be lawful. . . . Journeymen may each singly refuse to work, unless they receive an advance in wages, but if they refuse by preconcert or association they may be indicted and convicted of conspiracy. . . . The gist of a conspiracy is the unlawful confederation, and the offence is complete when the confederacy is made, and any act done in pursuit of it is no constituent part of the offence."

Influence on Later Cases. — From these early principles the conspiracy laws of the several states were developed. The stages have been by no means uniform. In some it has been shaped largely by statutory enactment while in others the modification has been accomplished through court interpretation.

Illustration from New York State. — In New York state, for example, the question was dealt with by statute. The laws of England became the basis of the state law in this commonwealth. They seem to have had their first extensive application in connection with the Revolutionary War and the efforts of some to conspire against the new government. Statutes were passed with this situation in mind. In 1813 a revision of the laws was made and the conspiracy section was included. It remained until 1828, the occasion of another general revision. This revised section made it a misdemeanor among other things to conspire to commit any act injurious to public health, to public morals, or to trade or commerce. In order to limit the interpretation of the older common law and keep it within the provisions of the statute, it was further declared that no conspiracies other than those enumerated in the law should be punishable criminally, and further that no agreement except to commit a felony, arson or burglary should be deemed a conspiracy unless some act besides such agreement be done to effect the object of the agreement. This new section was the work of a commission appointed for the purpose and it included all the cases usually considered as conspiracy except that of a conspiracy to injure an individual by means not in themselves criminal, and all that it seemed expedient to enumerate. To the list as finally adopted the commission had added one that the legislature rejected. This clause would have made it a criminal conspiracy to defraud or injure any person in his trade or business. From the backward look the commission evidently thought that this section should be included. The legislature, seemingly giving greater attention to present conditions, declined to incorporate it. The net result of the revision was to clear up somewhat the confusion that clung to the historical conception of conspiracy. Concerning these doubts and difficulties the revisors pointed out that "By a metaphysical train of reasoning, which has never been adopted in any other case in the whole criminal law, the offence of conspiracy is made to consist in the intent; in an act of the mind; and to prevent the shock to

common sense which such a proposition would be sure to produce, the formation of this intent by an interchange of thoughts
is made itself an overt act, done in pursuance of that interchange or agreement. . . . Acts and deeds are the subjects
of human laws; not thoughts and intents unless accompanied
by acts." The rejection of the clause bearing on the injury
to anyone in his business or trade has proved to be wise as
after events have shown.

Thus is seen in the experience in New York how conspiracy
rested primarily on the common law, how it was modified
to meet the new conditions of statehood, and finally how it
was revised so as to include all that was to be retained of the old
law in the light of the necessities of the day. The task succeeded
in gathering up from the common law those principles upon
which at the time it seemed desirable to base action against
conspiracy and expressing them definitely in statute form, thus
making the basis a statute law basis. It should be noted that
although there were several revisions of the statutes during the
following forty years, it was not till 1870 that this section was
modified again. With the steadily increasing activity of labor
associations and the growing recognition of their value, the
legislature in 1870 considerably modified the whole section dealing with conspiracy as far as the laborer was concerned. By
the act of that year the provisions of the former statute were not
to be construed "to restrict or prohibit the orderly and peaceable
assembling or coöperation of persons employed in any profession,
trade or handicraft, for the purpose of securing an advance
in the rate of wages or compensation, or for the maintenance of
such rate."

Scope of Conspiracy Law: Theory. — It should not be understood that the law of conspiracy was formulated purposely to
interfere with the activities of laborers. The points just stated
in connection with the early use in New York show that such
was not the case. In the trial of People *vs.* Trequier, in 1823,
it was brought out that the law relating to conspiracy had under-
gone a great alteration during the centuries just passed. Taken
formerly in a more limited sense, it had more recently become
a most useful method of dealing with almost every possible case
of combination. A variety of illustrations showed the wide
range of its application.

Practice. — Though such was the theory, it seems clear that this law was more easily invoked against laborers than against others. In the case to which reference has just been made the defendant workmen were charged with conspiring to refuse to work for a master hatter who had in his employ a journeyman who refused to be governed by the rules of the association which his fellow journeymen had formed. The evidence showed that the master hatters of the city had had a meeting to agree to reduce wages. To counteract this agreement among the employers the workmen had formed their society and agreed not to work for the new rate that the employers had named. Further the journeymen offered to prove a conspiracy among the master hatters not to employ any journeyman who left his last place on account of wages, in order to prove that the meeting of the journeymen was for a lawful purpose. This evidence was not allowed. The defendants also contended that their action was not unlike an earlier agreement of grocers and others not to purchase goods from auctioneers. This meeting the court held was for a lawful purpose — for the general advantage of the community. Concerning the meeting of the employers, the court dismissed the matter with the declaration that "one conspiracy cannot justify another." It seemed in this case easier to fasten the charge of conspiracy upon the laborer than upon the employer or the merchant. The case is typical. Though the offense was not limited in any way to the activity of labor associations, and though the principle covered a variety of activities and the records show that prosecutions were successfully made in many instances where laborers were in no way involved, yet, in practice, it came during this period to be a very convenient and very certain tool in the hands of employers to hold in check any combination that employees might make.

Even after the modification was made in the New York law in 1828, making it a misdemeanor to conspire to commit an act injurious to trade or commerce, the way was not easy for the laborers. In People *vs.* Fisher, 1835, a case was brought in the court charging that journeymen had formed "an unlawful club and combination" to prevent a fall in wages. The court summed up the issues in the question, "Is a conspiracy to raise wages an act injurious to trade and commerce?" The answer was in the affirmative. The mere raising of wages surely could not constitute an offense. Yet an agreement to do so was entirely a different matter. By a line of argument both ingenious and interesting the conclusion was very logically reached that such an agreement being a matter of public concern and it being possible to raise wages indefinitely, if at all, by this means, it would be very oppressive to the public and therefore would be highly injurious.

Its Definition. — The general form of expression and definition indicates how easy it was to find the law of conspiracy applicable to a variety of cases. The form of statement varied somewhat, though within narrow limits so far as meaning was concerned. A typical statement defined conspiracy as "an agreement or combination between two or more persons to do an unlawful act or to accomplish a purpose lawful in itself by means that are criminal or unlawful." "The crime is completed by the unlawful agreement." "The gist of a conspiracy is the unlawful confederacy and the offence is completed when the confederacy is made and any act done in pursuance of it is no constituent part of the offence."

Development of Definition. — Speaking somewhat more generally of the law of conspiracy, it may be said that its development seems to the layman peculiar, if not to the lawyer. In an interesting study of the Development of English Law of Conspiracy, Mr. J. W. Bryan has traced the stages in full detail. It is found in this study that the modern law of conspiracy "treats as a crime the mere combination to do certain acts;" regarding the offense as "complete as soon as the agreement is formed" and as "wholly distinct from any act performed in pursuance of it." But "the ancient law was otherwise. The conspiracy was an element to be taken into account but was not in itself a complete crime." During the long years from Edward III to George III the law was expanded and developed. One particular line of the development was the "rise of the principle that the bare unexecuted conspiracy is a complete offense." By the end of the eighteenth century the law had been developed in its essential elements. During the nineteenth century the courts were to systematize and generalize it: "to reduce the law to some degree of orderly and scientific arrangement." One phase of development was of particular importance. The courts held that to prove a conspiracy it was not necessary to show that the persons actually met in formal consultation to come to the agreement. Overt acts were to be conclusive of an agreement. "If you find," said a justice in 1837, "that these two persons pursued by their acts the same object, often by the same means, one performing one part of an act, and the other another part of the same act, so as to complete it, with a view to the attainment of the object which they are pursuing, you will be at liberty to draw the conclusion that they have been engaged in a conspiracy to effect the object." Again, as late as 1851, another justice said to the jury: "If you see several men taking several steps, all tending toward one obvious purpose, and you see them through a continued portion of time taking steps that lead to an end, it is for you to say whether these persons had not combined together to bring about that end, which their conduct so obviously appears adapted to effectuate."

The definition quoted in an earlier paragraph of this section has become classic: "to do an unlawful act; or a lawful act by unlawful means." This statement appeared in a charge delivered by Lord Denman in 1832. "The indictment," it was stated, "ought to charge a conspiracy, either to do an unlawful act, or a lawful act by unlawful means." As Mr. Bryan says, "It is clearly evident that the above antithesis was intended to limit the offence of conspiracy, not to define it." It is further pointed out that in the same case the justice added: "the words, 'at least,' should accompany" the statement. At a later time, commenting on his own statement, the same justice added: "I do not think the antithesis very correct." After citing the facts in connection with the formulation of the definition, Mr. Bryan adds: "In spite of its author's dissatisfaction with it, this antithesis has been treated as a definition ever since. As such it serves as the very foundation of the modern law of conspiracy. It has been cited, always with approval and without examination or criticism, in a long line of nineteenth and twentieth century cases, until its terms have become firmly embedded in the structure of the national jurisprudence. . . . The part which it played in the later decisions presents another very striking illustration of the accidental, unsystematic method by which the law of conspiracy has developed." One significant criticism of the law as thus developed may be added in the words of yet another justice: "It is never satisfactory, although undoubtedly it is legal."

It was through this period of development and application of the conspiracy law that laborers were seeking to establish a right to collective bargaining. The difficulties are obvious. The effect upon their spirit and temper is easily comprehended.

CHAPTER III

WAGE THEORIES

In the last chapter were related the events connected with the development and struggle out of which permanent associations of laborers emerged. The problems that accompanied these changes led in their day to much discussion, in which both theoretical and practical considerations were set forth in a pamphlet literature of some volume. During the earlier period of the development there was practically no such thing as a theory of wages. Customary relations were accepted as of binding force. They rested on precedent and needed no theoretical justification. Questions of trade expansion and national rivalry received much attention and gave rise to the body of literature in which Mercantilism was developed on a basis of theory. Incidental to the discussion of trade and national welfare, manufacture and foreign markets, wages came in for a share of consideration. This topic was prominent especially in the efforts to adjust taxation upon some legal basis that would stand the test of general principles and at the same time furnish the needed revenue. Running through the literature of this discussion appears a view of wages that is not only interesting in itself, but which furnishes evidence of a preference for a low wage rate based upon a view of wages generally accepted though not clearly and concisely formulated.

Benefit of Low Wages. — The opinion prevailed among a group of writers of the late seventeenth and early eighteenth centuries that the laborer was as a rule a heavy drinker, irresponsible, with no self-control; who could be kept at his tasks only by some form of stern necessity. He who will not labor shall not eat seems to have been the starting point of instruction and to this was added: he who earns but little can eat but little. Suspicion rested heavily upon the worker that with the slightest easement of living conditions he would abate his efforts, not to renew them until starvation again forced him to his task. From these opinions it was an easy step to the belief that low wages were necessary to keep laborers at their work, that advances in wages would increase idleness because it would make more idleness possible, and that industry among workers was necessary to enable England to seize and hold the foreign markets from her rivals. Professor Seligman has found the earliest trace of this idea expressed in 1669, when it was argued that high wages are injurious because "the men have just so much more to spend in tipple, and remain now poorer than when their wages was less, . . . they work so much the fewer days by how much the more they exact in their wages." The remedy was simple: "Subdue wages."

There are many other expressions to the same effect, so interesting that some will bear repeating. "If there be of food a plenty, laziness follows it." High wages mean debauchery and shorter time for work. The more the workman paid for provisions or the less he received with which to buy them the longer and the harder would he be obliged to work. Thus: "When the frame-work knitters or makers of silk stockings had a great price for their work they have been observed seldom to work on Mondays and Tuesdays, but to spend most of that time at the ale house and nine pins. . . . The weavers, 'tis common with them to be drunk on Monday, to have their heads ache on Tuesday and their tools out of order on Wednesday." "People in low life who work only for their daily bread if they can get it by three days' work in a week will many of them make holiday the other three or set their own price on their labor." Low wages became a public necessity, as it was reasoned: "The lower class of people if they are subject to little or no control, they will run into vice: vice is attended with expense which must be supported either by an high price for their labor or by methods still more destructive." "Men are as bad as can be described: who become more vicious, more indigent and idle in proportion to the advance of wages and the cheapness of provisions." As late as 1770 a book was published in which the argument was made to rest upon three principles, summed up as follows: "First, that mankind, in general, are naturally inclined to ease and indolence, and that nothing but absolute necessity will enforce labor and industry. Secondly, that our poor, in general, work only for the bare necessities of life, or for the means of a low debauch; which, when obtained, they cease to labor till roused again by necessity. Thirdly, that it is best for themselves, as well as for society, that they should be constantly employed." "The only way to make the poor temperate and industrious, is to lay them under a necessity of laboring all the time they can spare from meals and sleep, in order to procure the common necessaries of life."

As has been said, these views were expressed generally with reference to taxation. The immediate purpose was to raise revenue. This was to be done by levying on the laboring classes, accomplishing a double advantage of securing the revenue and improving the conditions of industry by lowering wages. It is but a slight modification of the argument, if any at all, to express it in terms of low wages as a factor in securing the same result. In either case the real wage was affected in practically the same way.

The Theory Questioned. — These writers did not occupy an undisputed field, however. In 1694 the reasoning was called in question and more and more frequently thereafter. By 1734 appeared a strong advocate of the idea that high standards of living for the laboring class are beneficial. "The working people can and will do a great deal more work than they do, if they were sufficiently encouraged. For I take it for a maxim that the people of no class will ever want industry, if they don't want encouragement." This should not be done by "making the poor fare harder." It is not the right incentive. The poor, it was further argued, belong to the great mass of consumers and to deprive them would "affect the consumption of things in general so mightily that there would be a want of trade and business amongst the other part of the people." Another writer, in 1754, urged that it was a fallacy to argue that industry could be forced by poverty. "When our workmen can no longer raise the price of their work to their mind, there still remain two great refuges to them from labor, the parish and robbing." The opposition continued in various forms of expression. One of the most forceful denied vigorously the proposition that "the poor will be industrious only in the degree that they are necessitous," declaring it to be "a doctrine which avarice in private life has greedily seized and has not failed to improve to its purposes. . . . A doctrine as false as it is inhuman." The discussion continued as a question incident to problems of expanding industry and was not cleared up in any comprehensive way until another group of writers appeared and opened a new era of discussion.

Classic School. — With the appearance of the Wealth of Nations Adam Smith began the work of systematizing economic thought. Following, however, the lead of writers of the day the chief concern of the work was indicated by its full title, An Inquiry into the Nature and Causes of the Wealth of Nations. Not until fully a generation after this did a definite theory of wages mature, though some authorities state that it had an earlier beginning. During this period the question of wages received more attention. The opening sentence of this great work declared that "The annual labor of every nation is the fund which originally supplies it with all the necessaries and conveniences of life." One of the great principles of the work is that labor is not only the cause but also the measure of value.

Closely following upon Smith's work Malthus published his essay on population. The combination of ideas that resulted from these studies together with what had been published before may be summed up in very brief form as follows. While labor is both the cause and measure of value yet wages are determined very directly by food supply. As the supply of food became more plentiful, marriages would be contracted at an earlier age and in greater numbers, families would increase in size until the population, thus increased by a rising birth rate and a falling death rate, would press upon the supply of food and the abundance would disappear. With the decrease in food supply would follow inevitably a decrease in the number of marriages, smaller families, a decrease in birth rate and an increase in death rate. Thus the pressure of population on food supply would gradually be relieved. This would be followed by relative plenty again and the events of the former cycle would be repeated. The introduction by Smith, the warnings of Malthus and the stern logic of Ricardo's reasoning give alike form and authority to this "iron law" of wages.

Wages Fund Theory. — But these statements were not developed into a theory with their first formulation. As the discussion progressed its expression became more definite, and it finally became known as the Wages Fund Theory. This development was so gradual that there is difference of opinion as to when it was first formulated. Professor Haney objects to naming Smith as its originator, though he says that "In the Wealth of Nations may be found traces of virtually every wage theory ever developed." This writer attributes the first statement of it to Senior, who "probably called into being the wages-fund doctrine which lies concealed in the writings of Smith and Ricardo." On the other hand, Professor Taussig claims that Ricardo "put forth a wages fund doctrine as unqualifiedly as any of the later writers with whom that doctrine is usually associated." Leaving this as a controversy that has no direct bearing upon this study, it may be said that this wages fund theory was generally accepted by English economists during a period of about fifty years, during the middle of the nineteenth century.

In its first form this doctrine sought to express the relation of wages to food. As Malthus said: "It may at first appear strange, but I believe it to be true, that I cannot by means of money raise the condition of a poor man, and enable him to live much better than he did before without proportionately depressing others in the same class. . . . But if I only give him money, supposing the produce of the country to remain the same, I give him a title to a larger share of that produce than formerly, which share he cannot receive without diminishing the share of others." The more definite statement of this doctrine was made with reference to the relation of wages to capital. Wages were paid out of capital and must be adjusted in their amount by what capital could pay out of its stock. Thus wages and profits, or interest, had a reciprocal relation; as the one increased the other of necessity decreased proportionately. As the laborer had nothing on which to draw for his support while he worked, he must be provided for out of the "funds" of capital as an advance. This could never exceed the amount of the capital and generally must be less than that amount by enough to provide the other needs of the industry. The maximum was thus fixed. The subsistence point was the minimum below which wages could not fall. Between these points the wage was regulated by bargaining, the determining factors being on the one hand population and on the other the amount of capital. Thus, as Professor Taussig sums it up, "Not only, as Adam Smith put it, are wages paid out of capital, and determined by a bargain in which the demand for labor comes from employers' capital: but the amount of that capital, compared with the number of laborers, fixes wages definitely." The proximate determination of wages depends, says Senior, on "the extent of the fund for the maintenance of laborers compared with the number of laborers to be maintained." James Mill sums up his view concisely by saying in his Elements of Political Economy: "Universally, then, we may affirm, other things remaining the same, that, if the ratio which capital and population bear to one another remains the same, wages will remain the same; if the ratio which capital bears to population increases, wages will rise; if the ratio which population bears to capital increases, wages will fall."

Mill's Statement. — The doctrine may be said to have its final statement in the writings of John Stuart Mill. The following extract sums up his view, an expression thought by him to be final: "Wages, then, depend mainly upon the demand and supply of labor; or, as it is often expressed, on the proportion between population and capital. By population is here meant the number only of the laboring class, or rather of those who work for hire; and by capital, only circulating capital, and not even the whole of that, but the part which is expended in the direct purchase of labor. To this, however, must be added all funds which, without forming a part of capital, are paid in exchange for labor, such as the wages of soldiers, domestic servants, and all other unproductive laborers. There is unfortunately no mode of expressing by one familiar term the aggregate of what may be called the wages fund of a country; and as the wages of productive labor form nearly the whole of that fund, it is usual to overlook the smaller and less important part, and to say that wages depend on population and capital. It will be convenient to employ this expression, remembering, however, to consider it as elliptical, and not as a literal statement of the whole truth.

"With these limitations of the terms, wages not only depend upon the relative amount of capital and population, but cannot, under the rule of competition, be affected by anything else. Wages (meaning, of course, the general rate) cannot rise, but by an increase of the aggregate funds employed in hiring laborers, or a diminution in the number of competitors for hire; nor fall, except either by a diminution of the funds devoted to paying labor, or by an increase in the number of laborers to be paid."

Attack on Wages Fund Theory. — So dominant was the influence of the classical school of writers that opposition was ineffectual until the last quarter of the century. At that time the attacks upon the doctrine by Longe and Thornton were so vigorous and spirited that they compelled attention. The attack has been summed up in a convenient form as follows: "The theory of a wage fund is untenable because (a) the capital or wealth applicable to the payment of the wages of labor in a country, at any time or during any period, does not consist of a definite fund which is distinct from the produce of labor; (b) because the dependent or laboring population in a country at any time, or during any period, does not constitute a supply of labor, or body of laborers, among whom the average wage fund or capital of a country could be distributed by competition; (c) because the supposition that such wage fund would be all distributed among the laborers of a country by the competition of the buyers and sellers of labor, if allowed free operation, involves an erroneous notion of the demand and supply principle." In his later writings Mill himself finally recognized the validity of these arguments and declared that the wages fund doctrine could not stand against such a presentation. The surrender of Mill is the beginning of the disappearance of the theory.

Productivity Theory. — With the passing of the wages fund theory, the field was open to all comers and a period of active discussion followed. Out of the newer views adapted to the newer conditions of industry developed slowly a new group of theories, those that now hold the field. According to one of these, wages are adjusted in the long run to the share of the product that is due to the labor factor. From this it takes its name, the Productivity Theory. The results of the productive process are divided among the factors that produce them, labor and capital being the ones chiefly considered under the assumption of free competition. The distribution of these shares lies in the hands of the entrepreneur, or responsible manager, and he assigns wages and interest on the basis of the marginal productivity of the labor and the capital. If he accepts an added "dose" of labor it will be because the product will be increased thereby. This addition to the product he hopes to take to himself temporarily as profits and for a time he will succeed in doing so. But competition with other entrepreneurs will eventually lead to a distribution of this sum as wages.

Thus added increments of profits become eventually added wages if the entrepreneur can be induced to add "doses" of labor. If, on the other hand, he adds capital (e. g., machinery or tools) then the profits pass to interest instead. Thus labor and capital are constantly offering themselves. The entrepreneur occupies a "zone of indifference," taking from either as he sees opportunity for temporary profit, finally passing it on as either wages or interest. Added increments of labor are subject to the law of diminishing returns. Since wages are determined by productivity, it must follow that when labor offers itself in too large quantities it must be content with smaller wages as its productivity is less. For in each group it is the marginal point that determines the productivity and thus the wages for all in the group. This is the limit of what the entrepreneur can pay.

Professor Clark has developed this theory most elaborately. "We not only admit, but positively claim," as he states it, "that there is a marginal region where wages are adjusted." Carrying the development further, he says: "The law of wages would stand thus: (1) By a common mercantile rule, all men of a given degree of ability must take what marginal men of that same ability get. This principle fixes the market rate of wages. (2) Marginal men get what they produce. This principle governs wages more remotely, by fixing a natural standard for them." This is not the final law, however. Later the summary statement is that wages and interest "are fixed by the final productivity of labor and capital, as permanent agents of production." Later still: "each unit of labor, then, is worth to its employer what the last unit produces." Summing up, Professor Clark concludes: "As real as gravitation is the force that draws the actual pay of men *toward* a standard that is set by the final productivity law. This law is universal and permanent: everywhere it will outlive the local and changeful influences that modify its operation. We are to get what we produce — such is the dominant rule of life; and what we are able to produce by means of labor, is determined by what a final unit of mere labor can add to the product that can be created without its aid. Final productivity governs wages." Professor Seager treats this theory in a briefer way, and sums up the statement of the law as follows: "Under conditions of free, all-sided competition the earnings of marginal, as of other, workmen tend to correspond accurately to the contributions which they make to production."

Exchange Theory. — A rival of the productivity theory is that of the Austrian School, a theory that has behind it no small weight of authority. Their theory is often called the Exchange Theory. In this theory wages are advances made by the employer to the workman in order that he will not have to wait for the completion of the product before he can receive his share. The time element is important in modern industry and this time space is bridged over by wages.

Socialist Theory. — During the time covered by these later developments another theory has been formulated. It had its first formal statement in the writings of Karl Marx, though like the other theories its first suggestions are found in the works of Smith and Ricardo. Taking the statements of these earlier writers that labor is the basis of value and value proportionate to the amount of labor, the Marxian theory develops and refines the idea and applies it in a way that very directly affects wages. If all value is due to labor then the value created belongs of right to those who perform the labor. From this brief proposition the reasoning expands into the full socialist philosophy. In this form it is not primarily a law of wages, but a reform program that seeks to reorganize industrial society and abolish wages. Wages as a bargain between those who work and those who employ them can never be fair since no division of product can be just when the product is due entirely to the efforts of the one.

The theory is difficult to state in brief because of the differences of opinion among its advocates. Marx himself did not develop it into a statement that has proved to be final. His followers in seeking to perfect it have not yet arrived at a point of definite agreement. As restated by two of his recognized followers, it takes a form as follows: "In common with Smith, Ricardo and other representatives of the classical school of political economy, Marx holds that the value of a commodity is determined by the labor time expended in its production, the labor time in question being defined as 'the labor time socially necessary to produce an article under the normal conditions of production with the average degree of skill and intensity prevalent at that time.'" (Hillquit.) "This is the problem of value which all great economists have tried to solve. Sir William Petty, Adam Smith, David Ricardo, John Stuart Mill and Karl Marx developed what is known as the labor value theory as the solution of the problem. This theory, as developed by Marx, not in its cruder forms, is one of the cardinal principles in Socialist Economic theory. The Ricardian statement of the theory is that the relative value of commodities to one another is determined by the relative amounts of human labor embodied in them; that the quantity of labor embodied in them is the determinant of the value of all commodities." (Spargo.) A brief form of the statement may be found again in Spargo: "The exchange-value of commodities is determined by the amount of average labor at the time socially necessary for their production."

The socialist theories proceed directly to a social program, involving a thorough reorganization of industrial society and a new socialist state. The value of the proposed program has had much to do with the acceptance or rejection of the theories upon which it is based. The glimpses of this new social order reveal generally a condition in which wages as such are abolished and income is distributed upon some plan either entirely new or greatly modified.

Employers' Interpretation. — While theorists have been giving their attention to the elaboration of the various views that have been summed up so briefly, the employer has been setting up for himself an interpretation of the situation. He would not assume to call it a theory. It is more real to him than theories usually are. To him there is a labor market where he buys his labor, just as he buys his raw material, on the most favorable terms. With the keen knowledge of experience he sorts his labor, always buying the qualities that best suit his purposes. He never uses a high grade piece of material where one of lower grade will do. Likewise he never uses a high price man where a lower price one will do. To him a good labor market is one plentifully stocked with a variety of labor enabling him to pick and choose and to have an advantage in bargaining. A market where labor does not show this variety is a poor labor market. This situation he sums up with the time-worn expression, demand and supply. Wages are fixed by demand and supply, the same forces that, to his mind, determine the prices of his raw materials and his finished products.

Laborers' Interpretation. — The laborer sees the situation from yet another angle. The theoretical considerations are to him not very real. He is so close to the exceptions, the variations that prevent tendencies from expressing themselves "in the long run," that he cannot see them in the large relations as the theorist views them. He must have something that to him seems real, and these theories lack the appearance of reality. But he has a standard of living to maintain and he fights vigorously against anything that endangers it. This is to him the one thing of unsurpassed importance. Whatever the conditions of the labor market may be, however the adjustment between demand and supply may vary, he must have enough to live on, — he and his family. Thus the standard of living and a wage that makes its maintenance possible are to him the decisive factors in all wage discussions.

The contrast between the last two views is strikingly shown in the following instance: In Chicago, a few years ago, there was a strike of oil wagon drivers. They were receiving $2 a day and were asking $75 a month. The method they adopted in urging their case was somewhat novel. A committee, headed by the business agent of the union, called upon the manager and made in substance the following statement: We want to show you what it costs the average family among our number to live. For rent, fuel, food, light and car fare it costs $1.97 a day. That leaves three cents a day for clothing for self and family, doctor's bills, and such other items as usually enter into the family budget. The manager was then asked if he could live on $2 a day or if he could suggest how his men could buy clothing and other necessaries on three cents a day. The manager's reply was frank. He did not believe he could. But the fact was that he could get plenty of teamsters who were willing to work for $2 a day. That, he added, is really what governs wages more than the cost of living.

Any effort to state in such brief form the various theories of wages must inevitably be unsatisfactory because inadequate. Yet it has been undertaken for the purpose of indicating their effects upon the movement of organized labor. As will be seen, the formulation of the first theory came at the time when combinations of laborers were beginning to appear but were not sanctioned by law. The period just prior to the formulation of the wages fund theory was the same as that of the Industrial Revolution and the enactment of the law (1799) against all combinations of laborers. The legalization of unions (1824) came at the time of the beginning of influence of the wages fund theory; and the beginnings of federated unions and amalgamations covered the period when economic science was being moulded into shape and taking on a definite form. The modern theories have been put forward at a time when unions were well established and were increasing in strength and influence.

Importance of Theories to Laborers. — There is little in any of these theories that has afforded much encouragement to the laborer. Certainly there was no consolation in a theory that dictated the reduction of wages for the purpose of encouraging or forcing habits of industry. With the appearance of the statement in the Wealth of Nations that all value is due to labor the outlook must have appeared more encouraging. Yet Malthus's turn to the discussion was disheartening in so far as the inevitable pressure on food supply and consequent poverty at regularly recurring intervals was an important factor. Again, the wages fund doctrine did not afford much encouragement. It was in the time of *laissez faire* when the government was to keep hands off and struggling interests were to adjust themselves. With a fixed sum of capital, however, to be distributed as wages among the laborers, the only outlook for gain was at the loss of some others of the same group.

The inevitableness of the increase of population and the consequent increase in the numbers of laborers is to this class a fact the reality of which cannot for a moment be doubted. This means a lowering of the margin and a consequent reduction in the wages of the group. The idea of fairness in the distribution according to the share produced is offset by the idea that the share produced must diminish. This appears as an inevitable result. The element of hope associated with the policy of increasing the efficiency of the labor units together with the increasing uses of the instruments of production, making industry as a whole more productive, is too far removed

w any ray of optimism on this theory. So it is that the
tivity theory cannot attract the laborers generally.

value theory of the socialist doctrine appeals to the work-
in large numbers. Yet it has associated with it the rad-
gram of social reorganization that encounters opposition
ial and political reasons and leaves it a problem as to
w influential this theory will become.

doubtful if any great weight of influence is to be at-
d directly to any of these various theories. In earlier
he habit of reading and discussion had not been formed.
eories were remote from the thought and the immediate
ns of laborers. Yet it cannot be doubted that there
me indirect influence. Parliament or Congress was the
n ground of exchange and through the activity of these
as shaped by the various theories their influence was
the spirit of the workingmen.

rough and ready explanation of the situation adopted
employer had a much more direct influence. If demand
pply affected wages, these factors could be controlled.
employer might adjust the demand so the laborers might
e the supply. Organization afforded the opportunity
his. If labor was a commodity to be bought in the cheap-
rket, organizations could be effected that would control,
t in part, this market.

CHAPTER IV

MODERN INDUSTRIALISM

Were there no reasons other than historical for the existe
of labor unions, these would explain much. The causes,
stages in their development, the form that characterizes t
organization and the spirit that animates their activity; t
are all intimately related with the past. But the present
its explanation as well. Modern industry explains much
modern life. Its form, assumed so largely in the last quar
century, has been the dominant factor in shaping our
twentieth-century civilization. In this new industry la
unions have their place. To its newer phases one may
for further reasons for their existence. Among these eleme
the following may be noted as important.

Changing Proportions of Capital and Labor. — The amo
of capital and the supply of labor are constantly chang
These changes are especially prominent in modern times. T
are not well adjusted to each other. When capital is a
mulated from savings it must be put to work. This can
effectively done only by combining it in proper proportions
labor. When the labor supply is increased modern industria
has no place for it except as it finds a complement of cap
Both of these factors of production are increasing. But
increase is neither systematic nor balanced. The changes
quite independent each of the other. Birth rate is contr
only indirectly by industrial demands for labor. Immigra
is regulated in amount by a variety of forces, industrial, polit
and humanitarian. Its distribution is quite unregula
Savings also have their stimulants and their checks, but
are by no means all industrial. Taxing policies, political p
and social ambitions act very directly on savings as a so
of capital. These suggestions make it clear that the importa
of capital and labor each to the other, so fully recognized w
measuring industry in terms of efficiency, is quite overloo

58

he matter of definite regulation and scientific adjustment. doubtless true that "in the long run" the birth rate, the ber of immigrants, expanding industry, increase of capital, automatically adjusted after a fashion. But this "long " is too long for the individual to contemplate with patience. exigencies are so pressing that they do not encourage osophical contemplation. In its effort to modify this malad- ment in favor of better immediate conditions for the la- rs, the labor organization finds one of the explanations s existence.

hile this phase of maladjustment in modern life has many ifestations, it is so general that its importance may not appear unless it is further indicated.

he Labor Market. — There is what is known as the "labor ket." Business outlook is frequently expressed in terms he condition of this market. But, as has been pointed out nother connection, a "good" labor market for an employer be "bad" for the workman. Much depends upon the t of view as between good and bad. In other words, this aining field has its antagonism and its frictions. The loyer seeks to create a favorable market when he goes to bargain for his labor. So the laborer tries to make the ket "good" for himself. Individually it is not easy for rers to do this. Collectively it is not so difficult. So or- zation is used in the accomplishment of this end.

apitalistic Production. — It is by no means unfamiliar to modern industry characterized as capitalistic. The sig- ance of this is not to be overlooked. Production is indirect. ls have yielded to machines. These in turn have grown e complex and interrelated until machinery has a meaning ewhat different from machine. Further, machinery has ged into plants. These vast complexes of capital goods inate modern industry. In them is carried to a point hith- undreamed of the division of labor and subdivision of esses. There are many meanings to such a situation. One at labor has been made more dependent upon conditions. e was when labor was the shaping factor in industry and s and implements were assistants. Now the relation is e reversed. Capital dominates and labor assists. This situation is important in at least three particulars. First:

there is a separation of the workman from his tools.
tools are now parts of an industrial plant. Without
labor is ineffective. With them production is enormousl
ulated. But empty-handed labor is at a tremendous dis
tage. Second: men formerly produced for purposes of con
tion. The relation was very direct. Now production is
more indirectly related to consumption. Formerly the
saw the result of his labor growing into a product the disp
of which, if not its consumption, would lie largely in h
hands. Labor now works for wages, scarcely knowing
it is producing. Its chief concern now is not the "crea
utilities," but rather it is getting and keeping a "job."
(and naturally following from these two) the workman
pendent upon others for the opportunity to work. Ind
initiative still has a high value and it should still be pr
in season. Yet there is more of pure rhetoric in it tha
was in former days. Where machinery is so complex
necessary to industry and where, because of this, it is
by the employer, the opportunity is quite entirely at t
posal of the employer. This creates a dependency that
real. To aid in protecting the interests of laborers ami
changes growing out of capitalistic production, labor
have appeared to many laborers as necessary.

Entrepreneur Régime. — In the previous paragraph
dustrial system has been spoken of as capitalistic. Th
has been generally accepted as fairly descriptive, but it
evident that industry has progressed beyond this charac
stage. To the use of capital goods has been added as
stage in development the specialization in its manag
Ownership and management are not so completely un
formerly. Indeed it is undoubtedly more accurate to c
the entrepreneur's stage of industry. The significance
becomes evident when it is related to another phase of d
ment. There is the historical change from "status" to
tract," a change the importance of which has been mu
phasized. Contract relations have occupied a large place
thought. But the entrepreneur is making one side of t
tract and the empty-handed laborer the other. This i
very real practical question in regard to the contract re
of modern industry. Some facts have already been stat

he laborer at a disadvantage in adjusting that particular
ct relation that is called the wage-bargain. Our boasted
ies in the fact that no better method has been found for
ng such questions than in an atmosphere of freedom of
ct. But a laborer cannot wait as an employer can if terms
: agreed upon at once. A day lost to a laborer cannot be
ıp. Necessity for a daily income flowing from daily labor,
sized by a dependent family, does not allow of a laborer
ıg for long an offer that will not be held open indefinitely.
ıt a heavy disadvantage in bargaining. He is offered em-
ent which he may accept or not as he may please. He is
-ed together with others in large numbers or "gangs"
is a "hand." He cannot always know where the labor
: is favorable to him, and if he knows he cannot always
' to it. Home ties, such as family relations, a house partly
ır on an instalment plan, education of children, — these
old him to a limited area. Such serious and practical
ıntages serve to upset that degree of equality in bar-
; power which is essential to the establishment and main-
e of practical freedom of contract. The unions seek to pro-
e laborers' interests against these disadvantages.

e of Industrial Change. — The very rapidity of the
s of recent years brings hardship as well as benefit. In-
ıls often pay the price of social benefit, but they seldom do
ngly. Nor does society always seek to compensate them
Changes in skill or craft are slow. An improved process
r an improved machine and an improved man. The im-
process is a saving to the employer and a benefit to the
ınity. The improved machine may be built and the old
crapped," it being charged against the industry. The im-
man is found in the vocational or trade school perhaps,
ıt it will not occasion very great delay before the young
taught. But the one skilled in the old process has so
skill that it is second nature and what is to be done with
It requires time to shape and fashion men to the right
ıd degree of skill for industry. They cannot be changed
uch after the shaping has once been done. These laborers
· situation from an angle of their own interests and act
ngly. Mutual concern leads to a use of the advantages
ıs for self-protection.

Labor's Replacement Fund. — Another unquestioned p
of industry is its speed. Machines are geared up to the p
that will secure the maximum of product consistent with
welfare of the machine which is intended to be short-lived a
way. This places a tax on the energies of men. The resu
premature old age. For the machine there is a replacem
fund. This takes the place of machinery when the latte
scrapped. For the men there are wages from which they
supposed to accumulate a "replacement fund."

For hired capital this replacement fund is taken care o
standard methods recognized by the rules of good busi
The lender looks after that before the loan is negotiated.
not so for the individual laborer. He cannot pay a commis
to an agent to place his labor for him, as a capitalist can
machine is built primarily to be used in this way. It is buil
speed. Men can become adjusted to such needs only by ev
tion and a process of the survival of the adaptable. This
slow process; too slow to amount to anything practically.
machine can be separated from its owner and can be used wit
danger. The laborer must be where he labors. He is not
from the danger of his labor. He takes his whole self, not sir
his industrial self, to his work. Nervous strain is felt on the
himself, the whole being. Monotony, strain, weariness, are
to the whole man and last after work hours are over. He ca
leave them in the factory. In fact he must not only carry t
away but he must return the next day without them. §
conditions are to be considered in explaining the existence
activities of unions.

Industrial Depressions. — The irregularity of business
ditions is a fact from which modern industry has not yet f
itself. Bad times follow good times and retrenchment is
essary. But interest and rent are more generally fixed tha
often realized. Long term leases create demands that mus
met. Long term notes, bonds, mortgages, preferred stock r
in charges that are fixed. When depression comes income
off and the convenience in meeting these charges is more or
curtailed. In such a situation a period of depression, a lean
is the harder to meet. This fact of irregular income on the
hand and the necessity for regular returns on the other, has n
the pay roll of special significance. Men can be laid off

ds cannot be set aside. Mills can be run on part time, but
head charges are continuous. Wages can be reduced, but
rest rates constitute a contract. This results in the pay roll
g a kind of buffer or shock absorber to ease the jolts in a
od of hard times. It is to make the pay roll more nearly con-
t, to prevent a resort to it whenever economies in the busi-
become necessary, that laborers resort to unions.

orporate Organization. — Finally, in even a partial list of
characteristic features of modern industry the spread of the
orate form of business organization must not be omitted.
corporation is the dominant form. This has changed the
ion between employer and employee from the personal to
impersonal. Directors determine policies. The officers of
inistration carry these policies into effect. This they do
ugh superintendents, foremen and bosses. The workman
es into intimate contact with the foreman and the boss.
sionally he may see a superintendent, but he does not know
He never speaks with one. The employer does not appear
im as a man with human interests and relations. The em-
er is a corporation. There is much of real psychological
rtance in this change. There is no individual to bargain
, because the foreman who has received instructions to take
fty or a hundred more hands has no authority to meet the
es of these hands as to any of the working conditions. His
se is set for him. The board of directors sitting around the
in the directors' room determine wages, hours and condi-
of labor and a man is taken on if he is willing to accept
. There is no bargaining. It is to restore something of
personal relations and to secure some degree of bargaining
wages that the men unite and authorize officers to act for
. An executive committee of a union with a thousand or
members can meet a board of directors and often gain a
ng. Through such an organization a thousand men can
as one man. Unions seek to take the place of the individ-
vorkman as corporations take the place of the individual
oyer and aim to restore something of the equality that pre-
ly existed.

aintenance of Dividends. — But while corporations have
rgely abolished the personal relations and personal bargain-
they have also been responsible for another important

change. In a previous paragraph it has been emphasize
fixed charges have become of large importance in b
finance. They have forced upon the pay roll a respon
that it has not always had to bear. To this must be a
practice in corporation finance that makes this burde
heavier. When times are good market quotations on co
stock run high because of large dividends. If these fa
business conditions continue over an extended period the
are capitalized. An enterprise with a comparatively
amount of real capital invested "cuts a melon," distr
more shares of stock to the same stockholders without
for any added investment or outlay on their part. The
stock issues become a fixed charge against further ea
Not in the same sense as would be true of bonds, to b
but yet virtually a fixed charge against the future earn
the industry. Regular dividends of the established amoun
be paid on them because the credit of the company is at
From two to four or five or more times the reasonable ret
the initial investment are thus paid as dividends. Str
laborers against high dividends to stockholders are no
occurrences yet. But it is not at all improbable that th
quency may increase. Union leaders are following very
ligently the reports of the numerous investigations into b
activity. They are learning more of these modern finance
ods. They are becoming more directly interested in then
organizations among laborers are becoming more ac
seeking to protect their own interests in these lines. It is
to be a very positive reason for some of the policies of or
labor.

EMPLOYERS' ASSOCIATIONS

One other element demands attention. Employers' a
tions are a power that has to be reckoned with. It n
admitted that they are of not quite the same significance
elements that have been named thus far in the chapter
ployers would explain their organizations often, if not alw
their answer to the organization of labor. In a sense this
Yet not entirely so. A more thorough investigation mig
to the question: who began it? No very satisfactory

could follow such an investigation. Nor does it need to be made. The situation is clear at the present time. Employers' associations exist. They are powerful. No one realizes this more fully than the laborer himself. To counteract their power and to secure to themselves a greater bargaining strength, the laborers seek to organize the more effectively. Each new element of organization on the part of one has led to a new move by the other, so that in the past few years it is probably in part true that each side can truthfully say that it is strengthening its organization because the other is doing the same.

Early Associations. — These associations of employers are not a purely modern invention. The early efforts of the laborers to speak collectively were met by collective replies from their employers. As early as 1832 the merchants and shipowners of Boston formed an association to deal with their laborers. They are reported to have voted to "discountenance and check the unlawful combination formed to control the freedom of individuals as to the hours of labor and to thwart and embarrass those by whom they are employed and liberally paid." They also "deplored the pernicious and demoralizing tendency of those combinations and the unreasonableness of the attempt, in particular where mechanics are held in so high estimation and their skill in labor so liberally rewarded." They finally resolved: "We will neither employ any journeyman who at the time belongs to such combinations, nor will we give work to any master mechanic who shall employ them while they continue thus pledged to each other and refuse to work the hours it has been and now is customary for mechanics to work." This combination is reported to have embraced one hundred and six firms in all. There were other associations during these early years, all formed for essentially the same purpose and expressing themselves in much the same manner as to the necessity for controlling the laborers in their organized activities.

Later Growth. — In 1864 the iron founders of Chicago recognized the necessity of an association in that city. As a result was formed the Iron Founders Association of Chicago. This body apparently agreed that the laborers might properly form their unions for purposes that concerned only themselves. Such activity must be kept, however, within proper limits. "When employees seek to enter the sphere of employers," they asserted, "and to dictate to them in the management of their business, it becomes not only the right but the duty of employers to check and suppress such movements by any lawful means."

It was not long before national associations came into the field. In 1875 the National Potters Association was formed. Then followed the Stove Founders National Defense Association (1886) which was further developed into the more comprehensive National Founders Association (1898). The metal trades came together in the National Metal Trades Association (1899). By 1905 several important trades were organized on a national basis. Among them were the stove and furnace industry, metal foundry work, lake transportation, machine construction, publishing and printing, marble cutting and manufacture of ready-made clothing. All of these became strong national organizations treating with the employees collectively by contracts. In addition to these larger ones, there were numerous local associations formed for the same general purposes.

The National Association of Manufacturers was formed in 1895. Its main purpose was to push export trade. It early became interested in the activities of labor organizations and developed its policies accordingly. By 1903 it had formed the Citizens Industrial Association of America. This last named association became at once very active in connection with labor unions. In 1903 the president of the older organization, who was made the first president of the Citizens Industrial Association of America, devoted his presidential address almost entirely to the relations of capital and labor. The policy made the association the leader in opposition to "trade union encroachments." It was evidently as the result of this address that the Citizens Industrial Association was formed. Together these two associations (which were in a sense a single organization) represented a combination of sixty national associations, sixty-six district and state organizations and three hundred thirty-five locals. One more step in the consolidation was brought about in 1907 with the formation of the National Council for Industrial Defense. This was made up of two hundred twenty-eight national, state and local organizations of business men. The Citizens Industrial Association of America was one of this group. The labor principles of the National Association of Manufacturers may be summed up in the following words: "The National Association of Manufacturers disapproves absolutely of strikes and lockouts, and favors an equitable adjustment of all differences between employers and employees by an amicable method that will preserve the rights of both parties."

Characteristic Form. — The usual form of the organization of these employers' associations may be briefly described in outline. The membership consists of employing firms. These members elect an administrative council. Dues are paid and become the basis for a "defense fund." Any employer who has trouble in his shop is bound by the rules to report the same to the council. If the trouble be serious, the council takes charge and under penalties more or less heavy the employer is bound to take no action not advised or approved by the council. The council investigates and endeavors to adjust the difficulties in accordance with the principles on which the association is based. If the adjustment cannot be made in this manner, then all the members of the association become in fact backers of the employer in his struggle. If the territory covered by the membership be large, the area is divided into districts and a chairman and vice-chairman named for each district. These, together with the officers of the association and the salaried executive secretary, constitute the administrative council. The executive officer investigates cases of trouble first. When he takes charge, the employer is bound to carry out any decision made by him and the administrative council. Pending such action and decision he cannot make a settlement in any other way. In case of strike, the association furnishes aid in various forms. Through employment agencies they may assist him in securing competent and docile workmen. They may provide for having his orders filled through other shops. They may provide him with necessary cash in case of need. They may engage a number of skilled men under yearly contracts who will be available to send to any shop where they may be needed because of a strike. They may issue a periodical or circular which will convey to all members such items as may be of interest. These various activities may of course be modified to suit the needs of either the locality or the industry. The thoroughness of the coöperation is sufficiently apparent.

Purposes: Employers' Statements. — Two lines of statements from such associations as these must be made in order to see their purposes as clearly as the laborers do. Taking the Citizens Industrial Association for illustration, there is first the set of resolutions adopted at their first meeting.

"Whereas, the strained relations between employer and employee are rapidly reducing the business conditions of the country into a state of chaos and anarchy, and the forces of socialism which are assuming control of the situation regard neither law nor the rights and the liberties of individuals, and

"Whereas, the Constitution of the United States provides that 'Congress shall have power to regulate commerce with foreign nations and among the several States,' and further provides that 'No person shall be deprived of life, liberty, or property without due process of law, nor shall private property be taken without just compensation,' therefore be it

"Resolved, that this convention demands that the officials, whether civic, State, or national, enforce the law of the land and see to it that every man, woman and child seeking to earn an honest livelihood shall be protected therein by the whole force of the State or of the nation, if it be necessary.

"Resolved, therefore, that in carrying on a firm and uncompromising contest with the abuses of unions as now constituted and conducted, at the same time acknowledging the free right of workmen to combine, and admitting that their combination when rightfully constituted and conducted may prove highly useful, we earnestly desire to act, and believe we are acting, in the true interests of the workingmen themselves, for our welfare is inseparable from theirs and theirs from ours; we are essentially interdependent, each is indispensably necessary to the other; and those who stir up strife between us are enemies of mankind.

"Resolved, that the Citizens Industrial Association of America is in earnest sympathy with every movement in the interest of labor. Believing that there can be no national prosperity where the working masses are ground down in hopeless poverty and ignorance, we hold, as happiest of all the results of the great industrial revolution achieved in the last half century, the greatly advanced and improved condition of the working-man at the present day."

The second line of statements appears in the suggestions and the plans of the organization. One of the purposes was the "protection of free labor." This was to be accomplished by a bureau of information for the use of the members. One of the purposes of the bureau was to "keep a carefully tabu-lated record of all lawbreakers and undesirable workmen." The union label was denounced as "a form of discrimination, in fact a species of the boycott." From the statement of the officials it is learned that "this is not the proper time to talk conciliation . . . since the principles and demands of organized labor are absolutely untenable to those believing in the indi-vidualistic social order. Neither is it the time to talk arbitra-tion or joint agreements."

Labor's View. — The laborer who is at all observant of this situation will be sure to be more impressed with the second line of statements than with the first. He will see in these combi-nations fighting organizations against which he must oppose some force or allow his liberties to be determined for him en-tirely by the employers.

These denunciations of labor organizations are not pecu-liar to any one group of employers. The list of quotations might be extended to much greater length. Yet one other state-ment must suffice to illustrate. "Since we," as employers, "are responsible for the work turned out by our workmen, we must therefore have full discretion to designate the men we consider competent to perform the work and to determine the conditions under which that work shall be prosecuted; the question of the competency of the men being determined solely by us. While disavowing any intention to interfere with the proper functions of labor organizations, we will not admit of any interference with the management of our business."

The description of this situation may be closed with the statement of an advocate of the employers' associations. "All the employers' organizations with which I am familiar are based upon the principle of dealing fairly with their workingmen and establishing equity and justice as between the two. . . . The real right or the real principle which should govern both bodies is a common interest." Doubtless every labor leader would subscribe to such a description of every labor union with which he is familiar. It is not the general statements on either side that count with each other. The acts of each prompt the other to continue the work of organization.

Conclusions. — Thus there appears an important group of reasons for the existence and the activities of labor unions. Taken together with historical developments they form a solid basis of explanation for their being. Their policies, their activities, their fighting spirit, all are easily enough accounted for when the explanation is fairly sought out. Without a review of these various elements, historical and current, it is quite impossible to understand trade unionism. To one whose mind is closed to these facts, labor organizations must appear quite incomprehensible. But to one who does see clearly the lines of current industrial life and who does trace them fairly into the past, their existence must cease to be cause for wonder.

One may or may not approve their policies. That is a question that comes later. One cannot fairly say that labor organizations have no reason for existence.

PART II
THE STRUCTURE

CHAPTER V

THE KNIGHTS OF LABOR

In spite of changing conditions and the fleeting nature of associations of laborers, efforts persisted for a larger organization, one that would in some way unite all elements of labor strength into a single unit in the interests of efficiency. The need was recognized more and more, and past efforts furnished both the warning and the inspiration to consummate the plan. The years during the Civil War and immediately following witnessed the formation of several societies that were of direct importance not so much for what they actually did as for the influence on the movement that finally did bring together into one organization a larger number of workmen engaged in a greater variety of trades than the country had yet seen.

Forerunners. — One that should be named in this list was the Knights of St. Crispin. This society was formed among the more intelligent shoe makers and had an unusual development. It began its career in 1867 with the first working lodge organized in Milwaukee. Its spread was rapid in the centers of the shoe trade especially in Massachusetts. In 1868 the first Grand Lodge meeting was held with about 600 chapters chartered. "For five subsequent years," as is stated in McNeill's Labor Movement, "the Order of the Knights of St. Crispin was a power in the land. It made and unmade politicians; it established a new journal; it started coöperative stores; it fought, often successfully, against threatened reductions of wages and for better returns to its members for labor performed; it grew rapidly in numbers, and became international in its scope; it is estimated that 400 lodges and 40,000 members at one time owed it allegiance; it became the undoubted foremost trade organization of the world." The causes for its decline, as given by its own members, were interference in politics, treachery of leaders, high salaried officers. Speaking more in the spirit of the times, the writer just quoted says that "to the dispassionate observer, it would seem as if a deeper reason exists for the failure. . . . The Crispins failed, not because they were a trade organization, but because, while seeking justice for their own members, they failed to be just to the workers outside their fold. The excessive restrictions imposed by local lodges on their members against teaching any parts of boot or shoe making to others, was as untenable a position as the 'iron-clad' of the manufacturers."

One other organization of this period that should receive mention was the National Labor Union. This was a delegate convention made up of representatives of local, state and national trade associations the membership of which at its height was reported to be 640,000. Seven annual conventions were held beginning in 1866. At first the powers of the national body were advisory only and its aim chiefly political. Its powers were strengthened somewhat as experience showed weakness. The convention was given authority to charter new locals and to exercise some degree of control over them. While the growth of this society was unusual it was nevertheless of a "mushroom" character. In 1871 the complaint was made that it was losing ground and the following year the annual convention proved to be a "funeral," the society dying of what Professor Ely has diagnosed as "the fatal malady, politics." The association had accomplished during its short life two noteworthy things, however. It had given a strong impulse to the eight-hour movement and contributed largely to the agitation for the establishment of bureaus of labor statistics.

Origin of Knights of Labor. — The movement that expressed itself in these and other forms at about the same time was to manifest itself in a society of larger proportions, wider influence, and greater degree of permanency, the Noble Order of the Knights of Labor. The more important facts in the history of this society may be related very briefly. The tailors of Philadelphia had had a strong organization. The cheap work by which government contracts had been filled for army supplies had undermined the standards of the trade and the Garment Cutters Union was losing ground. Among the members, however, were a few more farsighted who looked beyond the pending dissolution to something better. When the final vote had been taken which accomplished the dissolution of the union, some of these men immediately took up the plans that had already been partly formulated. The leader of this group was Uriah S. Stevens who became the founder of the new society. In 1869 the new relations were assumed and in 1871 the name, the Noble Order of the Knights of Labor, was adopted. The membership was at first limited to tailors. Soon others were admitted as associate members and after they became familiar with the aims were permitted to organize new societies among their respective trades. These were known as assemblies. With the formation of new ones the parent assembly became Assembly No. 1 and the others were numbered serially. No. 2 was organized among the Philadelphia ship carpenters. No. 3 was made up of shawl weavers. Then in turn came carpet weavers, riggers, while still other trades followed. Before the end of 1873 there had been formed eighty assemblies in various trades, some in territory outside of Philadelphia. By the close of 1876 there were over one hundred such local assemblies.

When five assemblies had been formed it began to appear necessary to have some authority uniting them. At first there was established a Committee on the Good of the Order made up of three from each local. Assembly No. 1 retained its prestige and was practically the center of influence and authority. By 1873 this temporary committee gave way to a delegated body known as the District Assembly. With the increase of local assemblies other district assemblies were formed designated numerically, as were the locals. The parent local of which Stevens was the Master Workman together with the other early ones formed District Assembly No. 1 with Stevens at its head. The increase of district assemblies led to the establishment of a national union. In 1878 this was consummated in a General Assembly with delegates from seven states representing fifteen trades. Stevens was chosen first Grand Master Workman. The year following delegates assembled from thirteen states. After that time conventions were held annually. Thus the new society grew on its organization side. Its membership increased with unparalleled rapidity. No very accurate information exists as to the numbers for the earlier years. The quarterly reports for the first year show that at the end of the first three months twenty-eight members were enrolled; the second quarter showed forty-three members; in the third this was increased to fifty-two and at the end of the year the number stood at sixty-nine. Rumor seems to have exaggerated the numbers. In 1878 the membership was reported to be as high as 80,000. This, in the opinion of Carroll D. Wright, was an exaggeration. He regarded the membership as probably small, "not counting far into the thousands." By 1883 the reports were more reliable and at this time the membership stood at 52,000. The next three years showed a phenomenal growth, expanding in 1886 to over 700,000. This was the high water mark. The authorities realized that it would be quite impossible to assimilate new members so rapidly and that there was danger that the ideals of the society would suffer. The growth was checked for a time for this reason. Other influences began to act also with the result that the numbers began to decrease.

One special feature of the Knights of Labor that characterized its early years was its close secrecy. Its name was not known but was designated by five asterisks. This caused it to be spoken of as the society of the "Five Stars." Considerable alarm was awakened by the fact that the appearance of certain cabalistic signs appearing mysteriously in a public place would bring together hundreds of workingmen. The clergy, both Catholic and Protestant, took notice of the fact and used their influence in public utterance against this unknown society. At the beginning the Knights had an elaborate ritual handed on by word of mouth but not reduced to writing. This ritualistic form later gave way to general laws of government which were slowly expanded into a constitution and laws controlling the relations of the several parts. The public hostility was somewhat modified by a partial removal of the injunction to secrecy. This was done first by making it optional with each local to decide whether or not secrecy conduced to the best results in its locality. Many came out in the open, and in 1881 action was taken by the General Assembly removing the secrecy from the Order generally. With the adoption of this new policy much of the keener opposition was removed and the membership began to increase rapidly.

Its Form. — At the height of its power the Knights of Labor was organized on the plan that has just been indicated. The local assemblies constituted the organization. These locals were composed sometimes of one trade and sometimes of several. It was not, strictly speaking, a trade society. The earlier locals were usually of a single trade while the ones formed later were more generally mixed. There were some instances of locals composed entirely of women, though it was not till 1881 that women were admitted to membership. The membership was made up generally of wage earners, however. Skilled and unskilled alike were accepted. In 1886 a mixed assembly in Chicago had a woman as its "Master Workman." Colored workmen were first organized in assemblies in 1883 and for a few years this class of membership increased rapidly. A later regulation declared that at least three-fourths of the membership of new locals must be of the wage earning class. The membership, open as it was, was not without limitation. The age limit was sixteen for unions already established but for new locals the membership must be entirely of those over eighteen years of age. A further restriction appears in the following section of the constitution of locals. "No person who either sells or makes a living, or any part of it, by the sale of intoxicating drink, either as manufacturer, dealer or agent, or through any member of the family, can be admitted to membership in this order, and no lawyer, banker, professional gambler or stock broker can be admitted." Prior to 1881 physicians also were excluded.

The district assemblies were formed sometimes on the basis of trade groups and in other cases the geographical bond united them. More recently the districts have come to be limited by state boundaries and the district assembly has become the state assembly. The General Assembly is a delegate body representing the entire membership. Usually the locals are related to the general body through the district or state unit, though this is not always the case. Some locals are independent of the district organization and are directly connected with the General Assembly.

Its Spirit. — With this organization the Knights of Labor has been able to make itself felt in industrial life. First it was powerful by virtue of its secrecy. With the passing of this phase the society took up with enthusiasm the policy of the strike. Though this was not entered upon without opposition yet the majority prevailed and strikes were popular in the Order. This counsel prevailed during the years between 1878 and 1883, after which the opinion changed. The constitution governing local assemblies was modified containing the following clause: "While acknowledging that it is sometimes necessary to enjoin an oppressor, yet strikes should be avoided whenever possible. Strikes, at best, only afford temporary relief; and members should be educated to depend upon thorough organization, coöperation, and political action, and, through these, the abolishment of the wage system. Our mission cannot be accomplished in a day or a generation. Agitation, education, and organization are all necessary." In the establishment of an assistance fund the Order was particularly careful to guard against the use of this money for strikes. "We declare," read this section of the constitution, "that strikes are deplorable in their effect and contrary to the best interests of the order, and therefore nothing in this article must be construed to give sanction to such efforts for the adjustment of any difficulty, except in strict accordance with the laws laid down in this article." In the sections that followed the law was made so rigid that it was practically impossible for a local to secure any funds for the conduct of a strike. Thus was brought to an end the possibility of a strike that had behind it the support of the Order as a whole. "We must teach our members," declared the leader, Mr. Powderly, before one of the annual conventions, "that the remedy for the redress of wrongs we complain of does not lie in the suicidal strike; but it lies in thorough effective organization. Without organization we cannot accomplish anything; through it, we hope to forever banish that curse of modern civilization, — wage-slavery."

Probably no society has ever looked out upon a more brilliant future than did the Noble Order of the Knights of Labor as it completed its organization with the General Assembly at its head. Its aims were noble and its ideals high. One of its founders in discussing the prospects for a new society at the time of the dissolution of the union of the garment cutters said that he had been looking all his life "for something that will be advantageous to the masses; something that will develop more of charity, less of selfishness; more of generosity, less of stinginess and meanness than the average society has as yet disclosed to its members." This is shown again in the words of another of the leaders when speaking of the fact that the Order of the Knights had grown out of a failure. It was, he said, "a failure of the trade union to grapple, and satisfactorily deal with the labor question on its broad, far-reaching, basic principle: the right of all to have a say in the affairs of one. It was because the trade union failed to recognize the rights of man and looked only to the rights of tradesmen that the Knights of Labor became a possibility."

Again the exalted ideals of the founders may be illustrated in the words of Stevens himself: "The few are millionaires; the many struggle for bread. Where, if not here in this Western World, shall the patriotism and statesmanship be found to preserve the race from destruction? Neither the bayonet, nor bullets from gatling guns can save us. Justice to all alone can do it. . . . Your presence here gives us life and hope. . . . Coming as you do from all over this continent, shows the magnitude of the awakening. It foretells the blessing of Heaven upon those who help themselves. It secures the coming 'to the fore' at an early day in industrial, political and social life of those principles and legal enactments that shall secure the physical well-being, the mental development and the moral elevation of mankind." These high hopes lived in the hearts of many who were inside the Order. Powderly, in closing his history says: "The historian of the future will record that the revolution inaugurated by the Knights of Labor and carried forward by the force of thought and ideas, won more for the cause of human liberty than the revolutions which spilled the blood of humanity's advocates through all the centuries of time."

In Simon's history the account opens with a most enthusiastic statement of the importance of the Order. "No labor organization in the world has ever had the strength, as well as the solidarity, of the Knights of Labor. It is a new factor in the labor problem, and one whose consequences can hardly yet be computed. In 1869 it had eleven members; it now has about 1,000,000 in the United States and 300,000 more in Canada. It is not a trades-union nor an assemblage of trades-unions. It accepts the unskilled worker to as full fellowship as the most cunning artisan. It is a society for mutual defence and united attack, which is so well intrenched that every careful thinker must recognize it as one of the social forces of the day. The marvelous rapidity of its growth is in itself the best proof of its utility. The fact that it lives and waxes strong is *prima facie* evidence that it has a right to live and to grow. At the present time it is the strongest weapon which civilization has put in the hands of labor." It is "an organization in whose power now rests perhaps the destinies of the republic. . . . The Knights of Labor may fail, but whether the organization dies or lives, it has taught a lesson which will never be forgotten as long as man shall earn his bread by the sweat of his brow. It has demonstrated the overmastering power of a national combination among workingmen. If the Knights of Labor were to dissolve to-morrow, on the next day a new society would be formed to push on their work."

Writing of this society in 1886 when it was in the height of its strength, Professor Ely describes it as "the most powerful and the most remarkable labor organization of modern times, established on truly scientific principles which involved either an intuitive perception of the nature of industrial progress, or a wonderful acquaintance with the laws of economic society."

Its Decline. — The decline in the influence of this society was no less striking than its rise. Within but a few years more than it had taken in building up its wide influence this had been lost, its membership declined, and though it still maintains its existence, it does so, to state it in the words of Professor Commons, as "a bushwhacking annoyance on the heels of its successor."

It should not be understood that the Knights of Labor did nothing but spring into prominence and out again. It had, in fact, an active life full of importance to its members. The truth of Professor Ely's statement is not to be doubted. In 1886 the organization not only had brilliant prospects but was adapted to its day remarkably well. It was a changing era, however, and the Knights came at the close of a period rather than at the beginning. It is not because the Noble Order of the Knights of Labor did nothing but exist for a brief period that it receives only a passing notice here. It belongs essentially to the past now and this is not primarily a history.

One of the elements of weakness in the Knights was its dual organization in a trade. During the last quarter of the nineteenth century the trade assemblies were forming on national lines. The Knights recognized these as important and sought to incorporate them.   In 1887 there were in the Order as many as twenty-two national trade assemblies.   These existed side by side with the labor assemblies making a dual organization. This proved undoubtedly to be an element of weakness.   From 1886, the year that registered the largest membership among the Knights, the decline in numbers and influence was steady. The causes for this have been stated in various forms and as of differing importance.   They may be summed up as four in number.   (1) The failure of expensive sympathetic strikes in which the Order became involved in spite of its professed disapproval of such acts in its later years.   (2) Activity in political affairs.   This was of course the result of experience and there was an abundance of precedent in favor of political action. It did not bring strength to the Order, however.   (3) The presence of the two distinct forms of organization mentioned above, the mixed labor assembly and the national trade assembly. These proved to be factors that undermined rather than built up the strength of the Order.   (4) The over-centralization of power in the hands of the general officers.   The promoters of the first assembly guarded very jealously their leadership. They were the source of authority.   This relation generated restlessness and suspicion in the place of strength.

CHAPTER VI

THE AMERICAN FEDERATION OF LABOR

Though the Knights of Labor had such conspicuous success, it must not be understood that it was the only such organization in the field. The period was one which saw many attempts to form larger consolidations among the laboring classes. As previously stated some of the national trade unions had already been established and were well on their way to permanency. Besides these there were numerous other associations formed especially after the recovery from the panic of '73. These societies were quite generally secret. Their objects were political after the example of their predecessors. All were transient, giving way to jealousy, imperfect organization and too great zeal in political activity. Among these are to be noted two that became of particular importance because of later developments.

Origin of American Federation. — The Knights of Industry and the Amalgamated Labor Union, the latter an offshoot of the Knights of Labor, united in issuing a call for a convention to meet at Terre Haute, Indiana, in August, 1881. Its object is supposed to have been to supplant the Knights of Labor. It soon developed that a majority of the delegates were opposed to a further extension of the labor societies and favored the extension of trade unions. As a result of this difference the secret organization was not formed. Another call was issued for a second meeting to be held in the fall of the same year. This call showed a realization of the dangers of so many organizations. As it declared: "We have numberless trades' unions, trades' assemblies or councils, Knights of Labor, and various other local, national, and international labor unions, all engaged in the noble task of elevating and improving the condition of the working classes. But great as has been the work done by these bodies, there is vastly more that can be done by a combination of all these organizations in a federation of trades' and labor unions." The result was a convention of about one hundred delegates representing more than 250,000 workingmen. At this meeting a permanent organization was effected, to be known as the Federation of Organized Trades and Labor Unions of the United States and Canada. This new society had a constitution and held annual meetings until 1886. In that year it was reorganized under a new constitution, the name being changed to the American Federation of Labor. In order to preserve the continuity in the organization this last Federation, in 1889, dated its origin and numbered its conventions from the beginning made in 1881.

The American Federation of Labor is at the present time the strongest organization in America and ranks high among the labor organizations of the world: "the sovereign organization," writes John Mitchell, "in the trade union world." Its history since its inception is one of steady growth, of consistent policy and aggressive management. The results appear in a powerful organization with all the force of a highly centralized body and all the power of a thoroughly democratic society. Its success may be attributed to a few important points of policy by which it has welded together the conflicting interests of many trades and held them with all the strength of a single purpose. It has avoided the shoals of politics which have wrecked so many strong associations in the past. It has consistently left to separate trades the direct control over the differing trade interests, thus avoiding the dangers of internal strife. The weakness arising from too many diverse interests in conflict has given way to the strength of united action where it is possible and to non-interference in trade interests where it is necessary. On these few simple principles the American Federation of Labor has builded well.

Its Form of Organization. — The Federation membership is made up principally not of individuals but of trade groups. It consists "of such Trade and Labor Unions as shall conform to its rules and regulations." The constitution sets forth in brief the object and form of organization. These may be described as follows, quoting freely from the pages of that document. They are: to secure the organization of local unions; to federate these locals into delegate bodies; to establish national and international trade unions and to promote the interests of such unions already formed — these unions based upon a strict recognition of the autonomy of each trade; to subdivide these unions into groups, called Departments, to be composed of unions in the same industry or having the same general interests.

The Convention. — With this form of organization it is inevitable that the real factors are the convention and the executive officers, and of these the former is the source of authority. The convention is a delegated body that assembles annually. The date of meeting, now fixed for the second Monday in November, has been chosen as best in that it comes after the excitement of election time, and just prior to the convening of legislative bodies, especially Congress with the President's Message. In this way, the leaders think, they can best get the public ear through the press reports of their proceedings and can most effectively bring their policies to the attention of the legislators. Even the President is thus provided with the latest word from Organized Labor and may shape his Message accordingly.

Representation. — The representation of the various unions in the convention is on the basis of membership. Nationals and internationals send one delegate for a membership of less than 4,000. Above this there is a proportionate increase of delegates: 4,000 or more, two delegates; 8,000 or more, three delegates; 16,000 or more, four delegates; 32,000 or more, five delegates; "and so on." Other bodies, not nationals, have one delegate each. The representation is allowed only if all dues are paid and all other obligations to the Federation properly discharged. In the convention of 1914 there were 369 delegates with 19,951 votes. These were made up as follows —

No. of Unions	Name	No. of Delegates	No. of Votes
95.....	Nationals or Internationals..........	248.....	19,825
22.....	State.............................	22.....	22
75.....	Central...........................	75.....	75
17.....	Trade and Federal Labor Unions....	17.....	28
5.....	Fraternal Organizations.............	7.....	1
214		369	19,951

Immediately on being called to order the President appoints the list of committees. The scope of the convention's work will be indicated by the names of the several committees. Each has a membership of fifteen. Rules and Order of Business, Report of President, Report of Secretary, Report of Treasurer, Resolutions, Laws, Organization, Labels, Adjustment, Local or Federated Bodies, Education, State Organization, Boycott, Building Trades.

Among the rules governing the proceedings of the convention some are of special interest. Resolutions of any character or proposals for changes in the constitution cannot be introduced in the convention after the fourth day, except by unanimous consent. All resolutions are referred for special consideration to the appropriate committee. A rule of procedure that might well be extended to lawmaking bodies is one requiring all matters referred to any committee to be reported back to the body. The report may be of any nature that the committee may decide upon, — favorable, unfavorable, non-committal, ambiguous, — but there must be a report. This prevents the killing of measures in committee and insures a fair and open consideration in true democratic style. The convention protects itself from its friends as well as from its enemies by a rule that none other than members of a *bona fide* trade union shall be permitted to address the convention or read papers therein except by a two-thirds vote of the delegates. Party politics, whether they be Democratic, Republican, Socialist, Populist, Prohibition or any other, shall have no place in the convention. To prevent the repetition of discussions already settled a rule provides that no grievance shall be considered by any convention that has been decided by a previous convention except upon the recommendation of the Executive Council. Grievances leave sore spots and these often do not heal within a year. The grieved party is thus prevented from seeking to establish his case after he has once lost.

Officers. — The officers of the Federation are President, eight Vice Presidents, a Secretary and a Treasurer, each elected at the last day of the convention. The term of office begins on the first day of January. If the elected officers are not chosen delegates to the convention the President and Secretary are *ex officio* members but without vote. All elected officers must be members of a union connected with the Federation. The duties of these officers are in general such as belong to the respective offices. The President presides at conventions, exercises supervision over the Federation and travels in its interests. He must file with the Secretary each month an itemized statement of his expenses and must make a full report at the annual convention. The President's report is one of the most important items of the convention business. It sums up the work of the year in a complete way, amounting to a current history for the twelve months touching all the activities of the Federation in particular and the labor movement in general. It further aims to point out as the lesson of experience means of strengthening the organization and discusses in a practical way the policies of the society.

In case of vacancy in the presidency the Secretary takes executive charge. A meeting of the Executive Council must then be called within six days for the election of a President for the remainder of the year. The Secretary has large responsibilities. With him lies the keeping of all books, records, documents, letters and accounts. He collects all moneys due the Federation, turning them over to the Treasurer, except a maximum sum of $2,000 for current expenses. This he may use only on approval of the President. All disbursements of the Federation must be shown by vouchers and a report that is carefully audited. With him are filed all reports and information called for from the unions affiliated with the Federation.

The office of Treasurer is relatively unimportant so far as the financial work is concerned. He receives funds from the Secretary, giving receipts for them and all orders for payment must be signed by the President and Secretary as well as by the Treasurer.

Executive Council. — The responsible administrative work rests with the Executive Council. This is composed of the Federation officers, eleven in number. This gives added importance to the Treasurer's office and provides work for the eight Vice Presidents. The constitution assigns to these no other work than that which is connected with the Council. Being made up of officers only, it very naturally takes to itself important powers. It is responsible virtually for carrying into effect the purposes of the Federation. It watches legislative measures that affect the interests of working people and initiates such legislation as the convention may direct. The work of organizing laborers into locals and nationals and of associating them with the Federation is carried on under the general direction of the Council.

The Council is authorized to send out speakers in the interest of the Federation whenever the revenues warrant such action. In a general supervisory capacity the Council has power to make rules to govern matters not in conflict with the constitution or with the constitutions of affiliated unions. Any rules so made must be embodied in the annual report to the convention. Vacancies in the Council (except in the Presidency) are filled by the Council itself by a majority vote.

Granting Charters. — In granting charters to unions that are to be affiliated with the Federation the Council must make sure of a positive and clear definition of the trade jurisdiction claimed by the applicant. If they regard it as a trespass upon any organization already in the Federation the charter cannot be granted without the written consent of that union. Other matters of a jurisdictional nature, such as changing a name of a union and the adjustment of membership with change of trade, are also under the direction of the Council subject to the approval of the Convention. The Council may revoke a charter once granted only when the revocation has been ordered by a two-thirds majority of a regular convention by a roll call vote. The Federation does not wait for unions to be formed and apply for membership. It is more aggressive than that. Paid organizers and advisors in addition to the officers are always at work. Wherever there is an opportunity of bringing men into an association or affiliating societies already existing, there the representatives of the Federation are at work. A recent case illustrates this. Until recently there has been trouble among steam shovel and dredge men. There were rival organizations fighting each other. After more than three years of effort these rivals were brought together on the basis of an amalgamation by the officers of the Federation. They have all come together as the International Brotherhood of Steam Shovel and Dredge Men, a national that has recently been chartered by the American Federation of Labor.

Activity of Officers. — The records of the Federation show that a large part of the activity of some of the officials consists in forming new associations and bringing them into the Federation. The annual report for 1914 contains a list of seventy-five national and international organizations formed from American Federation of Labor local unions alone in the last nineteen years. Some of these have not survived in the struggle so that the list cannot be understood as representing a net gain. In addition to this form of organization, which may be regarded as the final stage in the development, many charters are granted to local trade and labor unions, and to state and city central organizations. The total of these various charters for the eighteen years from 1897 to 1914, inclusive, was: internationals, 118; departments, 5; state federations, 43; city centrals, 1,294; local trade unions, 4,689; federal labor unions, 2,139;—a total of 8,288 charters in all.

Another phase of activity appears in the following incident in connection with the clothing trades. The Journeymen Tailors Union of America, one of the oldest of the trade unions, has been for a long time affiliated with the American Federation of Labor. The constitution of the Federation contains a clause requiring that before any affiliated organization can either change its title or extend its jurisdiction, it must receive the approval of the Federation. Before granting such approval, it would of course be the duty of the Federation's officials to see that the extension of jurisdiction or change of name did not conflict with the interests of existing unions. The Journeymen Tailors Union recently changed its name to the Tailors Industrial Union and assumed general jurisdiction over the garment making industry. This brought the newly named union, with its membership of 12,000, into conflict of jurisdiction with the United Garment Workers of America, with a membership of 60,000, and the International Ladies' Garment Workers Union, having 130,000 members. This action on the part of the journeymen tailors was reported to the convention of the Federation in 1914 as "not only unwarrantable and against the laws and practices of the American Federation of Labor, but against the interests of the entire tailoring or garment working industry." The action of the convention followed the recommendation of the Executive Council and "firmly and strongly rebuked the Journeymen Tailors Union for its unwarranted action and unjustifiable assumption of extension of jurisdiction." The tailors were instructed to resume the former title and cease to operate under an extended jurisdiction before a fixed date. The situation was complicated in this particular case by the fact that some locals of the United Garment Workers had seceded and had claimed to

be the real organization. These seceders joined with the journey-
men tailors in forming the new union and claiming the extended
jurisdiction. They assumed the label of the United Garment
Workers and claimed the right to authorize its use by the new
Tailors Industrial Union. In response to this the Federation,
through the Union Label Department, sent out notice that the
label no longer represented the American trade union movement.
The outcome of this pressure brought to bear by the American
Federation was to bring the unruly members back into line.
The tailors have resumed their former name and returned to
their earlier jurisdiction. It seems that if it had not been for
the strong coercive force of the Federation brought to bear
to prevent it, there would have been a serious fight before the
matter was finally adjusted.

That there was need for some change was recognized in the
report that was made to the convention. It was insisted, however, that changes in the trade looking toward a closer alliance
or amalgamation should be brought about through mutual
agreement among all the trades directly concerned and not by
the extension of one union arbitrarily to include all the others.

While the deliberate departure from the established rules of
the organization could not be overlooked by the officers of the
Federation, this drastic action is probably the beginning rather
than the end of the matter. Trouble has been brewing in the
clothing trades as a result of the confusion of relations between
unions. It is no longer a simple matter to distinguish between
custom made and ready made garments. The extension of
women's ready-to-wear garments has promoted the confusion.
There are now in addition to the Journeymen Tailors, the United
Garment Workers of America (workers on men's clothing) and
the International Ladies' Garment Workers Union (workers on
women's clothing) while the last named has six subdivisions
each operating more or less independently of the others. These
are (1) cloak, suit and skirt workers; (2) women's tailor made
garment workers; (3) dress and waist makers; (4) misses and
children's wear makers; (5) wrapper and kimono makers; and
(6) white goods or underwear makers. Overlapping among these
is the United Hebrew Trades. This is a situation that will
have to be cleared up in a constructive way before a permanent adjustment can be made.

It will readily appear that the Executive Council is the body of real importance, made up of eleven men practically always in session having large powers of direction and control and responsible only to the convention at its annual meetings. They are generally members of this convention and by virtue of their office would carry considerable weight of influence in case the Council is called upon to defend its course.

Revenues. — The revenues of the Federation are provided for by constitutional regulation. They are derived from a per capita tax upon the full paid up membership of all affiliated bodies as follows: national and international trade unions, a per capita tax of two-thirds of one cent per member per month; for local trade unions and federal labor unions, ten cents per member per month, five cents of which must be set aside to be used only in case of strike or lockout; local unions the majority of whose members are less than eighteen years of age, two cents per member per month; from central and state bodies, ten dollars per year payable quarterly. The prompt payment is assured by the rule that delegates shall not be entitled to a seat in the annual convention if dues are in arrears. If dues at any time are three months or more in arrears the union is automatically suspended from membership in the Federation and can be reinstated only by a vote of the convention after the arrears have been paid in full.

Regulating the Parts. — Means are adopted to avoid confusion in organization and to keep the Federation's interests intact. Central labor unions may not admit to their councils delegates from organizations that owe allegiance to any body hostile to any affiliated organization, to one that has been suspended or expelled, or to one that is not connected with any affiliated union. All nationals must instruct their locals to join central labor bodies, departments and state federations in their vicinity where such exist. Similarly, trades assemblies may be formed and if they exist all affiliated bodies must join. All such bodies, central labor unions, trades assemblies or departments, may act only within the limits of the rights of the Federation or the national unions. The laws of the two latter must not be violated by any regulations of the former named bodies.

To maintain this adjustment is clearly in the interests of peace though in fact a goodly amount of fighting is necessary to maintain it. It is a kind of fighting, however, that tends to unify the Federation in that it is directed against those who are urging plans that would beyond doubt greatly weaken the Federation as an organization. It closes the door against a large amount of internal strife.

To push the policy of organization further the Federation has a membership of locals directly with itself instead of indirectly with a national trade union. When its organizers are entering a new field it becomes necessary to organize locals of a new trade, possibly, or to bring together members of a variety of trades in a single local. The work in this line is indicated by the constitutional provision as follows: Seven wage workers of good character, following any trade or calling, who are favorable to trade unions, whose trade or calling is not organized, and who are not members of any body affiliated with this Federation, shall have the power to form a local body to be known as a "Federal Labor Union," and they shall hold regular meetings for the purpose of strengthening and advancing the trade-union movement, and shall have power to make their own rules in conformity with the constitution of the Federation and shall be granted a local certificate by the President of the Federation; provided the request for a certificate be indorsed by the nearest local or national trade union officially connected with the Federation, but not more than three federal labor unions shall be chartered in any one city. The President of the Federation has authority to appoint any member of any affiliated union to audit the accounts of any federal labor or local trade union and report the result to the President of the Federation. The books and accounts of such locals are open at all times to the inspection of persons so appointed. The fee for this certificate is five dollars which must accompany the application. The Federation before issuing certificates must refer applications from a vicinity where a chartered central labor union exists to that body for investigation and approval. These certificates of affiliation may not be granted by state federations of labor. It is vested solely in the Executive Council of the American Federation of Labor and the executive councils of affiliated national and international unions.

Departments. — One other phase of organization remains for emphasis, one that adds much to the strength of the Federation. Within the larger organization are formed subdivisions, called departments of the American Federation of Labor, and are sub-ordinate to the larger body. They may be established whenever the convention or the Executive Council may deem it advisable. Each department, once formed, manages and finances its own affairs. It is made up only of affiliated unions. Its laws must conform to and be administered in the same manner as the laws of the Federation, and through it are to be transacted such portions of the Federation's business as pertain especially to it. The departments hold their conventions either during or immediately before or after the convention of the Federation and in the same city. Its officers report all the activities of the department to the Executive Council in quarterly and annual reports, and either the president or secretary of each department must be present during some portion of every regular meeting of the Executive Council to take up matters of mutual interest. All affiliated nationals must become affiliated with any department in which they may be eligible, except the Union Label Trades Department.

Under these provisions five departments have been organized and maintain an active existence. They are the Building Trades Department, Metal Trades Department, Mining Department, Railroad Employees Department and the Union Label Trades Department. Each has its separate set of officers and executive council.

Its Character. — The American Federation of Labor is in reality a federation. Local trade unions generally are allied with the organization indirectly through their respective nationals. Of these nationals there are (report of November, 1914) 110 now affiliated. This number contains the majority of the larger unions. Of the 57 that have each a membership of 10,000 or more 40 are affiliated, and of the 100 that have a less membership 70 are enrolled in the Federation. These 110 unions represent approximately 22,000 locals most of which are in the United States.

In addition to these 110 national unions and the five departments, the Federation is made up of 43 state branches, each with a separate organization and character determined by the conditions in its own state; of 647 city centrals, delegate bodies with headquarters or places of meeting in the principal cities of the country; of 570 local trade and federal labor unions, all connected with the Federation in a manner already described.

State Organizations. — Of the state organizations a further word may be said that will throw some light upon their nature. The experience in New York State may be chosen as illustrative of the development in the older states. The Workingmen's Assembly was organized in New York State in 1865 as the result of the combined action of some of the labor unions in the preceding year. The events leading up to it were in brief as follows: A bill had been introduced in the state legislature in 1864 known as the Hastings Strike Bill. During the debate some amendments were added that so changed the nature of the bill that the originator withdrew his support and it became known as the Folger Anti-Trades Union Strike Bill. A strong opposition developed within the ranks of organized labor and the bill was finally defeated. The unions took to themselves the credit for defeating the bill. There followed a clear realization of the necessity for a more definite organization in order to secure protection "in relation to legislation as well as the question of wages and hours of labor." "From that victory in 1864," states one of the leaders, "the seeds of a great and grand organization were sown:" the Workingmen's Assembly came into existence. The defensive was soon laid aside and an aggressive and earnest agitation begun. Soon a high degree of complexity characterized this organization. It continued its separate existence until 1898. In the meantime other organizations came into being. In 1869 a district assembly of the Knights of Labor was formed. In 1888 the American Federation of Labor started its own state branch. These latter associations were formed in the state as a part of the regular spread of these two rival organizations, and for a time the three existed side by side. The rivalry was keen and so coöperation seemed impossible. In agitating for legislation in their interests the rival committees so confused the legislators that many measures which might have been won were lost because of the number of committees each claiming to represent the one authoritative body. This experience continued for several years after the necessity for unity had become apparent to some in the rival groups. During this time efforts were being made to secure some grounds on which a single organization could be formed. The acute rivalry between the two large national organizations made it difficult for them to come to-gether. The feeling on the part of the Workingmen's Assembly that it was first in the field and that its legitimate territory had been invaded by outside organizations made it difficult for it to surrender any of its prerogatives as a representative of the labor interests of the state. The growing strength of the Federation in all parts of the country made it a power that must be reckoned with, and so after years of deliberation and repeated experiences in the wastefulness of rivalry the two were united into the Workingmen's Federation of the State of New York in 1898. Under this name the new association remained until 1910 when it changed its name to the New York State Federation of Labor. The older leaders had passed out of control, the representatives of the Federation dominated and in the interests of uniformity of name the Federation secured the present title. For a few years after this amalgamation further efforts were made to secure a union with the state branch of the Knights of Labor. It seemed for a time as if this union might be accomplished. Details could not be satisfactorily adjusted, however, and the two have remained apart. With the increasing strength of the one and the waning influence of the other the adjustment seems now to be definitely settled, although a real difficulty remains in the handicap that comes to the work of both organizations as the result of their rivalry.

In the constitutions of the early Assembly and the independ-ently formed branch of the Federation there was but little difference. The constitution of the Workingmen's Assembly, as it stood in 1884, was practically the constitution of the Working-men's Federation as it existed in 1905, and these are essentially the same as the fundamental law of the state federation as it is at present. The objects of the organization remain embodied in the same form of statement in the latest copy of the constitution of the New York State Federation of Labor as was phrased in the earlier issues of the constitutions of the Workingmen's Assembly and the Workingmen's Federation. The objects as stated will show the nature of this particular branch of work.

Their Objects. — To agitate such questions as may be for the benefit of the working classes, in order that they may obtain the enactment of such measures by the state legislature as will be beneficial to us, and the repeal of all oppressive laws which now exist. To use all means consistent with honor and dignity so to correct the abuses under which the working classes are laboring as to insure to them their just rights and privileges. To use our utmost endeavors to impress upon the various divisions of work-ingmen the necessity of a close and thorough organization, and of forming themselves into local unions wherever practicable. Thus the two objects are expressed and they indicate fairly the field of activity of these state federations. They seek to influence legislation in their favor and act as agent for the larger organiza-tion in pushing the work of closer and more thorough organiza-tion of all laborers within the state. A plan to limit the work to the former of these two was adopted in 1889. It proved im-practicable and in the constitution of 1897 the restriction does not appear. The dropping out of the more restricted policy was doubtless the result of the consolidation that was effected at that time, the new organization retaining the purposes of the Amer-ican Federation of Labor. The present organization, then, is under the constitution of the New York State Federation of Labor.

The constitutions of these state organizations are essentially the same as that of the American Federation of Labor, varied only to meet the differing situations and the modified purposes of the states. The state federations consist of the annual conven-tion which is a delegate body. The membership, however, is generally not restricted to delegates from unions affiliated with the American Federation of Labor. The locals are represented directly instead of through national unions, and any local may be represented except such as may have seceded from or been expelled from a national union. The work of the several con-ventions is along the same lines. Officers chosen at the conven-tions constitute the executive council, a body that carries the authority of the organization subject to the approval of the annual conventions.

City Centrals. — In describing the organization of the city centrals it will not be necessary to add much. These bodies have a relation to the interests of labor in the city similar to the state federation and the state interests. They commonly meet more frequently, as once a week in the large cities. They are delegate meetings with the usual corps of officers necessary to administer their affairs. Their work consists in pushing organization, extending their representation in locals not affiliated with the central, and in considering wage scales, trade agreements, and other matters of a similar nature. At these meetings matters of a most intimate relation to the welfare of organized labor are freely discussed. Efforts are made to keep the discussions confined to questions that relate directly to labor affairs. This proves difficult indeed and the presiding officer not infrequently has to test the full extent of his authority in order to enforce the rules that bar all political discussion and all personalities. These men speak plainly in their discussions and seldom attempt voluntarily to conceal their impressions.

While these city centrals are now generally affiliated in the American Federation of Labor, such has not always been the case. Indeed they came into existence before the beginning of the Federation. Under the name of trades' assemblies they were formed soon after 1830. In 1866 there were thirty centrals organized. These were more or less active both in politics and industry according to the personnel of the leaders and the temper of the times. With the expansion of the American Federation of Labor these were gathered in one by one and new ones were formed, so that at the present time by far the larger number look to the Federation as their creator.

Policy of the Federation. — The American Federation of Labor has had from the start two distinct and characteristic objects of policy. It was peculiarly a trade organization, preserving the trade societies as the units; and it eschewed all purpose of "going into politics." The first point of policy was set forth in the preamble to the constitution adopted in 1887. "We therefore declare ourselves in favor of the formation of a thorough federation, embracing every trade and labor organization in America, under the trades-union system of organization." On the second point it declared itself more at length in a manifesto that Carroll D. Wright has declared to be "worthy of preservation in any history of the labor movement."

"We favor this federation because it is the most natural and assimilative form of bringing the trades' and labor unions together. It preserves the industrial autonomy and distinctive character of each trade and labor union, and, without doing violence to their faith or traditions, blends them all in one harmonious whole — a 'federation of trades' and labor unions.'

Such a body looks to the organization of the working classes as workers, and not as 'soldiers' (in the present deprecatory sense) or politicians. It makes the qualities of a man as a worker the only test of fitness, and sets up no political or religious test of membership. It strives for the unification of all labor, not by straining at an enforced union of diverse thought and widely separated methods, not by prescribing a uniform plan of organization, regardless of their experience or interests; not by antagonizing or destroying existing organizations, but by preserving all that is integral or good in them and by widening their scope so that each, without destroying their individual character, may act together in all that concerns them. The open trades unions, national and international, can and ought to work side by side with the Knights of Labor, and this would be the case were it not for men either overzealous or ambitious, who busy themselves in attempting the destruction of existing unions to serve their own whims and mad iconoclasm. This should cease and each should understand its proper place and work in that sphere, and if they desire to come under one head or affiliate their affairs, then let all trades' and labor societies, secret or public, be represented in the Federation of Trades' and Labor Unions."

In this statement appears clearly the determination of the promoters of the Federation neither to ask nor give quarter in their rivalry with the Knights of Labor. Seizing upon the weakness involved in the existence of both mixed labor assemblies and national trade assemblies in the same organization, they were quick to take advantage of it. The Federation rested squarely upon the trade association, and this form was the one that dominated. In 1894 the Federation resolved to hold no meetings or conferences with the Knights until the latter should abandon its dual organization in the trades. This resolution it was in position to make effective by a refusal to recognize in any of its unionized shops a card of a member of the Knights of Labor. As the trades were for the most part federated in the American Federation of Labor this refusal was a serious handicap in securing employment.

Comparison and Contrast. — With the formation and continued existence of the American Federation of Labor the historical part of the movement merges into the present. Other organizations now in process of formation or development in so far as they differ from those of the past are matters of current activity and it remains for the future to reveal their value. A backward glance over the several organizations that have had some degree of permanency in the past reveals some principles that are interesting as well as important. It is the work of the historian of the labor movement to bring these out in fullness. There are some lessons that even now are apparent. Out of the several forms of organization have developed two that have stood forth as rivals. These are the Knights of Labor and the American Federation of Labor. They were established at about the same time. Each gathered into itself what was by its founders thought to be the valuable lessons of the past. Yet they developed on quite opposite principles. The organization of Knights was based upon the principle that the interests of all laborers were identical, that "an injury to one is the concern of all" and that all members would therefore come to the support of any who needed aid. On this principle the assemblies were formed, not on the basis of trade membership but rather of mixed membership. Thus the Knights of Labor was an organization which undertook to bring all separate interests into subordination to the interests of the whole; a broad principle which in present society exists to any considerable extent in ideal only. In contrast with this the Federation has from the start admitted the conflict of interest even within the boundaries of the laboring class and has shaped its organization in such a way as to allow play for these conflicting interests without interfering with the unity at points where the interests were common. Its basis of organization has been regularly that of trade units joined into a federation. Considerable autonomy remains to these units and this is freely exercised, yet there is in the fact of federation opportunity for common action on common interests that is immensely increased in its efficiency from the absence of friction within the organization. This organization on the basis of a single vocation rests on the principle that "men who think alike should act together," a principle that is not so highly tinctured with idealism as that adopted by the Knights but one that has stood the test of time in various forms of association, one that has the virtue of being sternly practical. It "comes closer to human nature" in its preservation of individual interests. From the standpoint of idealism the Knights represent the higher development, while the Federation reveals the greater practical insight. From another point of view the difference appears in the degree of centralization attained in the two societies. With the Knights a higher degree of centralization was not only possible but natural, while with the Federation it was simply impossible. In one other particular the policy of the two has been unlike. The Knights, largely influenced by the example of former societies, aimed to exercise direct political control. The Federation, on the other hand, was warned by the same experiences and from the start has been able to muster sufficient strength to prevent political action from becoming a part of its policy. This has often led to some very bitter fights, especially on the part of the socialist members of the Federation. The non-political program has been steadily adhered to and still remains as one of the points on which the present leaders are most determined. These opposite policies and principles adopted by these two great rival societies have had opportunity to show their relative strength. For a time the Knights had a remarkable growth. The test of time has revealed the weaknesses of its foundation and the superior adaptability of that of its great rival. The American Federation of Labor, though admittedly not without its weak points, stands to-day as the most powerful organization that American workingmen have been able to create; a product of experiment, failure and determined effort of the past. It compares favorably with the organizations in other countries. It sums up for labor organizations the lessons of history.

CHAPTER VII

THE AMERICAN TRADE UNION

With the outline of the two great national associations set forth in their main features, it remains to describe that form of trade organization that is called the trade union. This is not an easy task. It is doubtful if any description of these units of the movement can be made that will be satisfactory. More than one hundred and fifty in number, each has its own definite structure or form of organization, its own constitution and set of laws. Each is an evolution and stands to-day as a product of many forces that have worked themselves out along varying lines. Historical development, peculiarities of particular trades, personalities of leaders, geographical area included within the scope of the society's activities: these are some of the forces that have had an important influence in shaping the particular form of a society. It is admittedly difficult, perhaps dangerous to the interests of clearness, to formulate a blanket description that will cover the form of organization of this group of societies that goes under the name of American trade unions.

Upon analysis, however, it becomes evident that an examination of a large number of unions reveals a unity of principle running through practically all of them. It is this common element that the present chapter seeks to describe.

Its Parts and Their Relations. — The American trade union is made up of three distinct parts with definite relations between them. There is, first, the central body, called by various names as The Union, The International, The General Union, The Grand Lodge, The Grand Division. Then there is the local body, generally called The Local. Between these two there is interposed in the larger unions a third body made up of locals within restricted areas and smaller than the central body. These are generally called Divisions, though various names are used as District Lodge, Joint Council, System Division. It may be that the particular needs of the union are such as to call for a fourth division. This is true of The United Mine Workers which has The International, The District, The Sub-District, and The Local. In this description the word union will mean the central body.

Generally speaking the locals are the source of authority in that they have the voting strength and constitute the units upon which the union rests. This authority is practically all delegated and rests in the central body or the union as a whole. This gives the largest importance to the central organization and causes it to stand as the union in all external relations. In the more detailed description, therefore, it will be best to begin with the first body, the union itself.

The Union: The Convention.— In the fundamental laws of organization of practically all of these societies the constitution asserts that the union is the "ultimate tribunal," the "supreme head," the "sovereign body," having jurisdiction over every interest that touches the welfare of the trade and every relation between it and the outside world of industry. The embodiment of this authority is the convention, a delegate body representing the locals. The basis of this representation is by no means uniform. It varies with the particular needs of the trade that it represents. The delegates are chosen by the locals in a ratio determined in the constitutions of their respective unions. There is no uniformity in this ratio. Each local is entitled to at least one delegate. Sometimes it is fixed at one delegate for each one hundred members or major fraction thereof. The total number for any one local may be limited, as in one case for example, it cannot be more than five, and in another the limit is ten. By another method in general use the representation is adjusted so as to give the larger locals proportionately less voting strength, as the following plan will illustrate. For 100 members, one delegate; between 100 and 500 members, two delegates; between 500 and 1,000 members, three delegates; for 1,000 or more, four delegates. In some cases each delegate has one vote while in others the voting is done by unions. Proxies are sometimes allowed. Occasionally the adjustment between the number of delegates and the voting strength is made in a more complicated way. The number of delegates is fixed by units of 200 members. The local, however, is entitled to one vote for the first 100 members and one additional vote for every additional 100 of membership. In this case the number of delegates does not equal the voting strength so as to have one delegate for each possible vote. Some delegates thus have in effect two or more votes each and each may vote following his own discretion. In case an odd number of votes falls to any local with an even number of delegates the delegate first elected is entitled to the extra vote. If the local is not represented by its full quota of voting delegates, those who are present may cast among them all the votes that the local is entitled to.

In order to encourage a large attendance of delegates at the conventions some unions pay the expenses out of a general fund. In other cases each local pays the expenses of its own delegation. In still other instances there is an adjustment by which the local pays entertainment expenses and the union the travelling expenses. Obviously the choice between these several plans will rest upon the financial condition of the organization and the importance attached to the work of the convention. Where there are funds for the purpose and where it is for the interests of the trade to have a large convention with all locals represented, the general funds will be drawn on for the expenses. If funds do not permit, but a large representative vote is desirable, then there will be the resort to proxy voting or the plan of more than one vote to a delegate. Some trades obviously do not attach so much importance to a large delegate meeting and then it is left quite entirely to the locals to decide each for itself whether it will send representation or not. In this latter case the larger locals will probably pay the entire expenses of the delegation. In smaller ones it is not unlikely that there will be some one among the younger men who is an enthusiastic unionist and is anxious to see the larger body at work and to try himself out among the leaders. In such a case some plan will be devised by which the local can have one delegate at least by sharing some part of the expenses. If the necessity for a representative body is great and the funds for securing such a body are small, there is the plan, resorted to in some cases, of levying a fine upon any local that is not represented by at least one delegate. This fine, however, is made revocable at the discretion of the union officials. In the Typographical Union, for example, the expenses of delegates are not paid from the general fund. The result is that the smaller locals are not represented. To meet this difficulty the plan has been adopted of having the meetings of the convention at different places in order that the locals within easy distance in one year may be represented, a privilege that at the next convention will come to the locals in another section. Thus the smaller locals have an opportunity for occasional representation. Professor Barnett has figured out that for the convention of this union at Washington in 1903, 180 locals out of 695 had delegates at the meeting. This was twenty-six per cent. These locals represented 33,486 members, which was 72.5 per cent of the total membership.

Meetings of Convention. — As to the frequency of convention meetings there is wide variation. There are unions that provide for annual conventions. Others meet every second year. Some have triennial sessions. Beyond this the probability is that the time of meeting is not fixed in the constitution but is left to the discretion of designated officials or to referendum vote. In one case a referendum vote is submitted on the question: "Shall a convention be called this year?" This referendum is taken each year except the one immediately following a convention year. At the time of such a referendum, it is necessary to secure a full discussion. In one trade paper, for example, is found this editorial notice: "Shall we hold a convention in 1913? That question should receive the careful consideration of every member, and should be discussed in every meeting between now and January, when the vote will be taken." Occasionally long periods will pass with no session of the convention. The Granite Cutters held a session in 1880 and did not convene again until 1912. At the present writing no time is set for another convention of this union. Such a time may be arranged for by an initiative proposition and a referendum vote. During the thirty-two years that intervened between the two conventions the general laws of the association were revised five times by a small revision committee elected by a general vote. The Cigar Makers convention of 1912 was the first to be held in sixteen years. This union pays the expenses of delegates from the general fund, and has found the referendum more economical and on the whole more satisfactory. In 1912 the International Molders held a convention after a five-year period. There were at this meeting 403 delegates, only 60 of whom had been present at a former convention.

There are very obvious advantages to be credited to the plan of holding frequent conventions. The enthusiasm that comes from numbers and from discussion of problems is inspiring, and the delegates return with a measure of this for their locals. Capable leaders from the various sections come together and in the discussions and planning it will often be that new talent will develop that may rise into higher positions. Against these advantages, however, other considerations may be placed. With a large union it is a stern fact that expenses are heavy. The enthusiasm is more difficult to preserve in its intensity while it is being scattered widely among numerous locals. The town in which the convention is held is anxious to be hospitable, and consequently an elaborate round of entertainment is prepared. This interferes with the calm discussion and careful attention that many of the difficult affairs of the union need. Writing of the printers Professor Barnett states that: "As a substitute for a small and representative council, the convention is an archaic and inefficient institution. In session for only a week, feted on every possible occasion by the entertaining union, with a membership so large as to make deliberation impracticable, the supervision which the convention can give the work of the officers is necessarily slight." One recent corrective suggested is the designation of a permanent convention city for this union. There are obvious tendencies in the direction of doing away with the convention quite entirely, as one after another of its duties are now discharged in other ways. Whether or not it is to pass entirely it is difficult to forecast. There are some very decided advantages accruing from it and these may be powerful enough to stem the present tide away from the plan. Enthusiasm is very necessary to unionism. Methods of keeping it alive are consequently of great importance. The convention is certainly a great factor in keeping members enthused. Delegates carry these stirring influences away with them. The trade journals print descriptions and pictures that arouse interest. Election as a delegate may be the incentive for much active work during the year. It is true that the convention's work may be done in other ways in part or for a limited time. It is not clear that it can be done away with entirely without some definite loss to the cause. For the year 1915 there were announced forty-four conventions of international unions.

The Business of the Convention. — The business of the convention is restricted to lines generally laid down in the constitution. A description of its powers is made difficult by the fact that in so many cases it shares its authority in a very real way with the referendum. When this latter method has not been arranged for as a substitute, the convention elects the officers of the union, amends the constitution, hears the reports of the officers and takes action on a variety of matters that are brought before it. A typical "order of business" is as follows: Report of committee on credentials; Roll call of officers and members; Reading of minutes; Reports of officers, commencing with the president; Receiving communications and bills; Reports and petitions of subordinate unions; Resolutions; Report of special committees; Nomination for and election of officers; Installation of officers; Unfinished business; General benefit of the organization; Adjournment. The list of committees may be taken as further indicating the scope of the convention's work. A typical list is as follows: on Constitution; on General and Local Division Statutes; on Ritual; on Grievance, Appeals and Petitions; on Subordinate Divisions; on System Division Statutes; on Mutual Benefit Department; on State and National Legislation; on Labor and Labor Statistics; on Finance and Salaries. Each of these has seven members. The following have three each: on Resolutions and Greetings; on Grand Officers' Reports; on the Official Organ; on Printing; on the Press; on Transportation; on Local Grand Division Session; on Rules.

Executive Officers. — At all times, whether in convention or during the interim, the executive officers stand for the union in a very real and practical sense. Of these the president is the center of influence and power. He is distinctively the leader. These officers are elected for a term and in a manner that are not uniform among the unions. There are two characteristic ways of choosing the chief executive: by vote of the convention and by referendum method. Generally in the unions that hold conventions either annually or biennially the president is chosen by vote of the convention for a term that corresponds to the frequency of the sessions. Either one or two years will be the length of term. In unions that do not hold conventions either annually or biennially, the election will be generally for a short term. This must not be regarded as the deciding factor in determining the method of election, as in some cases a union with triennial sessions will select a president by referendum every two years regardless of the convention year. The tendency is decidedly in favor of short terms for these officers. One or two years is the length that prevails very generally. In case of election by the convention there is nothing peculiar about the method of voting other than what has already been noted; the system of representation and the relative strength of voting as among the locals represented.

The organization of the executive staff is the direct result of necessity. In the earlier days of the unions the executive officers were numerous, following the manner of the locals. The occupants were not paid for their services and were chosen from widely scattered sections of the country. With the increase in work for these officers to do it became evident that some change must be made. Either all the authority must be concentrated in a single officer or a limited number must be chosen, brought together for coöperation and paid a salary. Wherever this option has presented itself the latter course has quite generally been chosen. This gave the president the usual corps of fellow officers, the vice president, the secretary and the treasurer. From the first short terms have been popular. Even in the most firmly established unions the terms of office have not been lengthened. Reëlection has made possible the equivalent of lengthened terms where that has proved to be desirable, keeping at the same time a high degree of democratic control. It was clearly the early tendency to change officers: to pass the office around. When the duties were simple and more or less routine this was easily possible. It had the added advantage of preserving the "labor" point of view in the office, as the occupant was not out of the shop for a long enough time to forget the "atmosphere" of the movement whose servant he was. With the growing importance of continuity of policy and the increasing difficulty of the problems that had to be faced, adminstrative and executive experience became a distinct asset to the union and this has led to reëlections for many successive terms in some of the strongest unions. In the early history of the Typographical Union for a period of forty years, from 1850 to 1890, there were thirty different presidents. Only two of these held office for as long as three years, and five were in office for two years each. In 1888 the term of office was made two years. Since 1890 aside from the present incumbent who is in his first term, there have been three presidents in the twenty-four years. The first had three terms or six years, the second but one term and the third had seven terms or fourteen years.

Before the election of John Mitchell to the presidency of the United Mine Workers of America only one occupant had exceeded a two-year term. Mr. Mitchell was president for ten years. In further illustrating the extent to which continued service has been secured with short terms of office it may be noted that a president of the Carpenters Union continued in office for twenty years, and that Mr. Arthur was at the head of the Brotherhood of Locomotive Engineers for twenty-nine years, or until his death.

The officers receive salaries paid out of the general funds of the union. The amount varies, depending upon the financial resources of the union, and the demands made upon the time and energies of the men. The president generally receives the highest salary though the secretary sometimes receives an amount as large. There is considerable variation in these amounts. One of the highest, perhaps, is $7,000. From this it ranges down to $1,000 or perhaps lower. For the stronger and larger unions it is probable that $2,500 or $3,000 is the amount generally paid. Mr. Mitchell, writing in 1903, and speaking of unions as a whole with no distinction as to size or strength, says: "I believe no national officer receives a higher salary than $3,000. The probable range of salaries for trade union presidents lies, at the present time (1903), between $1,000 and $1,800." The amount of the salaries is quite generally fixed in the constitution. There are cases, however, in which the determination is left to each biennial convention of the union. The vice presidents do not all receive salaries. In some instances they receive a *per diem* compensation for the time that they use in connection with the duties of their office.

President's Representatives. — With the increasing complexity of the duties of administration it has become more and more difficult for the president to discharge his duties successfully and efficiently. Vice presidents were chosen to assist him. These officers did not quite meet the needs in all cases. It was necessary for the president to know that the locals were living up to their obligations. Written reports from local officers were not sufficient. In some cases the president is assisted in this work by the vice president. The Boiler Makers have nine vice presidents, all on the road advising locals and assisting in organizing new ones. These needs have been met in other instances by the selection of special representatives of the president whose sole duty it is to travel about from local to local and to report conditions to the chief officer. These functions have been differentiated in the more advanced unions until there are the financier, the strike agent, the label agitator and the organizer, all representing the president and doing what it would be impossible for a single individual to do. These agents are more or less numerous as the particular demands of the several unions require. They all bear a very intimate relation to the chief executive, being in a very real sense his personal representative. An instance of the increasing need of this development and of its presence in most of the unions may be shown from a statement made by the president of the Molders Union, an organization that is evidently just at the point of realizing the need for this step in evolution. The constitution provides that the president and the four vice presidents shall act as organizers. This work, the president contends, they are not able to do. "The staff of vice presidents," he says, "has necessarily become a body of specially trained men whose time is fully occupied in taking up and adjusting those questions which our members have been unable to successfully dispose of locally. Experts and specialists are as much a necessity in an international union as in any other large enterprise, and our staff of vice presidents, to be successful, must be composed of men who, through their long training in the affairs of our organization, have become specialists and who, through their knowledge and experience, are able to give service which could not otherwise be rendered."

Executive Board. — One other important feature of the or-

ganization of the union remains to be noticed. It is usually
called the executive board or the executive council. There is,
in this branch of the organization as in others, some variation
in the structure of the council. There is variation in the number
of the membership. In some instances the number is as small
as three. In other cases it is as many as eight or even more.
Generally the president is a member of this board. His associate officers also have places, as the vice presidents, the
secretary and the treasurer. When the vice presidents are
numerous, as they are in some of the unions, only a part of
their number will be included. Officers whose terms have
expired are sometimes, by virtue of their former service, elected
to this body. Sometimes they are assigned to the place by a
constitutional provision that works automatically. Generally
the number will be filled out with others chosen directly for
the position, either by convention or by referendum vote.
There is more variety in the size and membership of these
boards than in the work they have to do. With reference to
this latter point they may be divided into two classes: one having
numerous duties of an executive nature, and the other acting
only as an advisory board with appellate duties in cases of
conflict or lack of adjustment between the other branches of
the union's organization. It has been the case in some instances
that this board has been permitted to transact its business by
correspondence, though this is not customary. Its evident
disadvantages have prevented its general adoption. If the
board be large in number it will generally be more purely an
advisory body. In cases where its membership is limited, as
to three, it holds a large power, as it can act quickly and has
only the limited number to consult in determining a policy.
The work of this board is naturally divided into two kinds,
the administrative and the judicial. These two functions have
not yet become very clearly differentiated in the organization.
The council will perform both functions indiscriminately. In
a few cases a judiciary board has been established to have
sole control of all business of a judicial nature when the union
is not in session. This judicial business consists in appeals
by members against other members, decisions on laws of the
union or disputes between locals or members of different locals.
In short, such a board will pass upon all questions relating to

the laws of the union or of any of the subordinate locals or divisions. Perhaps a typical list of functions of an executive board is that of the Cigar Makers Union. This board may substitute its judgment for that of the president in certain cases. It grants charters to new locals; levies assessments to replenish funds; acts as a board of approval of many executive acts, as in cases of appointment or removal, and in the employment of clerks as assistants. It can try the president if he be impeached by locals (a motion of one local seconded by one-fifth of all the locals impeaches). It can hear, as a court of appeal, all judicial decisions of the president. This might make it appear that the president of this union is limited in a very real way in the exercise of his functions. Such is not, as a matter of fact, the case. The separation of executive and judicial activities has not progressed to such a point yet that they are clearly definable. The consequence is that the president acts in such a way that his executive and judicial duties are often, in practice, hopelessly intermingled. "A study of the system of administration," writes one of the students of this particular union, "is primarily a study of the International President." While the various organs for the performance of all the several functions of this union have not yet been very clearly differentiated, it does not follow that the organization, in its results, is not effective. Speaking of the judicial system and its ability to accomplish results, the president stated in the annual report of 1912: "As already stated, the International Union is completely self-governing. Every member of the International Union possesses the right to first appeal to the local union against any action taken against him, and if dissatisfied with the result he may appeal to the international president, and from any decision rendered by the president he, or the local union, may appeal to the international executive board, and from the executive board, to popular vote, which plan completely safeguards the right of the member and the rights of the union. Under this plan of appeals there can be no such thing as autocracy on the part of any local union, the international president or the executive board. The final disposal and decision is vested in the hands of the combined membership."

With the continued development of the burdens of the administrative branch, the executive board will increase in importance. As conventions become less frequent, this will be still more accentuated. The executive board will tend to become the center of authority, subject to the will of the union of locals. With the Boiler Makers, for example, the executive council meets once a year for a two weeks' session. During this time it makes an inventory of supplies and property of the union, plans further campaigns of organization, considers and develops financial plans, and discusses the policy being followed in the strikes that are in progress. This may amount to as many as fifteen or more at the time of the session. Contrasted with this may be noted the executive board of the Molders Union. During the five-year period between the conventions of 1907 and 1912 this body held fourteen meetings at which was considered all the various business of importance pertaining to the work of the order.

Movement Toward Centralization. — There must be a limit to this centralization. Efficiency and economy both argue for its extension. But unionists sometimes care less for economy and efficiency than for some other things. They are jealous of authority and suspicious of its centralization. The official who spends his entire time for years in the atmosphere of a business office or in the duties of administration may be liable to the charge of losing touch with the shop and the atmosphere of shop work. The energetic workman with aspirations for leadership and demagogic tendencies finds in this departure from what he may term the democratic spirit the material that he can use with skill to his own advantage. It is doubtful if this tendency toward high centralization of management in the executive board and the growing infrequency of delegate conventions will continue for much longer without interruption.

The Local. — Next in importance to the national organization is the local. As a matter of fact, locals existed before the formation of the nationals in many cases and the amalgamation into the national has been a development that is in itself not without significance. The first realization of a community of interest would naturally appear with the extension of the trade and the local rivalry among employers. With this development it was not possible for the locals to remain apart. The first coming together was of an informal character, for the purpose of conferences and discussions of a common policy, with the locals free to accept or reject the conclusions. The necessities of the case soon made these conferences of increasing importance. The next step that has been pointed out is the exchange of membership. This grew out of the increasing tendency of members to seek work farther away from home. The advantages of this exchange soon became evident. Growing very naturally out of these exchanges was the necessity for some uniformity in the membership requirements. This we are told was the next step toward amalgamation. In this way, taken of course in outline only, the locals became more clearly aware of the importance of a closer union among the locals of the same trade, first in neighboring communities and later covering wider areas. In this way, it may be assumed, the nationals were made out of the existing locals. Yet this does not explain in full the relations that now exist. There is another side to it. The larger union has been instrumental in bringing into existence many of the present locals. These have not the traditions of separate existence and are not so insistent upon a large degree of "home rule." The analogy is helpful, if one thinks of the attitude of the original thirteen states and the new states of the union toward the question of "states rights." These new locals, in many cases, are relatively so numerous that it is quite correct to speak of the union as the parent of the locals.

Relation to the Union. — Any group of laborers, it is true, may form an organization. But they cannot ally themselves with a larger organization in their trade without conforming to certain specific requirements. These are laid down by the trade union in session in its convention and are enforced by its administrative officers. Thus the local must in a sense surrender a part of its autonomy if it is to become affiliated with a national or international organization. This many local societies refuse to do and they remain isolated societies, self-governing but without an influence commensurate with the needs of the day. The nature of the trade determines largely whether local societies form nationals or not. If trade associations took only this form there would be to-day, as there was in the earlier days, no trade union movement. Even is this more true since in recent times the small societies can exercise much less influence than their predecessors did. The newer local societies, having been brought into existence through the efforts of the national society, have not this feeling and they readily and naturally become united with the larger organization of the trade.

Charters: Membership. — The first step in becoming a local allied with a national is to secure the charter. Charters are granted by the international executive board to those who make application in the proper form. This will all be attended to, of course, by the organizer whose special work it is to prepare the new members for their organization. The number for a new local must generally be not less than seven. In some cases ten, or even more, is the minimum number of charter members. In case there is already a local of the trade in a city, its consent to the admission of the new society must be obtained. This is intended to prevent friction through the formation of rival locals or the possibility of factions withdrawing to set up an independent society. This factional fighting is not uncommon, but under the present regulations the new society must either "go it alone" or ally itself with some other organization than the national of its own trade. This is by no means an impossible thing, as will be shown later. There are often reasons why it is better that there should be more than one local in some trades and in some cities. With this provision in force such subdivision can be carried on in a friendly way and prevent the loss of advantage that otherwise comes. The terms of the charter fix the form of organization that the new local must take and establish its relation with the union, with the sub-district unit and with other locals in the union. After the charter is secured the local is "established." Members may then be added who conform with the union's requirements for membership. Activity in the trade is the first essential. Unlike the earlier societies the skill required to engage in the work of the trade must be shown, the ability must be sufficient to earn the standard wage paid to the craft in the locality. The age requirement shows considerable variation, while some unions discriminate on race and others on sex. These latter considerations are of force in a trade where the nature of the work and the section of the country offer reasons that are sufficient. The Order of Railway Conductors needs no sex requirement but on the matter of race it establishes the regulation that admits only white male persons who are actually employed as conductors. The Order of Railway Telegraphers opens its membership to any white person of good moral character who is eighteen years of age or over and is actually employed in the trade. The Retail Clerks' International Protective Association accepts any person regardless of sex between the ages of sixteen and fifty. Thus it is obvious that the nature of the trade is the leading factor in determining the nature of the membership. Given the name of the union it would be generally possible to guess with a fair chance of success what the membership requirements will be. That there are other requirements than these more general ones is evident from the fact that members on voting on a candidate may use the "black ball." This is not always used in its simplest form, however. One instance, at least, of a more complex use of this means of rejection is in vogue. If the committee on membership unanimously reports unfavorably on a candidate the matter is closed. If not, the members ballot. Three or more black balls reject the candidate. If, however, two black balls are voted the ballot is taken again. If for the second time two black balls appear the candidate is rejected. If on either the first or second ballot less than two black balls appear the candidate is elected.

Initiation Fees: Dues. — Initiation fees are very diverse. In some of the constitutions the amount of the fee is fixed. Some establish a constitutional maximum or minimum limit, or both, as for instance between $10 and $25. Sons of members, if between the ages of 14 and 17, for example, may be admitted at half rates. Initiation fees do not always remain with the local. The proportion of the division is determined by the central authority. Effort is made to keep all these as nearly uniform as possible. The locals are allotted only enough to meet local expenses. The balance goes to the general fund.

Freedom of Local. — In all matters where the interests are general the central body through its administrative officers and executive board exercises a very real control over locals. Within this limitation, however, the members have considerable scope of action. Their officers they choose for themselves, they have their regular meetings and transact purely local business as they may wish. Their discretion in fixing dues, fees and fines is large and the disciplining of members is quite entirely in their own hands usually with a reserved privilege of appeal. They must maintain certain standing committees, such, for

instance, as committees on grievances, on wages, on conciliation, and if there be any form of benefit fund, as there so frequently is, there must be a regular system for collecting the
funds. The officers, though chosen by the locals, are required
to report to the union headquarters the condition of their
respective locals. These reports generally consist in filling in
standardized blanks sent out from headquarters and calling
for such information as to membership and conditions of organization as experience may have shown to be desirable. Thus
the information is uniform and easily compiled at headquarters
into general statements. As a typical equipment of officers
for a local the following list will serve. President, vice president, recording secretary, financial secretary, treasurer, sentinel,
conductor, three trustees (usually so chosen as to be a continuous body), an executive board of five members, an auditing
committee of three, and a label committee of the same number.
All these are elected annually.

District Unit. — Between the national organization on the
one hand and the local on the other has developed the division
or district unit, a connecting link that has not the independent
character of the latter nor the authoritative control of the
former. It is the direct outcome of the growth of the larger
unions, necessary as an aid in administrative and judicial activity. These have but little that is distinctive in character.
Created directly to meet a practical need their form is expressly
provided in the constitution and their powers limited to those
that the document directly confers upon them. They are
made up of delegated members chosen from the locals of a
limited contiguous territory. Matters of comparatively minor
importance may be referred to them for consideration, and
even for final disposal subject to possible appeal to the national
body. Uniform wage scales for local areas are often determined
by these bodies. Differences of opinion between locals and
employers, when open disturbance would be more far reaching
in its effect than the limits of a single local, must be referred
to the subdivision before final action is taken. In the judicial
activity cases may be referred to them, as to a court of appeals,
with the privilege of carrying the case up to the supreme
court of the union, if it cannot be satisfactorily adjusted otherwise. The tendency in the larger unions is to make these sub-

divisions state wide in their jurisdiction. The meetings will be rather frequent, sometimes quarterly and sometimes annually. Among organizations of railroad laborers the unit for this form of organization is generally a line of railroad. The Railway Telegraphers have their system divisions.

The Referendum: Amendments. — The referendum has been developed by trade unions into an elaborate instrument for recording the popular will of the membership. In some directions it seems to be superseding the work of the conventions. Practically all of the great unions provide for this method of voting. It is used in particular for the accomplishment of two distinct ends. One of these is for the amendment of the constitution. In its simpler form it is used to ratify amendments proposed or endorsed by the convention. In such cases the resolutions for amendment are printed within a certain time limit after the convention adjourns, sent to all the locals with instructions to return the vote within a given time again set by the law of the union. These returns are then compiled and the results announced from headquarters. While in the earlier form of organization it was usual to vote upon amendments in the convention making no use at all of the referendum, there are now cases where all amendments in whatever way proposed cannot have a final endorsement in any other way than by referendum vote. The only weight that the convention carries in such cases is the influence that its endorsement may have when the members come to decide for themselves. In cases where annual conventions are not held it has been necessary to make more general use of this method. In such cases the initiative is added to it. Amendments may be proposed by any local. Then they must be endorsed by a prescribed number of locals as, in the case of a large union, forty not more than five of which may be in any one state. With this provision for initiative complied with, the referendum vote will be taken. Amendments thus proposed must ordinarily receive a majority (sometimes two-thirds) of all the votes cast, provided a designated minimum of all the members vote.

The Referendum: Election of Officers. — The second general use of the referendum is for the election of officers. Nominations are made by locals. The following requirements may be regarded as typical. Locals nominate by majority vote, each local being privileged to nominate one candidate for each elective office. These nominations are then sent to the national secretary. From these communications the list of nominees is prepared and published in the official journal of the union. The five who have been supported by the largest number of locals for each office become the nominees, provided that candidates for the office of president and secretary have at least thirty endorsers and all other candidates have at least ten each. The election is then held, the voting being for the candidates who have been nominated in accordance with this plan. For officers other than president and secretary the nominees having the highest number of votes are declared elected. For the two named offices the candidates must receive a majority of all votes cast. In case no one receives a majority, a second election is held to choose between the two candidates receiving the highest number of votes. In some unions the referendum is used for other purposes than these two. Laws involving an increase of taxation must in some unions be submitted by referendum vote. Measures initiated by the executive board may be thus referred. In some cases the referendum is coupled with the initiative in general legislation, fifty locals, or some other fixed number, being sufficient to require action.

The Referendum: Its Value. — Experience with the referendum has tended to reduce somewhat the optimism of those who have been its most persistent advocates. In cases of general interest it is not difficult to poll a large vote in the locals. If it be to determine some question relating to a strike the vote will be generally large. Any other question that touches directly the interests of the rank and file will call out a large vote. Constitutional questions seldom poll a large vote. Even elections for the choice of officials show a light vote with the exception of those locals from which the candidates are chosen. It has been necessary to place the percentage of voters actually voting very low in order to secure the passage of any legislation at all by this method. So striking has the apparent neglect become that it has even been suggested by some leaders that it may be a good policy to fine all members who do not vote on any measures submitted to locals for their consideration. The referendum plan of voting was called into operation to meet the difficulty of minority voting. Experience would indicate that the plan does not realize all that its advocates hoped for.

Conclusion. — This is in general terms the outline of government that the trade unions of America have adopted. It has evolved out of the necessity of the case and is not to be regarded as in any sense a permanent structure. The form is constantly changing, though slowly and at differing paces in different unions. There are clear evidences of greater uniformity as experience reveals the superiority of some forms over others. Natural selection is awarding the prize of relative permanency to the form that best meets the needs of the time. Others copy the strong points or are worsted in the struggle. This tendency toward uniformity is not without its definite limitations, however. Varying conditions of different trades will of necessity cause variations in form. Women in industry will mean women in unions. High degrees of skill will naturally lead to high fees and somewhat exclusive membership. Changes in division of labor will affect the membership requirements. There will remain variety in the midst of uniformity as each organization seeks to meet the general demands of labor's interests and at the same time the specific requirements of a particular trade. Though there is evident increasing uniformity and a slow approach to a type, it must not be understood that this type will be permanent. No type of labor organization has acquired permanency and it is not probable that any one will. Relative permanency is not only the only fact that is apparent but it is the only thing that is desirable. Stagnation would follow upon cessation of change. That there is little danger of this is only too apparent to one who sees the newer types that are already beginning to appear. Though of great consequence these do not yet belong to a description of what is, and so do not come in for consideration at this time.

Any study, based only on the printed constitutions, can give but a partial idea of the real organization. These documents are amended with comparative ease, and sometimes the departure from their requirements is not very summarily dealt with. Results are of large importance and if they are secured, the legality of the means is not always very carefully scrutinized. "To a certain extent," says John Mitchell, "the formal written constitution of a trade union is rather a state-

ment of principles and a formulation of the present policy of
the union than a hard and fast determination of its future
laws." With the more conservatively directed unions, this
is not so often the case. Age in unionism quite generally leads
to greater respect for the laws of unionism even when it may
mean the loss of some immediate object.

CHAPTER VIII

TRADE UNION STATISTICS

A complete and accurate statement of the numbers connected with unions is difficult to make. Until within the last decade a guess was the nearest possible approach. Within that time more accurate information has appeared. Unions have adopted the method of reporting only those members whose dues are paid up. This regulation has been brought about largely by the central authorities. Voting strength as shown by conventions and referendums as well as claims on benefit funds have been made dependent upon paid-up memberships. Names in arrears are automatically dropped from the rolls in accordance with the rules of the nationals. This method of keeping a membership account has contributed greatly to the accuracy of trade-union statistics. Yet it must be recognized that a considerable margin of inaccuracy still remains. In spite of the fact that all figures must be taken as approximate only, they must be admitted to have an importance that is not to be overlooked.

More recently the departments of labor in some of the states have undertaken to compile these statistics so that they are not only more available than formerly but also more nearly accurate.

GENERAL DATA

From the last statement of the New York State Bureau of Statistics and Information it is learned that there were in 1913 a total of 2,604,701 unionists reported in the United States and 149,577 in Canada, making a total for North America of 2,754,278. Most of these belonged to international unions. As the figures are from the official reports of paid-up memberships, they may fairly be regarded as a minimum.

The first of these reports was made for the year 1910 and was an estimate only. The total for America was then placed at 2,625,000. That this was an overestimate appears from the more reliable reports used in the following years based on paid-up membership as reported by the officials of the unions. The accompanying table shows the changes for the four years.

	1910	1911	1912	1913
United States.........		2,162,926	2,389,723	2,604,701
Canada..............		133,132	160,120	149,577
Total for America (estimated).........	2,625,000	2,296,058	2,549,843	2,754,278

These more accurate data make earlier estimates seem quite improbable, though they appear to have conveyed the reliable opinion of the day. In 1864 the total membership of labor organizations was estimated at 200,000. In 1903 John Mitchell asserted that there were probably at that time 2,250,000 trade unionists in the United States. Speaking in the annual report of 1912, President Perkins of the Cigar Makers Union said that thirty-five years before that time there were probably not over 40,000 organized workmen in the United States as against 2,300,000 at the time of the report.

Grouped according to trades and arranged so as to show the membership for each trade group, the result is as follows:

Groups of Trades	Total Membership
Mines and quarries..................	423,300
Building and stone work.............	543,460
Metal, machinery and shipbuilding.....	248,092
Woodworking and furniture...........	25,910
Textiles and clothing.................	240,964
Glass, pottery, paper and leather......	43,470
Printing and binding.................	101,522
Transportation......................	667,845
Food, liquor and tobacco.............	103,900
Restaurants and trade................	120,727
Theaters and music..................	86,627
Miscellaneous.......................	148,461
Total.........................	2,754,278

The number of members in unions at the present time cannot be accurately stated, because of the inadequacy of the records kept by many locals and the difficulty of gathering the data from those who do keep the more careful records. The most recent reliable estimate is that made by Professor Barnett for the Commission on Industrial Relations. "It may be roughly estimated," says the report, "that in manufacturing, mining, transportation and the building industries, if the proprietary, supervisory, official and clerical classes are excluded, twenty-five per cent of the workers twenty-one years of age and over are trade unionists." Further it is stated that the number of trade unionists is steadily increasing relative to the working population, in spite of the opposition to unionism manifested by the larger corporations and the employers' associations.

NON-FEDERATED UNIONS

Of the unions that still remain outside of the Federation, by far the largest group is that of railway employees. There are eight unions with a total membership of 373,339. Of these the largest is the Brotherhood of Railroad Trainmen, numbering 133,884. The Brotherhood of Locomotive Firemen and Enginemen has 88,840 members; the Brotherhood of Locomotive Engineers, 68,890; the Order of Railway Conductors, 45,782. The other four unions are the Car Workers, the Signalmen, the Station Agents and the Station Employees.

Outside of the railway orders the largest unaffiliated union is the Bricklayers, Masons and Plasterers Union,[1] having a total membership of 82,298. There are four other unions each with a membership of 20,000 or over that have not affiliated. These are the Letter Carriers; State, City and Town Employees; Post Office Clerks; the Electrical Workers (dissenting branch). The four have a combined membership of 103,145.

NUMBER AND DISTRIBUTION OF LOCALS

While it is evident that the number of locals varies greatly in the different unions, it is not easy to state the exact number for each. The universality of the trade will be the determining factor, of course, and such trades as the printers, the carpenters and the masons will have a large number of locals as well as a large membership, while trades like the granite cutters, diamond

[1] As this material is in press, the announcement is made that this union is about to affiliate with the A. F. of L.

workers, or powder workers will be comparatively small. In the Twenty-Third Annual Report of the United States Commissioner of Labor (1908) is a study from which it appears that in 73 unions there was a total of 17,235 locals; 16,299 being in the United States and 936 in Canada. The average number of locals for the entire 73 unions was 236, for the number in the United States the average was 223, leaving an average of 13 locals in Canada. There were 22 unions that had no locals outside of the United States. Deducting this number from the list, it leaves 18 as the average number for Canada among the unions that have any locals there at all.

The variety and distribution of the locals may be shown by a few cases taken as illustrative. The United Textile Workers had (August, 1915) a total of 195 locals, two of which were in Canada. These were distributed throughout 17 states of the union in addition to the ones in Canada. The Typographical Union shows also a large local list. In 48 states there were 620 locals. The District of Columbia had one, making 621 within the United States. Hawaii, the Philippines and Porto Rico had one each, and Canada had 45. In addition to these there were 19 German-American locals, 37 locals of mailers, 6 of newspaper writers, and 1 of type founders. These aggregated 732 locals, all of which were members of the international. These were joined into 196 allied printing trades councils and 18 state and district organizations. (Report of Secretary, 1914.) The Bricklayers, Masons and Plasterers had (June, 1915) a total of 945 locals. Of these, 883 were scattered throughout all the 48 states and the District of Columbia, and 62 were in Canada. These were joined in 23 state and provincial conferences. The Molders Union had (July, 1915) 410 locals. One was in Panama, 32 in Canada, and the remaining 377 were in 40 states of the union. The International Association of Machinists (July, 1915) had 819 locals; 754 in 48 states and the District of Columbia, 63 in Canada and 2 in Panama. The Cigar Makers Union (June, 1915) had 490 locals, of which 449 were in 43 states and the District of Columbia, 23 in Canada, one in Cuba and 17 in Porto Rico. The United Brotherhood of Carpenters and Joiners (Sept., 1915) had 1,898 locals, 141 district councils, 18 state and provincial bodies, all joined in the international. These locals were scattered through all of the states and territories, the Hawaiian Islands, Porto Rico and Canada. There are 7 general districts in this union, each with a member on the executive board of the union. The membership within these districts was as follows: 54,998; 28,777; 49,025; 7,528 (Southern states); 24,148; 32,121; 4,105 (Canada).

VARIATIONS IN MEMBERSHIP

That there is continual variation in the membership becomes evident upon a study of the official reports of the various organizations. Locals are continually being formed while others are dropping out or being officially dropped by the general officers. The facts showing this are numerous, yet no general compilation can be made that would be comprehensive. The Carpenters and Joiners reported in 1908 a total of 1,906 locals with a membership in good standing of 178,503. Two years later the number of locals was 1,825 and the total membership was 200,712. To these facts are added in the report the statements that 724 members are paid up but whose locals owe more than three months' tax and are not in good standing; and 30,710 members with dues over three and under six months in arrears. These are not included in the total paid-up membership stated above.

The reports of the Cigar Makers Union show the variation in that trade. On September first, 1912, the conditions were:

Number of unions in good standing, 1901 414
Number of unions organized since that date 192

Total 606

Number of unions dissolved or suspended, since 1901 118
Number of unions in good standing, Sept. 1st, 1912 488
Net increase since Sept., 1901 74

The growth of this union appears further from the following table:

Sept. Year	Locals	Membership	Sept. Year	Locals	Membership
1877	17		1896	350	27,318
1879	35	2,729	1897		26,347
1880	74	4,440	1898		26,460
1881	126	14,604	1899		28,994
1882		11,430	1900		33,955
1883	183	13,214	1901	414	33,974
1884		11,871	1902		37,023
1885	191	12,000	1903		39,301
1886		24,672	1904		41,536
1887	259	20,566	1905		40,075
1888		17,199	1906		39,250
1889	270	17,555	1907		41,337
1890		24,624	1908		40,354
1891	291	24,221	1909		44,414
1892		26,678	1910		43,837
1893	316	26,788	1911		42,107
1894		27,828	1912	488	41,500
1895		27,760			

Variations in membership are very general. But few unions escape this experience. There is no regularity in these variations, as the forces that cause them are irregular, varied and complex. The tables on pages 126 and 127 show these changes. It will appear that for many there is a fairly constant gain, for others there is considerable irregularity, while for a few the figures of membership remain comparatively constant.

NEW YORK STATE

The New York State Department of Labor has published data that show very clearly the development of organized labor in that state. From these figures the accompanying tables will indicate the conditions of growth; including the increase in the number of locals in New York City and in the rest of the state for each year and the increase in membership for the same sections of the state.

Unions Showing Increase	1909	1910	1911	1912	1913	1914
1. Order of Railway Conductors of America		39,649	42,349	43,627	44,329	45,782
2. Brotherhood of Locomotive Engineers		57,599	61,568	63,812	66,261	68,890
3. Brotherhood of Locomotive Firemen and Enginemen		63,548	71,398	77,338	85,292	88,840
4. Brotherhood of Railroad Trainmen		102,718	113,871	119,107	124,360	133,884
5. Bricklayers, Masons and Plasterers International Union of America		61,827	76,500	75,914	81,638	82,298
6. United Shoe Workers of America		4,500	8,857	15,213	22,210	14,000
7. United Mine Workers of America	267,000	233,700	250,400	267,000	370,800	
8. United Brotherhood of Carpenters and Joiners of America	104,000	190,400	194,600	192,300	210,700	
9. International Union of the United Brewery Workmen of America	40,000	40,000	45,000	45,000	45,000	
10. International Brotherhood of Electrical Workers	13,800	16,000	18,900	19,600	22,700	
11. International Glove Workers Union of America	800	800	900	1,100	1,300	
12. International Association of Machinists	48,400	56,900	67,100	59,800	71,000	
13. American Federation of Musicians	39,400	40,000	59,000	59,000	54,600	
14. Brotherhood of Painters, Decorators and Paper Hangers of America	59,600	63,500	67,600	68,500	70,900	
15. United Association of Journeymen Plumbers, Gas Fitters, Steam Fitters and Steam Fitters Helpers of the United States and Canada	18,400	20,000	23,700	26,000	29,000	
16. International Brotherhood of Teamsters, Chauffeurs, Stablemen and Helpers of America	32,000	35,800	38,200	41,500	46,900	
17. International Typographical Union of North America	45,500	49,100	51,800	54,700	56,400	

Unions Showing Irregularity	1909	1910	1911	1912	1913	1914
18. Cigar Makers International Union of America	39,800	43,200	43,600	41,500	40,200	
19. United Garment Workers of America	53,400	54,200	52,500	46,400	58,500	
20. International Ladies Garment Workers Union	1,800	18,700	66,800	58,400	78,800	

America...	6,300	5,400	3,100	4,000	5,400
23. Journeymen Tailors Union of America (Tailors Industrial Union)	13,200	11,700	12,000	12,000	12,000
24. International Broom and Whisk Makers Union............	800	600	700	700	700
25. International Longshoremen's Association...............	21,300	20,800	25,000	23,500	22,000
26. International Brotherhood of Maintenance of Way Employees..	10,000	8,700	10,000	9,100	8,000
27. Piano, Organ and Musical Instrument Workers International Union of America......................	4,000	4,000	4,000	2,000	1,000
28. International Brotherhood of Pulp, Sulphite and Paper Mill Workers of the United States and Canada........	1,000	700	2,800	3,500	3,100
29. Saw Smiths National Union.........................	300	300	100	100	100
30. International Slate and Tile Roofers Union of America.....	2,100	1,400	700	400	300
31. Tobacco Workers International Union..................	4,300	4,100	4,000	3,700	3,600
32. International Wood Carvers Association of North America...	1,300	1,200	1,200	1,000	1,000
33. American Wire Weavers Protective Association	300	300	400	300	300

Unions Showing Practically No Change

34. The Granite Cutters International Association of America......	13,100	13,400	13,500	13,500	13,500
35. Metal Polishers, Buffers, Platers, Brass and Silver Workers Union of North America......................	10,000	10,000	10,000	10,000	10,000
36. International Molders Union of North America...........	59,000	59,000	59,000	59,000	50,000
37. The Commercial Telegraphers Union of America.........	1,000	1,000	1,000	1,000	1,000
38. United Textile Workers of America..................	10,000	10,000	10,000	10,000	16,000
39. Brushmakers International Union....................	200	200	200	200	200
40. American Brotherhood of Cement Workers.............	9,000	9,000	9,000	9,000	9,000
41. Retail Clerks International Protective Association.........	15,000	15,000	15,000	15,000	15,000
42. Glass Bottle Blowers of the United States and Canada.....	9,300	10,000	10,000	10,000	10,000
43. United Hatters of North America...................	8,500	8,500	8,500	8,500	8,500
44. United Powder and High Explosive Workers of America....	200	200	200	200	200
45. The Steel Plate Transferrers Association of America......	100	100	100	100	100

NUMBER OF ORGANIZATIONS
(September, 1915)

Year	New York City	Remainder of State	Total	Gain + or Loss — Per Cent
1898.......... 440		647	1,087	
1899.......... 477		843	1,320	233 +
1900.......... 502		1,133	1,635	315 +
1901.......... 515		1,356	1,871	236 +
1902.......... 579		1,650	2,229	358 +
1903.......... 653		1,930	2,583	354 +
1904.......... 670		1,834	2,504	79 —
1905.......... 667		1,735	2,402	102 —
1906.......... 678		1,742	2,420	18 +
1907.......... 712		1,785	2,497	77 +
1908.......... 704		1,740	2,444	53 —
1909.......... 690		1,669	2,359	85 —
1910.......... 722		1,735	2,457	98 +
1911.......... 736		1,762	2,498	41 +
1912.......... 693		1,776	2,469	29 —
1913.......... 760		1,883	2,643	174 +
1914.......... 763		1,854	2,617	26 —

MEMBERSHIP
(September, 1915)

Year	New York City	Remainder of State	Total	Gain + or Loss — Per Cent
1898....... 125,429		45,638	171,067	
1899....... 141,687		67,333	209,020	22.2 +
1900....... 154,504		90,877	245,381	17.4 +
1901....... 174,022		102,119	276,141	12.5 +
1902....... 198,055		131,046	329,101	19.2 +
1903....... 244,212		151,386	395,598	20.2 +
1904....... 254,719		136,957	391,676	1.0 —
1905....... 251,277		131,959	383,236	2.2 —
1906....... 260,008		138,486	398,494	4.0 +
1907....... 286,180		150,612	436,792	9.6 +
1908....... 239,538		132,921	372,459	14.7 —
1909....... 243,157		129,572	372,729	0.1 +
1910....... 337,509		144,415	481,924	29.3 +
1911....... 357,071		147,243	504,314	4.6 +
1912....... 377,709		148,963	526,672	4.4 +
1913....... 491,793		173,455	665,248	26.3 +
1914....... 431,998		163,826	595,824	10.4 —

NUMBER OF UNIONISTS, CLASSIFIED IN OCCUPATIONS
(September, 1915)

Trades	1898	1903	1908	1913
Building, stone work, etc.....	59,676	110,173	120,010	138,738
Transportation..............	19,065	63,791	68,000	93,995
Clothing and textiles.........	26,444	40,981	31,409	226,528
Metals, machinery, etc.......	11,621	48,230	28,830	37,452
Printing, binding, etc........	15,090	23,915	25,181	30,730
Wood working and furniture..	4,468	16,916	10,194	14,762
Food and liquors............	6,469	15,757	14,753	17,995
Theaters and music..........	9,346	11,674	16,955	26,607
Tobacco....................	8,889	12,435	11,523	10,217
Restaurants, trade, etc.......	3,228	14,828	10,636	28,705
Public employment..........	1,880	9,753	15,097	18,304
Stationary engine tenders.....	3,738	11,166	11,984	11,655
Miscellaneous..............	1,153	15,979	7,887	9,560
Total.................	171,067	395,598	372,459	665,248

Of the 27 cities in New York State with 1,000 or more population, only 4 showed a decrease in the number of locals in 1913 compared with 1912, and but 4 suffered a loss of union members. In but 2 was there loss in both the number of locals and the membership. The total loss in membership was 1,933 and the gain was 139,322, making a net gain of 137,389. While there was a total loss of 5 locals, there was a total gain of 153. As previously shown, the gain in locals for the state was 174 and in membership 138,576.

Further evidence of centralization appears from an examination of the 9 largest cities of the state. In 1910 these 9 cities, having 65 per cent of the state's population, had 87 per cent of the trade unionists of the state, leaving but 13 per cent of the unionists in the remaining 35 per cent of the population. In 1913 the percentage of union membership in these 9 cities had increased to 90. Of these cities, New York with 52 per cent of the population had 70 per cent of the union men, in 1910.

Further, it is shown that in every industry there was a gain in membership, and in all but the tobacco industry there was a gain in the number of unions.

All these results must be understood to be net, for there were losses as well as gains. For example, in transportation there were large gains in spite of a loss of 2,000 members mainly in the navigation branch.

During the year 1913 one new local at least was formed in each of 13 different trades or branches of trades, a total of 292 locals in such trades. The number of trades with a membership of 2,000 or more in the state was increased by 5, making a total of 65 such trades. This is again a net result, 8 trades being added to the list and 3 cut off. Of these 65 trades the total membership increased in 54, decreased in 10, and in 1 remained stationary. Only 2 trades showed a decrease of as much as 2,000 members. Of the same list of 65 trades, 30 increased the number of locals, 27 showed no change, and 8 experienced a decrease.

VARYING SIZE OF UNIONS

The strength of influence of unionism is further indicated by the large membership of some of the unions. With centralized management the collective strength is greatly increased by numbers. The unity of action gives added force. There are three unions each with a membership of over 100,000. These are the United Mine Workers of America (370,800); the United Brotherhood of Carpenters and Joiners of America (210,700) and the Brotherhood of Railroad Trainmen (133,884).

Arranged in groups on the basis of the reported membership there appear:

Unions		Total Membership
3	over 100,000	715,384
11	between 100,000 and 50,000	734,128
14	" 50,000 " 25,000	503,327
29	" 25,000 " 10,000	450,768
68	" 10,000 " 1,000	275,819
33	less than 1,000	25,487

Of the entire number listed, 158 unions, the median of membership is 5,000.

THE AMERICAN FEDERATION OF LABOR

A further indication of strength is found in the relative numbers affiliated with the American Federation of Labor. The last report of membership in this organization at the time of writing was the annual report made to the convention in November, 1914. This shows a total membership of 2,020,671: about 73 per cent of the entire union membership of the country. This can be regarded as approximate only, for the comparison is not for the same years.

TABLE SHOWING AVERAGE PAID-UP AND REPORTED MEMBERSHIP AND NUMBER OF UNIONS AFFILIATED WITH THE A. F. OF L. 1897–1914

Year	Membership	Unions Affiliated
1897	264,825	55
1898	278,016	67
1899	349,422	73
1900	548,321	82
1901	787,537	87
1902	1,024,399	97
1903	1,465,800	113
1904	1,676,200	120
1905	1,494,300	118
1906	1,454,200	119
1907	1,538,970	116
1908	1,586,885	115
1909	1,482,872	118
1910	1,562,112	120
1911	1,761,835	115
1912	1,770,145	112
1913	1,996,004	111
1914	2,020,671	110

The average membership for the official year 1915 is reported as 1,946,347, the first decrease since 1909. The largest average monthly membership was for September, 1915, when the number was 1,994,111.

The changing nature of the membership is indicated by the following statement from the report: "Sixty-four national and international unions show an increase in their average membership over last year (1913) of 90,627 members; twenty-three organizations show no increase; twenty-three organizations show a decrease of 64,277 members; and the total membership of directly affiliated local unions shows a decrease of 1,683 members. The membership reported does not include all the members involved in strikes or lockouts or those who were unemployed during the fiscal year, for whom tax was not received."

Supplementing the above table are stated in the report the following facts for the one year 1914 as to alterations made in

the relations of other unions in their charter affiliations. One
national union with a membership of ten was disbanded. Two
were suspended. These had a combined membership of 1,172.
Of central bodies, eight were disbanded and one suspended for
non-payment of per capita tax. There were forty local trade
unions disbanded; 151 suspended; five joined internationals;
and the charters of two were revoked. Of federal trade unions
fourteen were disbanded; fifty-four were suspended and three
joined internationals.

The net gains made by the Federation do not indicate by
any means the extent of the changes either in the numbers or in
the variety of the associations. The report for 1914 contains
the following table which sums up the work of the officials in the
matter of charters.

CHARTERS ISSUED 1897–1914

Year	Internationals	Departments	State	Central	Trade Unions	Federal Unions	Total
1897......	8		2	18	154	35	217
1898......	9		0	12	129	53	203
1899......	9		1	35	303	101	449
1900......	14		5	96	484	250	849
1901......	7		4	123	575	207	916
1902......	14		6	127	598	279	1,024
1903......	20		3	171	743	396	1,333
1904......	11		5	99	179	149	443
1905......	3		1	67	143	73	287
1906......	6		4	53	167	87	317
1907......	3		1	72	204	93	373
1908......	0	2	4	73	100	55	234
1909......	3	2	2	40	77	52	176
1910......	2	0	1	83	152	96	334
1911......	3	0	0	61	207	55	326
1912......	2	1	2	57	149	49	260
1913......	2		1	63	197	59	322
1914......	2		1	44	128	50	225

That the Federation is making the larger gains is at once apparent from a brief comparison. The gain for the last year
credited to the Federation is 225,859 and to the unaffiliated
unions it is 2,307. According to these figures the Federation
can claim 99 per cent of the total gain for the year. This large
share of gain is due to the fact that a number of independent

unions either affiliated with the American Federation of Labor during the year or were amalgamated with unions that were already affiliated, while some of the independent associations disbanded. Especially large gains were made by some of the affiliated unions. The Mine Workers, for which John Mitchell claims the most rapid growth "of any trade union in the history of the world," increased by 103,800. The Ladies Garment Workers added 20,400; the Carpenters and Joiners, 18,400; and the United Garment Workers, 12,100.

The comparison of the numbers in the larger unions and in the smaller leads to the question of equity when these unions are federated. Are the smaller unions outvoted by the superior voting strength of the larger? Do they fear any such result?

Comparing the voting strength of the unions that are affiliated in the American Federation of Labor it appears that there is a wide variation. One union has 3,345 votes and as many as three have but one vote each. The second largest union has 2,128 votes while two unions have two votes each.

Arranging the unions on the basis of their voting strength in the Federation, it appears that

Unions		Have Votes		Total Votes of the Group
18	from	1 to 9	inclusive	74
16	"	10 to 19	"	202
7	"	20 to 29	"	187
8	"	30 to 39	"	275
6	"	40 to 49	"	262
3	"	50 to 59	"	162
5	"	60 to 69	"	318
2	"	70 to 79	"	150
1	"	80 to 89	"	85
4	"	90 to 99	"	387
70	"	1 to 99	"	2,102
16	"	100 to 199	"	2,342
6	"	200 to 299	"	1,543
4	"	300 to 399	"	1,401
1	"	400 to 499	"	400
6	"	500 to 599	"	3,260
3	"	600 to 699	"	1,906
2	"	700 to 799	"	1,498

From this table it appears that a combination of the two largest groups of votes would total 5,473 of the 21,185 votes of the convention. The total vote of the eleven largest unions is 11,126. The number of votes in the convention necessary to a majority is 10,593. This includes the votes cast by the centrals, locals and state branches, 1,260 votes in all. If this last group be left out of consideration, the total vote of the unions alone is 19,925 with 9,963 as a majority. The nine largest unions in the Federation have a total voting strength of 10,061.

As in this group of eleven large unions there are rival interests as well as community interests, the probability of their combining against the small ones is rather remote. The group consists of the United Mine Workers of America (3,345 votes); the Brotherhood of Carpenters and Joiners (2,128 votes); the Association of Machinists (754 votes); the Brotherhood of Painters, Decorators and Paper Hangers (744 votes); the United Garment Workers (607 votes); the Ladies Garment Workers (699 votes); the Federation of Musicians (600 votes); the Typographical Union (594 votes); the Hotel and Restaurant Employees (590 votes); the United Brewery Workers (520 votes); the Association of Street and Electric Railway Employees (545 votes). This group does not appear to have interests sufficiently unlike those of the smaller unions and at the same time of common importance to themselves to cause any immediate danger. Yet it is evident as a practical matter that the larger unions are in a position to wield by far the greater influence in determining the policies of the American Federation of Labor.

CHAPTER IX

WOMEN AND UNIONISM

There are very good reasons for considering the relations of women to the labor movement as a separate topic. While theoretically the welfare of laborers is a question broader than sex lines, as broad as labor itself, the methods of work, the purposes and spirit vary with sex as they do with trades, nationality or territorial sections.

Women in Industry. — It must not be supposed that the presence of women in the union movement is novel. Women in industry is a phenomenon much older than is popularly supposed. In America women in unionism is in fact about as old as is unionism itself. In the period prior to the Civil War women were appearing in one industry after another. For those who insist that the American labor movement had its beginning in 1825, the beginning of organization among women would be fixed by the same date. This should be taken to mean that women wage earners were a factor in industry, that they were assembling in organizations, asserting demands and even enforcing them by strikes. Records reveal during the first third of the nineteenth century the existence of unions among tailoresses, seamstresses and other needlewomen, cotton mill girls, women in book binderies, in boot and shoe factories, and in other trades open to women. These organizations were active and often successful in gaining their ends.

Condition of Early Unionism. — The description of the unionism of this early period given in a former chapter will serve to recall many of the conditions of these years. Many organizations of women, transient in nature, were formed. They were turbulent or peaceful according to the character of the membership. Their immediate objects once attained, they either disintegrated or reorganized on the lines of some broader reform movement, tending toward the political activity of the day. The appearance of women in the movement was, of course, new and in the growing mill towns of New England somewhat perversive of puritan traditions. Daughters of real New England stock, working in factories, living in boarding houses, dissatisfied with wages or hours of labor, organizing, drafting resolutions, adopting constitutions, going on strike, marching the streets in parades of hundreds, singing their extemporized songs and shouting their demands, must have startled the quiet towns so new to milling life. The editor who exclaimed "What next!" must have voiced the feeling of most of his readers.

Early Strikers. — The records of these early years are well stocked with accounts of strikes among women workers. Beginning in 1825 with a protective organization among tailoresses in New York, the number multiplies and spreads to New Hampshire, Massachusetts, New Jersey, Maryland, and Pennsylvania. It appears that practically all these strikes were for increase of wages, shorter hours of labor or improved conditions. The public took an active interest in the events, and the discussions of the period are interesting as well as instructive. As a writer in the Mechanics' Free Press said regarding a strike of mill girls in Dover, N. H., in 1829 the strike "formed the subject of a squib, probably for half the newspapers from Maine to Georgia. The circumstance of three or four hundred girls or women marching out of their factory in a procession and firing off a lot of gunpowder, and the facetious advertisement of the factory agent for two or three hundred better behaved women made, altogether, a comical story quite worth telling."

In 1836 the girls of the Lowell mills struck because of the increasing cost of living. In the earlier years of milling the corporations of necessity provided the boarding houses. The price of board was advanced from $5 to $5.50 a month because of an advance in cost of provisions. This increase the women insisted was equivalent to a reduction in wages. Thus early came the question of the relation of wages to cost of living. Resisting the paternalistic management of the Lowell employers who undertook to regulate the lives of employees, a Factory Girls' Association was formed numbering 2,500 members. It appointed officials through whom they would communicate with employers. "As our fathers resisted unto blood the lordly avarice of the British Ministry," declared these mill girls, "so we, their daughters, never will wear the yoke which has been prepared for us."

There were during this early period instances in which these associations were more permanent than the local strike which occasioned them. The National Trades Union had its Committee on Female Labor which was active in looking after the work assigned to it. In New York there was the United Tailoresses' Society which had some energetic women officials. At Lynn, Mass., women shoebinders about one thousand in number formed The Female Society of Lynn and Vicinity for the Protection and Promotion of Female Industry. Philadelphia had its Association of Shoebinders and Corders with its membership of several hundred women.

National Ideals. — Following the lead of the men's unions during the later years of this pre-Civil War period, these organizations became interested in the broader humanitarian ideals of the time. The shorter working day and better working conditions became more closely related to the expanding suffrage, greater political activity, slavery agitation, women's suffrage and the other movements of this remarkable reform period. The New England Workingmen's Association was made up of women as well as men delegates, coming from various reform as well as trade organizations. These women took a leading part in the work of the convention. Because of this, in 1846, the name was changed to the New England Labor Reform League. Two women were chosen among the seven members of the executive committee. On another important committee of eight, three were women. In 1845 was formed the National Industrial Congress. This led to a series of congresses that continued for ten years. By its constitution members were elected by associations of men and women which adopted its principles. This organization soon became interested in larger questions of reform and did not limit itself to problems of labor.

Permanent Organizations. — A strike and agitation among cotton mill operatives in Lowell, Mass., in 1845 led to the formation of the Lowell Female Labor Reform Association. The leadership was energetic and the work of the association commanded attention. This organization stated in its constitution that it "disapproved of all hostile measures, strikes and turnouts until all pacific measures prove abortive, and then it is the imperious duty of every one to assert and maintain that independence which our brave ancestors bequeathed us and sealed with their blood." Owing to the activity of the association's officials the Massachusetts legislature was appealed to and investigations were made into the labor conditions of the textile industry. To these women officials has been given the credit of creating the favorable public sentiment and starting the investigations and reforms that began the series of protective legislative measures in which Massachusetts has for so many years led the way. Through the further activity of this reform association a Female Department was maintained for several months in the Lowell Voice of Industry, a leading labor weekly paper. Later the women purchased the paper and continued its publication as a labor paper. After two years of activity the association changed its name to the Lowell Female Industrial Reform and Mutual Aid Society. Fees were raised and a sick fund established.

Following the Lowell model the women of Manchester, N. H., formed the Female Labor Association of Manchester, which had a membership of about three hundred and was characterized by energetic and aggressive action.

Outside of New England the principal organizations were the Female Industrial Association of New York and the Industrial Union of Philadelphia. Like their New England sisters these associations had practical difficulties to deal with and they sought to meet them in much the same way.

The pre-Civil War period for the women as for the men tells the story of disconnected and unrelated effort. There were organizations and associations, strikes and turbulence, victories and defeats. But there was no movement. The trade as a stratum in industry had not appeared as a permanent alignment. For this reason the organizations that were formed lacked permanency and specific purpose.

Character of Early Period. — Of this period the characteristic features may be stated briefly. The strikes apparently did not break out until a point of desperation had been reached. These led to a degree of persistence and turbulence that early secured for women the reputation of "good strikers." Demontrations were prominent and often boisterous. Street parades, resolutions scattered broadcast, poems and songs, protest meetings in the open, placards, and even more noisy agencies were used to attract attention and testify to determination. When these strikes were lost the defeat was but temporary. A few weeks or a few months and the women returned to the fight with renewed vigor.

The public and the press were divided on the issues. Chivalry brought some to the women's support who otherwise would have sided with the employer. The ideas of freedom embodied in the oratorical expressions of Revolutionary days were freely used and often effectively. Yet on the other side were the ideals of home, of the sanctity of woman's character, of the importance to the coming generations of preserving the womanly virtues. In the interests of these ideals it seemed unwomanly to strike.

Later Period. — With the period following the Civil War came the development of the trade unions into the nationals as they are known to-day, and the Knights of Labor. These new forms of union organization found women already entering many trades and their unions in many cases very much alive. Yet but few of the national trade unions admitted women to membership. Of the thirty or more that existed during the years from 1860 to 1875, only two extended their membership privileges to women of the trade. These were the printers and the cigar makers. Yet women did not cease to push their own interests. Women shoemakers formed themselves into a national union under the name, Daughters of St. Crispin, in 1869. They were guided by the Knights of St. Crispin, one of the strongest unions of the time. They had twenty-four locals, or lodges, most of which were in Massachusetts. Maine, New Hampshire, New York, Pennsylvania, Ohio, Illinois, Wisconsin, and California were also represented. This union was conspicuous for a time as an exception rather than as a type. The locals continued to represent the women in the various centers of industry.

The Cigar Trade. — In the cigar trade the women were at first organized locally and in unions of their own. These were active unionists and hated the "rat girls" with true union hatred. By 1867, the Cigar Makers Union came to the conclusion, after its three years of life, that women must be admitted to membership. Further experience of strikes being broken by poorly paid women workers convinced this union that more energetic measures were necessary. In 1871 special action was taken in convention to push the organization among the women workers. Opposition continued, however, in some quarters. In 1877 a Cincinnati union struck against the women and for a long time held out against the provisions of the constitution of the international. The trade proved easy for women to learn, and many immigrant women had learned it before coming to America. The employer was quick to seize the advantage. The union was slow to see the importance of unionizing the whole trade. The shock of awakening came when an employer secured women to break a strike and advertised on the boxes of his product: "cigars made by American girls." Necessity finally forced the decision. By 1880 female cigar makers were at work in large numbers. It became not a question of choice, whether the union men should or should not extend the privileges of unionism to the women. Self-preservation demanded that it should be done and it was done. American girls must be admitted and foreigners with them. As an officer tersely said: "It is better to have them with us than against us."

The Printing Trade.— In the printing trade there is very much the same story. The union printers were opposed to the entrance of women into the trade. Yet women were learning the trade. They could not do so by the regular apprenticeship method, but with the encouragement of employers they "stole" it and acquired sufficient skill to do the work. They at first formed their own unions. When in the unions they were loyal; but most of them were non-union and would take work at much lower wages than were paid to men. Realizing the dangers the male unionists first began to encourage and assist women to form unions. They hired halls, furnished necessary supplies, and paid all expenses necessary to start a woman's union. But this was not the end. The regular unions of men began to receive applications for membership from women. In 1869 the unions one at a time began to receive them. The reasons for the change are clear enough. As with the cigar makers, it was self-protection. Their admission was coupled with demands for equal pay for equal work and insisting that women unionists must demand the union scale.

In other trades confusion still dominated. The industries were not sufficiently mature and the methods of work were not clearly enough distinguished to make possible anything more than transient local effort.

The Knights of Labor. — With the appearance of the Knights of Labor a new spirit prevailed. It will be remembered that the struggles of the former years were around two principles. One was that of trade interest and of rivalry with employer only within the trade area. This did not afford a positive platform upon which the men unionists could stand and urge the organization of all working women. The other principle was the broadly humanitarian idealism that reached well into the clouds but did not rest upon the ground. It led to no solidly practical results. It was for the Knights of Labor to attempt to find a working program that could rest upon both of these principles. The spirit of this organization has already been noticed. Its principle, an injury to one is the concern of all, was an ideal that was to be taken literally. It began with calling for the abolition of the labor of children and for equal pay for equal work for both sexes.

Women were admitted to membership in the Knights of Labor in 1881. Both as separate and in mixed locals the membership of women increased rapidly. The 1885 convention provided for a special committee of women to investigate conditions of women's work. At a later convention all of the sixteen women delegates were appointed a special committee to promote the interests of the women. Investigation showed women to be poorly organized generally, with hard work, long hours and low pay. The cause of their lack of interest in organization was reported as "largely due to their own ignorance of the importance of the step, yet much blame can be attached to the neglect and indifference of their brother toilers." For the first time systematic work was undertaken in this field. The investigator was made a general officer of the Knights and given a free hand to push the work. Cities were visited and interest aroused in the unions. Circulars were sent out and information furnished wherever needed. The female membership of the Knights was raised in a few months by a number probably between 11,000 and 12,000 representing about thirty different trades. For four years the organizing and educating work was energetically and systematically carried on. Then came the leaner years of the Knights of Labor. Membership was shrinking. The treasury was low. With the general waning of interest came the decline in the work of the women's department. Finally the energetic field organizer and general officer married and withdrew from the "field of industrial life to the quiet and comfort of a home." The position was offered to the one sole woman delegate at the convention of 1890. Upon her declining to accept the office the woman's department of the Knights of Labor came to an end. It is idle to present figures of membership during this period. Reports were irregular and incomplete. It is estimated that the largest membership was about 50,000.

The American Federation of Labor. — The work of the Knights of Labor was not lost even though the order itself declined in influence. The strengthening of the national unions in the various trades and the rise of the American Federation of Labor brought to the front again an active interest in the women. From the first the American Federation committed itself to the policy of organizing women workers. In 1885 it was resolved in convention to "call upon and advise working women of this country to protect themselves by organizing into unions of their respective trades and callings" and further the legislative committee was pledged to render assistance whenever possible. Again in these early years the president of the Federation urged that "first and foremost we should bend our energies to the organization of laboring women in trade unions." This should be done in order that girls and women "may learn the stern fact that if they desire to achieve any improvement in their condition it must be through their own self-assertion in the local union." Later a resolution was favorably received calling for the appointment of women organizers to confine their attention especially to pushing the formation of unions among their own sex. Though this was the opinion definitely expressed in the conventions, the executive council did not respond promptly and the matter of getting these organizers into the field proceeded slowly. Though so definitely committed to the policy in a general way the practical side was not pushed with vigor, only occasionally was an organizer actually appointed and then the work was limited to a few months. More recently the work has gone forward with greater energy.

The National Women's Trade Union League. — At the 1903 convention a new departure was undertaken. It took the form of a National Women's Trade Union League and was to include in its membership all working women whether in trade unions or not; and also all women who sympathized with the organization movement though themselves not of the "ranks of labor." One other organization should be named in this connection. The Women's International Union Label League, organized in 1899, has been active in pushing the interests of the union label. Its objects are somewhat broader than those of the Women's Trade Union League, yet their relation to the unionizing movement among women is very real. It has stood for the encouragement of union-made goods, the universal eight-hour day, equal pay for equal work regardless of sex, early closing and Sunday closing, sustaining fair employers, and in general any movements related to these. The more direct work of this league has been in connection with the union label. Its membership includes not only women members of trade unions, but the wives and daughters of unionists also. These two organizations in particular have been working in close coöperation with the American Federation of Labor. They are represented by delegates at the Federation's annual conventions and a close coöperation is maintained in the organizing work.

The Nationals. — It appears from the records to be the present policy of the Federation to push the work of organization among women largely through these associations and through the affiliated national trade unions. Among them the field is covered. In the addresses of the president the work is referred to and the delegates are strongly urged to have women organizers put into the field by their respective nationals, especially by those in trades where women are entering in large numbers. In 1913 and the year following special assessments were levied the proceeds of which were to be used in assisting the Women's Trade Union League in furthering its work.

Work of the Women's Trade Union League. — This one cent assessment for the first year to organize women workers led to the expenditure, between the last of February and the first of October, 1914, of $10,857. Eighteen organizers were put into the field of whom five were women. The work was done largely in the New England field (except Vermont); in New York, New Jersey and Pennsylvania; and in the Carolinas. Georgia and Alabama; these sections being the centers of the

textile industry. The assessment voted by the 1914 convention
the Executive Council did not deem it wise to levy, owing to
conditions that so greatly modified all industrial activity after
the outbreak of war. The work for the year ending with the
1915 convention was carried on in a more limited way, the
officers making use of some available funds that were already
in hand. Two women organizers were kept in the field for the
year. Somewhat more than nine thousand dollars were spent
in the work. Efforts were made particularly among garment
workers, textile workers, manufacturers of electric supplies and
silk workers. The textile workers again received the greater
amount of attention.

In its present form and as equipped for carrying forward this
work the League comprises, as stated by its Secretary in the 1915
report, nine local leagues in as many different cities (Boston,
New York, Chicago, St. Louis, Springfield, Ill., Kansas City,
Mo., Baltimore, Denver, and Philadelphia), forty members at
large, the Illinois State Committee, and the Los Angeles Committee of the National Women's Trade Union League. Affiliated directly are six international unions, five state federations of labor, twenty central labor bodies, one local union and
one trades council auxiliary.

The president has just issued a call "to the 7,000,000 women
workers in the United States, nearly half of whom are under
twenty-one years of age," to organize for better conditions of
labor and to become affiliated with the Women's Trade Union
League and the American Federation of Labor. Thus is the
work being vigorously pushed in accordance with the coöperative policy of these two organizations.

Results of the Efforts. — In the unionizing work, each trade
has its peculiar problems, its successes and failures, the details
of which are too numerous and varied to be included in so brief
a sketch. There are, however, certain underlying facts that
are important in understanding the movement and in account-
ing for the degree of success as well as for the degree of failure.

Attitude of Union Men. — The attitude of union men has
been very significant. From the earlier days when, in the
twenties and thirties, it was becoming evident that women
were pushing their way into certain trades, even down to the
present the attitude has not changed fundamentally, though

it is manifested in a different way. If it was a case where women were just beginning to enter the trade, they were opposed by the men. To organize them would be to encourage their permanency as rivals. As in one trade after another the women came in ever increasing numbers and became established, the opposition was reluctantly withdrawn. It slowly gave way to a more or less spontaneous enthusiasm for their organization. At first the opposition was so pronounced that the men in some trades, as the tailors in 1819 and again in 1835, either went on strike or flatly refused to work for employers who gave work to women. These early days saw similar trouble with bookbinders, shoe workers, and cotton mill hands as well as in other trades. As the rivalry of women workers appeared inevitable the alternative was to unionize them. This slow change the men have been making as gracefully as possible until at present the admission of women to the trades is taken as a fact. This has settled the matter of organizing and the work is being pushed and encouraged by the men themselves. At the 1914 convention of the Federation a resolution was introduced in which it was resolved "that we do our very utmost to restore individual, social, and racial health by restoring the women to the home and the children to the school and to such play as shall help them to grow up and become efficient men and women." As this came from the resolutions committee and was finally adopted by the Federation, it was resolved to restore health "by making the employment of women as congenial as possible and by sending children" to the school and playground. The discussion revealed two reasons for the change. The convention realized that it could not by mere resolution take women out of industry. They are in industry to stay. Even if it were possible to do this, the convention realized the pertinency of the question: what would become of those who are dependent upon industry and have no homes? The voting sense of the convention recognized the inevitable. The same idea appears in the comment made by the president at the same convention: "More and more it is realized that women do not live apart from the political, social and economic organization of society, but that they are responsible members and should share in its burdens and contribute to its progress. What has been done in organization this year is a mere beginning whose results are not yet appreciable. The work should be continued with un-remitting vigor. Women wage earners must be organized or they will retard the progress of all organization." Speaking of the economic dependence of women the more recent attitude of the Federation appears in the statement of the report of the Executive Council at the 1915 convention. "There are often many criticisms advanced that women do not understand the spirit and the methods of collective action of organization in trade unions, and that therefore they cannot protect themselves through economic organizations. Again and again this asser-tion has been proved false. Women can be organized, they can and do understand the principles of trade unionism, and they are able and willing to fight for the cause."

Attitude of Women. — While the attitude of men has finally become positively aggressive and no longer constitutes a serious obstacle to the spread of organization, it cannot be said that all difficulties have been removed. The women themselves are in a sense their own handicap. This fact appears evident from any careful analysis. In the first place women as a class may have become permanently industrialized but the same is not true of the individuals. Marriage is looked forward to with more or less definiteness. This may not affect the situation where women continue to work at a trade after marriage, but these are rela-tively unimportant. The prospect to the single working girl is marriage and a home life. Though not always realized, it is important while as a prospect it continues. Because of this they care less for organization and the sacrifices necessary to maintain it. For the same reason the wages are not of such importance. Low wages help out and no part of them seems necessary to provide for the future. They become even more anxious to escape the conditions of low-paid labor than to im-prove them. Unionism offers a present sacrifice for a future benefit. The working girl appears unwilling to make the sacri-fice. It is even claimed that successful unions are a detriment to permanency of organization. The ends sought are immediate. If these ends are attained, the organization goes to pieces, leav-ing a serious wreckage in the way of forming another union in the future.

Again it is claimed that the youthfulness of women wage earners is a handicap. Census reports show that in by far the larger number of cases they are under twenty-five years, leaving but few experienced heads for council and conservatism. Another fact not to be overlooked is the feeling of pride and of social distinction between workers. The former of these leads some to hesitate to join a union openly for fear of being rated too publicly as working girls. The latter offers a serious barrier in that girls of one trade look down upon those of another and would not "stoop" to being associated with them in a union.

Finally, it is to be noted that while women are admitted to membership, they have but little to say in determining policies. Rarely indeed are they chosen to office. Attendance upon meetings is often impracticable because of the location of meeting rooms, the tobacco smoke and the boisterous language of the men. It is still true that mixed unions are not successful in securing attendance of women, much less in making use of the administrative and executive ability of the women members.

Attitude of Employer. — The employer also is an important factor. Experience has revealed to him the necessity of checking union movements at the beginning, realizing that if they acquire momentum they may pass beyond control. As women are generally more timid than men, a firm stand by the employer can often defeat entirely a movement for organization among them. Women in many trades have been valuable as strike breakers. They are valuable in a labor supply because of the relative ease with which their wages may be adjusted to necessary or desired economies in expenses. They are quite too valuable to lose as an unorganized group of labor.

Activity of Industrial Workers of the World. — The activity of the Industrial Workers of the World is accountable in two ways for the situation so far as unionism among women is concerned. First, its propaganda among unskilled workers has been fruitful for a time of large membership in industrial centers where it is openly at work. This membership does not prove to be permanent. Evidence of this appears in the Massachusetts figures. In 1911 there were 1,292 women unionists. The following year showed 16,546 in the membership. These were largely textile operatives in Lawrence, Lowell, New Bedford, Fall River and other localities where the Industrial Workers were organizing strikes among mill-workers. In 1913 the total membership fell to 9,157, a shrinkage of over 7,000 in a year.

This variation, which the state report mildly characterizes as "somewhat transitory membership" is not out of accord with the policy of the Industrial Workers. They regard all unskilled workers, both men and women, as their source of strength, even though comparatively few are enrolled formally as members. However disturbing it may be to the statistician who likes to see his figures plot into graceful curves, the irregularity of membership does not in the least dampen the ardor of the leaders of the Industrial Workers of the World.

Second, the Industrial Workers have imparted an incentive to the leaders of trade unionism. This has reacted in creating a renewed interest in the problem of unionizing the women wage earners. At the time of the Lawrence disturbance not alone the strike leaders but others who were entirely on the outside were openly criticizing the officers of the trade union of textile workers for their neglect to organize the unskilled foreign girls and women. Though these trade union officials defended their actions with much zeal, the net result appeared to be that the neglect was inexcusable. It was made to appear that the trade union of textile workers was something of an aristocracy, seeking to promote the interests of some of the workers at the expense of others. However this may have been, the developments of more recent months are interesting. As has been said above, special assessments were levied by the American Federation of Labor to be used by the Women's Trade Union League. As stated in the annual report of the president of the Federation: "The textile industry was selected as one of those upon which efforts were to be centered." The effect appeared also in another way. In the government investigation which covered the movement to 1909, it was stated that the prospects for large increases of membership were gloomy. Before the report was published a supplementary statement was made covering nearly all of the year 1911. In this latter statement much of the gloom disappears. "Since 1909 there has been a most marked growth in the number of women's unions, a still larger growth in the membership in the unions, and an improvement the most marked of all in the general interest taken in women's unions in all portions of the country and in almost all trades in which there is any organization at all. . . . The gain seems to have come suddenly. There was little evidence of real vitality or dynamic force in the period prior to 1909." The figures presented from New York State bear out the impression that the year 1909 was a year of change. It would not be right to attribute this sudden progress to any one cause. The recovery from the depression of 1907, the reverses in court sustained by laws intended to favor women in industry, these and other forces were undoubtedly active. It must not be overlooked, however, that the Industrial Workers of the World was organized in 1905 but that the first three or four years were occupied with dissension and internal adjustment. In 1909 the new organization stepped into the field relieved of its incumbrances and ready for business. The incentive that this new and radical organization imparted both directly and indirectly must not be left out of account. While it may be responsible for a large amount of transitory membership among women, it must be held accountable also as an important factor in increasing the membership both in its own organization and in many of the trade unions as well.

STATISTICS OF WOMEN IN UNIONS

As to the number of women enrolled in the membership of unions there are no data that are both comprehensive and accurate. The efforts are so new that they have not been made general. The policy adopted has been one of concentration in particular localities and trades. The activities of the Women's Trade Union League have been centralized in a few cities especially, though not entirely confined to them. In but few of the states are there reports that give any comprehensive information. The Massachusetts Labor Bulletin shows that 181 unions in that state had a female membership of 25,749 at the close of 1912. One year later there were 195 such unions with a total female membership of 30,513. The gain of 1913 over 1912 was eighteen and one-half per cent. This compares unfavorably with the gain of the previous year which was fifty-nine and one-half per cent. The municipalities having one thousand or more women unionists were:

City	Women Unionists
Boston	8,089
Brockton	4,138
Fall River	3,484
Lynn	2,543
Lawrence	2,187
New Bedford	2,106
Haverhill	1,018

Boston had 39 locals; Brockton, 15; Lynn, 13; while in the other cities the number of locals was smaller.

Of the 195 unions referred to there were 18 whose membership was made up of women alone, to the number of 7,226, while 62 unions each numbered 100 or more in its membership.

By trades the entire 30,513 women were distributed as follows:

	Number	Per Cent of Total
Boot and shoe workers	11,901	39.
Textile workers	8,682	28.5
Garment workers	3,185	10.4
Telephone operators	2,548	8.4
Retail clerks	876	2.9
Cigar factory workers and tobacco strippers	650	2.1
Bookbinders	583	1.9
Other occupations	2,088	6.8
Total	30,513	100.0

The following tables indicate some of the facts in a more detailed way. Each may be left to explain itself.

1. Table showing trade unions reporting 10 or more women members, their female membership, and the estimated proportion women form of total union membership. (From the History of Women in Trade Unions, p. 136: Vol. X of Report on Conditions of Woman and Child Wage Earners in the United States. Government Printing Office.)

	No. of Unions	Female Membership	Estimated Per Cent Women form of Total Union Membership
Bookbinders.................	25	3,628	40
Boot and shoe workers........	40	5,443	17
Cigar makers................	32	3,490	10
Garment workers (men's)......	133	17,212	40
Garment workers (women's)...	13	1,217	70
Glove workers...............	13	652	58
Hat and cap makers..........	14	5,385	54
Musicians...................	60	1,323	7
Printers (typographical workers)	17	621	3
Retail clerks (saleswomen).....	42	1,308	4
Shirt, waist and laundry workers	41	3,229	75
Textile workers..............	33	6,142	45
Tobacco workers.............	33	5,020	72
Waitresses..................	22	1,928	5
Miscellaneous...............	28	7,391	
Total..................	546	63,989	3

2. Table showing estimated number of women in unions, number 16 years old and over engaged in the trade, per cent who are union members of women and of men occupied in the trade, and proportion of women and of men occupied in the trade, United States, by trades. (History of Women in Trade Unions, p. 138.)

	No. of Women who are		Per Cent who are Union Members of		Per Cent of Persons 16 yrs. of age and over, occupied in the trade who are	
	Members of Unions (No. estimated)	Occupied in the trade, 16 yrs. of age and over	Women occupied in the trade	Men occupied in the trade	Women	Men
Bookbinders.........	3,600	14,303	25.2	35.6	50.5	49.5
Boot and shoe workers	5,400	49,535	10.9	27.2	34.2	65.8
Garment workers (men's)...........	17,700	75,468	23.5	45.9	56.2	43.8
Garment workers (women's)........	1,200	72,242	1.7	1.2	62.9	37.1
Glove workers.......	700	7,170	9.8	11.6	62.6	37.4
Hat and cap makers..	5,400	7,049	76.6	30.6	32.4	67.6
Musicians...........	2,800	52,010	5.4	91.2	56.9	43.1
Retail clerks (sales-women)...........	2,100	142,265	1.4	10.8	24.1	75.9
Shirt, waist and laundry workers...........	3,200	47,180	6.8	4.8	69.8	30.2
Textile workers......	6,100	231,458	2.6	3.0	50.0	50.0
Tobacco workers.....	9,000	37,125	13.5	2.2	30.9	69.1
Typographical workers	1,300	15,353	8.5	32.5	10.3	89.7
Waitresses..........	1,900	41,178	4.6	58.1	39.6	60.4
Miscellaneous.......	9,600	1,317,159	0.7	20.3	13.2	86.8
Total..........	70,000	2,109,495	3.3	20.5	17.5	82.5

3. The reports from New York State are much more complete and extend over a longer period of time. Though they indicate the conditions in that state only, they afford opportunity for comparative study within that area. The following data from the reports of the State Industrial Commission show the status of organization in New York State.

Year	Number of Women Unionists	Year	Number of Women Unionists
1897	5,764	1906	11,625
1898	7,505	1907	14,231
1899	8,088	1908	10,698
1900	11,828	1909	12,410
1901	14,618	1910	28,123
1902	15,509	1911	35,402
1903	14,753	1912	37,170
1904	12,817	1913	78,522
1905	12,265	1914	67,449

4. CHART SHOWING THE PROPORTION, IN PER CENT, OF WOMEN TO ALL UNIONISTS IN NEW YORK STATE, 1897–1914.

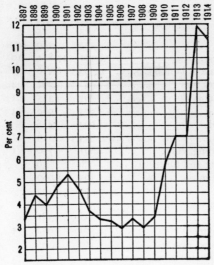

5. CHART SHOWING THE MEMBERSHIP OF WOMEN IN UNIONS IN
NEW YORK STATE, 1897–1914.

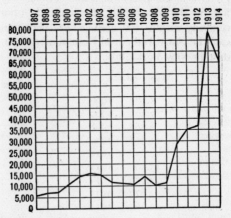

6. Table showing the number of union women in the several trades, in New York State, for September of the two years 1913 and 1914.

	1913	1914	No.	Unions of Women Exclusively Sept., 1914 Membership
Railways.....................	13	15		
Telegraphs...................	257	289		
Garments....................	51,512	47,811	10	1,345
Shirts, collars and laundry......	9,363	6,426	1	12
Hats, caps and furs...........	2,942	3,204	4	618
Boots, shoes and gloves........	367	335	1	170
Textiles.....................	3,225	988	3	472
Iron and steel................	622	438		
Other metals.................	13	16	1	16
Printing, binding, etc..........	1,891	1,770	1	1,230
Wood working and furniture....	36	39		
Theaters and music...........	3,395	2,080		
Tobacco.....................	2,390	2,297		
Hotels and restaurants.........	301	1		
Retail trade..................	352	381		
Public employment............	1,501	952	1	800
Paper and paper goods........	106	5		
Leather and leather goods......	25	100		
Mixed employment............	32	11		
Other distinct trades..........	179	291		
Total....................	78,522	67,449	22	4,663

7. Table showing national unions affiliated with the American Federation of Labor with the members of each sex in the locals of New York State (1915):

	Men	Women	Total
Bookbinders........................	1,649	1,282	2,931
Boot and shoe workers...............	1,032	268	1,300
Cigar makers.......................	7,552	2,207	9,759
Railway clerks......................	373	15	388
Retail clerks........................	458	286	744
Cloth hat and cap makers............	2,900	771	3,671
Commercial telegraphers.............	846	228	1,074
Electrical workers...................	7,676	438	8,114
Fur workers........................	8,074	2,055	10,129
Garment workers....................	43,965	11,787	55,752
Ladies' garment workers.............	65,799	40,521	106,320
Musicians..........................	10,862	453	11,315
Printing pressmen...................	1,427	58	1,485
Pulp and paper millers...............	1,986	5	1,991
Railroad telegraphers................	3,397	61	3,458
Journeymen tailors..................	1,226	66	1,292
Textile workers.....................	2,196	806	3,002
Tobacco workers....................	165	76	241
Leather novelty workers.............	425	100	525
Typographical union................	11,175	274	11,449
Upholsterers and trimmers...........	1,748	13	1,761
Actors.............................	7,000	1,000	8,000
[1] Twenty-five other international unions	4,295	78	4,373
[1] Local trade and labor unions........	8,968	1,619	10,587

8. Table showing the national unions not affiliated with the American Federation of Labor with the members of each sex in the locals of New York State (1915):

	Men	Women	Total
Actors.............................	1,213	589	1,802
Bookbinders........................	1,425	125	1,550
Post-office clerks....................	4,444	77	4,521
Industrial Workers of the World......	3,610	19	3,629
Musical and theatrical union.........	1,622	3	1,625
Shoe workers.......................	1,684	34	1,718
[1] Sixteen other international unions....	2,730	74	2,804
[1] Local unions......................	36,437	2,058	38,495

[1] Not all these have women in membership.

PART III
COLLECTIVE BARGAINING

CHAPTER X

THE STRIKE

DEFINITION

To define the terms strike and lockout seems comparatively simple. Yet there is not an unqualified agreement as to what the definitions should express. The need for clearness becomes apparent as soon as any analytical study of labor disturbances is begun.

Federal Bureau of Labor. — In the earlier reports of the Federal Bureau of Labor, little attention was given to formal definition. "A strike," it explained, in the Sixteenth Annual Report, "occurs when the employees of an establishment refuse to work unless the management complies with some demand; a lockout occurs when the management refuses to allow the employees to work unless they will work under some condition indicated by the management. It appears, therefore, that these two classes of industrial disturbances are practically alike, the main distinction being that in a strike the employees take the initiative, while in a lockout the employer first makes some demand and enforces it by refusing to allow his employees to work unless it is complied with." Three years later the definitions used were more formal and a degree more exact as well. As used in the 1904 report a strike is "A refusal by the employees of an establishment to work unless the employer complies with some demand made by the former or withdraws some obnoxious demand made by himself." A lockout is "A refusal by the employer to allow his employees to work in his establishment unless they will comply with some demand as to the conditions of employment made by him." The principal distinction, as pointed out, is "in one case the employees take the initiative in regard to discontinuance of work in an establishment and in the other case the initiative is taken by the employer."

Two years later the Bureau stated a third form of the definition again somewhat more exact. "A strike is a concerted withdrawal from work by a part or all of the employees of an establishment, or several establishments, to enforce a demand on the part of employees." "A lockout is a refusal on the part of an employer, or several employers, to permit a part or all of the employees to continue at work, such refusal being made to enforce a demand on the part of employers." For purposes of the classification made in accordance with them these definitions served well, but they cannot be accepted as in all respects satisfactory.

Another type of definition is important. A good instance is that taken from the Canadian Industrial Disputes Act: a strike is "the cessation of work by a body of employees acting in combination, or a concerted refusal or a refusal under a common understanding of any number of employees to continue to work for an employer, in consequence of a dispute, done as a means of compelling their employer, or to aid other employees in compelling their employer to accept terms of employment."

Comparison of these definitions and others that might be added reveals two quite separate considerations. In one the strike is regarded simply as an act of stopping work. In the other it is looked upon as essentially a means of inducing or compelling an employer to yield to certain demands.

Legal Definition. — When approached from the standpoint of legal definition another interesting distinction appears. A Federal Circuit Judge has given in one of his opinions (Farmers' Loan and Trust Co. *vs*. Northern Pacific R. R. Co., 60 Fed., 803) an interesting analysis. Recognizing that the legality of a strike must be determined largely by the meaning of the term, the Judge examines a variety of definitions from dictionaries, both literary and legal. His conclusion is that there are in the group of definitions two controlling ideas: "extorting by compulsion from the employer certain concessions" and "cessation of labor, but not the abandonment of employment." Both these elements, it is urged, are present in any strike. If the latter be omitted from the definition, then the term comes to represent the ideal, never existent in fact and certainly not the strike of history. The definition that he offers is: "A combined effort among workmen to compel the master to the concession of a certain demand, by preventing the conduct of his business until compliance with the demand." To this he adds: "The concerted cessation of work is but one of, and the least effective of, the means to the end; the intimidation of others from engaging in the service, the interference with, and the disabling and destruction of, property, and resort to actual force and violence, when requisite to the accomplishment of the end, being the other, and more effective, means employed."

That this view does not go unchallenged among jurists appears in the opinion reviewing this case before the court of appeals. Here it was asserted that the court was not prepared to go as far in defining the term. "A combination among employees, having for its object their orderly withdrawal in large numbers or in a body from the service of their employers, on account simply of a reduction in their wages" is a strike as that term is commonly used. To this the Justice adds the simple statement of Sir James Hannan of the Queen's Bench; a strike is a "simultaneous cessation of work on the part of the workmen." (Arthur vs. Oakes, 63 Fed., 310.)

From these statements it will appear that while in the matter of an exact definition there is not entire agreement, yet there are certain elements that are necessary to any definition. With these in mind a strike may be defined as a cessation of work by a group of employees by preconcerted agreement for the purpose of enforcing a demand concerning the conditions of employment. Such cessation may concern a single department, branch or subdivision of a shop, or it may extend to factories in different unrelated industries. The strikers may or may not insist upon retaining a claim to the places struck against. Though doubtless of much importance as a matter of tactics in the conduct of the strike, such a claim is not an essential element. The strikers, confident of the dependence of the former employer upon them, may withdraw entirely and await the time when he will feel obliged to yield to their demands and offer them their former positions. Such incidental features are often of much consequence in determining the kind of strike or the tactics used in its conduct. They are not, however, essential elements.

The Lockout. — After discovering the elements of the definition of a strike, there remains the lockout. The only difference, as pointed out in the earlier definitions, is that of initiative. If the employees start the disturbance it is a strike; if the employer acts first, it is a lockout. This may serve as a basis of tabulation, but it is lacking in thorough analysis. The employees may be pushing their demands and threatening a strike. The employer, seeing some tactical advantage in not allowing his men to act first, may turn the key to the workshop door just as he thinks the men are ready to walk out. A day later the disturbance would have been a strike. A day earlier it is a lockout. The difference between a strike and a lockout then becomes not so much the initiative in the dispute. It is simply a difference of twenty-four hours. Or, again, the employees may be pushing their demands. Knowing that a strike on the question of wages is inevitable the employer may suddenly break off negotiations, refuse to treat with the union officials and lock out the men for the ostensible reason that his business is his private affair and that he refuses to recognize the union. This then is a strike over wages if left till to-morrow but a lockout over recognition of unions if called to-day.

"Attack Strike": "Defense Strike." — Obviously the initiative in bringing about the cessation of work is not the same as the initiative in starting the dispute. The Massachusetts Bureau of Labor has recognized this difficulty and has sought to meet it by a classification on the basis of the party that raised the point about which the issue centers or that first makes the demand for change to which the other party refuses assent. This eliminates the difference between strike and lockout and so it has been proposed that the terms be dropped. As substitutes this department has suggested the terms "attack strike" and "defense strike." An attack strike is one in which "cessation of employment results from a movement begun in the first instance by the employees"; a defense strike is one in which "cessation of employment results from the initiative taken by the employer in making some change in the conditions of employment." A classification made on this basis is more satisfactory. It is more important to know, as far as possible, the real cause of the disturbance than to try to tell who first caused the stoppage of work; more significant to know what troubles led to the outbreak than to have the knowledge limited simply to the beginning of open hostility. Though the use of the terms attack and defense strike is more scientific and leads to keener analysis, they will undoubtedly be slow of adoption because it is so difficult to adjust them for comparative purposes to data already recorded.

Of strikes prior to the last quarter of the nineteenth century little is known. Their occurrence attracted but slight attention at the time. Those that occasioned more than local disturbance found their way into the passing records of the day, but these were soon lost. Only a more recent and thoroughly organized search for these lost accounts has brought some of them to light. These findings are of course incomplete, yet they warn us very positively against the error of supposing that the strike is in any sense a modern device. The importance attached to it in recent years is a relative one only. The strike is old, older in fact than labor organization itself.

Resorted to, as they were, with steadily increasing frequency and carrying with them consequences more and more serious, strikes attracted public attention to such a degree that the Tenth Census (1880) embodied a special report on the subject. The Federal Bureau of Labor then took up a more thorough investigation, beginning with the year 1881.

The first strike in the United States of which record has been discovered occurred in 1741. References found in the literature of later periods refer to a strike in that year among the journeymen bakers (probably) of New York City. For over half a century after that time, no serious trouble of this kind appears to have occurred. If there were strikes during this time, the records of such have not yet come to light. Fifty-one years later, 1792, there appears the first record of the existence of an organization among the journeymen shoemakers of Philadelphia. These workmen appear to have been more than ordinarily aggressive. They called a strike in 1796, one in 1798 and again in 1799. The first two of these were for an increase in wages and were successful. The last was against a reduction of wages and was only partly successful. About one hundred men appear to have been concerned. In 1805 these same journeymen "turned out" again in support of a demand for more wages.

This strike was not successful. The masters brought charges of conspiracy against the leaders in the Mayor's Court of the city of Philadelphia. The trial lasted three days and aroused unusual interest. The decision rested on the doctrine that a combination to raise wages is conspiracy and as such is unlawful. The defendants were found guilty and fined eight dollars each and costs.

During this early period the journeymen shoemakers were among the most active workmen in resorting to the strike. Other early cases are found among sailors, printers, shipbuilders, hat workers, spinners and weavers. Eight separate strikes of shoemakers during these early years were of sufficient importance to lead to trials in court and the cases were tried in various cities in Pennsylvania, New York, Maryland and Massachusetts.

The period prior to 1881 may be divided roughly into three subdivisions. Before about 1835 the strikes were few and of small consequence. Investigation shows that in all the years previous to 1835 there were possibly twenty-four strikes of which the records have been preserved. Most of these related to wages and in over half of them it is not known whether they were successful or not. From 1835 to 1870 the change is quite noticeable. To be sure, the records of these years are better preserved and consequently our information is more satisfactory. Yet in addition to this it remains to be emphasized that the spirit of reform agitation was active and expressed itself in demonstrations of workingmen, sometimes involving but a few and at other times including several hundred. In this period the record shows about three hundred strikes, most of which dealt with wages and hours of labor and a large proportion of which did not succeed.

In the seventies more serious disturbances began to occur, and assume proportions that were regarded as alarming. By that time industrial changes had come about that made strikes more disastrous. The associations of workingmen were not only more numerous but more powerful. Experience was beginning to show that stronger organization was necessary. Immigration was responsible for large foreign elements more turbulent and less amenable to American methods of control.

The great railroad strikes of 1877 mark the first serious disturbances. These struggles began over a ten per cent reduction in wages. Other grievances over which the employees had been brooding for months stimulated the men and the strike spread. In the same year began a series of strikes in the Ohio coal fields which continued intermittently over several years, at times resulting in serious rioting and conflicts with the militia. In the seventies alone there were nearly four hundred disturbances. Though a large number of these still dealt with wages, an increasing proportion arose over other causes.

Though the tabulation of strikes prior to 1881 is of course incomplete, an analysis of the table shows that in the thirties and forties strikes varied from one to eleven a year, the average being three. The average for the fifties was 6.3; for the sixties, 7.1; and for the seventies, 30.6.

Though the numerical value of such a count is small, yet, allowing for the increasing certainty of finding records of strikes in the later years, the evidence is clear that strikes were steadily increasing in number as well as seriousness. The summary of the table shows a record of 1,491 strikes prior to 1881, 1,089 of which related to wages. Success followed in 316, failure resulted in 583, while 154 were compromised and in 438 instances the outcome is unknown.

Such information as has been brought to light indicates that during the nineteenth century there was a generally accepted idea that strikes were somehow inevitable. They did not deal exclusively with wages and hours of labor. Wages were of course an ever present source of friction. Hours of labor were not easily adjusted. Customary long hours withstood with some strength the reform movements in favor of a shorter day. Strikes for the ten-hour day were frequent. Most of them failed, and that largely because the influx of immigration furnished a supply of foreigners ready to work the longer hours. In 1831 a machinists' strike involving about sixty men was called to secure permission to quit work at sundown. The employer was requiring work till seven-thirty o'clock. The strike failed, the records tell us, because there were found plenty of men to take their places. At about the same time a strike for shorter hours was successfully resisted on the ground that it was "customary" for men to work the longer day.

Conservatism did not always fight on the side of the employer. Somewhat later some coal operators sought to introduce some improved methods of blasting in the mines to avoid slack and secure larger lumps of coal. The miners opposed the change and demanded the right to blast the coal as they thought proper. They struck to maintain the old system. The temperance agitation that swept the country did not pass without its effect. In 1817 a Medford shipbuilder determined to abolish the grog custom. It was usual to furnish drink to the workmen at intervals during the day. The men struck upon the announcement that grog would not be furnished. They did not like the innovation. They could not carry their point and later returned to work. In 1839 the records tell us that the employees of a railroad struck demanding an increase in pay and more whiskey. Their allowance at the time was one and one-half pints each per day, dealt out in nine doses. During the seventies a writer tells us that it appeared to be the general opinion in many parts of the coal regions that "unless there occurred a general strike on the average of two years, things did not seem to be exactly right." Both employers and employees regarded the strike as a necessary evil.

ANALYSIS OF STRIKE STATISTICS

Number of Strikes. — Strikes have come to be more than mere incidents in industry. Their importance has led to serious effort to learn as much as possible of their industrial significance. Complete and accurate information is not easy to obtain, important as it would be. The Federal Bureau of Labor has gathered the most complete data and on this it is possible to base some conclusions. The information covers a period of twenty-five years, 1881–1905. During this time there occurred in the United States 38,303 strikes and lockouts that lasted twenty-four hours or longer. (In the five-year period, 1901–1905, the government investigators found 641 "fractional day" strikes, leading to the actual closing of 326 establishments out of a total of 790. In these 790 establishments the strike was successful in 551 and partially successful in 42.) These disturbances involved 199,954 establishments and a total of 7,444,279 employees. Others were thrown out of work as a direct result and this number raises the total by 2,000,000 more. To trace the results numerically farther than this is not possible. It is evident, however, that within a quarter-century more than 10,000,000 persons ceased work during the adjustment of the conditions that caused the strike or lockout.

Of course this large number was not out of work at one time nor should it be inferred that that number of separate individuals was involved. Statistically considered, however, that is a showing formidable enough to indicate the seriousness of the strike and lockout as an industrial problem.

Of this entire number slightly less than ten per cent were females. The percentage of females that went out on strike (9.4%) is noticeably smaller than the proportion (15.8%) that was locked out.

It is not possible to state accurately the amount of time lost in these disturbances. Of the entire 199,954, the average duration was 30.8 days. But neither strikes nor lockouts necessarily result in closing an entire establishment, though generally work is stopped. Taking 124,000 cases, or 85% of the entire number, the establishments were actually closed an average of twenty-three days. Lockouts appear to last longer than strikes. The average length of strikes was twenty-five days and of lockouts eighty-four days; the average time of actually closing up was for strikes twenty days and for lockouts forty days.

TABLE NO. 1

Year	Number of			Number of Establishments			Number of Employees Involved			Number of Employees Thrown out of Work		
	Strikes	Lockouts	Total	Strikes	Lockouts	Total	Strikes	Lockouts	Total	Strikes	Lockouts	Total
1881	471	6	477	2,928	9	2,937	101,070	655	101,725	129,521	655	130,176
1882	454	22	476	2,105	42	2,147	120,860	4,133	124,991	154,671	4,131	158,802
1883	478	28	506	2,759	117	2,876	122,198	20,512	142,710	149,763	20,512	170,275
1884	443	42	485	2,367	354	2,721	117,313	18,121	135,434	147,054	18,121	165,175
1885	645	50	695	2,284	183	2,467	158,584	15,424	174,008	242,705	15,424	258,129
1886	1,432	140	1,572	10,053	1,509	11,562	407,152	101,980	509,132	508,044	101,980	610,024
1887	1,436	67	1,503	6,589	1,281	7,870	272,776	57,534	339,310	379,676	59,630	439,306
1888	906	40	946	3,506	180	3,686	103,218	13,787	117,005	147,704	15,176	162,880
1889	1,075	36	1,111	3,786	132	3,918	205,068	10,471	215,539	249,559	10,731	260,290
1890	1,833	64	1,897	9,424	324	9,748	285,900	19,233	305,133	351,944	21,555	373,499
1891	1,717	69	1,786	8,116	546	8,662	245,042	14,116	259,158	298,939	31,014	329,953
1892	1,298	61	1,359	5,540	716	6,256	163,499	30,050	193,549	206,671	32,014	238,685
1893	1,305	70	1,375	4,555	305	4,860	195,008	13,016	208,024	265,914	21,842	287,756
1894	1,349	55	1,404	8,196	875	9,071	505,049	28,548	533,597	660,425	29,619	690,044
1895	1,215	40	1,255	6,973	370	7,343	285,742	12,754	298,496	392,403	14,785	407,188
1896	1,026	40	1,066	5,462	51	5,513	183,813	3,675	187,488	241,170	7,668	248,838
1897	1,078	32	1,110	8,492	171	8,663	332,570	7,651	340,221	408,391	7,763	416,154
1898	1,056	42	1,098	3,809	164	3,973	182,067	11,038	193,105	249,002	14,217	263,219
1899	1,797	41	1,838	11,317	323	11,640	308,267	14,698	322,965	417,072	14,817	431,889
1900	1,779	60	1,839	9,248	2,281	11,529	399,656	46,562	446,218	505,066	62,653	567,719
1901	2,924	88	3,012	10,908	451	11,359	396,280	16,257	412,537	543,386	20,457	563,843
1902	3,162	78	3,240	14,248	1,304	15,552	553,143	30,304	583,447	659,792	31,715	691,507
1903	3,494	154	3,648	20,248	3,288	23,536	531,682	112,332	644,014	656,055	131,779	787,834
1904	2,307	112	2,419	10,202	2,316	12,518	375,754	44,908	420,662	517,211	56,604	573,815
1905	2,077	109	2,186	8,292	1,255	9,547	176,337	68,474	244,811	221,686	80,748	302,434
Total	36,757	1,546	38,303	181,407	18,547	199,954	6,728,048	716,233	7,444,279	8,703,824	825,610	9,529,434

In Table No. 1 is shown by years for this quarter-century period the number of both strikes and lockouts, the number of establishments affected, persons engaged in the strike, and persons thrown out of work because of the strike in each year. The irregularly rising curves (as shown in Charts 2, 3, 4) indicate the increasing frequency of strikes, numerically considered. The further seriousness is shown by the curves of establishments involved and of employees on strike and thrown out of work. The period of relatively least disturbance was from 1881 to 1885 and of greatest disturbance centering around 1903. Between these times the wave-like appearance is significant of alternating storm and calm that necessitates much reading between the lines.

Value of the Count. — Any statistical summary of strikes and lockouts, while being of unquestioned importance, must not be taken as saying the final word. The industrial significance is shown only so far as numerical statement goes. One strike is by no means the equivalent of another, though each counts one in a table. Counting establishments involved helps to remedy this defect. The number of persons engaged in the strike and the number thrown out of work as a direct result shed further light on their significance. In Chart No. 5 the curves show the changes in each of these particulars. The steady rise of the curve of number of strikes tells its own story. Much more irregular are the changes in the number of establishments affected. The number of strikers and persons thrown out of work reveals the most irregular situation. At three previous points is the line higher than at its end. From 1890 to 1898 the number of strikes shows a decline. The number of establishments reveals the same except there are greater variations. In both of these curves the 1890 point is higher than the 1898 point. Neither of these curves reveals so clearly the situation in 1894 as does that of the number of strikers. From 1899 to the end the relative changes in the curves are less.

Other considerations are of great consequence both industrially and socially. These cannot be measured statistically and therefore are not capable of being introduced into a table or plotted in a curve. High or low wage labor amounts to more than a simple estimate of total wages lost. High wage and therefore skilled

CHART NO. 2

NUMBER OF STRIKES AND LOCKOUTS COMBINED

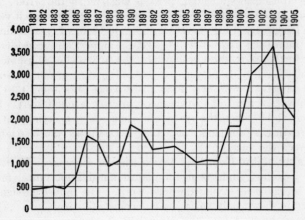

CHART NO. 3

NUMBER OF ESTABLISHMENTS

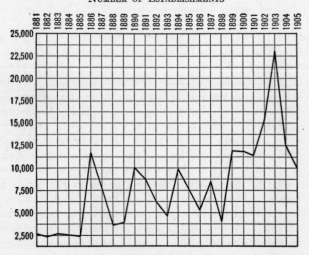

CHART NO. 4

NUMBER OF STRIKERS AND PERSONS THROWN OUT OF WORK

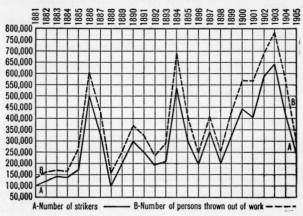

A-Number of strikers ——— B-Number of persons thrown out of work — — —

CHART NO. 5

STRIKES AND LOCKOUTS: ESTABLISHMENTS AND STRIKERS

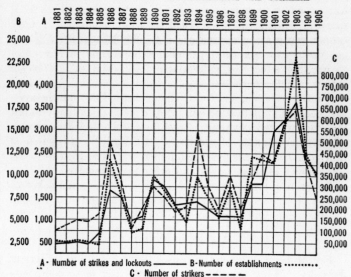

A - Number of strikes and lockouts ——— B-Number of establishments ··········
C - Number of strikers — — — —

labor can better afford the financial strain of a strike. Even a short strike of low-wage laborers may be more serious in its effect upon the strikers than one of somewhat longer duration in which high-wage workmen are involved. Similarly complexity of plant and character of machinery and other equipment greatly modify conclusions drawn solely from duration of a strike.

Again the nature of the industry is important. Here the matter is one of broader social significance. A public utilities strike is at once recognized as serious. The line is not easy to draw because the differences between public utilities and private enterprises are after all differences of degree rather than kind. An anthracite coal strike converts many to the policy of public ownership of mines. Serious railroad strikes always start public agitation for compulsory arbitration and government ownership. Manufacturing establishments that supply the markets with luxuries might be closed for months without causing much comment outside of a narrow circle of consumers in addition to the employees and employers directly concerned. On the other hand, let the bakers of a city go on strike for a day and the entire populace is disturbed. Necessities, necessary comforts, comforts, luxuries are difficult of definition. Their elasticity of demand does not yield to accurate analysis. They cannot easily be subordinated to tabular statement. Yet no one can doubt that they demand consideration in any effort to measure either the industrial or the social significance of strikes and lockouts.

It must be remembered that the average strike like the average man is a statistical fiction. No strike is at all likely to last the average length of time. Much less probably will it involve the average number of workmen. Similarly in no period of time will there be the average number of strikes, with the average amount of time, wages and other losses incurred.

Statistics of strikes have a meaning and their compilation is a distinct service. Their value should be measured in relation to other facts and must not be overestimated.

CAUSES OF STRIKES

The problem of assigning causes to strikes is one of serious difficulty. Many troublesome elements enter in to contribute to the confusion. The distinction pointed out between attack strikes and defense strikes, if consistently made, would aid in clearing up some of the confusion. There are, however, other points that remain.

Value of Stating Causes. — The support of public opinion is coming more and more to be regarded as a valuable asset in time of strike. This leads to statements of causes that are framed for their effect on public opinion. To the extent that this is done a classification of causes becomes unreliable. A few years ago a desperate strike occurred on the street car lines of a large eastern city. The system was completely tied up and the city finally put under practically martial law. The strike began because two or three men refused to join the union that had recently been formed. The men demanded their discharge; the company refused; and the strike was called. A committee of the strikers consulted a lawyer to secure his services as counsel during the strike. He refused to act in such capacity unless the strikers changed their demands and asked for an increase in wages. The company was very unpopular. For months the city government had been trying to secure transfers and these the company steadily refused to grant. Even policemen and mail carriers were obliged to pay fares. The profits of the company were popularly supposed to be large. It was thought that while a demand to unionize the lines would not meet with general support, a struggle for an advance in pay would win popular approval. The change in tactics was made and the strike fought through on the question of wages. In the final settlement a wage increase was granted, while the non-union men were retained in the service of the company but with the understanding, however, that they should be used only as barn men, not to be given routes. The cause of this strike was unionism. It was fought through with the public understanding that an advance in wages was the issue. The result was that wages were advanced while the question of unionism was compromised. An aggressively fought teamsters' strike in Chicago in 1905 was ostensibly undertaken in defense of the garment workers, though, as Jane Addams explains, it really arose from causes "so obscure and dishonorable that they never yet have been made public." The laundry workers of Chicago more recently met and drew up a set of demands for their employers' consideration. There had just been formed the Laundry Owners' Association. When the demands were presented, they were promptly refused and the next day the laundry workers found themselves locked out from their own concerns and also from every other laundry in the association. On a large interurban trolley line a hard fought strike arose in which the strikers demanded more pay and better hours. Investigation afterward showed that this strike was really a case of a union newly formed with aggressive young men as leaders trying themselves out.

When the question of legality may be involved, the statement of causes becomes still less reliable. In a strike of bricklayers in Massachusetts, the employers appealed to the court to have the strike declared illegal. Before the court four causes or objects of the strike were named: increase of wages, shorter day, foremen to be members of the union, and free access to the buildings for the business agents of the union. In writing the opinion the judge considered the lawfulness of these causes. The first two were lawful objects of a strike. The third and fourth raised "more difficult questions." But the judge found it unnecessary to deal with that difficulty. The employer had replied to all four demands with a refusal. That, in the opinion of the court, made the strike simply one for higher wages and a shorter day, and therefore a lawful strike. Had the third and fourth demands been urged alone the outcome might have been quite different. (Willcutt vs. Bricklayers' Union, 85 N. E., 897.) Here is a method that unionists may be quick to take advantage of in those states where the legal rights of the strike are more restricted. To whatever list of grievances the workmen may have it needs but the addition of one or two concerning wages and the hours of labor and the legality is assured. The legal security gives a fighting advantage, but such tactics will greatly obscure statements of causes of strikes.

From these several considerations it is evident that to formulate clearly the specific causes of strikes is extremely difficult, quite entirely defeating scientific accuracy. At the same time the analyses that have been made and those that will continue to be made have a practical usefulness. They assist in revealing tendencies. They approximate a sufficient degree of exactness to enable them to be used safely as bases for programs of regulation if such programs are carefully framed and revised at intervals.

Classification of Causes. — An elaborate analysis of causes appears in the federal government report already referred to. Fourteen causes are named as covering the field. These are, (1) For increase of wages; (2) Against reduction of wages; (3) For reduction of hours; (4) Against increase of hours; (5) Concerning recognition of union and union rules; (6) Concerning employment of certain persons; (7) Concerning employees working out of regular occupation; (8) Concerning overtime work and pay; (9) Concerning method and time of payment; (10) Concerning Saturday part holiday; (11) Concerning docking, fines, and charges; (12) Concerning working conditions and rules; (13) In sympathy with strikers and employees locked out elsewhere; (14) Other causes not specified above. As strikes so frequently result from several causes, it is necessary to double the list, including for each particular cause named another in which that cause enters as in part responsible. As in case of a strike because of wages, it may be solely for an increase or it may be for an increase of wages combined with one or more other causes.

Of the several causes named, the most important are those growing out of wages, hours of labor, and recognition of the union. Of these the question of wages has during the twenty-five year period been the most disturbing. As a single cause it resulted in 16,918 strikes, or 43% of the entire number. Coupled with other causes there were 3,425 (9%) more. Hours of labor were responsible for a total of 1,996 (5.4%) as a single cause and combined with other causes the result was increased by 1,853 more strikes or 5% of the total. Recognition of the union or of union rules alone caused 6,926 strikes (19%). As a contributing cause it led to 1,658 (4.5%) more. If these are combined, it appears that wages either alone or joined with other grievances led to a total of 20,343 (53%); hours of labor 3,849 (10%); and union recognition 8,584 (23%) during the quarter-century covered by the investigation. Employment of certain persons caused alone 2,693 (7.3%) strikes and sympathy with other strikes or with lockouts led alone to 1,346 (3.6%). These last two causes do not enter into combination so frequently as the three that have already been named. Under the last group of causes (14) there were 1,624 strikes (4.5%).

It is evident that the most disturbing factor is wages, while

hours of labor yields second place to disputes over union prerogatives. When the relative importance of these factors is
considered the conclusions are somewhat modified. The curves
in Chart No. 6 indicate that in recent years wages do not cause
so large a proportion of the strikes as formerly. The curve,
though irregular, falls very perceptibly. On the other hand,
union recognition, at first of relatively small consequence, quite
steadily increases in importance until at the close of the period
it successfully rivals wages in significance. During the same
period in which these two factors show a tendency to change
places, the question of hours does not vary in importance to
any great extent, remaining in its relation below both of the
others during practically the entire period.

If the question of complex causes be raised, it is seen from
Chart No. 7 that there is but little change. Causes of strikes
have generally been single causes. Combinations of grievances
have been subordinate in importance, with a slight tendency to
increase in the last ten years of the period. Of the entire number
of strikes for the period, 32,710, or 89%, grew out of a single
grievance.

Causes of Lockouts. — The above statement pertains to
strikes only. As to lockouts the importance of the causes
changes somewhat. Recognition of the union and union rules
head the list. These causes combined led to 43% of the entire
number of lockouts during the period. These causes were very
persistent, no one of the twenty-five years under review passed
without one or more lockouts occasioned by them. The number
was generally well distributed. In 1881 there was one such
lockout. After that year the lowest number was six, in 1882,
and the largest was 76 in 1903.

Disputes over wages ranked second in importance among
lockouts, being responsible for 25% of the number, while hours
of labor caused only 7%. (See Chart No. 8.)

RESULTS OF STRIKES

It is difficult to measure the results of strikes and lockouts.
The consequences to industry and to society are both far-reaching and complex. No tabular statement can be made to em-
brace them all. It should not be overlooked that a strike may

CHART NO. 6

STRIKES CONCERNING WAGES, HOURS AND UNION RECOGNITION

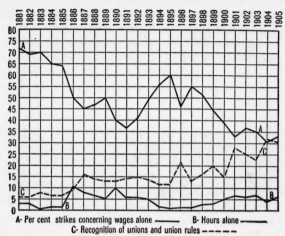

A- Per cent strikes concerning wages alone ——— B- Hours alone ———
C- Recognition of unions and union rules ————

CHART NO. 7

STRIKES FOR COMBINATION OF CAUSES

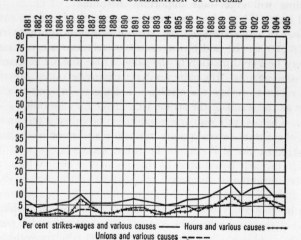

Per cent strikes-wages and various causes ——— Hours and various causes ++++++
Unions and various causes ————

CHART NO. 8

LOCKOUTS DUE TO WAGES, HOURS AND UNION RECOGNITION

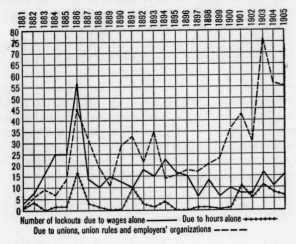

Number of lockouts due to wages alone ———— Due to hours alone +++++++
Due to unions, union rules and employers' organizations — — —

be brought to a close by the strikers returning to work when this is but a tactical move only. It may appear that a temporary yielding will give some important advantage which may be used later. Then when the later time arrives the strike is called again. It may show from the point of figures as another strike. Yet so far as the underlying industrial relations are concerned it may be a continuation of the same strike; the same strike in two or more acts. If a more limited meaning be taken, however, it is easier to review the results. If strikers win what they are after as the result of the strike, that strike may be called a success. The opposite outcome would then be called a failure. In case there were several points in dispute and some were gained by strikers, the strike might be called successful in part, or a failure in part, determined by the point of view. Within this limited meaning of the terms, an analysis of the strikes shows the following results. Taking the number of establishments as a basis of analysis it appears that strikers won their point in 48% of the establishments, lost in 37%, and succeeded partly in 15%. This analysis shows the larger net result favorable to strikers; though, if the employers be allowed to count partial successes as also partial failures, then slightly over one-half of the results (52%) were against the strikers. The fact that each side must add the partial results to secure a clear net gain indicates how uncertain, after all, the outcome is and how nearly matched the opposing forces really are.

A similar analysis of lockouts indicates not quite the same conclusions. Employers succeeded in enforcing their point in 57% of the establishments, failed entirely in 32%, and succeeded partly in 11%. Here the employers have a clear majority to their credit, though not a very wide margin of safety. Presumably the employer is better able to estimate his chances of success and can act with greater promptness and suddenness. These advantages doubtless account for the comparatively large proportion of successes that attend lockouts as compared with strikes. (See Table No. 9 and Charts Nos. 10 and 11.)

TABLE NO. 9

SUCCESS OF STRIKES AND LOCKOUTS

Year	STRIKES				LOCKOUTS			
	Total Establishments Involved	Percentage of Establishments in which Strike			Total Establishments Involved	Percentage of Establishments in which Lockout		
		Succeeded	Succeeded Partly	Failed		Succeeded	Succeeded Partly	Failed
1881	2,928	61.37	7.00	31.62	9	88.89	11.11	
1882	2,105	53.59	8.17	38.24	42	64.29		35.71
1883	2,759	58.17	16.09	25.74	117	56.41		43.59
1884	2,367	51.50	3.89	44.61	354	27.97	.28	71.75
1885	2,284	52.80	9.50	37.70	183	38.25	3.28	58.47
1886	10,053	34.51	18.85	46.64	1,509	21.18	13.11	65.71
1887	6,589	45.64	7.19	47.17	1,281	34.19	1.25	64.56
1888	3,506	52.22	5.48	42.30	180	74.44	3.89	21.67
1889	3,786	46.49	18.91	34.60	132	40.91	25.76	33.33
1890	9,424	52.65	10.01	37.34	324	65.74	5.56	28.70
1891	8,116	37.88	8.29	53.83	546	63.92	14.29	21.79
1892	5,540	39.31	8.70	51.99	716	69.13	25.28	5.59
1893	4,555	50.86	10.32	38.82	305	41.90	18.31	39.79
1894	8,196	38.09	13.50	48.41	875	11.31	2.40	86.29
1895	6,973	55.24	9.94	34.82	370	13.24	.27	86.49
1896	5,462	59.19	7.47	33.34	51	80.39	1.96	17.65
1897	8,492	57.31	28.12	14.57	171	60.82	3.51	35.67
1898	3,809	64.21	6.38	29.41	164	63.41	.61	35.98
1899	11,317	73.24	14.25	12.51	323	18.01	.62	81.37
1900	9,248	46.43	20.62	32.95	2,281	94.30	.31	5.39
1901	10,908	48.77	17.13	34.10	451	37.03	42.13	20.84
1902	14,248	47.31	22.85	29.84	1,304	78.22	4.06	17.72
1903	20,248	40.87	23.40	35.73	3,288	81.39	5.17	13.44
1904	10,202	35.28	15.28	49.44	2,316	55.91	23.06	21.03
1905	8,292	40.17	11.45	48.38	1,255	31.60	32.64	35.76
Total	181,407	47.94	15.28	36.78	18,547	57.20	10.71	32.09

CHART NO. 10

SUCCESS OF STRIKES

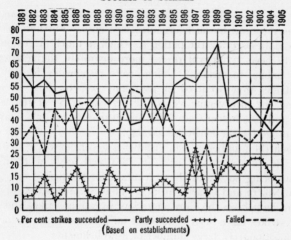

Per cent strikes succeeded ——— Partly succeeded +++++ Failed - - - -
(Based on establishments)

CHART NO. 11

SUCCESS OF LOCKOUTS

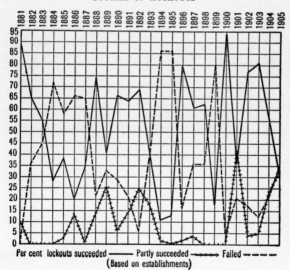

Per cent lockouts succeeded ——— Partly succeeded +++++ Failed - - - -
(Based on establishments)

ORGANIZED LABOR AND STRIKES

By no means do all strikes involve labor organizations nor are they caused by such organizations only. Further analysis of the data covering the period to which so much attention has already been given will reveal more definitely the relation of labor unions to strikes. Unions were responsible for 47% of the strikes that occurred in 1881 and 75% of those in 1905. During the intervening years the percentage never fell below 48% and rose higher than 82%, the median being 65% and the percentage for the entire period 69%.

When the number of establishments is considered, it is found that the unions caused 77% in 1881 and 92% in 1905, the median being 89% and the percentage for the period 90. (See Table No. 12 and Chart No. 13). Thus it appears that organizations have been the more aggressive in calling strikes and that these strikes have been conducted on a larger scale, involving a proportionately large number of establishments.

PROPORTION OF STRIKES ORDERED BY UNIONS AND BY NON-UNION MEN

Year	STRIKES Per Cent Ordered by Unions	STRIKES Per Cent Ordered by Non-unions	ESTABLISHMENTS INVOLVED IN Per Cent Ordered by Unions	ESTABLISHMENTS INVOLVED IN Per Cent Ordered by Non-unions	ORDERED BY LABOR ORGANIZATIONS Succeeded	ORDERED BY LABOR ORGANIZATIONS Succeeded Partly	ORDERED BY LABOR ORGANIZATIONS Failed	NOT ORDERED BY LABOR ORGANIZATION Succeeded	NOT ORDERED BY LABOR ORGANIZATION Succeeded Partly	NOT ORDERED BY LABOR ORGANIZATION Failed
1881	47.35	52.65	76.88	23.12	64.99	6.71	28.30	49.33	7.98	42.69
1882	48.46	51.54	76.20	23.80	56.36	9.54	34.10	44.71	3.79	51.50
1883	56.69	43.31	84.74	15.26	64.07	18.31	17.62	25.42	3.80	70.78
1884	54.18	45.82	83.10	16.90	55.62	3.25	41.13	31.25	7.00	61.75
1885	55.35	44.65	72.81	27.19	62.42	10.58	27.00	27.05	6.60	66.35
1886	53.28	46.72	87.87	12.13	33.46	20.48	46.06	42.07	7.07	50.86
1887	66.34	33.66	87.22	12.78	48.36	7.19	44.55	27.08	7.24	65.68
1888	68.14	31.86	87.44	12.56	56.17	4.99	38.84	25.00	8.86	66.14
1889	67.35	32.65	79.74	20.26	45.61	21.37	33.02	49.93	9.26	40.81
1890	71.33	28.67	90.58	9.42	53.99	10.17	35.84	39.86	8.45	51.69
1891	74.83	25.17	92.00	8.00	38.46	8.10	53.44	36.76	11.68	51.56
1892	70.72	29.28	91.16	8.84	39.33	8.75	51.92	39.19	8.16	52.65
1893	69.43	30.57	87.93	12.07	53.94	10.89	35.17	28.42	6.19	65.39
1894	62.83	37.17	88.72	11.28	37.35	13.67	48.98	43.94	12.12	43.94
1895	54.25	45.75	87.51	12.49	59.25	10.05	30.70	27.21	9.18	63.61
1896	64.59	35.41	89.97	10.03	62.47	6.55	30.98	29.93	15.69	54.38
1897	55.29	44.71	91.83	8.17	59.67	29.51	10.82	30.83	12.54	56.63
1898	60.42	39.58	84.54	15.46	69.74	6.15	24.11	33.96	7.64	58.40
1899	62.05	37.95	92.24	7.76	76.33	14.19	9.48	36.56	14.92	48.52
1900	65.43	34.57	91.07	8.93	48.06	21.95	29.99	29.94	7.03	63.03
1901	75.85	24.15	91.97	8.03	50.36	17.19	32.45	30.59	16.44	52.97
1902	78.24	21.76	94.14	5.86	48.31	23.72	27.97	31.58	8.74	59.88
1903	78.82	21.18	95.49	4.51	41.72	23.77	34.51	22.86	15.43	61.71
1904	82.14	17.86	95.42	4.58	35.75	15.59	48.66	25.48	8.78	65.74
1905	74.72	25.28	92.43	7.57	41.58	11.30	47.12	24.04	13.22	62.74
Total	68.99	31.01	90.34	9.66	49.48	15.87	34.65	33.86	9.83	56.31

183

CHART NO. 13

PROPORTION OF STRIKES ORDERED BY UNION AND NON-UNION MEN

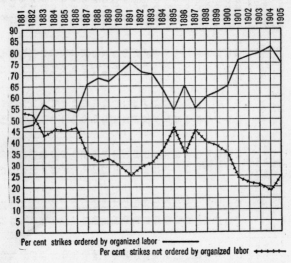

Per cent strikes ordered by organized labor ————
Per cent strikes not ordered by organized labor +++++

In terms of results a distinction may again be made between strikers acting through organization and those striking by some concerted action that could not properly be called a labor organization. Speaking in terms of establishments and referring to the strikers as union or non-union, it appears that in 1881 the unions succeeded in 65% of the establishments, partly succeeded in 7% and failed in 28%. In 1905 success came in 42%, partial success in 11%, and failure in 47% of establishments, the median being 54% success, 12% partially successful, and 34% failure; and the percentages for the entire period being respectively 49%, 16%, and 35%. Compared with this showing for organized strikes, the non-union strikes show, for 1881, success in 49% of the establishments, partial success in 8%, and failure in 43%. For the last year, 1905, the respective percentages are 24, 13, and 63. The medians for the three are 31%, 9% and 58%, and the percentages for the period are 34, 10, and 56. (See Charts 14, 15.)

On the whole the figures throw doubt upon the ability of unions to hold their own as striking organizations. The same

CHART NO. 14

SUCCESS OF UNION STRIKES

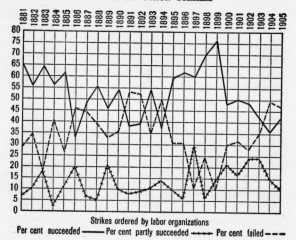

Strikes ordered by labor organizations

Per cent succeeded ———— Per cent partly succeeded ++++ Per cent failed ---

CHART NO. 15

SUCCESS OF NON-UNION STRIKES

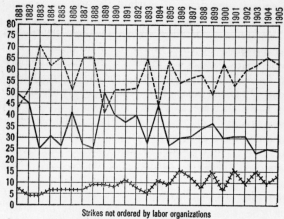

Strikes not ordered by labor organizations

Per cent succeeded ———— Per cent partly succeeded ++++ Per cent failed ----

seems to be true in establishments where the strikes are not ordered by the labor organizations. Unions are more aggressive, perhaps too aggressive to assure success. Unorganized groups on the other hand may defer a strike until conditions become so serious that when they finally do undertake a strike their chances for success are much greater.

Difficulty of Interpretation. — Much interest centers around the question whether or not strikes are increasing in number and importance. Though the data gathered for the period of twenty-five years are so abundant in details, there is difficulty in interpreting them. The changes in industrial organization have altered materially the number of establishments as well as the relations existing between them. The number of employees is changing in proportion to establishments. Unions are increasing in number, are including steadily larger proportions of unskilled workmen, and are adopting new policies. All of these as well as other changes exert an influence on strikes which makes any comprehensive interpretation of their number uncertain. Though, as has been said, the data thus collected covering a period of twenty-five years have a certain value, they are important because suggestive rather than otherwise. The fact that no effort is being made by the Department of Labor to continue the reports serves in itself to indicate that they are not of enough importance to warrant the necessary expenditure of time and money.

In two different detailed studies of these figures may be found expression of their significance. With regard to the effect of unionism on strikes as shown by the past, Huebner says in the Twelfth Biennial Report of the Wisconsin Labor Commissioner: "On the basis of the number of strikes the effect is to check the increase as trades unionism becomes older and more experienced; on the basis of the number of employees and establishments affected by strikes, the effect is to accelerate the increase. The character of the strike is being changed by the union so that it is becoming of increasingly widespread importance to both parties and to the community at large. . . . Union strikes are not becoming more successful even though unionism is being more and more thoroughly organized. . . . Furthermore, trades unionism affects the causes of strikes by reducing the importance of the purely standard causes (wages and hours) and increasing the importance of trades unionism (closed shop, union rules, etc.) as a cause of strikes."

In an elaborate study of strike statistics Professor Cross analyzes the figures from many important angles and sums up his conclusions in ten points.

"(1) That strikes have increased absolutely; that, as compared with the growth in population, they have increased relatively, although there may be some doubt as regards their relative increase when compared with the increase of wage earners in the manufacturing industries.

"(2) That the number of union strikes has increased more rapidly since 1896 than ever before.

"(3) That it is not so much the restraining influence of unionism as the loss of membership and bargaining power, together with some decrease in the number of unions, that causes a decrease in the number of union strikes during periods of business depression.

"(4) That, as strikes increase, the average number of strikers, establishments, and employees affected per strike decrease, and, as strikes decrease, the size of the average strike increases.

"(5) That the average number of strikers, establishments and employees affected per strike, — i. e., the size of the average strike, — has tended to decrease since 1896.

"(6) That, as unions grow stronger, the tendency is for the average union strike to decrease in size and importance.

"(7) That the percentage of successful strikes decreases during periods of business prosperity and increases during 'hard times.'

"(8) That compromised strikes are becoming more numerous.

"(9) That union strikes are not becoming more successful, even though unionism is being more thoroughly organized.

"(10) That trades unionism affects the causes of strikes by reducing the importance of hours and wages and by increasing the importance of union rules, closed shop, recognition of the union, etc., as causes of strikes."

CHAPTER XI

THE STRIKE (Continued)

VIOLENCE

Violence in strikes is a stumbling block to many would-be defenders of labor organizations. Its presence leads many to assume that a peaceful strike is quite impossible. It is not to be wondered at that this confusion exists. Even judges whose minds have been trained to the task of drawing correct inferences have been so fully impressed with the prevalence of violence that they have been led to make somewhat exaggerated statements. "Of the ideal strike," writes Judge Jenkins from the United States Circuit Court Bench, the objection is "that it is ideal, and never existed in fact." "It is idle to talk of a peaceable strike. None such ever occurred. The suggestion is impeachment of intelligence. From first to last . . . force and turbulence, violence and outrage, arson and murder, have been associated with the strike as its natural and inevitable concomitants. . . . A strike without violence would equal the representation of the tragedy of Hamlet with the part of Hamlet omitted." (Farmers' Loan and Trust Co. *vs.* No. Pacific R. R. Co.)

Mr. Justice Brewer declares "the common rule as to strikes" to be not merely to quit employment but the employees "forcibly prevent others from taking their places. It is useless to say that they only advise; no man is misled." If the training of judges does not protect some of them against such generalizations, it is not surprising that others fall into much the same error.

A generalization equally erroneous would be one asserting that violence is never an essential element in strikes. Few fall into such an error. Perhaps the labor leaders themselves come as near to it as any. Their general belief is not only that strikes may be conducted without violence but that they are so conducted. John Mitchell may be regarded as their spokesman when he declares that violence should never be tolerated by strikers or leaders. It is a tactical error. Better lose a strike, advises this leader, than resort to violence to win it. Speaking of the actual occurrence of violence he says: "The amount of violence actually committed is grossly exaggerated and that which is fairly traceable to the officials of trade unions is almost infinitesimal." As to the seriousness of this form of violence he asserts that more men are killed every Fourth of July from accidents associated with the celebration of the day than are killed "in all the strikes in all the cities of the country on all days of the year." Further, Mr. Mitchell pointedly adds that during the five months of the great anthracite coal strike of 1902 the number of men killed was only eight, while on the basis of accident records in the mines he estimates that if the mines had been operated during this time no less than 200 men would have been killed and 600 seriously injured.

Unsatisfactory Evidence of Facts. — Though many opinions have been expressed on the subject of violence, but little actual evidence is at hand as to the facts.

An investigation has been made extending from Jan. 1, 1902, to Oct. 1, 1904, based on a search of newspaper records for that period. The results were published in the Outlook, in December, 1904. They show much of the characteristic newspaper attitude of exaggeration and varying degrees of sensationalism. Taking these figures at their face value, the investigation showed that during these thirty-three months serious violence attended strikes in 30 states. The total number killed was 198, of whom 125 were non-union men; 56 were union strikers; and 17 were officers. The total number injured was 1,966: non-union men 1,626; strikers 173; and officers 167. The total arrests were 6,114: 415 non-union men, and 5,699 strikers. The claim is that this report includes only the accounts that found their way into the papers and that it should be offset by the counterclaim that the reports are doubtless exaggerated. As these two counterclaims are not of equal force, it still leaves in doubt the truth to be read from the figures.

Comparing strike violence with violence growing out of other causes one authority finds the former "as dust in the balance." In this same period, as it is pointed out, lynching parties caused more deaths by 70% than strikes. In New York City there are four times as many arrests for assault and battery as for similiar violence due to strikes in the whole United States. Taking the field of industrial accidents, it is further emphasized that reliable estimates show that for the same period 2,400 persons were killed in industry, 20,400 disabled for life, not to list the scores of thousands disabled only temporarily. During the period of thirty-three months above referred to, it is asserted by the editor of the Mine Workers Journal that no less than 900 men lost their lives in coal mines, and in every one of these cases a coroner's jury found the accident to be the result of willful violation of law on the part of the mine operators.

To such a comparison other authorities object. The trade unionists belong to the more intelligent and more peacefully inclined members of society. Their depredations in time of strike are not to be minimized by placing them alongside of events and people between whom and themselves there is no fair basis of comparison. Among other objections to statistical tabulation of strike violence it is urged that they are radically incomplete and generally untrustworthy.

Is Violence Increasing? — Whether violence is increasing or not it is impossible to establish satisfactorily. Between the two extremes of statement, the one by the opponent of all labor's activities and the other by union officials, there seems to be plenty of middle ground.

Older unions are supposed to exercise greater influence toward peaceful methods. Moral suasion and the "silent treatment" are undoubtedly sometimes very effective. One who claims to have been personally connected with the management of 200 strikes denies any knowledge of strike violence, either spontaneous or systematic. The worst was "a few personal brawls magnified into riots by news-hungry reporters."

After a careful study of a large number of strikes extending back into the early years of the last century, Professor T. S. Adams concludes that "in any strike of a given size there is less likelihood of violence to-day than there would have been sixty years ago; but owing to the undoubted increase in the number of strikes the aggregate volume of violence has grown enormously."

While definite data of a statistical nature are very unreliable and while it is exceedingly difficult to draw any reliable conclusions as to whether or not it is increasing, it remains true that after all allowances have been made for misrepresentation and error, an amount of actual and open violence is far too great to redound to the credit of a civilized people. It will be remembered that during the anthracite coal strike of 1902 there was much difference of opinion based on conflicting reports as to the amount of violence. The operators were accused of exaggerating their side while the strike leaders were declared to be concealing the acts of strikers. After the heat of the conflict had passed and a deliberate investigation could be made, the commission made some pertinent comments. "It is true that exaggerated accounts of the disturbance were published and that there was testimony from reputable witnesses tending to minimize them and vouching for the good order of the communities in which such witnesses live." "Justice requires the statement that the leaders of the organization which began and conducted the strike, and notably its president, condemned all violence, and exhorted their followers to sobriety and moderation." This temperate attitude was not followed by the leaders in the local organizations. The result was that "disorder and lawlessness" existed "to some extent over the whole region, and throughout the whole period." "It is admitted that this disorder and lawlessness was incident to the strike. Its history is stained with a record of riot and bloodshed, culminating in three murders, unprovoked save by the fact that two of the victims were asserting their right to work, and another, as an officer of the law, was performing his duty in attempting to preserve peace. Men who chose to be employed, or who remained at work, were assailed and threatened, and they and their families terrorized and intimidated. In several instances the houses of such workmen were dynamited, or otherwise assaulted, and the lives of unoffending women and children put in jeopardy."

Many other strikes involving large numbers and important issues serve as evidence of the truth of the statement that violence is very general. West Virginia, Michigan and Colorado are too fresh in mind to need more than naming as further evidence.

Because of the difficulty in finding accurate data it is not easy to decide whether violence is increasing or decreasing in strikes. Many facts that make comparisons unreliable cannot arbitrarily be set aside. The spread of unions among unskilled, illiterate, and less law-abiding classes of laborers, the appearance of the Industrial Workers of the World openly advocating violence and the opposition to this organization by the trade unions; these and other developments make it very difficult indeed to measure violence in terms of statistics.

Some Conclusions. Passions Aroused. — Reasoning along another line, one not by any means unsupported by a generous array of facts, some tentative conclusions may be stated. Strife means inevitably the arousing of passion, and where passion dominates, the orderly procedure is very likely to be broken over. The more important the issues involved in a contest the more deeply stirred the contestants will become. Primitive emotions come to the surface, and unchecked by cooler reason they express themselves in lawless ways.

The "Sacred Cause of Labor." — The laborer has been thoroughly taught his history lesson. Labor's path in the past has not been strewn with roses. Obstacles on every hand have been met and overcome only by insistent struggle. Consequently "labor's cause" is inevitably and necessarily "dear to the hearts" of all good union men. Heavy sacrifices have been made for the cause, and the cause must not suffer. This exaggeration leads very easily to a loss of perspective, a failure to see issues in their correct proportions. A blindness of reason through the enhanced importance of an issue the imminence of which is so clear leads to an unbridling of forces held in check in ordinary times. Violence results.

The "Tantalizing Employer." — The employer, schooled to different methods, conscious of a certain advantage, more self-contained, not having an aggressive cause to advocate, has less to say. Diplomacy is his weapon, a weapon in the use of which his contestants have been quite wholly unskilled. The very coolness and apparent indifference toward what the striker so clearly sees as the "human element" becomes a cause of aggravation. Unable to break down the employer's resistance by means peaceful, other methods are adopted, less peaceful in their nature.

Expecting such a result, the employer of course prepares for it. Mayor, chief of police, constable, sheriff; one or all receive notice of danger to property. Forces are marshalled as a warning. As a matter of fact this display often proves aggravating. It invites violence. This result may come from two causes. A massing of force in too leisurely a manner, or in too small numbers may encourage strikers to feel that the legal opposition to their purposes is but half-hearted and will not be pushed further. This of course invites the more turbulent element to try the issue. Or again it may appear that the sheriff's posse or the line of blue coats is being used ostensibly to preserve peace but actually to help the cause of the employer. The distinction between these two is in some instances by no means easy to make. If there were opportunity for cool deliberation the distinction might be thought through by the strikers. In a strike this is not likely to be done. The authority of the law appears to be used to defeat a strike and strikers cannot always stand peacefully by during such an interference.

With the decided advantage often afforded by the presence of officers of the law, the employer may find it to his advantage to create a necessity for their presence. Believing, as strikers so often confidently do believe, that the employer himself incites a mild oubreak of lawlessness in order to justify a call for protection, it is difficult to restrain open opposition to these authorities.

Two Kinds of Lawlessness. — Recent investigations have made it clear that in many cases the employer is not altogether law-abiding. His lawlessness is of a different brand. It is more finished, much less primitive, but none the less lawlessness. To the strikers, who so often realize this, their own violations of law are to themselves justified under the "fight the devil with fire" formula. The community is often much less clearly conscious of the kind of law violation in which the employer may be implicated. It is of the less apparent kind. The violence of the striker is an outbreak of primitive passions and almost inevitably expresses itself in destruction of property or in inflicting personal injury on those who in any way obstruct their purposes. Far cruder forms of lawlessness characterize the methods of the striker. For this reason they attract wider attention. Investigations, reliable in themselves but not published until the trouble is over, have recently revealed more clearly to the public some of the methods of employers. Sheriff's posses or even state militia are often equipped and paid by the employer, detective agencies, the successors to strike-breaking organizations, furnish an element that is naturally lawless and easily excited. Recent disturbances in more parts of the country than one have brought clearly to the public attention the reality of these facts.

While these considerations are in no sense quantitative they are vital to any analysis of strike violence. As long as these elements remain there will be violence. It is simply a cause and effect sequence. If they can be cleared away or minimized in importance the results will be modified accordingly.

Attempts are sometimes made to ascertain who started the trouble. This is quite impossible of accomplishment. Even if it could be stated finally and reliably, it is very doubtful if it would help. The complexity is far too great. Whoever started it, the methods now adopted are so complex as to be quite impossible to trace to first causes.

Developing Public Sentiment.— It seems evident that there is developing a very strong public sentiment against violence. This offers a ray of hope. So much depends upon popular support in a strike that it is often the determining factor. The reality of this appears in the agility displayed by each side in its effort to fix on the other all responsibility for violent outbreaks of lawlessness.

The Older Unions. — Older unions, with a fund of experience, able officials who have a strong following in their membership, are more likely to conduct strikes free from violence. On the other hand, they are less likely to strike. New unions strike more easily. The officials have less real authority as leaders. They are often following instead of leading. Unskilled trades are likely to be more turbulent than skilled. Since it is easier to fill their places, terror must do for them what high skill does for others in keeping strike breakers away. Foreigners are sometimes less easy to restrain because they know less of our law and are easy prey to self-seeking leaders of a demagogue type.

Stable Leadership. — Whether or not the number be increasing, it is as a matter of fact true that there exists to-day a group of strong, able and influential leaders who openly oppose violence and do all within their power to restrain it. No one without actual experience can comprehend the difficulties of their task. They have been successful and their influence is spreading. This group will undoubtedly increase in number. Its influence will also increase. As they recognize more and more clearly the importance of a favorable public sentiment, they will give increasing attention to its demand that these collective bargaining contests must be reduced to a more orderly and law-abiding method of procedure.

So long as public responsibility is clearly related to the increasing power of strong unionism the situation is favorable to the reduction of violence to the lowest terms. It is doubtful if it can be entirely eliminated.

DEVELOPMENT OF THE LAW

One of the most important questions relating to strikes is that of legality. To state it as a general proposition that strikes are lawful may be helpful in many ways, but it does not dispose of the question satisfactorily. Through the years in which strikes have been increasing in number and have been held by union laborers as a weapon of increasing importance, there has been a slow evolution of legal opinion concerning them. In the earlier stages the courts were seldom asked to deal with them. Prior to 1850 less than two score cases were taken to court of which any record has been preserved. These cases were similar in their essential elements. The demands may be summed up as two in number; for higher wages and for discharge of workmen who would not join and pay the dues of the associations that were being formed among them. Most of these cases were jury trials.[1]

Early Cases. — The law applied in the first of these early cases was the English common law of conspiracy. It is of more than ordinary historical interest to refer again to the positions taken by the contending parties in the first case, that involving the Philadelphia cordwainers in 1806. The prosecution contended "that no man is at liberty to combine, conspire, confederate, and unlawfully agree to regulate the whole body of workmen in the city. The defendants are not

[1] For a complete record of these cases see A Documentary History of American Industrial Society, volumes three and four. In these volumes may be found either the record of or the reference to every known labor case that occurred prior to 1842. For a brief account of the legal arguments of these cases, see the author's Attitude of American Courts in Labor Cases, chapter 3.

indicted for regulating their own individual wages, but for undertaking by a combination to regulate the price of the labor of others as well as their own." To this the defense replied with a counter-proposition. "There is no crime in my refusing to work with a man who is not of the same association with myself. Supposing the ground of my refusal to be ever so unreasonable or ridiculous, . . . to be in reality, mere caprice or whim . . . still it is no crime. The motive of my refusal may be illiberal, but it furnishes no legal foundation for a prosecution: I cannot be indicted for it. Every man may choose his company or refuse to associate with anyone whose company may be disagreeable to him, without being obliged to give a reason for it: and without violating the laws of the land."

In his charge to the jury the judge stated that "A combination of workmen to raise their wages may be considered in a twofold point of view: one is to benefit themselves; the other is to injure those who do not join their society. The rule of law condemns both. . . . One man determines not to work under a certain price and it may be individually the opinion of all: in such a case it would be lawful in each to refuse to do so, for if each stands alone either may extract from his determination when he pleases. . . . But they were bound down by their agreement, and pledged by mutual engagements, to persist in it, however contrary to their own judgment. The continuance in improper conduct may therefore well be attributed to the combination."

In the cases that followed it was quite generally insisted by those whose duty it was to interpret the law to the juries that while the indictment did not rest on a demand for higher wages, journeymen were free, each acting singly, to refuse to work. When they acted "by preconcert or association" they became liable for conspiracy. The gist of the conspiracy was held to be in the unlawful confederation and the offense was complete when the agreement had been made. "It was never doubted," said one judge (1815) "that where diverse persons confederate together by indirect means to impoverish or prejudice a third person, or to do acts unlawful or prejudicial to the community, they are indictable at the common law for a conspiracy."

Results of Early Cases. — The logical outcome of such law began to be apparent. A reëxamination followed. In 1821 the certainty of the common law of conspiracy was called into question. The unquestioned application of English precedents appeared to restrict too much the principles of American freedom about which so much was heard. Instead of being in its final form, the law of conspiracy was referred to as being in an unsettled state arising from its gradual extension from one case to another through force of precedent without an accurate examination of the "nature and principles of the offense" and leading to "an unusual want of precision in the terms used to describe the distinctive features of guilt or innocence". Before this preliminary analysis the principle that "the union of persons in one common design is the gist of the offence" began to waver.

The feeling between the two sides directly concerned in these struggles was strong and each felt that with its own success and the defeat of the other side was linked those eternal principles of liberty and justice for which the nation had been established. The one side was most anxious to see the law put "an end to those associations which have been so prejudicial to the successful enterprise of the capitalists" of the country and blot out of existence in all the cities those "combinations which extend their deleterious influence to every part of the union." On the other hand, the journeymen were just as insistent that strong effort be made to rescue "the rights of mechanics from the grasp of tyranny and oppression."

The view of the law in this period was fairly representative of the spirit of the age. English political struggle had ushered in the era of *laissez faire*, but it was an era of relative freedom for the merchant and manufacturer class from restrictions of king and lords in Parliament. There was no thought of any practical extension of the new privileges to journeymen and laborers. The American Revolution had won political independence from Great Britain, a movement based on new principles of freedom. But this also had been a movement in which the capitalist classes had been leaders. They little thought that American freedom would be of any different brand than that of England except a greater degree of freedom from a King and parliament. Further developments were necessary to secure the extension of the nation's rights and privileges to its workingmen.

Period of Change: Massachusetts. — The great reform agitations centering around the quarter-century year, 1825, were slowly expressing themselves in definite form. Organizations of laborers had become a recognized fact, one that law could neither overlook nor suppress. In 1842 the Massachusetts Supreme Court handed down an opinion (Commonwealth vs. Hunt) that first expressed judicial appreciation of the possible good in labor organizations, the first suggestion that even a violation of law by their members should not be made an occasion for denouncing the association as such. In this case the charge of the indictment was that of associating together, a charge that before other courts in earlier years had been successfully maintained. The case was the first one to be brought to trial in Massachusetts and came before the lower court in Boston. There the view held in previous cases in other cities of the Union had been adopted and the defendants found guilty. The decision was appealed to the supreme court of the state. As there were no precedents within the jurisdiction of Massachusetts by which this court was bound, it was possible to look at the facts in quite a different way. The laws of England regulating wages and other matters pertaining to laborers were not adapted to the new conditions of the colony and so were not adopted and confirmed by the constitution of the Commonwealth. For the first time in common law it was held that the manifest intent of the association of laborers was to induce all engaged in the same occupation to become members. Such a purpose was not unlawful. The fact of association gave the members a power that they otherwise would not have, a power that might be exerted for useful and honorable purposes, or for dangerous and pernicious ones. For example, the court indicated some of the beneficial purposes that might be served by an association, as "assistance in times of poverty, sickness and distress; or to raise their intellectual, moral and social condition; or to make improvement in their art." It was held to be necessary in order to charge the guilt of a criminal conspiracy that it must be proved that the object was criminal. Further it did not appear that the means used by the association had been criminal. The members had refused to work for any person who should employ anyone not a member of their society. In the absence of any contract binding them by its conditions to remain at work, the persons were "free to work for whom they please, or not to work, if they so prefer." It further did not appear that it was criminal "for men to agree together to exercise their own acknowledged rights, in such a manner as best to subserve their own interests."

The principle of right insisted on by the court in this case was that "every free man, whether skilled laborer, farmer, or domestic servant, may work or not work, or work or refuse to work with any company or individual, at his own option, except so far as he is bound by contract," and further that men may agree together to exercise these rights. Wherever this option had the authority of law, two important changes resulted. Mere association was no longer criminal conspiracy, and a right to stop work belonged to all and could be lawfully exercised by agreement.

New York State. — Much the same change was brought about in New York State but in a different way, as has been shown in a former chapter. In that state conspiracy had early been made a matter of statutory enactment; though it was not made specifically applicable to laborers. In 1828 the legislature enacted a law which brought together all legislation on conspiracy into a single statute. The commission in its report proposed to make it criminal to conspire "to defraud or injure any person in his trade or business." This was not adopted by the legislature. As finally enacted the statute declared it to be a misdemeanor for two or more persons to conspire, "to commit any act injurious . . . to trade or commerce," and that "no conspiracies other than such as are enumerated" in the act (six in all) shall be punishable criminally, and further that "no agreement . . . shall be deemed a conspiracy unless some act beside such agreement be done to effect the object thereof by one or more parties to such agreement." This law stated in definite form what should be regarded as conspiracy and put an end to all common-law conspiracies not included in the new statute. In the report the revisers made a clear comment on the legal supposition that an agreement not carried into effect could be a conspiracy when it said: "By a metaphysical train of reasoning, which has never been adopted in any other case in the whole criminal law, the offence of conspiracy is made to consist in the intent; in an act of the mind; and to prevent the shock to common sense which such a proposition would be sure to produce, the formation of this intent by an interchange of thoughts is made itself an overt act, done in pursuance of that interchange or agreement. . . . Acts and deeds are the subjects of human laws; not thoughts and intents unless accompanied by acts."

The first case brought under this statute was a strike of shoemakers for higher wages, and was held to be an agreement to commit an act injurious to trade or commerce (People *vs.* Fisher, 1835). The common-law ideas seemed to have held over for a time, but cases since then have not followed the reasoning of this opinion.

The Newer Developments. — The legislation of 1828 in New York State and the decision of the Massachusetts court in 1842 opened the way for new developments. Conspiracy ceased to be a sufficient charge of guilt and the strikes that became subjects of litigation were submitted to more rigid scrutiny to reveal the methods adopted and the objects sought. The confusion has slowly disappeared in the light of full discussion of principles. At least one book of some authority, a book intended as a text-book on strikes and boycotts, written obviously from a somewhat biased point of view still declares that "all strikes are illegal. The wit of man could not devise a legal one." At the same time in another book, also intended as a text-book on labor laws, one obviously written with strict impartiality, it is declared that "instead of saying no strikes are legal, we should now say all strikes are legal; that is, all plain and simple combinations to quit work when there is no breach of a definite time contract in so doing, and where it is not complicated with any element of boycotting, or marked by any disorder or intimidation."

Present Difference of Opinion. — The present situation reveals one important difference of opinion. It is not so much a difference in view touching combination and concerted cessation of work as it is the reasons that prompt the act. In the opinion of Judge Vann of New York there is general if not universal agreement. According to this view a man is entirely free to agree to or to reject any conditions of labor, as he may wish. Terms of employment are subject to mutual agreement without interference from anyone. The right of one to act is not changed by his acting in concert with others. "Whatever one man may do alone, he may do in combination with others, provided they have no unlawful object in view. Mere numbers do not ordinarily affect the quality of the act." Thus far there is intended to be the statement of a general right. Following this an application is made. Workmen have a right to organize to secure higher wages, shorter hours of labor, or to improve their relations with the employer. This pertains to organization. Further they have the right to strike provided the object is not to gratify malice, or to inflict injury upon others, but to secure better terms of employment for themselves. "A peaceable and orderly strike, not to harm others, but to improve their own conditions, is not a violation of law."

Importance of Motive: Massachusetts View. — With this view so generally held comes a parting of the ways. Some courts rest here. Others have carried their reasoning farther, holding different conclusions. Of the one view, which may be characterized as the more conservative, the Massachusetts court has been the most influential exponent. In the opinions of this court appears a decided determination to insist on the importance of the reason for the strike. Also there are echoes of the old idea of strength in combination. In 1906 the judges in this state were impressed with the fact that in most cases a successful strike gave the employees such a control over labor that the employer was obliged to yield to their demands. "A single individual may well be left to take his chances in a struggle with another individual. But in a struggle with a number of persons combined together to fight an individual, the individual's chance is small, if it exists at all. It is plain that a strike by a combination of persons has a power of coercion which an individual does not have." That the reason is of deciding importance appears in the view expressed in 1908 by the same court. "It is settled in this Commonwealth," declares the judge, "that the legality of a combination not to work for an employer, that is to say, of a strike, depends (in case the strikers are not under contract to work for him) upon the purpose for which the combination is formed—the purpose for which the employees strike." This statement of the law throws upon the court the duty of examining into and revealing the real reasons or purposes of the strike before they can pass upon its lawfulness. As already stated the purposes usually accepted are such as deal with increasing wages, lessening the hours of labor, or improving relations with employers. The position may be regarded as a final one, if it be taken in the general terms in which it is expressed. It is a constantly changing one, however, in that it is left to decide in each new case as it arises whether or not it comes within any one of the three general purposes stated. The strict construction or loose construction attitude toward this "sweeping clause" becomes of great importance.

The position taken by this court is that of the larger number of courts throughout the country. It was in this same state and as late as 1908 that the case already referred to arose in which four reasons for the strike appeared in the four demands made by the strikers. Of these the court found that two (increase of wages and shorter hours) were "properly enforceable by a strike." In as much as it was lawful to strike for these two reasons, the validity of further reasons did not call for consideration. Such an interpretation seems to break down the restriction placed by the court so far as any practical considerations are concerned. The strikers need but to add to whatever demands they may have a request for an increase of wages and shorter hours, and to do this in such a way as to cover up the purpose from the court and any strike may be lawful. If the employer sees fit to yield to the wages demand thus forcing the employees to continue the strike for other reasons it cannot relieve him for any considerable length of time, as new wage demands may be made continually.

This policy of inquiring into purposes has the further positive authority of Justice Harlan. Legality and illegality in strikes, he holds, must depend upon the means adopted for enforcing a strike and on its objects. Strikes may be criminal, illegal, or innocent. A strike is criminal if its purpose be to injure or molest masters or men; illegal if it be the result of an agreement depriving those engaged in it of their liberty of action; innocent if the result of a voluntary combination for the purpose only of benefiting themselves by raising wages or any other lawful purpose. In considering these statements it must be kept in mind that in some cases the authorities referred to have in mind the acts performed in enforcement of a strike as inseparable from the strike itself while others think of the strike as separate in its essence from any acts that may be resorted to to enforce it.

Importance of Motive: New York View. — The more advanced view is held by the New York court and was first expressed by Justice Parker. It holds the statement of purposes as above named and usually made in opinions as "illustrative rather than comprehensive." The right to stop work, and to join with others in stopping is given its logical application without restriction. Any reason regarded by the employee as sufficient must be regarded by the employer, society and the court as sufficient. "Their reasons may seem inadequate to others, but if it seems to be in their interest as members of an organization to refuse longer to work, it is their legal right to stop. The reason may no more be demanded, as a right, of the organization than of an individual, but if they elect to state the reason, their right to stop work is not cut off because the reason seems inadequate or selfish to the employer or to organized society." This view carries the application of the right to stop work in combination with others to a logical conclusion from which it is not easy to shrink. It separates the act from the motive, refuses to consider the motive and rests the act on the general right to perform the act. Applying the logic of this view, the judges of the California court have declared that "in case of a peaceable and ordinary strike, without breach of contract and conducted without violence, threats, or intimidation, this court would not inquire into the motives of the strikers. Their acts being entirely lawful, their motives would be held immaterial."

Summary. — The evolution of strike law, then, has passed through clearly defined stages. Bound at first to the precedent of conspiracy there has been a steady movement toward a more liberal view. Personal rights have been more fully recognized as applicable. Traces of the effects of conspiracy still appear but with less frequency and with diminishing authority. There is a possibility for its revival, however, should such seem to the courts the best way to preserve individual rights as they understand them. The rather radical view that motive has no place in determining lawfulness in connection with strikes is one not held in all jurisdictions, but it appears to be one that will gain rather than lose in influence unless strikes become characterized by greater lawlessness and more pronounced selfishness against unorganized labor.

CHAPTER XII

ARBITRATION

DEFINITION OF TERMS

To find a means of settling labor disputes and to bring an end to strikes and lockouts after they have been started has long been a hope of many. Plans have been devised and suggestions made that lack nothing in variety. Yet the difficulty is still recognized and the means of avoiding it still inadequate. Arbitration is a term that has as its general meaning the agencies and methods by which strikes are ended or avoided. In much of the discussion it is used in this general sense and the result is much vagueness and misunderstanding. It is becoming, however, more and more evident that clearer distinction in meaning is necessary before the desired progress can be attained. Especially does this need become apparent when terms of more recent general use are brought into a discussion. Conciliation and mediation are terms now almost as familiar as arbitration. These are often used quite indiscriminately. Even in our statutes and in commissions organized by their authority there is much confusion. There are boards of conciliation and arbitration, boards of mediation and arbitration, boards of conciliation and mediation, and boards of conciliation, mediation and arbitration. These various terms and combinations do not indicate with sufficient accuracy the functions of the particular boards. Indeed there is much less variety in functions than in names. As Mr. N. P. Gilman rightly declares: "Arbitration is probably the most misused term in the vocabulary of industrial peace."

It is important at the outset of any discussion that as clear a meaning as possible be attached to each of these terms. That there be some overlapping in meaning is perhaps a practical necessity since the terms refer to different stages in a process and the limitations may be somewhat arbitrary. Yet if this process be followed through from its beginning the several terms will appear quite clear enough for intelligent practical use.

Collective Bargaining. — It is inevitable that differences of opinion should develop between employer and employee. When men are organized and the employer deals with them in groups there is *collective bargaining*. If the bargain thus made is drawn up in a formal way and is agreed upon for some definite time it becomes a *trade agreement*. Minor disputes over interpretation or application of the terms of the trade agreement may then be settled by methods provided for in the agreement itself, if it be a trade agreement of the model type. This is the *joint conference*. Thus far there is only an adjustment or a working agreement by which things are kept moving. Some question of larger importance than any covered by the trade agreement or, it may be, the drawing up of such an agreement itself, may cause serious trouble and an attack or defense strike may be called to enforce the demands of one or the other side. Collective bargaining in its special form of joint conference under a trade agreement is then at a standstill. It is at this point that it becomes important to analyze other stages and apply other terms with definiteness.

Conciliation. — Though the men are not at work and any former agreements may for the time be void, still there may be communications or conferences between representatives of each party. The difficulties may be settled and working relations resumed as a result of these conferences carried on between the parties directly concerned, with no outside assistance that is openly recognized as such. This would be *conciliation*. It is an affair that is dealt with exclusively by the men and their employers. It arises at the point where a trade agreement does not automatically adjust the differences. The strike is called off and work is resumed.

Mediation. — If the two parties fail to reach an agreement in this way and the strike continues, it may be terminated in another way. Conciliation failing, it may be that third parties may have influence and by "tendering their friendly offices" may bring the warring parties together for further discussion, find some basis of agreement and thus effect an end of the struggle. This would be *mediation*.

Arbitration. — In the event of a struggle that continued beyond the efforts of conciliation and mediation, there are yet other possibilities. Either through conciliatory efforts or through the agency of a mediator, it may be that an agreement can be reached by both sides to submit their contentions to an impartial body that will after a hearing render a decision of settlement. This is *arbitration*. When the agreement to arbitrate is voluntarily entered into it is called *voluntary arbitration*. With the act of arbitration is another inseparable from it. The disposition of the award may give rise to trouble. Usually of course it would be understood that when the parties agree to the arbitration they would also agree to accept the award. This agreement is, however, voluntary and cannot be enforced if either party chooses for any reason to reject it. Thus it becomes more fully characterized by the term *voluntary arbitration with voluntary award*. This is the form of voluntary arbitration more usual in practice. Thus far any of these processes may be adopted without any reference to legislation or interference on the part of any public official. As laws have been enacted dealing with the question, it is obviously a possibility that the organized power of the state may step in and exercise an authority in the matter. First to consider is the state's authority to compel publicity in cases of strikes on the ground, now so familiar, that the consumers as a third party have a right to know what the struggle is about. This information it may furnish by authorizing an *investigation*. The only result of this course would be to compel witnesses to testify before the investigators under oath and thus separate the kernel of truth from the large amount of chaff or rumor, furnishing to the public a statement of the facts so far as they pertain to the question of the strike.

Compulsory Arbitration. — The state may go further and insist that the differences shall be submitted to an impartial body for adjudication and award. This is *compulsory arbitration*. It does not in this form declare what shall be the status of the award after it has been formulated. If its acceptance is left to the judgment of the contending parties, permitting them to agree to accept it if they choose, it is *compulsory arbitration with voluntary award*. If, on the other hand, the requirement is made in the law that the award shall be binding on the parties named in the law for a specified time, it is *compulsory arbitration with compulsory award*.

These then are the several stages at any one of which a strike may be settled. Collective bargaining, trade agreement and joint conference are activities that belong rather to the pre-strike stage and are devices for the automatic adjustment of differences before they become acute enough to cause an open breach in the industrial relations. When the strike once begins or is threatened, it may be terminated by conciliation, if the adjustment is effected by the parties concerned directly. If third parties intervene to bring the parties together so that they finally reach an agreement of their choice it is mediation. Arbitration implies third parties called in or allowed to form an agreement for the contending parties. If they are agreed upon or accepted by the strikers and the employers of their own choice, it is voluntary arbitration. If they are compelled to accept them it is compulsory arbitration. So with the award of the arbitrators, it may be voluntary or compulsory. Compulsory investigation deals only indirectly with the settlement, its purpose being to strengthen the force of public opinion.

Importance of Distinctions. — For this special use of these terms there is authority, and authority may also be found against them. The dictionary meanings of conciliation and mediation furnish both support and refutation, as they are in some sense synonymous. Perhaps the most striking difference between the above classification of terms and that used by many is the clearer distinction here urged between conciliation and mediation. These terms are frequently used synonymously, referring alike to the intervention of a third party for the purpose of bringing employers and employees together on some common ground of discussion and agreement. Jevons in the State in Relation to Labor uses the single term conciliation to cover both when he says: "A conciliator is one who intervenes between disputants in order to promote calm discussion, to draw forth frank explanations, or to suggest possible terms of compromise." This he distinguishes from arbitration in the following terms: "An arbitrator, on the other hand, is one appointed, either by the consent of the parties, or by superior authority, to inquire into the facts, to receive explanation from both sides, and then, with or without the concurrence of the disputants, to assign the terms of arrangement." Following the classification above presented, conciliation is not presented by Jevons, but rather mediation is defined.

While many authorities use conciliation in the sense in which mediation is used here, it seems clear that there is reason for the distinction. True the choice of terms may be arbitrary, but the two distinct ideas are not to be confused and each must have its separate term. When a trade agreement in the organized territory of the coal mining industry expires it is not uncommon to have a strike. On the day of the expiration of the agreement the men quit work. This is the situation which the daily papers are so fond of capitalizing into large headlines and sensational warnings. The strike is on, so far as the facts go, but the machinery of adjustment still operates and a new agreement is finally reached and the men return to work. There is no interference, friendly or otherwise, by third parties. The miners and the operators confer and out of the conferences comes a conciliation of the difficulties and work is resumed. If conciliation is to mean the same as mediation, then another term is needed for a situation such as just described in coal mining, for example. It is collective bargaining, but not of the normal kind. If that term is to be generalized by that much it cannot stop till it has been made to cover the entire list including compulsory arbitration with compulsory award.

The *bringing* together of employers and employees for the settlement of their differences by peaceable negotiation should be called mediation, as it implies an outside agency. The *coming* together voluntarily of employers and employees for the settlement of differences by peaceable negotiation is conciliation. In this sense there can be no board of conciliation as a permanent public or legal body. There may be boards of mediation, boards of arbitration, and boards of mediation and arbitration. These may be government boards or boards organized through private agencies. If there be any permanent group of conciliators, it would be a joint conference acting under a trade agreement and would belong to the pre-strike period.

Other Distinctions. — A further distinction is sometimes made between primary arbitration and secondary arbitration. "By primary arbitration," it is explained, "we mean the authoritative settlement by impartial arbiters of the terms of the employment contract itself. By secondary arbitration we mean the adjudication of those minor disputes growing out of the interpretation of an existing contract. Secondary arbitration is judicial and easy. Primary arbitration is legislative and difficult." Then is added: "Unless otherwise stated, primary arbitration will be understood to include and assume secondary arbitration." This distinction seems of no practical importance beyond the very evident fact that some cases of arbitration settle questions unlike other cases, and that some are difficult while others are easy.

It is to be hoped that out of the confusion of terms now in use there will evolve soon a definiteness and regularity that will both contribute to clearness in handling practical situations and make unnecessary such lengthy discussion of definitions in dealing with the topic.

That this necessity has been recognized before is evident in many writings. Gilman realizes it when he says, "There is, in fact, a great amount of laxity, inaccuracy and confusion in the popular use of different terms for methods of composing labor disputes, and there can hardly be said to be more than the beginnings, as yet, of a true scientific use of them in the careful writings of the day. A more precise use of the various words commonly applied would make discussion more profitable and lead more quickly to lasting conclusions." Following this recognized need this writer distinguishes between the several forms in a chapter given up to the subject. The definition of conciliation is made clear enough by this writer but when, in the latter part of the chapter, mediation and arbitration are defined, the definitions seem confusing and lacking in practical distinctions. This appears when it is stated that "so long as the parties accepting mediation have not bound themselves to accept the award, the mediator is still only a 'conciliator,' i. e., one trying to reconcile. If then, in fact, when the award has been made by him, both sides accept it, without a previous agreement to do so, this is an instance of conciliation, not of arbitration. In case the award is rejected by one or both parties, it is an instance of unsuccessful attempt at conciliation." Again he says, "The mediator's offer of his services, however, may produce so good an effect upon the two parties that they agree to accept his award when it shall be made. In this case, it is common to say that they have accepted him as the 'arbitrator' of the case." Thus the distinction between the mediator on the one hand and the conciliator and the arbitrator on the other is lost in vagueness. The position of the mediator between the conciliator and the arbitrator is so indefinite that whatever he does of practical value he loses his identity by very reason of his success. If he fails, he is a conciliator but an unsuccessful one. If he succeeds, he is an arbitrator. He is a mediator only because he has not yet completed his work.

This distinction cannot be regarded as satisfactory. In the first place, it conceives the mediator as making an award. That is not his function in the classification that has been proposed. The essence of mediation is to bring about a settlement through the intercession of an outside party who proffers his services. The settlement may be largely one of his own forming, but it is not openly so. He can make suggestions which the parties to the strike may accept and embody as an agreement. Indeed the really skillful mediator in practice will not let it appear that the terms of settlement originate with him. That being the case, the more skillful the mediator, the less apparent is it that there is mediation. If he does make an award, upon the invitation of the parties, he becomes an arbitrator.

One other basis of distinction between terms has been offered and is worthy of consideration. It is a classification of terms on the basis of the questions at issue between the employer and his workmen. It may be the interpretation of an agreement previously made; an agreement expiring by time limit to be renewed for another term of years; or the making of an agreement for the first time. The term arbitration is limited to such cases only as hang upon an interpretation of a "previous agreement, a violation of which is asserted by one party or the other." Mediation is restricted in meaning to the work of drawing up an award which shall become an agreement. This seems not only impractical but inadequate. Trouble may arise and call for settlement where there is no agreement of a formal kind and no probability of forming one. Yet such trouble must be adjusted. It matters not so much in practice whether the strike is for one cause or another or for a group of causes. It is not of prime importance whether both sides agree that the dispute is over the interpretation of an agreement, or only one side insists upon that while the other denies it. The practical phase of the situation is that work has ceased, or is about to cease, and something must be done to secure a restoration of amicable working relations.

The only practical basis of working definition is that proposed at the beginning of this chapter. With the distinctions proposed between conciliation, mediation, voluntary arbitration and compulsory arbitration, the four leading terms, the application can be made with clearness and definiteness to all situations that arise in industrial relations.

Our Lack of Interest in Arbitration.— In ordinary times there is too little discussion of policies of arbitration. Following every serious strike the topic is revived for a time but interest soon lags and the discussion is dropped till another disturbance awakens it. That no definite results issue from such a course is to be expected. While the public mind is excited with the rumors of industrial warfare and irritated by the deprivations and hardships sometimes incidental to such strife, proposals appear and are seriously discussed. When the struggle is ended, these same proposals that seemed so reasonable begin to appear quite too rash for serious thought and they are laid aside. In time of industrial peace the consideration of such topics is naturally quite foreign to our habit of mind. The spirit of *laissez faire* is still with us, and the habit of looking at business from the individual rather than the social viewpoint makes it difficult to gain a hearing for any plans that seem to interfere with the timeworn principle that a man may run his own business in his own way. The result of this situation is easily told if not foretold. Nothing of a constructive nature is accomplished. The industries of America stand in need of some definite policies of adjustment in labor struggles. They are lagging behind other industrial countries in this respect. With each serious disturbance, however, some progress is made. There are now many who are earnestly committed to a policy of compulsory arbitration with compulsory award applicable to all public utility enterprises. A smaller group goes further and insists upon compulsion in all industries involving a minimum number of men. On the other hand, these are opposed by extreme individualists who stand strongly in favor of the application of the methods of the past.

Between them the public at large is not greatly stirred in ordinary times. It is evident, however, that each serious disturbance finds the ranks of the former class somewhat augmented even if there does not appear to be much depletion in the numbers of the latter.

EARLY DISCUSSION — COMPULSORY ARBITRATION

It is not easy to assign any definite time when open discussion of arbitration began in the United States. The early labor disputes were brought to an end generally in one of three ways. They were closed by an agreement voluntarily reached by the parties. They were fought to a finish. Or they were taken to court. The second method was the most usual. European countries were developing definite and permanent organizations through which arbitration was applied. The knowledge of these spread to this country. Workingmen especially became interested in them. As the possibility of a peaceful method of settling disputes became a matter of more general knowledge, it began to attract more favorable attention. By the early eighties results began to appear. The Knights of Labor was in the full height of its influence in these years. It took a positive stand on the subject. "In the management of great or small concerns," wrote Mr. Powderly, in the Story of Labor, "each trouble or difference, whether in relation to discipline or wages, should be talked over in a conciliatory spirit and *arbitrated*. Joint boards of arbitration should be formed between manufacturers and workmen all over the country." It was the general policy of the Knights to discourage strikes and to emphasize particularly the principle of arbitration. In the Preamble to its constitution it stated as one of its aims: "The enactment of laws providing for arbitration between employer and employed, and to enforce the decision of the arbitrators." Later in the same Preamble it further declared: "We will endeavor to associate our own labors . . . to persuade employers to agree to arbitrate all differences which may arise between them and their employees, in order that the bonds of sympathy between them may be strengthened and that strikes may be rendered unnecessary."

This agitation, following as it did upon the series of strikes of the period, gained serious attention. The result was generally speaking a step forward in the stages of development through which we have passed. State legislatures were appealed to and laws were enacted that established state boards to act as arbitrators.

The Unions and Compulsory Arbitration. — For a time compulsory arbitration was called for by organizations of laborers and demands were made for laws embodying such a policy. This period of agitation was pretty closely associated with the years of Knights of Labor supremacy. In New York State especially the records of the proceedings of the Workingmen's Assembly show a distinct demand on the part of that organization for compulsory arbitration between 1888 and 1894. The Assembly had secured in 1886 a State Board with powers of voluntary arbitration. The hopes that were entertained for the work of the board were not realized. The disappointment found expression in a search for some way to compel employers to submit differences to the board. Compulsory arbitration seemed the natural way. In 1888 the convention of this state organization resolved: "in view of the fact that in most cases the spirit of the law is evaded by the refusal of employers to arbitrate with the state board . . . we demand" amendments to the law to "compel the submittal of all existing trouble to the said Board of Arbitration when deemed necessary." Again in 1893 the convention passed the following: "Whereas, Recognizing the fact that compulsory arbitration would be one of the best measures in the interest of labor; therefore, be it resolved, that we demand at the hands of the state legislature an amendment of the present law making arbitration compulsory, thereby enabling the Board to enforce their decisions." That this board was of the same opinion as the association of workingmen appears from the fact that their annual reports favor the adoption of legislation providing compulsory arbitration.

As the Workingmen's Assembly was largely under the influence of the Knights of Labor it is not surprising that such an attitude should develop. The change to opposition was also a natural one. So far as the records of the organization show, the change is accounted for easily. While the demands for a compulsory arbitration law were being asserted the leaders sought legal advice. They were told that the courts might uphold a law compelling corporations to submit to arbitration but a law compelling an individual to arbitrate would in all probability be held unconstitutional. In the language of the proceedings: "Seeing that it was useless to bother with the matter it was dropped." Another series of events doubtless had much to do with this change of policy. The Workingmen's Assembly had a rival organization and after some years of negotiation a new adjustment was made. The result was that the Workingmen's Assembly and the New York State Branch of the American Federation of Labor were amalgamated in 1898 into the Workingmen's Federation of New York State. This organization, since become the New York State Federation of Labor, was dominated by the methods and principles of the American Federation of Labor. That national body has from the beginning quite consistently opposed anything looking toward compulsory arbitration. Doubtless this change had much to do with the passing of that period in which organizations of laborers actively urged compulsory arbitration. Other reasons have been assigned for the change. It is urged that as the laborer usually has supreme confidence in the justness of his claims and is unable to see anything favorable in the claims of the employer, it was good policy to enforce compulsory arbitration as it would compel the adoption of a verdict that was certain to be favorable to laborers. It is further urged that experience with voluntary arbitration revealed the real possibility of a finding in favor of the employer, in which case the worker would be compelled to accept some condition of labor against his will. The truth of this explanation is not easy to establish. It is a fact that tribunals not infrequently found the employer justified in his position. It is also a fact that these awards the workers were not willing to accept. This situation, stated thus rather concretely, has been generalized and is the form of opposition that practically all organizations of labor now show when compulsory arbitration is suggested. When a compulsory arbitration bill was before the New York State legislature in 1900 it was actively opposed by the state Federation not because of its particular provisions but because of the principle involved. "We cannot afford," said the president of the Federation, "to endorse a proposition which carries with it the possibility of a man being compelled to work for an employer or under conditions obnoxious to him, with the alternative of fine or imprisonment. This seems to be the consensus of opinion among trade unionists."

Current Interest. — That the issue is still alive appears at intervals in the periodical literature at various times, as well as in the labor press. A recent visit to America by prominent Australian leaders stirred up the question anew. Prominence was given to the issues in which these men were interested. Interviews were printed, their addresses were published and the magazines of the day took up the discussion. These Australian visitors had much to say about compulsory arbitration. Judge Higgins, President of the Commonwealth Arbitration Court of Australia, was very outspoken in favor of the plan and very positive of the benefits that resulted to the country from its adoption. His statements were not allowed to go unchallenged, however. The labor press did not look with favor upon them. It declared that "Judge Higgins has been a member of the court during the greater part of its existence and, as is to be expected, approves of the court and its policies." It hastens to add that "his is the view of one who looks at the labor movement and labor problems from the outside. He has a legal conception that unions must exist because the whole system of compulsory arbitration rests upon responsible unions. 'Should it be necessary,' he naïvely states, 'the attorney general is given authority to create a union.'"

To counteract the statements favorable to compulsory arbitration, other authorities from the same country were interviewed and their opinions given equally wide circulation. These views are, in the minds of the American leaders, of much greater weight since they come from "those who view the labor movement from within the ranks of the workers and who have had long and intimate experience with conditions in Australia."

Mr. H. P. Hickey, General Secretary-Treasurer of the United Federation of Labor of New Zealand, was quoted: "Let me say that I have read from time to time of your strenuous opposition to compulsory arbitration. Believe me, if you could see the curse it is in this young country with all its ramifications and oppression and repression your antagonism would be even greater.

Here it is simply crushing the heart of labor and unless the repeal of some of the legislation is not swiftly secured in the direction of giving the right to the workers to use their organizations in the direction the majority see fit, I am much afraid the result will be chaotic in the extreme."

It is further stated in the labor press that "Mr. Albert Hinchcliffe, a member of the Australian printers' union and of the Parliament of Queensland, recently made a trip through the United States and visited the headquarters of the American Federation of Labor. In discussing this phase of Australian legislation Mr. Hinchcliffe said to us it had determined the effectiveness of labor organizations by making the workers look to outside agencies for better conditions and had thereby stunted the initiative and growth of organizations. Like Mr. Hickey, he said it had taken the heart out of the movement."

The subject was regarded as of sufficient importance by the Anthracite Coal Strike Commission to be given notice in its report. It said:

"There are some who have urged the Commission to recommend the adoption of compulsory arbitration, so-called, as the means of securing this desired result (settling trade disputes in the coal industry), but we can not see our way to recommend any such drastic measure. We do not believe that in the United States such a system would meet with general approval or with success. Apart from the apparent lack of constitutional power to enact laws providing for compulsory arbitration, our industries are too vast and too complicated for the practical application of such a system.

"We do believe, however, that the State and Federal governments should provide the machinery for what may be called the compulsory investigation of controversies when they arise. The States can do this whatever the nature of the controversy. The Federal Government can resort to some such measure when difficulties arise by reason of which the transportation of the United States mails, the operations, civil and military, of the Government of the United States, or the free and regular movement of commerce among the several states and with foreign nations are interrupted or directly affected or are threatened with being interrupted or affected."

STATE LEGISLATION AND ARBITRATION

The agitation for compulsory arbitration did not lead to the adoption of any specific measures. Indirectly it strengthened the growing feeling of the day that strikes should be settled in such manner as to avoid their serious consequences. This led to the adoption of laws passed by a number of state legislatures providing for public agencies for the settlement of industrial disputes. Between 1878 and 1890 thirteen states placed upon their statute books laws looking to this end. By 1900 ten more joined the group. By 1915 this number had been increased to thirty-two states. The plans comprehend all varieties and combinations of mediation, and voluntary arbitration together with compulsory investigation. In a comparative study of this group of legislation and its results Dr. Leonard W. Hatch divides the laws into four classes: Laws providing for (1) local arbitration with no permanent agency therefor; (2) permanent district or county boards established by private parties; (3) arbitration or conciliation (mediation) through the agency of state commissioners of labor; and (4) a special state board or commission for the settlement of industrial disputes. A detailed description of all these laws will not be necessary here. There was much copying in drafting the later ones, as the earlier ones proved their strength.

Forms of State Legislation. — The central idea running through them all was the desire to arrange a method whereby the state government could in an official way either offer its services or give public legal sanction to some private agency for settlement. This, as has been shown, was especially favored by the workingmen. They became, through their various organizations, active in securing the laws and frequently looked upon them with especial favor as the product of their own work. As to results Dr. Hatch disposes of the first group with the comment: "all turned out to be practically dead letters." Of the second class, permanent local boards established by private parties, he further says "much the same verdict of failure as above must be pronounced." The plan of intervention by a state commissioner appears to have worked somewhat better. Reports show positive results though falling in fact far short of expectations. The later enactment of a law in some of these states establishing a state board is in itself evidence that the single commissioner plan did not meet with the success that was anticipated.

The State Boards. — It is in connection with the state boards that the most serious and profitable work has been done. This plan has been adopted in by far the larger number of states including the leading industrial commonwealths, as New York, Massachusetts, Connecticut, New Jersey, Ohio, Illinois, Missouri and others. The importance of this class of laws and their accomplishments warrants more detailed description. New York and Massachusetts led off with their laws both in the same year, 1886, and they were in a sense models for the other states of this class. Boards were constituted by appointment by the governor, confirmed by the senate. In Massachusetts the provision was that employers and employees both be represented by a member of the board and that the third member be chosen by the other two and appointed by the governor of the state. In New York the personnel was different. The appointments were all to be made by the governor, one to be selected from each of the two largest political parties and the third from a labor organization. This has been changed in more recent legislation so that the bipartisan character of the New York board has disappeared. The work is now under the direction of the Industrial Commission created by the 1915 session of the legislature. If partisan at all, it has, of course, the complexion of the party in power. The Massachusetts principle of representation of employers, employees and the state has been retained in that Commonwealth. These boards were intended to act as boards of mediation or of voluntary arbitration giving their services when called in by the parties concerned. The award was intended to be binding upon the parties, the invitation to arbitrate being understood to be an agreement to accept the award. The plan was not intended in any sense to be an application of the compulsory arbitration principle, as the award is binding only by voluntary assent that it be so.

An important feature is the provision for public or compulsory investigation. The New York board was simply authorized to make an inquiry into the causes of the trouble and publish the same, and the Massachusetts plan authorizes the board to go further and fix the responsibility for the outbreak. In this state such investigation is obligatory. This brief outline makes no attempt to describe the details of the provisions of either of these two state boards or to enter into any discussion of those of other states. New York and Massachusetts have been admittedly leaders in the provision for such arbitration. The other states have freely copied their plans. "The prevailing type (of state board), judging by the number of states adopting it, is that of the New York laws," says Stimson, in his Handbook, though he thinks that perhaps the Massachusetts law has worked rather better in practice.

CHAPTER XIII

ARBITRATION (Continued)

Results of State Boards. — The results accomplished by this method of state arbitration are not easy to estimate. Much difference of opinion exists. Dr. Hatch, writing in 1905, divided the seventeen state boards then existing into two groups. One included "those which have been active relatively little or not at all." This group included nine states. The other included "those with records of some considerable activity ever since their establishment." Of these there are eight: New York, Massachusetts, New Jersey, Ohio, Wisconsin, Illinois, Indiana, Missouri; all of them important industrial states with large and complex industries.

The New York board, the pioneer board of the movement, was first organized as a board with appellate jurisdiction only. Local boards provided for in the law must be called in first, and only on their failure could the state board act. Events forced a change almost immediately. Two strikes of some magnitude occurred. Ten thousand laborers, chiefly women in the collar industry at Troy, were involved in a combination strike and lockout. In this same city 2,500 hands were on strike in the steel and iron works. The board was ready to act and public and press joined in a call for its action. But in the opinion both of the board itself and of the attorney general of the state, the law gave the board no authority to act on its own initiative. Yielding to popular demand the board did offer its services in mediation and succeeded in bringing the parties together for a settlement. In six other instances similar action was taken within a few months though such action had no legal justification. At the next session of the legislature the provisions were changed giving the board direct jurisdiction when appealed to by the parties, and also extending its authority in mediation and investigation. This placed the law on a more permanent basis. Referring to the possibilities under the law the commissioner states in his report for 1913: "In the nature of the case, as the law now stands, what shall be done in this field depends mainly upon the policy of the Commissioner of Labor. The Department may intervene at any time for purposes of conciliation (mediation), and it may publicly investigate any dispute at any time. It can do nothing through arbitration except as parties in dispute agree that it shall, but outside of that its activities in the line of friendly reasoning or investigation on behalf of the public depend upon the policy of the Department." The commissioner emphasizes the possibilities of public investigation, and states it as a part of the program "to make freer use of this power of public investigation, whenever the public interest seems to warrant. This power has been but little used in the past in this state, but the experience we have, and especially experience elsewhere, indicates that this is in line with modern progress."

Estimate by Officials. — If the officials themselves be left to speak on their usefulness it cannot be said that modesty stands in the way of candid expression of their conception of the value of their work. In a report of a western state a commissioner says: "Wherever difficulties of any kind have occurred between employers and employees your commissioner has invariably been called upon as a mediator, and in nearly all instances his efforts have resulted in a speedy and satisfactory adjustment of all difficulties." For a period of ten years the reports of this bureau show 71 strikes. In three only did the commissioner intervene. One intervention was at the request of the governor, another was on his own motion and the third was at the request of the parties. The reports do not show that he brought about a settlement in any one of these instances.

Writing for the American Federationist, in 1894, a member of the New York State Board presents rather a vivid picture. "Arbitration is growing." If employer and employee "have differences, let an entirely disinterested party appointed by the state be called in and settle the points at issue. That this is feasible has already been amply demonstrated. . . . Arbitration by the state has already accomplished much in New York. . . . The Arbitration Commission is ever watchful and its good offices always in demand. The sanguine striker in the first flush of the battle may ignore the peacemaker, but returning reason accepts his intervention. The just employer recognizes the utility of this state official. The hostile forces are brought together by the arbitrator, reason and justice sit down on the same bench and the result is the workman returns to his shop."

Results as Shown in Reports. — During the first fourteen years under the law, down to the end of 1900, there were in New York State 6,189 strikes and lockouts reported. Of these the board intervened in 390 cases (6.3%). Of this number the board took preliminary action only in 135 cases. There was positive intervention in 274 cases. In 119 of these the result was a settlement and in 155 cases the board failed to secure a settlement. This gives a net result of securing a settlement in less than 2% of the strikes during the period, though there was aggressive intervention in nearly 4.5% of the disturbances. Of the 119 settlements effected, 97 were by mediation, 21 by arbitration and one through public investigation. Of the cases in which the board acted (1886–1900) the request came from employers in 16 cases, from employees in 34 cases, and from both in 8 cases. In 58 cases in all, or about one-seventh of the number of interventions, were the services of the board sought. During the last two years for which figures are available, 1912 and 1913, the reports show again the results of the work of this board. In the two years there were 452 strikes and lockouts. Of these 244 were settled either wholly or partly in accordance with the demands of employees, 185 were settled by direct negotiation between the parties, 53 by mediation of the state bureau, one by mediation of outside agencies, and 5 by arbitration. Thus it appears that of the 452 strikes, 5 were successfully arbitrated by the state board, and 53 successfully mediated. Of the 131 interventions made in the two years, 37 were made on request.

On the basis of these figures the report of 1913 says: "The State Department of Labor through this Bureau has exercised a growing influence in the prevention of strikes and the settlement of industrial disputes. The Bureau has intervened in all of the important disputes of the year and is recognized throughout the state as a fair, impartial body; employers and workmen alike usually welcome its activities."

In the experience of Massachusetts a few months were sufficient to show that the law as at first passed did not give the board sufficient scope. It was amended at the first opportunity, by giving the board the power to intervene of its own motion, and to conduct public investigation as well as mediation or arbitration. Summing up the work of the first eighteen years (as shown in Dr. Hatch's study), there were 2,628 strikes and lockouts in the state during the period. Of these the board acted in 524 cases, or 20%. Of action taken before suspension of work there were 419 cases, making a total of 943 interventions, 36% of the number of strikes. Of these 943 interventions, 69 were on invitation from employers, 154 from workmen. In 255 cases both parties joined in the invitation, a total of 478 instances, leaving 465 cases where the board intervened of its own initiative. In 27% of the total number of cases of intervention the invitation came from both parties. In a total of 409 cases the workman showed confidence in the board and in a total of 324 instances the employers were willing to seek the board's assistance. The success of the board is shown by 185 cases of preliminary action only, 460 settlements effected and 298 failures. The disputes settled by mediation numbered 229, and by arbitration 224. Public investigation was the means of settling 3, and 4 were decided on submission of one party.

Comparison between the work of these two boards for these years shows that the Massachusetts board has been the more successful in arbitration.

Obstacles to Success of State Boards. — In spite of these evidences of success on the part of the state boards, there remains a drawback that has very seriously hindered them in the past and must continue to do so as long as they are composed as they are. This drawback is the charge of political influence. As they are appointed, they can hardly be expected to escape all consideration of political advantage. As the members are more or less directly connected with the political fortunes of their party, it is difficult for them to make it clear that they are acting without reference to party welfare. Employers in a private way are very outspoken on this point. It is not uncommon for them to refuse because they have the suspicion that the board is looking for a chance to make campaign material for the next election. The larger the numbers involved in the strike the greater the temptation to "play politics" in the efforts to bring about a settlement. No one is quicker than the shrewd employer to detect such a motive. Many of them rebel against such a use being made of the situation. One prominent among organized employers declares that "a politically created state board cannot by the very nature of its being render just and impartial decisions in labor disputes." The evidence in support of such a contention is not easily gathered and cannot be tabulated in mathematical form. It is not a matter of public record. It is to be discovered by reading between the lines and by listening to both employers and other representative men when they are not talking for publication. It comes from experience and observation. It impresses itself upon those most directly concerned while they are having the practical experiences of labor troubles to be settled. Many an employer is too suspicious of the motives of the members of the board and of their methods of work, even while for expediency's sake he submits to mediation at their hands. This difficulty is beyond doubt a real one. The boards themselves in many instances by their very methods of work have aroused and strengthened the suspicion against them. However glowing may be the accounts of their own work as stated by themselves in their official reports, the fact remains that the suspicion of politics forms a very real barrier to the expanding usefulness of the state boards.

FEDERAL LEGISLATION AND ARBITRATION

The serious strikes of the eighties had an effect on arbitration that was not confined to the commonwealths alone. In Congress the matter was given serious attention. The result was the beginning of a development that has not yet reached a conclusion.

First Legislation. — In 1886 a special Presidential message was addressed to Congress urging action. In 1888 the first federal law was passed. Recognizing the constitutional limitations on Congress the law was made applicable only to transportation agencies and to disputes that affected interstate traffic. As an arbitration measure it was provided that if the parties agreed, two should be selected, one by the railroads and one by the employees, and they two should select a third. Such a board was given power to secure evidence similar to commissioners appointed by courts. The award was to be reported to the United States Commissioner of Labor and by him published. The publication of the report ended the existence of the board. The parties could accept or not its decrees. This was as far in the direction of arbitration as it was thought safe for Congress to go and the plan was one of voluntary arbitration with legal authority for the arbitrators to secure evidence.

Legal Investigation. — The bill contained also a provision for legal investigation. It gave the President power to appoint two commissioners who together with the Commissioner of Labor should constitute a board of inquiry. The authority of this board was the same as in the other case. It might be called into existence in any one of three ways: at the instance of the President, upon request of one of the parties, or upon the request of the governor of the Commonwealth. This was the provision similar to the compulsory investigation plans adopted by several of the states. This law providing for voluntary arbitration and compulsory investigation was an experiment. Many had hopes that it would be useful. These expectations proved not to be well founded, however. No arbitration occurred during the ten years of its life and there was but one investigation. The Pullman strike of 1894 came to an end about the middle of July. The Cleveland Commission of investigation was appointed on July 26th. There being then no dispute to settle it proceeded to investigate the events of the strike and made some valuable recommendations. In November the report was made to the President and submitted by him to Congress in December. It could hardly be called an effort to settle the strike. Yet the report was important in that it revealed conditions and made recommendations that led to a new law. Four years later, 1898, the new law was passed. The investigation feature was dropped and provision was made for mediation and arbitration. The same constitutional limitations were recognized and practically the same questions were subject to the jurisdiction of the board. Mediation was evidently not regarded as offering very hopeful prospects. If requested by either party to the dispute, the Chairman of the Interstate Commerce Commission and the Commissioner of Labor were to extend their aid in mediating the controversy. In case they did not succeed they were then to attempt to secure arbitration.

The New Law: Arbitration Features. — The larger part of the law was concerned with arbitration. This was of course to be voluntary. The steps toward organization were strengthened by authorizing the Chairman of the Interstate Commerce Commission and the Commissioner of Labor to name the third member in case the two appointed should not within five days agree upon the third. In still another respect the new law was much more positive. In case the board of arbitration was constituted, both parties must bind themselves to accept the award, refrain from strike or lockout pending the arbitration, and observe the award for at least thirty days. This was made enforceable by court procedure.

Five specific things must be agreed to by the parties. (1) Pending the arbitration the status prior to the dispute must remain. (2) The award must be final unless appealed and set aside on points of law. (3) The award must be executed and was enforceable in equity. (4) For three months neither party could sever the employment relation without thirty days' written notice. (5) The award was to continue in force one year with no new arbitration on the subject unless an appeal should set the award aside.

Mediation Features. — In mediation a gain was made in this law in establishing a permanent agency for that purpose. This made it easier to secure this form of action. On the other hand, it was undoubtedly a loss in that the new law allowed action only on request of one or both of the parties, whereas under the former law the President could of his own initiative start the mediation.

In arbitration the law was changed from voluntary arbitration with voluntary award to voluntary arbitration with compulsory award.

If any new hopes were attached to this revision of the law, they were destined to be deferred, for during its early life the law was not invoked in either of its provisions. Some efforts were made by the two designated officials to bring about arbitration but to no satisfactory purpose. The familiar reply was made by the railway companies refusing to arbitrate.

Inactivity of First Years. — For eight years the law remained practically a dead letter, only one effort being made during the time to use it and that proving a failure. The general opinion prevailed that the attempt had come to naught. About 1906 the law was revived in practice and since that time it has been a factor of great importance in adjusting railroad labor controversies. The arbitration provision that was so fully elaborated in the law has been distinctly subordinate in practice, while the mediation provision has proved to be by far the more important.

For the seven years ending 1911, the law has been invoked in a total of forty-eight cases, and as some of these involved more than a single controversy the number of controversies totals nearly sixty. Of these, nineteen cases came by application from the companies, thirteen from employees, and sixteen were joint applications. While the number of cases in which the employer showed willingness to mediate by appealing to the law is not so much larger than the other, it is of some importance to note that these nineteen cases involved a total railroad mileage of 390,000 miles and 126,000 men, a mileage and a number of men far greater than in either of the other cases. The total for the whole forty-eight cases was 505,000 miles and 163,000 men. This difference is explained as being due to the fact that when a strike is threatened that may become really serious, it is the company rather than the employees which desires to bring about a settlement through the friendly offices of the mediators. Of all these cases only two came prior to 1907. This revival of the law has been a very hopeful feature to those who advocate mediation and arbitration through government agencies. The cases involve a wide variety of controversies touching practically every possible point that is raised in determining working relations between railroads and their employees. The frequency of the appeal is also marked in the latter years. In five years only once was there a period as long as three months during which mediation was not invoked.

Reasons for Slow Development. — Doubtless the slowness with which this Erdman Act was brought into working operation was largely due to the provision that arbitration meant an acceptance of the award and there was no provision for mediation except upon the initiative of one of the parties in dispute. It was not until those made responsible in the law for carrying into effect its provisions began to assume the initiative that the law began to revive. This initiative was of course extra-legal. By indirect methods, however, the officials brought to the attention of one of the parties their desire to assist. This was usually so adroitly done that the pressure of public opinion was made to count and a refusal to invite mediation would mean a loss of public sympathy. By this skillful method the obstacles to the working of the law were removed. The proportion of mediation to arbitration indicates the relative importance of the two in practice. Of the forty-eight cases four were arbitrated directly without mediation. Of the forty-four remaining cases, thirty-six were settled by mediation, and of the remaining eight that were carried on to arbitration the greater number of points in controversy were mediated. By the skill and tact of the officials concerned the law was saved and mediation was brought into action again. Arbitration with compulsory award still remained the dream of those who gave to it so large a place in the Erdman act.

One other point noted from the experience with this act is of especial importance. In both mediation and arbitration cases the employees have been members of organizations and have carried on their part of the proceedings through their official representatives. These are usually the national officers of the respective unions involved in the trouble. In the words of the Commissioner of Labor: "Although the law applies equally to organized and unorganized workers, it is difficult to see how its provisions could be carried out with any degree of satisfaction except in cases where organized employees are dealt with. Much of the success which has marked the operation of the law thus far is probably due to the fact that the classes of employees with whom it deals are strongly organized and well disciplined groups."

Growing Confidence. — The steadily growing confidence in this act is shown by the facts. Prior to 1906 the provisions were invoked but once. This case was one in which the employees sent the request for mediation and the railroad officials refused to consider either mediation or arbitration. Since that date, as the reports state, "there has been no single instance in which mediation has been definitely rejected in any case of consequence in which a strike was seriously threatened. . . . As a rule, whenever an application for mediation has been made by either side in any serious case, the other party to the controversy has cordially accepted the mediators' tender of friendly offices, and negotiations have been undertaken which have uniformly resulted in an amicable adjustment of the pending controversy."

Though this law has been on the statute books since 1898 and has had at least five years of active application the Commissioner of Labor in 1912 said of it, "In spite of the large number of serious controversies successfully handled, the law may be said to be in an experimental stage, and it is too early yet to predict that it will meet the exigencies of the future as it has those of the past five years."

Recent Changes. — The unsatisfactory result of the arbitration in the case of the Locomotive Engineers on the eastern railroads, in 1912, was keenly felt by the parties concerned. In this case fifty-two roads and over thirty thousand engineers were involved. Public opinion was satisfied because a strike was averted. The influence of the public as decisive was evidenced by the fact that the difficulties were arbitrated at all under the Erdman Act. The railroad managers objected to so small a number as three on the arbitration board and finally it was agreed that without legal authority the board should be enlarged by the addition of four more, making a board of seven, five of whom were regarded as representatives of the public. When in the spring of the next year the firemen of the same district presented similar demands they insisted upon arbitration under the Erdman Act. The railroads finally yielded under protest, and a board of three members was agreed upon.

This was followed immediately by demands from the conductors and trainmen. They also proposed arbitration under the same law. The roads again objected on the ground that a board of three, made up as it was, virtually left the decision in the hands of one man. The matters involved were quite too important and too complex to be settled in this way. The roads and the workmen had both had experience within a few months, once with a large board and once with a small one. These two controversies had served to bring to light other defects of the act also. While negotiations were pending in this third case, representatives of both the railroads and the brotherhoods of workmen came together in agreement on a bill that should take the place of the Erdman Act. The understanding was that if this new bill should at once become law the pending controversy would be settled by an application of its provisions. The bill was put through practically without opposition and the case of the conductors and trainmen was the first to be adjusted by it.

Character of New Law. — The new law, known as the Newlands Act, became effective in the summer of 1913, fifteen years after the Erdman law was enacted. It repealed its predecessor. In its place there was established a board of mediation with a commissioner, an assistant commissioner and not more than two other government officials appointed by the President and Senate. The commissionership is a permanent office, the appointment being for seven years. The board is to deal, as did the former one, with such disputes between interstate railroads and their employees engaged in train service over question of wages, hours of labor or conditions of employment as may threaten serious interruption of business. Either party may appeal to the board for mediation or for its services in bringing about arbitration. Also the board may at its discretion offer its services of its own initiative. Arbitration boards are provided for to consist of three or six members as the parties may agree. One-third of such board is to be named by each party and the remaining third selected by these. In case they come to no agreement in the choice of members the board of mediation appoints them. The award of the board must be accepted by both parties, though this provision is qualified so as to protect individual rights that might otherwise raise the question of constitutionalty. The board must confine itself in its award to questions that are regularly brought before it in the agreement and in the hearing.

As the first permanent organization of the board of mediation the President has appointed the minimun number, adding to the commissioner and assistant commissioner one other member (the law permits the appointment of not more than two). In the first case under the new Newlands law the arbitration board consisted of six members. In one other case since that the board has been made up of the larger number. In two other cases, three have constituted the board of arbitration.

First Applications. — Unlike the Erdman Act this new arbitration plan received a severe test at the beginning. It seems thus far to have established its superiority. Its very existence is strong witness of the importance of public opinion as an influence against railroad strikes. Clearly one thing the public demands, and that is that whatever the difference of opinion may be as to what constitutes a fair working bargain, it must be adjusted without cessation of work. This was clearly evident in the agreements to arbitrate during the last two years of the old measure. Though neither party was satisfied with the fairness of the plan they agreed to submit to it. The new plan aims to remove some of these objections and probably does. The public has all the stronger reason for expecting the adjustment of differences without tying up interstate traffic. Though it may prove to be somewhat over-sanguine, there is much reason for agreement with the optimism of one of the chief promoters of this new law, the Executive Secretary of the National Civic Federation, when he says that the new law "may reasonably be taken to mean that we are to have no more strikes on the railroads of this country."

The procedure in the case of these brotherhoods and their demands upon the railroads reveals an interesting phase of the development. The pressure of public opinion was so strong that not only was each unwilling to accept the responsibility of resisting it, but a law was enacted expressly for the purpose of opening the way for a settlement. A provision in the law requiring arbitration would have been in all probability unconstitutional. Virtual compulsory arbitration was secured through the pressure of public opinion. It may be that we are about to enter upon a régime of arbitration made compulsory by the force of public opinion, a force that cannot be submitted to the constitutionality test and that cannot be resisted with impunity by either party. This would be virtually compulsory arbitration in all of its beneficial elements without the objections that are raised against the legal compulsion of the parties. It is to be hoped that this public opinion form of compulsion will be given a thorough trial before further steps are taken in the direction of legal compulsion.

Possible Weaknesses. — If it has been clearly established that the public has a voice, it is not so certain that the best plan has been formed by this new law. It was hurriedly passed, more to meet an emergency than to formulate a satisfactory plan. It has defects, and some of these are already being discussed. Among them may be mentioned the following:

(1) The problems with which a board has to deal should not be regarded as simple because they deal only with wages, hours of labor and conditions of employment. In the conductors' and trainmen's case seventeen articles were submitted, extremely complex and technical in their nature. These were offset by eight articles submitted as counter propositions by the managers for the railroads. To these the labor representatives objected most vigorously and they were finally withdrawn though not without protest. The matter is one on which the railroads may be expected to insist, however, as from their point of view they cannot be expected to allow the employees to present demands, some or all of which may be allowed, without themselves standing also to gain something from the arbitration. It seems but reasonable to hold that if adjustments are to be made both sides should have a chance at the same time of making any propositions it may choose before the arbitrators. Otherwise it will be only a question of how much or how little the workman can gain, which restated may read how little or how much the roads must lose.

(2) The Newlands Act makes no provision for unorganized laborers to appeal to it. This may appear a serious matter, but it loses its seriousness in the face of the policy that practically all of the railway brotherhoods adopt of insisting that their agreements shall apply to all employees whether members of the organization or not. So long as the law applies only to employees concerned in train operation this objection has but little more than academic value.

(3) It is proposed to extend the provisions of the law so as to include all classes of railroad men, instead of train operatives only. This would doubtless raise legal objections that should not be forced for consideration yet.

(4) Again it is suggested that this board, so influential in adjusting wages, should be more directly united by working relations with the Interstate Commerce Commission, the body that is responsible for adjusting traffic rates.

(5) Further extension of the law is also proposed, making its

provisions applicable to a far wider field, those industrial corporations that are subject to Congress. These two later propositions can well be left for a time until the new plan has had
a more thorough trial. To carry the degree of public confidence
necessary to guarantee peace in the railroad world the boards
must establish themselves firmly by the excellence of their
work. Development has proceeded slowly in the direction of
settlement of railroad labor disputes. Yet it has been along
sound and profitable lines. It should not be hurried. By it
within the past few months troubles have been amicably settled
that might in former days have caused an industrial struggle
more costly than any that the past has experienced.

New Powers of Secretary of Labor. — While progress of a
very positive kind has been made in government mediation
and arbitration in railroad disputes, this is not the only development. With the creation of the separate department of labor
another step was taken that opens large possibilities. Among
the powers conferred upon the Secretary of Labor was one that
authorizes him "to act as mediator and to appoint commissioners of conciliation (mediation) in labor disputes whenever
in his judgment the interests of industrial peace may require
it to be done." This is clearly a recognition of the value of the
work of the Anthracite Coal Strike Commission appointed
extra-legally by President Roosevelt. It gives the Secretary
of Labor large discretionary power which may be used as an
effective agency through which public opinion may work.

What use the Secretary of Labor would make of this power
thus conferred upon him by the law was the subject of much
discussion at the beginning. His first statement was only in
the most general terms. "The policy to which I shall adhere,"
he is reported to have said in a public address, "during my
administration will be to do all I can to bring labor and capital
together in mutual conferences, so that they may settle their
own differences." The developments since the organization
of the department do not indicate that the first secretary in-
tends to allow the opportunity to pass unnoticed. "Commissioners of conciliation" (mediation) have been appointed and
the work of mediation has been carried on in a variety of cases.
During the year ending June 30, 1915, the good offices of the
department had been extended in thirty-two disputes involving,

directly and indirectly, 94,289 men. Of these disputes twenty-four were amicably settled and five were reported as still pending at the close of the year. Since that date the work has been carried on in the same manner and during the first four months of the next year about thirty-five cases were mediated, twelve of which were brought to a successful termination and eighteen were still pending. These records show that it is the intention of the department to develop this line of mediation as fully as the conditions will permit. Though the actual number of cases for the entire period is not great, the large proportion of successes is a favorable indication of further possibilities.

In railroad disputes the first year of activity of the board of mediation and "conciliation" shows results that are worth while. Twenty-eight cases of differences were taken up by the board, involving a total of 125,000 employees. In most of these cases, — all except two, in fact, — strike votes had been passed before the services of the board were requested. Of the twenty-eight cases dealt with, twenty-one were adjusted through mediation alone. The others were settled in part by mediation and in part by arbitration.

Influence of Public Opinion. — The foregoing descriptions make it evident that whenever danger arises public opinion is keenly alive to the necessity for securing some means by which costly strikes may be averted. The serious lessons of the past serve as warning not to rely solely on individual effort by way of conciliation. Personal interests, ambition for control, recklessness of community interests have often been powerful enough to sweep aside all efforts at conciliation. Yet the principle of conciliation is still dear to the popular mind. It means no interference from outside. Cases of serious strikes have each time led to a popular demand for settlement and cessation of hostilities. Then mediation or arbitration seems more reasonable. State boards have been created and have in many cases justified their existence. When the public hears the reply "nothing to arbitrate," it loses its respect for those personal rights upon which such a reply is based and a clear cry is heard for government interference. Just how this is to be brought about does not readily appear. Individual rights and government interference in industry do not mix well in making up a policy. So it is that generally speaking the public is hesitating between the remnants of *laissez faire* on the one hand with its application in conciliation, and compulsory arbitration with compulsory award on the other. Each serious outbreak forces it further along toward the latter, while in times of peace it is difficult to get a serious hearing in its favor. The practical middle ground is occupied by a variety of state boards that are intended to deal with all cases. These boards are vested with a variety of powers extending to a point just short of compulsion on one hand and on the other tied down so closely to *laissez faire* as to be of no service at all.

Where the industry partakes of the character of a public utility, there is ground for more positive interference and the government agencies are armed with more authority. The climax of government activity has been reached in case of the federal government and train operation on interstate railroads. Here there exists practically compulsory arbitration as a last resort so long as the boards constituted under the law continue to inspire public confidence. This they have at present in sufficient degree to make the plan effective. The nearest open door to an enlarged field of federal government operation is the authority now given by law to the Secretary of Labor. It would seem that there is sufficient legislation, or, at least, there is as much as can at present be based on a favorable public opinion. The problem of the present is to adjust means under these laws whereby no hardship may be imposed upon either workmen or employers, and the public may rest in the confidence that a fair deal is assured and traffic uninterrupted.

PRIVATE AGENCIES

While these elaborate methods have been developed as a means of government activity in arbitration private agencies have also been at work. It is not possible to enter upon a detailed description of all of them in this place. They are far too numerous. Yet many of them are worthy of careful attention. Notable among them is the National Civic League, an organization composed of representatives of employers, of employees, and of "publicists" as representing the "third party." This organization divides its work into numerous branches one of which is mediation and arbitration. Working both directly and indirectly this League has been a potent factor for industrial peace.

The New York Clothing Industry. — Among numerous more or less permanent associations of this general character one other stands out perhaps most prominently of all and cannot be passed without notice. It is the outgrowth of the series of strikes in the clothing industry, particularly in New York City. In the summer of 1910 the unions joined in a strike that was bitterly fought on both sides, lasting for two months and involving about 60,000 men and women workers. The events of the struggle attracted wide attention and the strikers were subjects of much popular sympathy because of the prevailing ideas as to sweat shop work and the varied nationalities represented among the strikers. Propositions and counter-propositions were made in an endeavor to reëstablish working relations. "Disinterested agencies" were instrumental in bringing about conferences, but these were of no avail. The issues were finally narrowed down to the question of the "open shop" or the "closed shop" and on this issue there appeared to be no compromise. At the end of the two months of bitter struggle the noted Protocol was signed and peace was restored. This "treaty of peace" was an agreement made between the two contending organizations, the Cloak, Suit and Skirt Manufacturers' Protective Association of New York City with a membership of 123 manufacturing firms (since increased in number) and 9 locals of the International Ladies' Garment Workers Union. It included all matters in controversy, minimum wage scale, a fifty-hour working week, and three other features that have made the Protocol so justly noted. These are (1) the joint board of sanitary control; (2) the preferential union shop; and (3) the plan for adjusting disputes in the future. The first and second of these are dealt with in some detail elsewhere on these pages. It is the plan for settling differences that is of special importance here. It comprehended a Board of Grievances and a Board of Arbitration with equal representation in each case for both manufacturers and employees. Both sides bound themselves to accept the awards of these boards.

The Board of Grievances was composed at first of four members, later increased to ten, an equal number from each party. In cases of deadlock the dispute was to be referred to a Board of

Arbitration, consisting of three members, one representing each party and one the public, the latter chosen by the other two and in case of their failure to agree, by the governor of the state.

The way of these boards has been difficult indeed. Employers of varying ability and experience pushed by the keenest kind of competition could not always agree upon what many of them would doubtless have liked to do. Employees, representing a variety of nationalities, difficult to organize and to train to stand together and new to American life, were not easily amenable to the hardships that their new life involved. A group of determined and able leaders was bound to maintain organization at all hazards seeking to amalgamate the 10,000 more or less of immigrants that annually come into the industry. A consuming public anxious for cheap prices eagerly sought bargains to offset a steadily rising cost of living.

The board faced these trying conditions and at the same time found it necessary to work out a plan of procedure and a set of rules that would be suitable to the situation. This was finally done after some further conferences. The procedure was established as follows: Any individual having cause for dissatisfaction might appeal to the Board of Grievances. A Clerk of this Board first took up the matter, and adjusted it, if possible, in accordance with established procedure. If this failed the matter was considered by the Board of Grievances. In case there was a tie vote or no decision reached, the matter went to the Board of Arbitration and its decision was final as both parties to the Protocol were bound by it. The success of this plan can best be indicated by the figures brought to light in a recent investigation of its working. From April 15, 1911, to Oct. 31, 1913, a total of 7,656 complaints were filled. Of these 7,477 (97.7%) were adjusted by the clerks. The 179 that were passed on were considered by the Board of Grievances. Of this number 159 were settled, leaving 20 cases to go to the Board of Arbitration. These 20 cases did not involve that many separate issues. There were but 9 different cases or issues passed on to the Board of Arbitration in the two and one-half years.

The abandonment of the Protocol by the parties concerned in the summer of 1915 brought an end to this particular method of settling their differences. In August a new agreement was signed in the industry and peace again restored. This new plan provided a somewhat different form of organization for conciliation and mediation as well as for arbitration. A more detailed description of this new contract appears in the chapter on The Closed Shop.

CHAPTER XIV

THE BOYCOTT

The practice of refusing relations with those whose policies are not agreeable is certainly no new thing under the sun. Applied to business there evolves nothing essentially new. Business relations, buying and selling, are voluntary acts. When one decides not to buy of another, it is not usual to demand a reason. As the relations of employer and employee become strained, human nature does not change any. The employer wishes both to secure the services of employees and to sell them his products. The employee, on the other hand, wishes an opportunity to work and to buy products of labor. Exchange markets have developed, both of labor and of products, but they are presumably voluntary, and so are subject to choices, whatever may prompt them.

The idea expressing all the variety of practices under these circumstances existed before it had a name. When Captain Boycott was sent by the irate Lord Erne into Connemara to take charge of the tenants who were demanding concessions that Lord Erne refused to make, he was met with such opposition that finally the Captain and his family were completely cut off from all association with the people of the district. For want of a word to use as a name for such a situation, "Boycott" came into use. This was in 1880. Few words in our language have had such a remarkable growth as this one. In a quarter century it has spread wherever labor troubles arise and its meaning is familiar to all English-speaking people.

For Americans the invention of the term was timely. The period immediately following its first use was that in which union leaders were making frequent use of this method of coercion. Not at all unlikely the suggestion of the new name had some effect on popularizing the boycotting methods that had such a general use during that same period. While originating from a struggle between tenant and overseer on an estate in Ireland, it now stands for a much wider variety of contest.

Definition and Classification. — In spite of its wide popularity and general use as a term, it is not an easy term to define accurately. The standard English dictionaries give the usual general definition. In one of these it is defined as follows: "To combine (a) in refusing to work for, buy from, sell to, give assistance to, or have any kind of dealings with, and (b) in preventing others from working for, buying from, selling to, assisting, or having any kind of dealings with (a person or company), on account of political or other differences, or of disagreements in business matters, as a means of inflicting punishment, or of coercing or intimidating."

When a reader turns aside from the general consideration to a discussion of the particular field of labor activity, the efforts to define become more elaborate. In Adams and Sumner's Labor Problems is found a somewhat more specific definition. "The boycott, as used in modern labor disputes, may be defined as a combination to suspend dealings with another party, and to persuade or coerce others to suspend dealings, in order to force this party to comply with some demand, or to punish him for non-compliance in the past." On the basis of the various methods adopted a classification of boycotts is then made. There is the primary boycott, in which there is no attempt to coerce third persons to suspend business relations; the compound boycott, where efforts are made to coerce third parties. The latter is what the work referred to calls the "ordinary form" of boycott. Then there is the fair list or union label and the unfair list.

For another classification one may turn to Laidler's Boycotts. Here the definition is introduced in the following words: "A boycott in labor disputes may be defined as a combination of workmen to cease all dealings with another, an employer, or, at times, a fellow worker, and usually also to induce or coerce third parties to cease such dealings, the purpose being to persuade or force such others to comply with some demand or to punish him for non-compliance in the past." Then follows the classification that this authority adopts. First there is the negative boycott and the positive boycott. To the former belong the union label and the fair list. To the latter, the unfair or we-don't-patronize list and the boycott proper. Then the boycott proper, itself a subdivision of the boycott, is subdivided into four kinds. First, the primary boycott; "a simple combination of persons to suspend dealings . . . involving no attempt to persuade or coerce third parties." Second, the secondary boycott; "a combination of workmen to induce or persuade third parties to cease business relations with those against whom there is a grievance." Third, the compound boycott; this "appears when workmen use *coercive* and *intimidating* measures as distinguished from mere persuasive measures in preventing third parties from dealing with the boycotted firm." This compound boycott is of two varieties, (1) involving threats of pecuniary injury and (2) involving threats of actual physical force and violence. Fourth, the tertiary boycott; "frequently applied to the most indirect forms." To emphasize the distinction between the secondary and the compound forms it is said "persuasion only is used in the secondary boycotts, while the compound boycott is accompanied by threats or coercion, the threats, at times, however, being mere threats to boycott."

In a pamphlet of the Wisconsin Free Library, prepared by G. G. Huebner, the boycott is again classified. There is the compound boycott, involving third parties; the primary boycott, involving only the persons directly interested in the dispute; the unfair list, not always regarded as a boycott; the fair list, the opposite of the unfair list, and legally not included under boycotting; and the union label, legally not included in the boycott and nowhere in the United States illegal.

Legal Definition. — Though several definitions have been offered, they do not seem to be sufficient. When one enters the legal realm, one might expect to find the matter cleared up. But not so. "The most casual observation," wrote Judge Halloway of Montana in 1908, "will disclose that scarcely any two courts treating of the subject formulate the same definition." "The word is not easily defined," said Judge Carpenter of Connecticut. Chief Justice Grant of Michigan declared on the other hand that he did not believe that the word had not an authoritative meaning. The term has been defined, he insists, by both lexicographers and courts. Judge Halloway, after stating three definitions, in an opinion adds: "We prefer a broader definition, and one we deem more consonant with present-day conditions." This one he states in the following words: "I think that the verb 'to boycott' does not necessarily signify that the doers employ violence, intimidation, or other unlawful coercive means; but that it may be correctly used in the sense of the act of a combination, in refusing to have business dealings with another until he removes or ameliorates conditions which are deemed inimical to the welfare of the members of the combination, or some of them, or grants concessions which are deemed to make for that purpose."

The law dictionaries give different definitions, taken from various court opinions. Black's Law Dictionary and The American and English Encyclopedia of Law characterize the boycott as a "conspiracy formed and intended directly or indirectly to prevent the carrying on of any lawful business, or to injure the business of any one by wrongfully preventing those who would be customers from buying any thing from or employing the representatives of said business, by threats, intimidation, or other forcible means." In the words used in Anderson's Law Dictionary, "The purpose is to constrain acquiescence or to force submission on the part of the individual who, by non-compliance with the demand, has rendered himself obnoxious to the immediate parties, and perhaps to their personal and fraternal associates."

The statement that seems to carry the greatest weight of authority in law is that made by Judge Taft from the Bench of the United States Circuit Court in connection with the efforts of railway employees to boycott other railroads. "As usually understood," says Judge Taft, "a boycott is a combination of many to cause a loss to one person by coercing others, against their will, to withdraw from him their beneficial business intercourse, through threats that, unless those others do so, the many will cause similar loss to them. Ordinarily, when such a combination of persons does not use violence, actual or threatened, to accomplish their purpose, it is difficult to point out with clearness the illegal means or end which makes the combination an unlawful conspiracy; for it is generally lawful for the combiners to withdraw their intercourse and its benefits from any person, and to announce their intention of doing so, and it is equally lawful for the others, of their own motion, to do that which the combiners seek to compel them to do. Such combinations are said to be unlawful conspiracies, though the acts in themselves and considered singly are innocent, when the acts are done with malice, i. e., with the intention to injure another without lawful excuse." (Toledo &c. Ry. Co. *vs.* Penn. Co., 54 Fed. 730.)

This definition forms the basis for the distinction so generally held in legal circles between the lawful purpose of self-help and the unlawful purpose of willful injury or malice. The essential legal element of the boycott is that it is malicious. This view is summed up by Stimson who concludes in his Handbook that the boycott belongs to the class of unlawful conspiracies "wherein the intent becomes of importance. . . . The prime question in the law of boycott is that of intent," and boycott means "exclusively an unlawful conspiracy."

An analysis of these definitions indicates that the word should have a more definite meaning. Even this will not solve all the difficulties connected with it but it will assist in no small degree.

Boycott and Strike. — The two terms boycott and strike should be more clearly separated. The need for this appears in the necessity for some degree of scientific accuracy, and further in the fact that in law strikes are generally lawful and boycotts are unlawful. To call an act a strike or to call it a boycott creates in the very term a presumption as to its lawfulness.

Strikes deal with labor relations, the withholding of labor and the inducement of others to withhold their labor. The latter is called the sympathetic strike. There is no good reason for calling it a boycott. Boycotts deal primarily with that other relation of business, the buying and selling of goods. Yet all efforts to influence such relations should not come within the meaning of the term. A "negative boycott" seems an unnecessary refinement. The "union label," the "fair list" are in the class with trade-marks and brands, with advertising and the guarantee of advertised goods, with the arts of salesmanship in their numerous refinements. They are intended to promote the sales of goods, not to prevent them. It would be considered highly unsatisfactory to say that a traveling salesman who was urging the reliability of the trade-mark of his house was boycotting the line of goods of a rival. To class under "positive boycott" the "unfair list," the "we-don't-patronize list" and the "boycott proper" is not a logical subdivision, for the first and second are but methods used in connection with the boycott proper. This separates from the term some of the extraneous material. The "boycott proper" is the boycott. Its further subdivision into primary, secondary, compound and tertiary boycotts is carrying it too far to serve practical purpose. It may profitably be divided into two kinds. Beyond this the lines of division are too much a matter of opinion to be of real value. These two kinds may be called the simple boycott and the compound boycott. The latter might be called the sympathetic boycott, making the terminology consistent with that used in case of the strike, where these are spoken of as a simple strike and a sympathetic strike. The term simple boycott applies to efforts to prevent sales of goods to laborers and their immediate sympathizers. The latter, the compound boycott, should be used only in connection with the more widely organized efforts, such as to prevent sellers of raw materials from selling to, and jobbers and traders from buying from, the boycotted. The line of division here is made between the direct and the indirect, between such influence as the boycotters can exert directly, and such as they can bring to bear indirectly through others not of their own class. This distinction offers objections that are real. The line of division is not so clear as scientific accuracy would demand. It is practical, however. It follows the distinction between the strike and the sympathetic strike. This differentiation is sufficient for practical purposes. There appears no need for primary, secondary, compound and tertiary strikes, though there is a variety both of kinds and of reasons that would make such distinctions possible. To make a distinction of definition that hinges upon the difference between "induce or persuade" and "coerce or intimidate" is to use as a basis of distinction a difference that is constantly shifting and always vague.

In the legal form of definition a serious objection is found in framing the statement so as to imply unlawfulness in the word. To do this is very unfortunate. "To refuse to have business relations with another until he removes or ameliorates conditions which are deemed inimical" seems a very innocent act. If it is to be called a boycott, as some judges would allow, in an indictment, then it begs the question, for as has been seen in the definitions that have been quoted, the word conspiracy is used in defining the term, as in the expression, "exclusively an unlawful conspiracy."

As in the strike a distinction is admitted between the act of striking and other acts that may or may not be done in connection with the strike, so the boycott should be separated from some of the acts that are done in connection with it. In its essence an industrial labor boycott is a form of collective bargaining that aims to improve the conditions of labor by securing concessions from employers through the means of stopping the sales of their products. In its simplest form it consists in the laborers themselves refusing to purchase and in inducing those who are actively in sympathy with them to do the same. In its more complex form it takes on a specific organization to accomplish the result by bringing pressure to bear upon other employers to induce them to withhold business relations until the issues in dispute are settled. A great variety of methods has been adopted to make the boycott effective. Some of these are unquestionably lawless. Force and violence that are unlawful in themselves are necessarily so when used in connection with boycotting. In connection with many of the methods used there is wide difference of opinion as to their lawfulness. Courts have generally regarded these methods as inseparably a part of the boycott itself and accordingly held the opinion that boycotts are in and of themselves unlawful.

Labor Boycotts and Other Boycotts. — It is difficult to see clearly the difference between boycotts that are organized by labor unions and those that are carried on by other groups for essentially the same purpose. A widespread movement was organized against the high price of meat by which through open agitation consumers were exhorted to cease buying meat from those who charged a price that the leaders thought was too high. Either the dealer must reduce the retail price regardless of what he paid for it or see his business ruined. What was the motive? In a city campaign in the interest of wholesome conditions in bakeries, the shops were inspected by a group of women. If the conditions were found satisfactory, the name was printed on a list. If unsatisfactory, the name was not printed. Consumers were then urged to patronize only the listed places. This committee of inspection was a voluntary association. It forced the bakers to do as they wished them to, or suffer heavy losses in their business. The method was arbitrary. What was the motive?

A group of men may strike to secure better conditions of labor. Their motive is laudatory. If for the same purpose they withhold their trade through the same organization that might have called a strike, the motive is malice. It is not alone the acts that they do in seeking to make the boycott successful that are unlawful. It is the act of ceasing to trade through agreement or in response to an order of an officer who is vested with the authority to issue it.

Condemnation of Boycotts. — That much general discussion is yet necessary before there can be formulated anything approaching a "public" opinion on this subject is obvious to anyone who attempts to follow both sides of the controversy. Those who condemn the boycott do so in no uncertain terms. A literature of considerable size and characterized by much extravagance of expression has already appeared, for the most part in pamphlet form. The vigorous efforts of the American Anti-Boycott Association represent this style of discussion. This is an organization the membership of which at the start was secret and whose pamphlets first appeared without the imprint of the publishers. Later the secrecy has been dropped. In the first part of March, 1915, an annual meeting of the association was held in New York City with a banquet at the Waldorf-Astoria. An elaborate gift was presented to the leading attorney with much speech-making. There were also mutual congratulations on the Association's having attained to its thirteenth year of life and having expanded from an initial membership of one hundred to a present roll of nearly one thousand members. It is in the literature of this organization that we read that the boycott is "a gigantic engine of tyranny," by the use of which is established "literally a reign of terror;" "the result of an elaborate and premeditated scheme to bring to disaster and ruin all non-union manufacturers and employees and to deprive them of their inalienable right to the unimpeded pursuit of a livelihood." The direct motive of boycotters is "the injury and the ruin of the manufacturer. To be sure their ultimate object is the amelioration of their own condition, but that is too remote to permit the boycott to be termed by any such

euphemistic name as competition." It is a "monstrous conspiracy to put up prices, to stem all the forces of economic laws,
and rise upon the ruins of their victims;" an "appalling tyranny
and outrage practiced on free and independent citizens;" a
"glaringly unjust conspiracy by which a part of that fair return
of wages which economic laws have given to all labor is taken
from him and appropriated to fatten the pocketbook of the
union man."

Such form of expression can hardly be characterized as judicial or temperate. A work intended to be a serious discussion
of the law of boycotts uses such language as the following:
"Men who will wantonly conspire to boycott inanimate objects, simply because men of their own trade and calling who
did not belong to their association built them, are monsters
who place themselves outside the pale of the law and should
be exterminated from the face of the earth. They place themselves on a level of the anarchist, whose religion and creed is
the destruction of all existing systems of property, society,
government and religion." The sentences that follow this
quotation grow more rather than less extreme.

Again we find the boycott described by the Brooklyn Eagle
as a "dragon, slimy and repulsive, which had, for more than
a quarter of a century, been a vague terror to independent
workers and to large employers, at all times, materializing now
and then as a concrete foe, insidious, treacherous, often triumph-
ant." A grand jury described a boycott in a case before them
as a "hydra-headed monster, dragging its loathsome length
across the continent, sucking the very life blood from our trade
and commerce, equally harmful to employees and employers."
Records of the American Bar Association contain the statement: "As frequently applied it is one of the most heartless
and brutal manifestations of private revenge recorded in history and is calculated to call forth the abhorrence and just
reprehension of all men who respect law and love liberty."
A Virginia judge declared from the bench that the acts are
"incompatible with the prosperity, peace and civilization of
the country, and if they can be perpetuated with impunity
by a combination of irresponsible cabals and cliques, there
will be an end of government and of society itself." Still other
statements of this character may be found in Laidler's Boycotts.

Very much more dignified and satisfactory is a statement found in an address by President Emeritus Eliot of Harvard: "The boycott is a method of combat which is eminently a method of ill-will, being an attempt to ruin the business of a person or corporation that will not conform to the regulations of the unions in the manufacture or distribution of its product. It is a gross interference with a just industrial liberty, and it is often extremely cruel in purpose if not in achievement. So far as it goes, it makes good will between the employing class and the laboring class impossible. It is a combative method and nothing else. Although seldom an effective weapon, except in places where the unions control a clear majority of the population, it is a weapon much dreaded not only by manufacturers but by merchants and other distributors of goods."

Approval of Boycotts. — Contrasted with this method of expression is that of those who insist upon their right to use the boycott when they wish. Naturally it is the union laborer who insists upon this right. That many irrational statements may be found emanating from this side of the controversy is to be taken for granted. It is useless to repeat them. It is sufficient to say that they come from the more radical, the less well informed and really the less influential sources. This cannot be said of the statements urged on the other side. Of numerous statements that might be used by way of illustration one may be selected that is quite typical. It appeared in connection with the discussion of the Buck Stove and Range Boycott and was printed in several of the labor papers during the year 1909.

"Neither the defendants in this case or other union men destroyed a Buck's stove or the factory where they are manufactured. They probably injured the sale of the stoves, but we deny that this is a property right. And that is where our protest against the ruling of the court comes in. If we assume that a boycott to injure the sale of a product injures a property right, then we assume that the manufacturer has a property right in the customer; and no man has a property right in a customer or in the laborer who works for him. The sooner we make this clear the sooner shall we get the relief we are asking for."

Commenting on this statement, the editor of one of these papers says the distinction "is absolutely true. To destroy

physical property, or to dissipate intangible property secured
as such by the law, is a radically different thing from turning
customers away from a seller of goods. The seller neither has
nor can have a legal property right in his customers. To erect
such a right upon the foundation of property rights in the good
will of the business, is either to beg the question or to abuse
the good-will principle. No one can have a property right in
the good will of his customers which the customers are bound
to respect. They may quit patronizing him at any time and
from any motive. If they do so from fear of personal injury,
it is they and not the seller whose rights are assailed. If they
quit not from fear of the boycotter but from information which
he supplies, then the boycotter's offence depends upon whether
his information was true and legitimate; and on these issues a
jury and not an injunction judge must decide. As to the legiti-
macy of the information upon which the customer acts, anything that would affect a free man's decision in buying goods is
legitimate information about those goods — provided only
that it is true. If the merits of the Buck stove, for instance,
were fraudulently extolled by the maker, the publication of
that fact ought to be and would be lawful. The Buck stove
customers have a right to know the truth about this important
element in determining their action as buyers. But customers
are influenced by other considerations than the inherent merits
of the commodity they buy. Good men and women would not
like to buy a commodity streaked with the blood of factory-
foundered children. It is therefore no wrong to let them know
the fact, if it be a fact, and to appeal to them in the name of
humanity not to buy. They might not like to buy commodities
produced by underpaid and overworked labor. It is therefore
no wrong to let them know this fact, in cases in which it is the
fact, and to appeal to them not to buy. And so of those who
prefer 'union-made' goods to 'scab-made' goods; the manufacturer has no property right in secrecy as to that fact. Unless persons who abhor the death-dealing child labor of our
factories; those who shudder at the oppressive conditions which
employers' unions, taking advantage of unfair social institutions,
are forcing upon working people; those who believe in encouraging labor organizations — unless these may unite to divert
their custom from the establishments that turn human blood

into dividends, both their personal freedom and their property rights are destroyed. For it is everybody's personal right and his property right to trade with whom he pleases."

Contrast of Opposing Views. — Contrasting the two views more pointedly, it appears that the opponents of the boycott more generally rely upon implications inferred from the terms used in stating their propositions. The expressions already referred to furnish evidence of this. They also rely upon precedents of courts and dicta of judges as finally settling the question. Opposed to these statements the advocates use the familiar expressions of individual rights, liberty to do what one wills with his own, and other well-known phrases that are very general, if not abstract. More particularly they insist that new and complex phases of industry make necessary new and different interpretations and applications of rules formerly held to be satisfactory.

Against edicts of courts that boycotts are unlawful, being violative of constitutional rights in protection of life, liberty and property, are opposed the constitutional statements of rights accorded to all citizens of life, liberty and property, rights that cover and protect the boycott. Against precedent based upon past pronouncements of courts are placed new conditions that should not justly be brought within the scope of these precedents. One side says that any person may work "when he will, where he will, for whom he will and at what wages he will," and when an organization is formed for the purpose of preventing any man from exercising these rights, that organization "violates the essential rights of labor." The other side replies that if anyone may work when, where, for whom and at what wages he will, certainly he may work with whom he will. It follows that he may refuse to do any of these things if he so wills. Further, if any organization to prevent the doing as one may will violates any essential right, it must be that an organization that protects laborers in the right to do as they will must be an important protection of an essential right. And, finally, if an organization to protect a right on the part of some violates that right on the part of others, there is in the final outcome a protection rather than a violation of essential rights. Thus the reasoning leads to no conclusion; certainly not to the very positive conclusion that essential rights are being violated instead of protected. And what is true of a person's right to labor is also true of his right to spend. He may spend what he has honestly earned, just as he may spend what he legally possesses, when he will, where he will, for what he will and at any price he will. Any organization to prevent this is in violation of an essential right. But any organization to secure this method of expenditure is in protection of an essential right.

Then, to pass to the final stage, if the right to do what one will be used to secure indirectly another and larger object, there is a new difficulty. For one side says that the exercise of this right results in damage to the other party, the one with whom the working or buying relations are to be established; it is malicious. The other side says that this right of spending is used to further the ends of the spender, namely, to promote the purposes of trade unionism, the securing of better conditions of labor and a better economic life. These ends are both lawful and laudatory. The object is not destructive but constructive. If motive or intent be of any consequence at all in giving legal color to these acts, the motive or intent is that of self-interest, the ultimate securing of those laudable objects sought through organization of labor.

CHAPTER XV

THE BOYCOTT (Continued)

Conclusions of an Exhaustive Study. — A recent study of the boycott: Boycotts and the Labor Struggle; Economic and Legal Aspects, by Dr. H. W. Laidler, has furnished a most exhaustive and timely elaboration of this perplexing subject. From it the following propositions appear.

New Name: Old Practice. — Though the word is comparatively new, the practice is very old. In great variety of forms history reveals it. In modern times consumers' boycotts, employers' boycotts, political boycotts, international boycotts, trade boycotts (in which employers have used against each other the same methods that are under discussion), farmers' boycotts, Abolitionists' boycotts, prohibitionists' boycotts — these and other forms are not unfamiliar. "The working class, in its fight for better and more humane conditions, is not the only element in society which uses its purchasing and selling power to force other groups to grant concessions. The general public resorts to the boycott to force a reduction of monopoly prices; the class conscious capitalist uses it to silence the organs of public opinion; the employer ruthlessly employs it to crush the union spirit among his workmen; the merchant wields it to cut the market from beneath unmanageable competitors; the citizen uses it to place his friends in office; the peoples of one country practice it to gain concessions from other countries or to prevent aggression; labor, business, social, ethical, religious, political, educational associations fashion it to their ends — some for the weal of society, some for its detriment."

Should Boycott be Legally Recognized? — There are social and economic reasons why the boycott should be legally recognized. It is true that it is often used unscrupulously and with blind and misdirected zeal. Yet the difficulties that the laborers have to encounter are real and very great. From his position of advantage the employer in order to break up organizations of labor uses means that are secret, underhanded and unscrupulous. Labor is handicapped heavily when operating individually against employers, whereas the employer has the distinct advantage of wealth and social position. Supplementing this, he forms powerful and often secret employers' organizations, uses secretly the blacklist in direct violation of law, employs secret agencies and detectives to spy out the acts and purposes of employees, secures appointment of private detectives in his own employ as sheriff's deputies with all the authority of the state to back them, influences the press and even the pulpit and, when open violence is resorted to, he calls in the militia and the courts to keep order and protect his rights. The chapter in which this proposition is elaborated is particularly valuable as setting forth many facts not generally known.

If labor is deprived permanently of the use of the boycott, the laborers will be driven to secret practices, always more harmful than those conducted in the open, to political action and to the tactics of the Industrial Workers of the World. If the boycott is legalized, it will be used more sparingly, more and more will it be safeguarded from abuses.

Finally, Laidler concludes: "In view of the effectiveness of the boycott in many trades, in strengthening the hands of labor, and thus, indirectly, in advancing social welfare; in view of the weapons which are constantly being brought into play against the laborer in his struggles, necessitating the use of weapons additional to the strike and the picketing; in view of some of the substitutes which may be resorted to if the boycott is not available; in view of the decreasing likelihood of any great abuse in the employment of the boycott, and the laws on the statute book which take due care of many of the perversions complained of; and in view of the greater number of peaceful settlements which would probably result from its potential use, the writer (Laidler) is in favor of legalizing this weapon. By this he means that neither the injunction nor the civil nor criminal process should be employed against the primary or the secondary boycott, nor against that form of the compound boycott which involves only the threat to injure the business of another by the withdrawal of patronage or labor. He, of course, would not include in this exemption the threat of actual violence to person and property.

"In advocating this legalization, he (Laidler) believes that there will probably be some abuses in the employment of the boycott, as there are in the exercise of every right; that at times the use of this weapon is less effective than that of others at the disposal of labor; but that such abuse and such occasional ineffectiveness do not constitute any sufficient argument for rendering the boycott illegal."

An Answer. — There is abundant reason for agreeing with this position, as stated by Laidler, though to many it will seem advanced or even radical. Its result will be to deprive the employer of some of the privileges he now has under the law and to extend to employees a corresponding advantage. If a greater equality of privilege and advantage be the result, there can be no rational objection, and only on the securing of such a result can be based any argument in favor of the change. As has been so often pointed out, the equalization of rights and privileges often necessarily involves a taking from one to give to another.

The Answer Conditioned. — It seems clear that if the present status of the boycott is to be permanent, it must be clear that the permanency rests squarely upon industrial equality; for the purpose of the law must be to secure such a result. If it is to be changed, the change must be clearly shown to be in the direction of such equality, else there can be no reason for the alteration. For this there is abundant justification found in the familiar maxim that the law adjusts itself to social changes, preserving justice as a constant fact amid the ever-changing phases of social evolution.

A Change Imminent. — That such a change is imminent seems evident. There is inconsistency between the law of strikes and the law of boycotts. Why motive or intent should not be either equally important or equally negligible is difficult to explain on any basis of reason. Clearly the difference rests on an historical foundation. This difference will cease to exist in time, for the retarded development has had its ways smoothed by its forerunner, and will sooner or later catch up.

Is Boycott an Attack on Property Right? — There is one element that is present in reality but is overlooked in that discussion which holds that boycotting is an attack upon a property right for which its owner may claim legal protection. When an enterpriser starts a business he assumes many risks that he cannot shift. The reward offered him by society is large returns in the form of profits, if profits there be; but the responsibility for the losses, if profits there be not. These profits are variable in amount and exceedingly illusive. Naturally the enterpriser does what he can to protect his profits. To do this many business practices have grown up that do not stand the test of morals and have consequently been condemned both in public opinion and in law. Among these risks is that of being able to get and keep a market. This is purely a matter of competition, and many influences are at work to change market conditions, to build up or overthrow one's trade. The right to enter or to refrain from entering into business relations is not open to question. It is fundamental and is not affected by the fact that others join in doing the same. If it is to the interest of one to refrain, it may be to the interest of a hundred or a thousand similarly placed to refrain. If they recognize this interest by consultation, come to the conclusion by agreement and unite in common action, no one of the group has done what, as an individual, he has not a legal right to do. Moreover, if their interests lie to them in refraining from assuming the business relation, they are simply furthering their own welfare, and this is, of course, a worthy motive. That they refrain from the relation cannot be interpreted as a loss to the other party to the case. It is true that such relations are entered into for mutual gain. If one desires the relation for his gain and the other refrains because he does not see it to his interest to assume the relation, it does not mean that there is a loss. It is true that an opportunity for gain cannot be taken advantage of, but that is not a loss. One cannot be said to have suffered a loss of a thousand dollars because he has never found a thousand dollars.

But further, so long as buying and selling are but two views of the same act, an act of voluntary business relation, and so long as the relation must be one of mutual agreement, it is difficult to see where the property right enters in. One's business is of course his property. So, in a sense, may one's labor be called his property. When one offers for sale and another refuses to buy, there is simply a refusal to exchange property for property. When one points out to another or to many others that it is to his interest not to buy, there is again simply the refusal to exchange. When many meet and decide together or agree not to buy, there is concerted refusal to exchange. To interpret

this as a malicious destruction of one's business, which is property, and even to interpret it as an infringement of a property
right is a manifestation of solicitude for one form of property
(a business) at the expense of another form (labor) that is not
easy to justify. The man who goes into business assumes the
risk of failure together with the chances of success. If failure
comes, it is his risk, so long as it comes from the refusal of others
to buy, and is his loss, but it is not a loss for which those who
refuse to be purchasers can be held reponsible. Clearly the
essential difference is in the combination and in the motive.
But it is at just these two points that the opinions show a tendency toward a change of view. Combination and conspiracy
are not so fully synonymous as they have been. Motive is
not so material as it has been. Plenty of *obiter* utterances may be
found to show this change. With the further modification of
these older views will come further modification of the court's
attitude toward the boycott.

A Conclusion. — It seems evident that the law will have to
attach more importance than it has to the contention of those
who insist upon the legality of the labor boycott. It is true that
a person's business is his own only in a restricted sense. Good
will does not belong inseparably to a business. The customers
are independent in their patronage. If in the sale of a business
a certain amount be added to the purchase price as covering
good will, the purchaser certainly has no control over the wishes
of the customers if they do not transfer their patronage to the
new owner. There is no legal recourse for recovery of any part
of the price paid unless the former owner violates some provision
expressly stipulated in the contract. If good will is a part of a
business, then it cannot be said that one's business is entirely
his own. Store, stock-in-trade, fixtures, these are property
that are protected by law. Good will is not subject to protection
of the same kind for it is a personal relation, mutually entered
into, and from which a party may withdraw at will. In strikes,
courts refuse to compel a man to work, avoiding every coercion
of the person. In trade relations they must take the same view.
As one cannot be made to work, so he cannot be compelled to
trade.

The Court's Conclusion. — This line of reasoning can be offset by extracts from the opinions expressed by the courts. That

is to be expected, as they do not accept these general principles. They conclude that the boycott is not socially justifiable and is unlawful. So long as they hold to these views, it will be unlawful and must be recognized as such. But the principles upon which their conclusions rest were laid down in a different age when conditions were unlike those of to-day. As the conditions change, the principles of social welfare change, and as these latter change, the laws change also. But legal changes are much slower than social. In this matter of the boycott the legal changes have not moved far enough in the direction of social changes.

EARLY EXPERIENCE IN BOYCOTTING

At one time in the development of labor's policy the boycott seemed a very hopeful weapon. Between 1880 and 1890 the Knights of Labor, as a nation-wide organization, reached the height of its power. During the same period the American Federation of Labor came into being. Both organizations were enthusiastic and saw labor's millennium just ahead. With eagerness the boycott was seized as a convenient weapon for fighting. While there is no complete information available as to the number of boycotts that were instituted during this period, the facts that have been collected show that its use touched a wide variety of trades, and that the outcome in a large proportion of cases was successful to the workers. Especially favorable did the method of attack prove against the newspapers, publishers, manufacturers of cigars, hats, clothing, stoves, against flour mills, hotels and theaters. A very complete record of boycotting was published by the New York Bureau of Statistics of Labor during the eight years, 1885 to 1892 inclusive. Covering that time records were compiled of 1,352 boycotts. In the first year there were 59. The year following the number increased to 163. The number remained large (hovering around 180) until the last year when it dropped to 88. The results of these boycotts are not fully reported. At first the success appears to have been relatively large. In the year of the largest number the successes appear least numerous. Many cases reported were not followed up to record the outcome. Of 686 cases, the conclusions of which were noted, 461 were reported as succeeding, leaving only about one-third as failures. This should not be taken as of too much weight, as it is possible that those of successful issue were more likely to be reported than the failures. In 1888 the Commissioner of Labor in whose office these facts were compiled was of the opinion that the boycott was losing rather than gaining in its effectiveness. At first it seems to have caught the employers unawares and they did not know how to oppose it. The peculiar persistency with which boycotts were fought did not carry the support of public opinion. Appeals to the courts met with success. The conspiracy law was interpreted by the judges as covering the cases and decisions were rendered against the boycotters. These legal appeals were made with increasing frequency. In one year over one hundred boycott leaders were sentenced to the penitentiary in New York City alone.

Conclusion from Experience. — An analysis of the data of boycotts during the eighties and nineties of the last century shows some interesting conclusions. Of those that were brought to a final termination, from two-thirds to three-fourths were successful, and, generally speaking, the greatest successes came to boycotts against primary necessities. It also appears that "the success of boycotts is likely to be in inverse ratio to their frequency; that those boycotts which do not act effectively within the first few months are much less likely to succeed than those vigorously pushed from the very beginning; also that the causes underlying the boycott are among the determining factors in its success." Further it appears that while boycotts are subject to abuse, such abuse is liable to prove a "boomerang against labor." With its continued use, the abuse tends to become less. The facts of the period indicate also a growing conservatism on the part of unions in the use of the boycott.

Factors Affecting Success of Boycott. — Several factors appear as of leading significance in determining the success of a boycott when no appeal is made to the court for legal interference. The following list is suggested by Laidler: the character of the market for the commodities boycotted; the strength of the boycotting organization; the frequency and regularity with which the article is purchased; the location of the boycotted firm; its capital; nation-wide extent of its trade; the degree of monopoly; the manner in which the unionists concentrate on one firm; the publicity secured; the ease with which the boycotted goods are distinguished; the character of the competition against the firm; the directness of the boycotting attacks; the causes leading to the institution of the boycott; the vigor with which it is pushed at the very outset; and the care used in its inauguration.

An Illustration. — That the boycotts of this period were "carried on in many cases in a most arbitrary, annoying and offensive manner, resulting in an outburst of popular sympathy for the boycotted and of popular indignation against the boycotters" will appear if two cases are described in some detail. One was the case of boycott against a music hall. Theiss was the proprietor and he employed an orchestra of thirteen pieces, with a force of waiters, bartenders and other helpers. His investment was given at $300,000. Among his employees were members of Waiters Union No. 1, the Carl Sahm Club and Bartenders Union No. 1. The demands presented to Theiss were that he discharge the orchestra, who were themselves union musicians, though not of the same union, and employ only members of the Carl Sahm Club, paying union wages; also that all non-union waiters and bartenders be discharged, — this within twenty-four hours, on pain of boycott. Theiss's son-in-law was head bartender and his son was head waiter. The leaders employed fifty men to conduct the boycott, supplying them with refreshment and arranging them in relays. They wore hats with boycott labels on them, passed out posters signed by the boycott committee of the Central Labor Union denouncing Theiss as a foe to labor. At times the crowd attracted in front of the hall was five hundred or more. The police arrested the leaders but the magistrates discharged them. Growing bolder, the men entered the hall, pasted labels on the tables, discolored the frescoed walls, set fire to substances which filled the hall with smoke and offensive odors, and destroyed some of the stage scenery. This continued for fifteen days. Theiss purchased his mineral waters of Shultz. They threatened Shultz till he would not sell to Theiss. Ehret, a brewer, was called on and asked to refuse to sell beer to Theiss and to foreclose a mortgage on his place or be boycotted by the Knights of Labor. At this stage Ehret arranged for a meeting in his office between Theiss and his boycotters. The outcome was that Theiss finally yielded at every point. Then the boycotters said that they had incurred an expense of $1,000 in pushing the boycott, printing circulars, paying the fifty men and other expenses, and that Theiss must pay this amount. He paid it. When taken to court the men were found guilty and sentenced accordingly. "We are told," said the judge in this case, "that it has been the custom to rob in that manner (by the boycott) and that such atrocities have been frequent in our midst."

Another Illustration. — Another case of boycott had quite a different course. A bakery was being operated by a Mrs. Gray and was charged with being non-union. An effort was made to raise wages and unionize. On refusal of Mrs. Gray to meet the demands a boycott was established. The customers were notified of the boycotters' claims, circulars were distributed and pickets were posted. Grocers who purchased her bread were in turn boycotted. The delivery wagons were followed and customers warned or threatened. Large placards were posted: "Boycott Gray's Bakery." Soon the boycotters added to their demands the payment by Mrs. Gray of $2,500, on account of expenses of pushing the boycott. The case received wide publicity through the papers and the general opinion turned in favor of Mrs. Gray. Orders increased and business prospered. The place became famous for the time. Pickets were arrested and fined for obstructing the sidewalks. In addition to the increase in business came checks from "prominent citizens"; "hundreds of letters" of encouragement and checks with large orders for bread to be sent to charitable institutions, till the resources of the establishment were unable to meet the new demands of business. The boycotters were persistent, however, and only continued indictments following arrests put a stop to their activities.

Other Cases. — The Fifth Avenue Hotel was boycotted by the Painters Progressive Union, pickets waylaying public men who were stopping at the hotel and requesting them to go elsewhere as an alternative to being boycotted in business or at the polls. A large brewery was boycotted because the proprietor had a wagon repair shop as a department of his business. A label manufacturing company suddenly saw its employees walk out. Later the managers received a demand for increase in pay, but the places had in the meantime been filled. A few days later two men from the Central Labor Union called, but on hearing that the former employees had left before making any request they went away apparently satisfied. Within a few days the firm was advised by one of its largest customers that it was boycotted and that they were forbidden to buy anything. The firm then discharged the new men and took back the former ones, paying the Central Labor Union fifteen dollars for the expenses of the boycott. An employer was boycotted for the sole reason that his men refused to join a union. In another instance a boycott was resorted to in order to compel two engineers, belonging to a rival organization, to join the union of the boycotters. A passage quoted from a number of the New York Boycotter indicates the spirit of these undertakings. "In boycotting we believe it to be legitimate to strike a man financially, socially or politically. We believe in hitting him where it will hurt the most. We believe in remorselessly crowding him to the wall; but when he is down, instead of striking him, we would lift him up and stand him once more upon his feet." Even with these views the same editorial adds that boycotting should be a last resort because it is such a drastic remedy.

In 1892 the New York Commissioner reports the decrease in the number of boycotts. One reason he assigns is that organized labor has attained a development where it finds it necessary to wield the "potent weapon" with caution. Doubtless the success of indictments in court had its effect also in securing caution. The newer and more radical the union, generally the more readily the boycott was used in its more offensive form, often continuing the boycott after the demands had been granted, and driving the victim out of business as an example to others, or demanding payments of money as a most open form of blackmail.

Effects of Early Experience. — With such a spirit as boycotters manifested during these early years of its general use, it is not to be wondered at that the public mind turned against it, that the employers resorted to every means afforded by law to fight it, and further that judges, impressed with the dangers of its spread, afforded such protection as the elastic conception of conspiracy made possible. From such a beginning the boycott has had a serious time in restoring itself to some degree of respectability even in the minds of those whose sympathies incline them to recognize the broad significance of the fight that laborers are making.

LATER DEVELOPMENTS

With the fuller realization of power on the part of some of the stronger unions, the boycott has come to be somewhat more conservatively handled. Yet once called into use, it becomes a matter of serious fighting. In connection with a strike on the Toledo, Ann Arbor and Northern Michigan Railroad, the strikers through their organization sought to boycott that road by compelling connecting roads to refuse to handle its freight. The matter was taken to the court where an injunction was issued against the union officials. In connection with this litigation Judge Taft wrote one of the strongest opinions against the boycott. The great Pullman strike of 1894 led to another systematic effort to boycott all roads that operated Pullman cars. This effort was made by the American Railway Union, an organization just formed through the leadership of Eugene V. Debs. There was much litigation as well as much lawlessness in this struggle, though the strike itself was more directly responsible for the disturbances.

Two Recent Cases. — Recent years have witnessed two great contests in which the boycott has figured as the leading if not the sole means adopted by the unions to secure their ends. These two are what are known as the Hatters' Boycott and the Buck Stove and Range Boycott. The latter began in 1906. The former was a part of a campaign for a closed shop begun by the Brotherhood of United Hatters of America in 1897. This campaign had been successful in a majority of shops. But when the shop of Daniel Loewe was attacked, he made a firm resistance and the machinery of a well-organized boycotting system was turned against it in 1902. Both of these cases were taken to court and made the cause of a desperate legal fight. Opinions went steadily against the boycotters. The Buck Stove and Range Case assumed the form of a struggle between the company of that name and the American Federation of Labor officials. Injunctions were issued forbidding the continuance of the boycott, the injunction was appealed and sentences that had been pronounced for its violation suspended pending the appeal. The case was finally brought to a settlement in the United States Supreme Court in accordance with which the accused were not required to serve sentence that had been imposed by lower courts nor were the principles in the case authoritatively decided.

The Loewe Case was brought under the Sherman Anti-Trust Act. The final decision of the United States Supreme Court in this case, after many years of trial and appeal, holds the boycotters, the individual members of the local union, individually liable for three times the damages sustained by the Loewe firm.

REASONABLENESS OF PRESENT LEGAL STATUS

Even a cursory examination of the law cannot fail to impress upon one that the boycott is not lawful generally in the United States. This situation arises not so much from statutory enactment directly dealing with boycotting as from the common law and from statutes of a more general nature. In every part of the country the common-law principles are generally the same and are to the effect that "at common law every person has individually, and the public also has collectively, a right to require that the course of trade should be kept free from unreasonable obstruction." Moreover, in at least thirty states there are statutes directed to the prohibition of interference with labor and against intimidation in any form. The tendency to define boycotting in terms of coercion and intimidation easily brings the act within the prohibitions of the statute.

In 1903 Alabama enacted the first state law in the United States in which boycotting is dealt with by name, declaring it to be illegal and subject to fine or imprisonment. The provisions of this statute are very rigid, making it a misdemeanor for any one to have printed or circulated any notice that a boycott "exists or has existed or is contemplated." Colorado, Illinois, Indiana and Texas have also placed anti-boycott laws on their statute books. These laws are similar in their general provisions.

As to the legality of boycotts there can be but one opinion. "As simple strikes are nearly always lawful, so boycotts are nearly always unlawful." Boycott has come to mean generally in law "an unlawful conspiracy." What the law is admits of no discussion from laymen. It is simply a fact, enacted by a legislature or declared by a court and a fact, of course, to be accepted. But what the law ought to be is certainly a topic open to discussion.

It is the question of how the law came to be what it is, and what it should be, that will occupy attention. It seems very doubtful if the law will remain as it is, and further it is even more doubtful whether it should remain so.

Legal Transition. — As already pointed out, the development of the common law of boycott is passing through much the same stages as that of strikes and is influenced by much the same forces. It has been shown how in the earlier days the strike was an unlawful conspiracy, how the broader "rights of man" forced the modification of this view by sheer weight of logic, until the lawfulness of these means is now generally recognized. The legal history of boycott, starting as it has from the same point of "unlawful conspiracy" must follow essentially the same line of development.

The Contrast: Strike and Boycott. — The differences that now exist may be summed up in the statement that the intent is of greater import in the boycott than in the strike. In the boycott "the intent becomes of importance." "The prime question in the law of boycott is that of intent."

This seems to be a distinction that cannot logically be insisted upon. Men may withhold their labor by agreement but they may not withhold their trade. Men may prevail upon their fellow laborers to withhold their labor, may be induced to join in a strike. They may not induce the same fellow laborers to withhold or withdraw their trade. In Massachusetts they jointly withhold their labor to raise wages but may not jointly withhold their trade for the same purpose. In New York they may strike for any reason or for no reason, but may not boycott whatever may be the reason. In other words, in a strike to enforce demands, the purpose is self-help, but a boycott to enforce even the same demands is malicious. Judicial opinions of to-day on the boycott sound so very similar to judicial opinions of two generations ago on the strike that the historical view seems to be the only valid one in explanation of this difference. Organized strikes are not new and the rights and obligations in connection with them have been somewhat adjusted to the "rights of man." Organized boycotts are new, and such rights and obligations as logically belong to them have not yet been properly subordinated to the more fundamental "rights of man." It does not seem possible that any reasoning can endure for long that views the intent in a strike as of itself virtuous and that of a boycott as of itself vicious.

From this point of view it is difficult indeed to follow the logic of Judge Taft's argument on the illegality of boycotts. As Judge Taft himself has later told us, the opinion was written "to explain what was the illegality of the boycott." It has been widely quoted and has been as influential, perhaps, as any opinion written. The opinion recognized ordinary competition as involving chances, and if one suffers from recognized and approved acts of competition, he has no ground for action. If an employer's profits are reduced by a refusal on the part of his workmen to remain in his employ unless wages are increased, the loss arises from the exercise of the workmen's lawful right to work for such wages as they choose, and to get as high a rate as they can. Even if called on to work with material that for any reason is not satisfactory to him as a workman, he may lawfully refuse to work it. The loss sustained by the material man by such a refusal gives no ground for action. In these matters, the opinion further states, what one may do many may combine to do without giving any right of action against those who cause the loss. If the workmen refuse to work at a critical time when the loss would be serious to the employer "and they intentionally inflict such loss to coerce him to come to their terms, they are *bona fide* exercising their lawful rights to dispose of their labor for the purpose of lawful gain." From this line of reasoning, so generally recognized as valid, the transition to the boycott is made in the following words: "But on this common ground of common rights, where every one is lawfully struggling for the mastery, and where losses suffered must be borne, there are losses willfully caused to one by another in the exercise of what otherwise would be a lawful right, from simple motives of malice." "The normal operation of competition in trade is the keeping away or getting away patronage from rivals by inducements offered to the trading public. The normal operation of the right to labor is the securing of better terms by refusing to contract to labor except on such terms."

If the distinction be that between the laborer's right to dispose of his labor and the right to spend his money as a purchaser, it is not a true distinction. Normal competition in trade and normal competition in labor cannot be successfully made to appear as two distinct forms of normal competition, with different laws controlling them. A withholding of labor and a withholding of trade may, and in most instances doubtless do, have the same intent or the same purpose, namely, the general purpose of the laborers to improve their conditions. It seems inevitable that this distinction between strike and boycott should be removed. It is but the simplest element of logic that what men may lawfully do in the disposition of their labor they may do in the disposition of their trade.

CHAPTER XVI

THE CLOSED SHOP

In approaching the topic suggested by the title of this chapter, the Closed Shop, we are face to face with one of the most perplexing questions of unionism. It is extremely difficult to find solid ground on which to stand in making an analysis. Nothing seems fixed. To one side, the matter seems simple enough. So too with the other. But when one seeks to bring the two sides together, the position accepted as determinative by one is most summarily rejected by the other.

An Old Issue. — That the issues involved are not new is evident at once upon a brief historical review. They have, however, assumed a new importance in more recent agitation and this has brought them into greater prominence. The Webbs in their Industrial Democracy assure us that the closed shop began with the beginning of unionism. "Any student of Trade Union annuals knows that the exclusion of non-unionists is coeval with Trade Unionism itself, and that the practice is far more characteristic of its older forms than of any society formed in the present generation. The trade clubs of handicraftsmen in the eighteenth century would have scouted the idea of allowing any man to work at their trade who was not a member of the club."

Instances of efforts to oust the non-union man appear early in American trade union history. The case of the Philadelphia Cordwainers in 1806 was one "not of every day's production" in which certain workmen formed an association and fixed a union wage which they sought to establish with their employer. They further agreed not to work for any employer who kept in his employ workmen who did not belong to this organization and obey its rules and by-laws. In 1809 the Baltimore Cordwainers were brought to trial for compelling an employer to discharge certain men who would not submit to being unionized. In the same year the New York Cordwainers "did unlawfully assemble and meet together and . . . did . . . unjustly and corruptly conspire, combine, confederate and agree together that none of them, the said conspirators . . . would work for any master or person whatsoever . . . who should employ any workman or journeyman . . . not being a member of the said club or combination." In 1815 the Cordwainers of Pittsburgh undertook to enforce the same rule. By 1850 the closed shop policy had been very generally developed in the leading trades. It came to be most strongly insisted upon that all workmen must join the trade association and that no employer should be allowed to retain in his shop any non-member.

A Complex Issue. — The issue is not an easy one to analyze because of its many sides. The lines cannot be drawn so clearly as to enable one to choose between two general propositions of universal application: between a shop open only to union men and a shop in which the employer chooses his own men without being influenced by union officials. Were this the real form of the issue it could become no more than a theoretical question, affording opportunity for endless discussion and never a final conclusion. It is essentially a relative issue, relative to the time, to the nature of the industry, to the disposition of the employer, to the character and degree of skill of the men employed, to the nature of the policies of the unions concerned, both local and national, and to the personnel of their leaders. With all these conditioning facts to consider, it is no wonder that as an issue for discussion it is as far from settlement as ever, and as a policy for adoption it has reached various stages. Thus the question becomes one of "practical exigency in a given time and place," and not primarily one of principle.

Definition of Terms. — Before any conclusive opinion can be formed on the industrial and social consequences of such a rule or policy, the terms must be more clearly defined than they often are in popular discussion. Open shop, closed shop, union shop, mixed shop; all have a meaning that is relative rather than independent and the terms are not used with a uniform meaning.

Early Meaning. — In earlier days the distinction was one made by the workingman himself from his union point of view. A closed shop was one to which the workman was supposed not to go because of strike, lockout, or boycott against the shop. By his own decision it was closed to him as a union workman. The open shop was one in which as a union man he might seek work. The open shop as thus understood was favored of course, while the closed shop was a shop condition in which temporarily at least as a loyal union man he could not work. Since this time the meaning has been practically reversed.

Employers' Definitions. — When one looks for accurate definition, adapted to the present time, a variety of usage appears. From the employer's point of view there exists what may be called a set of definitions, each term having its separate meaning. In a paper presented before the American Economic Association in 1904 there appears a four-fold group of terms, each presenting a situation and each given a name, as the employer sees the situation.

First, there is the union closed shop. This situation indicates a shop in which union conditions prevail and none but union men are employed. Second, there is the employers' closed shop; a shop closed by the employer to union men. Third, the nominal open shop (called also the "so-called open shop"). Here there is nominal freedom from discrimination. The employer is not supposed to discriminate against union men nor do the union employees, presumably, seek to intimidate or coerce the non-union workmen. Fourth, the true open shop; a shop in which the above suppositions are realized in fact; a shop "where the rights of the individual are respected, where reward is measured by merit and where law and order prevail." That such a distinction is logical, will not be denied. Yet it is too cumbersome for practical uses. As the issue now exists there appears no place for such definitions.

Workers' Definition. — On the unionist's side there is no serious attempt at such elaborate definition. The idea of what is wanted is sufficiently clear and practical to serve as a goal and in a very businesslike way the necessary steps leading to it are taken. There are, as the unionist sees it, but two conditions and so but two terms are needed. The closed shop: one closed to the dangerous rivalry of the non-union workman; the open shop: one in which the employer is left free to work out in practice any application of non-unionism that he may desire.

The "Union Shop" — To a union leader, however, is due

the credit of making real a third term in the laborer's vocabulary. It is the union shop. As this unionist, Mr. Henry White, former Secretary of the United Garment Workers, views the situation the open shop is one in which the conditions of work are set by the employer after trying conclusions with the union and establishing his independence. The closed shop is one in which terms of work are made by union officials after a strike or show of force to which the employer has yielded. A union shop, unlike either of the two, is one in which the union workmen have demonstrated to the employer their superior efficiency and thus made themselves the voluntary choice of the employer. While the open and the closed shop indicate compulsion, the union shop grows out of mutual advantage. The term union shop is "made to apply to places where only union members are employed without the employer's agreeing to follow this course, while in the closed shop the employer expressly agrees to exclude non-unionists."

In defending this conception of the union shop this writer says:

"There is a vital difference between being forced to give up a right, and deciding to suspend its exercise for practical reasons. This distinction may seem to be finely drawn, yet some of the largest disputes have taken place because of neglecting it. Many an employer will readily accommodate himself to a situation and employ only union men, but he will strongly protest against being bound by contract to do so. Even should he employ union men exclusively, he may reserve the right to employ others if he so desires. And so with the union workmen. When unable to help themselves, they will work with non-members; but they will resist an attempt to make them agree to do so at all times. The method by which the open or closed shop is upheld is the real question. There is no difficulty as to principle, if the acknowledged rights of either side are respected. The one condition that the union can justly insist upon is that there shall be no discrimination against its members, and that the employees shall be treated with through their representatives. The natural disadvantage of the laborer entitles him to that consideration, and public opinion sustains him to that extent. . . . Undoubtedly the employer would be inclined to discriminate, but that is a situation the union must meet by better organization. The employer could allege also on the same grounds that, by employing union men, he would lose control of his shop, and workmanship would deteriorate. The task of each side is to prevent the other from making unfair use of its power, not to seek to protect itself from oppression by curtailing the liberty of the other."

This distinction between a union shop on the one hand and a closed shop and an open shop on the other has been clearly made by Professor Commons. First he insists that the confusion of terms is due to the adoption of different points of view. The employer sees it from the side of the contract or the trade agreement with his men. It is legal or contractual. On the other side, the union sees the actual situation as it exists in the shop. With these facts in mind Professor Commons presented to the American Economic Association, in 1904, a definite distinction in the following words:

"It is evident that with these different points of view it is difficult to reach an understanding. Clearness would be promoted by adopting a use of terms which would bring out the above distinctions as they are found in practice. In doing so the closed shop would be viewed from the side of the contract, and would be designated as one which is closed against the non-unionist by a formal agreement with the union; the open shop as one, where, as far as the agreement is concerned, the employer is free to hire union or non-union men; the union shop as one where, irrespective of the agreement, the employer, as a matter of fact, has only union men. Thus an open shop, according to agreement, might in practice be a union shop, a mixed-shop or even a non-union shop. The closed shop would, of course, be a union shop, but the union shop might be either closed or open."

The Definitions do Not Define. — With these statements it will be clear that in current discussion the open shop is one open by the employer to the employment of anyone whom he may choose to hire. The closed shop is one which the unions have by the force of their organization closed to the employment of non-union men. The union shop is one in which, by mutual agreement and interest, unionists are preferred above non-union workmen.

Even so simple a terminology does not clear up much of the

issue. Instead, it perhaps confuses some phases of it. In this connection it must be noticed that the employers in presenting their side of the question have very clearly outmaneuvered the workingmen in the choice of terms. The unions have usually had the advantage of public sympathy, aroused to no small degree by the terms used. Such words as liberty, freedom, Americanism always have an appealing force. In this controversy the employers have seized upon these words. "The closed shop is Un-American!" This is a moving statement. "The open shop preserves the liberties of the American workman!" This is also appealing. In defending the open-shop policy a well-known employer proclaims boldly: "We will stand up for stalwart Americanism wherever we see it. When we do not see it we will endeavor to create it." Bascom emphasizes this when he says that the words open and closed "cast a deceptive light on the controversy between labor and capital." They suggest "liberty" *versus* "tyranny." "If we substitute for them the far more descriptive phrase, 'an unorganized as opposed to an organized shop,' the illusion disappears and we are thrown back on the old problem."

Employers' Description of Situation. — The deception is further revealed if some evidence is introduced as to the real conditions that prevail under cover of these various terms. To allow the employer to tell his story we learn the real situation as he sees it. Before the Industrial Relations Commission an employer active in his insistence upon the open shop referred to the "free, unfettered, non-union worker" in glowing terms. "Every employee has a right to be free to work when he will, for any employer and for such a wage as the two, standing face to face, may agree upon. The independent, non-union workman does not strike or boycott. He goes willingly to his work, and, free from interference, earns more than the union worker. Such a man is a good worker, a good citizen, and a true son of the Republic."

The employers have no doubts in their own minds as to what will be the inevitable outcome of allowing the union men to have any influence over the selecting of the workmen. It means in the end a closed shop. They charge the union men with bad faith in carrying out any understanding that may have been reached. The beginning of the difficulty, as it is pointed out, is in the tacit recognition of the union with the admission of the union men to employment. These men have their officers who represent them in making the wage bargain. They become spokesmen for the men when differences arise. Even when the situation develops no further than this, the non-union men become dissatisfied if not discouraged. Many of them do not stay. But developments go further than this. The union men become active in adopting policies and attitudes toward their rivals that in the end force the non-union men to leave. They are practically driven out as the result of the treatment that they receive from their fellow workmen. In cases where there may be no open violence, there are petty annoyances, minor persecutions and social ostracism that after a while make life so miserable that the men are glad to escape to a new job. The impression of the employer is very distinct that a shop cannot remain "open" if there is any considerable proportion of union men in his employ, especially if these men are of the aggressive type. It may be summed up in the words of a representative employer: "From my experience in manufacturing, I believe there is practically no difference between the closed shop and the nominally open shop. The non-union man stands no show in the nominally open shop."

A Representative Employer. — Stated somewhat at length, as it was elaborated in the American Economic Association discussion of 1904, the opinion of a representative employer runs as follows:

"The open shop, open to both classes of employees, is essentially and practically unstable. As usually found to-day (the so-called open shop) means, in the end, unless organized labor is met with an equally well organized and powerful employers' association, a 'closed shop.' The chief reason for this condition seems to arise from the inability or unwillingness of union men to abide by the implied contract which exists, or should exist, in such a shop, the terms of which are that the employer shall make no discrimination between union and non-union men; shall impose no objection to the men joining the union and shall in no way interfere with the reasonable exercise of the functions of the union or its officers, and that the union or union men shall do nothing to in any way interfere with, or restrict, the free initiative of the non-union man. There is, no doubt, ground for argument that certain employers fail equally in their recognition and observance of this contract. In the so-called open shop a most important difficulty appears to be that it tacitly admits union men and that, to a certain extent, recognition is thereby given the union and union officers who become spokesmen for the men in the case of misunderstandings which may arise. . . . Even though no more 'recognition' is accorded than at first suggested, the effect upon the non-union man is discouraging, and the actual results are that in an open shop, as is usually found where the unions are even fairly well represented, the non-union man does not stay. An employer writes: 'From my experience in manufacturing in Chicago, I believe there is practically no difference between the closed shop and nominally open shop. The non-union man stands no show in the nominally open shop. His life is made so miserable, if not by violence, by small annoying persecutions and by social ostracism that he will not stay. This class of persecution is so skillfully carried out that, in the majority of cases, the employer cannot locate or prevent it. The agreement idea is utterly worthless. So long as the agreement operates in favor of the union, everything goes along smoothly, but the moment an attempt is made to construe any question so as to give the manufacturer protection, the union official at once says that he cannot control his men. The only way a manufacturer can secure his rights under an agreement is by facing a strike. A strike may not come; it is an ever present possibility, and the employer, nine times out of ten, will put up with rank injustice rather than take the risk. The ideal condition would be the open shop where union and non-union men could work peaceably and pleasantly side by side. There is no question but that a great many skilled workmen belong to the union and it would be most desirable to be able to draw from that body without feeling practically certain that it would lead, sooner or later, to a closed shop. While in any well regulated, fairly well managed shop, union men and non-union men can work amicably side by side, if let alone, the moment there comes a preponderance of union men, the pressure of union officers is so great that the old story of persecution and annoyance begins. I am a firm believer in grievances of any kind among the men being listened to, corrected promptly and fairly, and in the vast majority of shops

I have no doubt that this would always be done. The trouble comes from a grievance that is manufactured outside of your shop and is forced upon the men against their will by leaders who have to make a showing of some kind in order to hold their positions. I can conceive of ideal conditions with the union, officered by intelligent, conservative and honest leaders, when the terrible annoyances that now exist would be done away with, but the time certainly has not come for this yet.'"

Unionists' Description of Situation. — When the union man speaks, a very different situation is revealed. As they see it, it is the employer that does not act in good faith. It is frequent among open shop rules to find the assertion that there shall be no discrimination for or against any workman on account of membership or non-membership in any organization. The employer is to have full power to hire or discharge as he sees fit; membership in a labor union to have no influence in either hiring or discharging. The unionist charges the employer with ignoring such agreements. "The employers promised not to discriminate, but they had no sooner begun to adopt the open shop than we saw the wholesale discharge of union men."

Employers declare openly that they must deal with the workman individually without giving reasons for what they may do and restrained by no conditions. This would pave the way for doing what the unionists charge. Another employer is frank enough to say: "When unions are weak I would make individual contracts with non-unionists who were often willing to start at almost any wage. I can then play these men against the union, eventually break the contract, and defy the union. If the union would permit us to employ non-union men we would do so, and the union could demand anything it chose. It could demand ten dollars a day if it wanted to. A year or so ago . . . I had 297 union men. I have succeeded in eliminating all but six, and I hope before long to have, not an open shop, but a closed shop — closed to the union."

In one instance there had been formed The Merchants', Manufacturers' and Employers' Association which began to use its organized influence against the growing strength of the unions. This they were to accomplish by the establishment of the open shop. All employees were to be dealt with as individuals. No employee was to be dealt with through a union official, though any man might belong to a union if he so desired. This situation appeared to the editor of a labor paper as so inconsistent that the wording of a part of the article can best set forth his idea. "This open shop," he writes, "is closed absolutely to the unions. It is not closed to the individuals who individually belong to the unions, but it is closed to their unionism, and it is closed to them except in their individual and therefore non-union capacity. And this prohibition of collective bargaining to the wage earners is enforced by a collective bargain of the wage payers. This denial of organization is made by an organization. This demand that the workmen make each his separate bargain is made by employers who have first bound themselves and each other to a collective bargain. The one class organizes to prevent the other class from organizing — or from being dealt with as an organization, if it does. And the class organization of the employers appoints its agents to refuse to receive any agents of the employees, and to deal with them only separately, without agents. Unions can do anything but function."

To sum the matter up: The employer says that unless the unions concede the open shop it will mean their destruction. The unionist says that if they do concede the open shop unionism is doomed.

Necessary Qualifications: Suspicion. — Neither of these groups of statements must be taken as universally or even generally true. There are employers who live up scrupulously to their shop agreements. Likewise there are unions that strictly observe the terms of their contract and are conspicuously fair to the non-members. Yes, says the employer, they are fair because temporarily it is to their advantage. Let conditions become less favorable and it will be seen how sincere they are. So the employee says of the employer. They may observe scrupulously the agreement not to discriminate, but let it appear that there is any advantage to result from a less scrupulous observance and there will be a change. This is one of the essential points involved. There is mutual suspicion. Each side is confident that it is entirely in the right and cannot bring itself to believe that there is any genuine sincerity in the opposite camp. No broad statement can be made that will be universally true, in regard to the various charges and counter-charges.

They all have at best but limited application. Yet there is much ground for believing that in the hands of an employer with determination and a self-interest to serve an open shop need have no union men at all in it. It is fittingly expressed in the summary statement, "An open shop can only mean one in which those who enter and those who leave do so at the suggestion of the employer. Its freedom is the freedom of the man who keeps it."

Likewise it is beyond question that in well-authenticated instances a well-organized union has succeeded in driving away all workmen who were not members. This in turn makes it a shop in which those who enter and those who leave do so at the suggestion of the union officials. Its freedom becomes the freedom of the union men who work in it.

Employers' Words and Deeds. — The statements made by many employers when set down beside their acts tend to reënforce the suspicions of the workmen. It is not always clear whether the employer is entirely sincere in what he says. Either he is sincerely interested in the personal rights of the employee and genuinely believes that it is his duty to protect them, or he uses the expressions that carry such a defense as a cloak to conceal the working out of his own business interests. When it is the one and when the other, it is by no means easy to say. Very plausible language is sometimes used that carries much weight until placed side by side with the actions of the user. "We must recognize the good which is in labor unions as well as the evil," writes a leading employer. "We must not condemn all the labor unions for the offences of some of them." "The employer," he adds, "who would like to strike down all the labor unions indiscriminately is blind to his own interests as well as faithless to his duty to the general public." This employer was at the time president of the National Association of Manufacturers and the Industrial Alliance, the latter association especially known in union circles as a most uncompromising foe of organized labor.

Before the Industrial Relations Commission an employer who is one of the most rhetorical advocates of the open shop as well as one of the most strenuous fighters for it, was asked about discriminations and grievances arising because of them in his shop. He replied that committees of workmen were allowed in his open shop. "If the men make out a good case, we try to redress it. If it is a poor case, we try to argue them out of it." On being asked who makes the final decision as to whether the case is a good one, he replied, "We decide." Some of his questioners expressed a doubt as to whether the workers were properly safeguarded under such a system. There were no such doubts in the mind of the witness. "Why," he replied, "the interests of both sides are safeguarded, aren't they? If the employee doesn't like the adjustment, he can quit."

Importance of " Principle." — It should not be inferred that the employers are always openly insincere. The difficulty lies deeper than that. The error lies in his supposition that there is a "principle" involved, a fundamental obligation that he owes in the name of society to the man who seeks work but does not join a union. He does not think the thing through. His own business interests, his own profits, must be protected. A union leader has tersely expressed this truth in the following words, applicable alike to both parties: "What is called 'principle' is sometimes another name for 'self-interest.' When the employer proclaims the open shop as a principle, it is often not so much the ethical question involved that he has in mind, as the opportunity it gives him for increasing his profits; and it must be confessed that, when workmen raise the question of the closed shop, what they have usually in view is the means it affords them to increase wages. The principle at issue, therefore, is mostly a matter of larger profits and higher wages, but it is discussed, on either side, as though it involved something divine. When the employer finds that he is able to enforce the open shop, he suddenly becomes aware that there is a 'principle' at stake, and that if he were to recognize the closed shop his business would become subordinate to the union. Likewise, unionists discover, when able to enforce their demands, that if they were to tolerate the open shop it would lead to the union's destruction. . . . By repeatedly asserting a proposition as a principle, one may become so imbued with its ethical importance as to be confident that unless it be acquiesced in dire consequences must follow. This is the habit of mind that both employers and workmen are rapidly getting into over the controversy."

Opposition to Unionism. — To many employers their opposition to the closed shop lies not alone in the objection to eliminating the non-union man. It goes further into opposition to unionism itself. To them arguments against the closed shop include all the charges that are to be brought against unionism. To such employers the demand for the closed shop presents an array of dangers that becomes to him very formidable. The platform of the National Association of Manufacturers calls, as a first issue, for the open shop, followed by the demand for no boycott, no sympathetic strike, no sacrifice of the independent workman to the labor union, no compulsory use of the union label. At its 1915 convention it endorsed the following resolution: "Resolved that the N. A. M. in convention assembled does again reaffirm its condemnation and opposition to the closed shop and of every form of closed shop agreement and that we again pledge our unalterable adherence to the principle of industrial freedom as exemplified by the open shop."

In an agreement made in 1903 between the Bridge and Structural Iron Workers and two organizations of employers, the National Association of Manufacturers and the Structural Steel Erectors' Association, it was required of the workman that there should be no union control over the appointment or the work of the foremen; no sympathetic strike; no outside persons to interfere with workmen during working hours; that the employer should have full power to hire or discharge as he should see fit; membership in a labor union to have no influence in either hiring or discharging; that there should be no interference with laborers while loading or unloading materials; and that employees were to be at liberty to cease work at any time.

Unionists' Defense of Closed Shop. — To all of these various charges against unionism the leaders reply briefly but positively — not so. But their attitude is not solely one of denial of false charges. The unionist has a positive defense for his closed-shop policy that is to him both clear and convincing. It rests upon the same general propositions that he relies upon for all his defenses. It is a part of union policy and, as a means to an end, is justifiable. It is a device. As the employer so openly poses as the friend of the non-union laborer, so the unionist insists that he is "fighting the battles of all labor." The laborer who does not join the union places himself in a situation where the employer is able to exploit him. Unless organization is maintained all labor is liable to exploitation. The interests of the laborers are the aims of the unions, and those who join secure benefits not only to themselves but to all laborers. While the persistence of many in remaining outside the ranks of the unionists appears to be the exercise of a personal right, yet the earnest unionist cannot admit the right of any of them to place personal interest above the group welfare. So aggravated do they become that they often express sentiments that do not reveal a very tender feeling toward the non-union man. Yet no one can be justified in supposing that the advocacy of the closed shop is merely an unreasoned prejudice against the non-unionist. If the non-unionist cannot see his own needs then he should be made to see them and labor should be denied to him until he can see himself as having interests with all laborers. This seems very rational to the man who sees "labor's cause" clearly.

Placing the matter upon the clear grounds of competition, President Gompers argues that the union man does not deny the non-union man the right to work. He does, however, seek contracts to supply the employer with labor wherever it is possible. This is based on the belief that in the long run the best interests of all laborers are served in this way. "We hold," it is argued, "that it is morally wrong under modern conditions for a man to remain outside the union in his trade. If he does so it is his legal right, but the union should have the right to treat him as a competitor."

Teaching of Experience. — Again, experience has convinced many leaders that the only alternative to what the unions ask, a shop closed to the non-unionist, is in practice a shop closed to the unionist. When they make up their minds to this, their course is clear; the shops must be closed by them rather than to them. Somewhat rhetorically the President of the American Federation of Labor declares: "As the immortal Lincoln said, 'This country cannot long remain half free and half slave,' so say we that any establishment cannot long remain or be successfully operated part union and part non-union."

In much the same line it is urged that in view of the long fight that labor has had in establishing union standards of wages and hours of labor it must be insisted, "that if the hours of labor are eight and the wages are two dollars a day, no one should be allowed, if we can help it without violence, to sell his labor below the scale or agree to work longer."

Estimate of Opposing Opinions and Policies. — In such a complex situation with so divergent and conflicting views, the truth cannot be found at either extreme. If the unionists are seeking to close all workshops to non-members of their unions for the purpose of dictating absolutely to the employers and dominating the industry through a monopoly advantage, seeking always and solely their own interests as laborers, then there can be no two views about it. They are wrong. Such a policy cannot be tolerated consistently with social welfare. And if, on the other hand, employers are seeking to close all shops to unionists, so that they, in fact, can dictate absolutely to the employees and dominate the labor market, making it "favorable" to themselves, again there can be no two views about such a situation. The employers are wrong. Society cannot tolerate such a policy with any degree of safety to itself. The policy of "union smashing" is as anti-social and as Un-American as the policy of which the unions are accused. When each side sees so clearly the evil in the position of the other and yet denies so stoutly that its own position is wrong, the truth cannot lie with either.

It must be emphasized that there is no general proposition to be laid down as a practical working rule. In some instances there is one set of forces that seem to control and in other cases other factors dominate. In different trades developments have been different. There are trades in which it would be held disgraceful for a man to ask for employment for himself. The Industrial Commission says that among hatters a man looking for employment must approach a journeyman who is already employed, and be introduced by him to the foreman as a man of the trade "on turn" and desiring to be "shopped." This is an ancient custom, antedating any general organization of the hatters; but it is sanctioned by the existing union, and any foreman who hires a man in violation of it is liable to a fine of twenty-five dollars. There are other trades, however, in which it would be regarded as unmanly to seek employment through another instead of asking for it oneself.

Conflicting Experiences. — In some of these instances an understanding has been reached that appears to be satisfactory to both sides. Such an adjustment need not be called to question. When either side gains any marked advantage and begins selfishly to exploit it a reaction immediately sets in. The steel workers were taught a severe lesson when they sought to dominate the steel mills of the country, as one may learn from Fitch's account in The Steel Workers. The employers in this industry, now in full control of their labor, may wisely profit by the warning that is sounded in this same story by Mr. Fitch. There is reason in the statement made by one of the most farsighted leaders when he says: "The management of most of the non-union plants to-day are unwittingly doing their best to force their employees into the unions. The conditions in these places are usually a ten-hour day, wages slightly lower than the union scale, time and a quarter for overtime, and straight time for Sundays and holidays. These conditions alone furnish the organizers with all the necessary ammunition."

On the other hand, there is the experience, by no means exceptional, of the employer who has recognized the reasonableness of union control and does not seek to root it out. Some of these have discovered that the labor question is really less troublesome under the organized shop than when it is unorganized. In the former the men have become confident that the employer is not going to take advantage of them, and so the leaders join him in holding the men in line with proper standards. In such a situation it has developed that the continual fighting of the employer, so common in the unorganized shop, has given way to steady coöperation. This may be explained as growing out of the fact that the men know that the dismissal of one union man will be followed by the employment of another. Consequently they do not inquire so carefully into the reasons as they would if they believed that a dismissal of a union man would mean the employment of a non-union man in his place.

John Mitchell with his clear insight into the various phases of the labor movement views the situation with confidence so far as the future is concerned. "With the rapid extension of trade unions," he says, "the tendency is toward the growth of compulsory membership in them, and the time will doubtless come when this compulsion will be as general and will be considered as little of a grievance as the compulsory attendance of children at school."

Conflicting Principles: One View. — It has been said that the issues cannot be determined on a basis of any broadly stated universal principle. Nor are the issues the same regardless of industry, trade, or locality. Yet it must not be understood that no fundamental tests are to be used at all. Here two somewhat antagonistic principles appear. The first may be expressed by reference to a leading authority. Carroll D. Wright in arbitrating an agreement in the anthracite coal industry declared: "There can be no doubt that the employer has a perfect right to employ and discharge men in accordance with the conditions of his industry; that he is not obliged to give any cause for discharge. . . . This right to discharge must be maintained. Any other view of the case . . . would compel employers to employ men whether they had work for them or not, and whether the men were competent or not, and would thus stagnate business and work to the injury of all other employers."

In accord with this same view, Section IX of the award of the Anthracite Coal Strike Commission read, "no person shall be refused employment, or in any way discriminated against, on account of membership or non-membership in any labor organization; and there shall be no discrimination against, or interference with, an employee who is not a member of any labor organization by members of such organization." Such expressions seek to adjust the issues on the basis of an individualistic philosophy. It has a familiar sound and an appealing force.

Another View.— Opposed to it are the views of others equally sincere and equally disinterested. Mr. John Graham Brooks voices them in the following terms: "Employers are going to the tilt in the name of 'liberty,' but organization on both sides has introduced something so like a revolution that the truth is, we do not know what liberty means as applied to the new situation. It has still, in its applications, very largely to be worked out. If, for example, the closed shop brought about without any violence and with the consent of the employer, as in some of the cigar factories, results in a good living wage with eight hours and improved conditions, and the entire exclusion of children; while outside the union there rages a destructive competition and many children employed, is it not grotesque to make words like liberty and Americanism synonymous with that kind of haphazard competition? Liberty is not adequately defined in terms of the employers' pecuniary interest. It also has social connotations which we are only beginning to learn."

Professor Seligman emphasized this principle by making it the theme of a Presidential Address before the American Economic Association in 1903. In reply to possible objections against reiterating this "thrice told tale" he insists that we are wrong in that "we grasp the form but not the substance. We think that we appreciate the social basis of economic law, but in reality our appreciation is fragmentary. We do the theory lip-service but not brain homage."

Speaking directly to the trade-union problem and the open shop, he said:

"While there is indeed only too much truth in the contention that many of our unions are steering perilously close to the rocks of monopoly and extortion, the problem cannot be solved simply by emphasizing the right of the individual laborer. The right of the individual to work is, indeed, as Turgot told us over a century ago, a sacred and imprescriptible right; but the conditions under which this right is to be exercised are by no means a matter of mere individual discretion and of social unconcern. We are beginning to see that the securest guarantee of liberty is the social sanction — that true and permanent freedom is at bottom an outgrowth of the social forces, and that individual bargaining results in a mere empty husk of freedom. Liberty — to quote Carlyle again — is a divine thing; the liberty to die by starvation is not so divine. If this is true, then the real sacredness and imprescriptibility attach to that wise and collective action which will secure a higher and more effective liberty for the members of the group, and which it goes without saying must be so devised as not to close the door of opportunity to either the unfortunate or the peculiarly gifted. To magnify the individual at the expense of the social group is to close our eyes to the real forces that have elaborated modern liberty and modern democracy, not in the backwoods of a frontier community but in the busy marts of commerce and the complex home of industry."

These two sets of views, each expressed by recognized authority, cannot easily be set aside. Yet it is not easy to reconcile them. Individual interest and social interest, individual right and social right, are not in all cases the same thing. They often are in conflict. In this particular case, the antagonism is clear. There are three cases of individual rights, those of the employer, the union workman and the non-union man. They are in conflict. The case calls for an adjustment. The rights must be modified, and the modification must be made in accordance with some correct principle. The determination of this principle lies at the bottom of the solution of this practical difficulty.

A Determining Factor. — Even in face of this difference, there is a determining factor. It must be admitted that the whole issue is really one of means, not of end. Whether or not shops should be organized, thoroughly unionized, closed to all who are not unionists, depends upon the purpose, upon the relation of this fact to other facts of the union movement. It is so directly related to collective bargaining that in a fuller analysis it becomes a question of maintenance of this collective activity. This is discussed more fully elsewhere and here the present topic leads so directly to it that the real issue loses itself in the larger question. Professor Ross has expressed the relation vividly when he said: "It seems to me so important that the sellers of labor should equalize themselves in bargaining power with the buyers of labor and therewith command for their labor its true market worth, that if you can show me that the closed shop is essential to such a condition, I approve of the closed shop. . . . If in many cases and in many trades it is impossible for labor successfully to carry through the collective bargain principle without the closed shop, as it seems to be, what hollow mockery it is for us to approve the purpose of labor organizations and yet deny them the use of the only legitimate means by which they can fulfill that purpose."

CHAPTER XVII

THE CLOSED SHOP (Continued)

LEGALITY OF CLOSED SHOP

What shall be said of the legality of the closed shop? If a contract is entered into between an employer and his men agreeing that none but union labor shall be employed, is that contract valid? There is some basis for a conclusion on this question, though not sufficient to make such conclusion final.

In a closed-shop contract that led to a trial in the Massachusetts court (Berry *vs.* Donovan, 74 N. E. 603) it had been definitely agreed that the employer would hire only members of the union in good standing and further that he would not retain in his employ any worker after receiving notice from the union that such worker was objectionable to the union, whether such objection was based on the worker's being in arrears for dues, disobedient to the rules or laws of the union, or for any other cause.

In accordance with this agreement a workman was discharged who had been in this employ for nearly four years. He brought suit for damages on the ground that the agreement had injured him by bringing about his discharge when it would not have occurred otherwise. While the term of employment was not for a fixed time, yet it appeared to the court that the agreement authorized the union "to interfere and deprive any workman of his employment for no reason whatever, in the arbitrary exercise of its power." With these two points in mind the court was of the opinion that "whatever the contracting parties may do if no one but themselves is concerned, it is evident that, as against the workman, a contract of this kind does not of itself justify interference with his employment by a third person who made the contract with his employer." It seemed that the motive was one to injure and so damages were awarded. The decision rested solely upon the fact that the injured person had been in the employment for about four years. What would have been the law of the case if it had been brought by one seeking employment and unable to secure it because of the agreement, is a point that is not discussed.

In the New York courts the question came up in a different form, somewhat more satisfactory for the discussion of the general principles involved. The parties had agreed that no employee should be allowed to work for longer than four weeks without becoming a member of the union. The court argued that public policy and the interests of society favor the utmost freedom in the citizen to pursue his lawful calling or trade. If a combination of workingmen interfered with the fulfillment of this purpose through contracts with employers, coercing other workingmen to become members of the organization, such action militates against the principle of public policy which prohibits monopoly and special privileges. "It would tend to deprive the public of the services of men in useful employments and capacities. It would impoverish and crush a citizen for no reason connected in the slightest degree with the advancement of wages or the maintenance of the rate." Concluding, the court says: "While it may be true that the contract was entered into, on the part of the (employers), with the object of avoiding disputes and conflicts with the workingmen's organization, that feature and such an intention cannot aid the defence, nor legalize a plan of compelling workingmen not in affiliation with the organization to join it, at the peril of being deprived of their employment and of the means of making a livelihood." (Curran *vs.* Galen, 46 N. E. 297.)

Later another case came to the same court. The agreement was a very elaborate one, as will be seen from the following abstract taken from the opinion of the court (Jacobs *vs.* Cohen, 76 N. E. 5): "The contract is in substance as follows: The defendants were the party of the first part; their own employees, 'by Barnard Kaplan, their representative and attorney in fact,' party of the second part; and the Protective Coat Tailors' and Pressers' Union, Local No. 55, of the United Garment Workers of America, a voluntary association organized by the parties of the second part, acting 'through Barnard Kaplan, its secretary,' party of the third part. It consists chiefly of restrictive stipulations against the employers, who agree to employ the persons already in their employment . . . each in his own capacity and for no other work than that he was engaged for,' during the period of one year. After fixing the number of working hours per week, it was agreed that ' under no circumstances shall work be carried on by the parties of the first and second part at any other hours than herein specified without a written consent of the party of the third part, executed by its duly authorized officer.' It was further agreed 'that the party of the first part shall not employ any help whatsoever other than those belonging to and who are members of the party of the third part and in good standing and who conform to the rules and regulations of the said party of the third part; and the said party of the first part shall cease to employ any one and all those employees who are not in good standing and who do not conform to and comply with the rules and regulations of said party of the third part, upon being notified to that effect by its duly credentialed representatives. The party of the first part hereby agrees to abide by the rules and regulations of the party of the third part, as known in the trade, and to permit and allow representatives of said party of the third part to enter their shop or shops at any and all hours of the day and night for the purpose of inspection and enforcement of the terms of this contract, as well as all the rules and regulations herein referred to. The party of the first part shall not engage any help whatsoever, even those who are members of the party of the third part, without their first having produced a pass card duly executed and signed by the authorized business agent of the party of the third part, said card to show that the bearer thereof is a member in good standing of the party of the third part and that he has complied with the rules and regulations thereof in force at that time. The party of the first part shall not employ more than one helper to every two operators, or one helper to two basters, and under no consideration to employ any apprentices.' The parties of the second part also agreed not to employ apprentices and to abide by the rules and regulations of the party of the third part. 'In the event of any one of the parties of the second part not remaining and continuing during the entire period of this contract in good standing, or does not in all respects conform with the rules and regulations of the party of the third part, then the party of the first part shall cease to employ such employee whoever he may be. . . . That the parties of the second part may quit work during a so-called "sympathetic strike," provided no new demands are made by them. Such quitting of work on their part shall in no way affect the validity of this agreement or suspend its operation.' A minimum scale of wages was agreed upon, and finally the party of the first part agreed to deposit 'and hereby does deposit with the party of the third part a promissory note in the sum of two hundred dollars . . . as security for the faithful performance by the party of the first part of all the covenants and conditions herein contained . . . as liquidated and ascertained damages upon the commission of any breach or violation of any of the covenants herein above set forth on the part of the party of the first part. . . .' The only stipulation on the part of the union was that it would 'furnish any and all help it may have on its application books' which it was to keep for the benefit of the other parties without charge of any kind to any person."

In this instance the court held that the agreement was not unlawful. It was voluntarily entered into by the employers. If the employers chose to enter into such an agreement they were free to do so. It seemed to the court that the employers had come to be released from an agreement into which they had voluntarily entered with the expectation of profit to themselves. If they regarded it as beneficial to themselves "does it lie in their mouths now to urge its illegality?" The view of public policy seems to have changed. "That, incidentally, it might result in the discharge of some of those employed, for failure to come into affiliation with their fellow workmen's organization, or that it might prevent others from being engaged upon the work, is neither something of which the employers may complain, nor something with which public policy is concerned."

Other cases have been brought to the courts but these do not set forth so clearly the principles involved. In an Illinois case (O'Brien vs. People, 75 N. E. 108), the employers had refused to sign a closed-shop agreement and the employees had gone on strike to compel them to sign. Such an act the courts would not uphold. It was coercive and unlawful, violative of the legal right of the employer, and it was "unjust and oppressive as to those who did not belong to the labor organizations." In Massachusetts an employer had posted a set of open-shop rules that were to go into effect at a stated time. (Reynolds *vs.* Davis, 84 N. E. 457.) A strike was called to prevent the rules being put into effect. The legality of such a strike was questioned before the court. To the court the purpose seemed to be to close the shop arbitrarily to all workmen not members of the union, "not because such workmen were personally objectionable in any particular, nor because there was not work enough for all the members of the union if non-union men were employed, but to compel all workmen to join the union for the purpose of creating a monopoly in the labor market, whereby to be able to contend successfully with employers whenever a controversy should arise." A strike for such a purpose "would not be justifiable on principles of competition, either as against non-union workmen or as against the employer, but would be unlawful."

For reasons other than the principles involved in the closed-shop contract, it may be unlawful to form an agreement that will result in the discharge of workmen already employed at the time of the making of the agreement. It may be the basis for damages. Also it appears that a strike to compel the adoption of a closed-shop agreement may be unlawful. That involves the more general question of the legality of strikes, whatever may be their purpose. That topic has been discussed in the chapter on Strikes. In the last case referred to, it appears further that the question of competition and monopoly are not foreign to this discussion.

The judicial attitude, then, is not settled into agreement. Of course violence and intimidation will, if used by one of the parties to secure the agreement, free the other from the binding force of the contract. There is uniformity on that point worked out through other channels and applicable in all cases. But coercion aside, there remains the uncertainty as to how the courts will view a contract of this kind. It may come within the right of the contracting parties so long as the agreement is entered into voluntarily. It may, on the other hand, be viewed as a monopoly against which even the freedom of contract will not stand.

THE IRON AND STEEL INDUSTRY'S OPEN SHOP

One concrete illustration of this struggle is of particular interest. The iron and steel industry is in many important respects a typical American industry. Its position in the industrial world is commanding. Its policies are therefore of more than ordinary importance. The experiences of unionism in this field are instructive. The tale is one full of interest. John Fitch in his study of The Steel Workers has presented the case at first hand and in full detail. He recounts at some length the struggle of unionists through the series of strikes culminating in the Homestead Strike of 1892, the death knell of unionism for the steel workers of the United States. The powerful United States Steel Corporation had been formed and stood ready to bring its immense concentration of force against unionism. Since that time its labor policy has been that of the open shop. Here is an opportunity to see what the open shop has been in relation to unionism and Fitch has furnished us with a full account during the period covered by his inquiry. A paternalistic attitude has been steadily maintained. Coal and gas from the company supplies were furnished at cost. Houses rented below the rates charged by other owners. Money was loaned for building on terms more favorable than local building and loan associations charged. A system of stock purchase for employees was introduced. A liberal pension and insurance plan was inaugurated. In these respects the paternalism was beneficial. Against these were offset an increase of the less intelligent classes of foreigners, and their distribution so as to prevent any class conscious feeling, an increase of pay for skilled and decreased pay for unskilled labor with the extensive introduction of machinery to eliminate at every possible point the need for the skilled. This has greatly increased the proportion of unskilled. Many workmen are cited as having found it in accord with their own experience that the reductions in wages from time to time approximately equalled their savings as revealed to the company by their savings deposits or their purchases of company stock. To these adverse conditions must be added the speeding up system in all its ramifications followed by the "judicious cuts from time to time in the rate of pay per ton, which make the men put forth the last ounce of energy to prevent a wage loss." Such is the record under the "employers' régime" as portrayed by Fitch.

Forms of Discrimination. — But what of membership in unions? Were workmen chosen without discrimination, as the open-shop principle would dictate? In 1895 a reduction in wages was posted. A mass meeting was held in protest. The following day men were discharged in groups for attending the meeting. Secret meetings were held and a local organization of twenty-five men formed in one of the mills. It was but a short time before the officers of this local were discharged and the president was informed at the time that he was dropped for forming the organization. In 1901 a secret organization was formed with a thousand members, and very soon several hundred of them were discharged. It is, as Fitch states, "a matter of common report" that one particularly active organizer "is blacklisted in every mill of the Steel Corporation." This lead of the managers of the Corporation was closely followed by the independents, so that the unionist fares the same throughout the district. In one of the independent plants it was decided to hold a meeting of protest against Sunday work. The superintendent called the leaders together and threatened them with discharge if they did not abandon the plan. Then at the time announced for the meeting together with several mill policemen he stationed himself in plain sight where he could see anyone who entered the hall. No one attempted to go in and there was no meeting. To his account of these instances Fitch adds the statement: "The officials of the steel companies make no secret of their hostility to unionism, and I have been told by leading employers that they would not tolerate it. Any movement toward organization, they assured me, would mean discharge. That this is no idle boast is evident from the records of all attempts at organization since 1892."

To insure the effective working of this policy the companies organized an elaborate secret service. Its agents were supposed to be employees working shoulder to shoulder with the men and quick to detect and report any movement toward agitation and organization. This has made the men very suspicious and very cautious. "I doubt," says Fitch, "whether you could find a more suspicious body of men than the employees of the United States Steel Corporation. They are suspicious of one another, of their neighbors, and of their friends."

THE PREFERENTIAL UNION SHOP

Contrasted with this struggle between the steel manufacturers and their workmen is that of the clothing workers of New York City. It began in 1910. The strikers through their union officials presented a list of grievances and demands which dealt with conditions of labor generally and which included the charge that union men were discriminated against and the more active leaders were blacklisted. There were many efforts at mediation by public-spirited citizens and finally a conference was arranged with an advance agreement that the closed shop should not be a subject of discussion.

In the proffer of settlement made by the organization of manufacturers many concessions were made. One clause, however, indicates their view on the employment of union labor. "We know of no discrimination against union men in our ranks and no blacklisting, but we are prepared to discipline rigorously any member of our association who hereafter shall be proven guilty of violating the pledge (not to discriminate) already given."

Negotiations reached the point of amicable adjustment on all important points except one. The employers would not concede what they considered to be a closed shop. The union leaders believed that the rank and file of the strikers could be satisfied only by the adoption of such a policy. Conferences came to an end and the strike was renewed with increased vigor. For a month efforts at mediation were persisted in with the final result of renewing the conferences. In previous discussions the employers are reported to have shown a willingness to employ a majority of unionists, and also to act in cooperation with the unions in securing many of the ends for which they were striving. But they flatly and steadily refused to go further.

A Compromise. — It was at this point that a compromise that had slowly been formulating was proposed. An open shop would not be accepted by the unionists because of fear of discrimination. A closed shop was rejected by the employers because of fear of union domination. A "preferential union shop" was suggested. This was finally accepted as involving essentially the main points for which each side contended. The Protocol was finally drawn up, signed and put into effect on the second day of September, 1910.

The Agreement. — The agreement as to the conditions of union employment was embodied in section fourteen of the Protocol. This read as follows: "Each member of the manufacturers is to maintain a union shop, a 'union shop' being understood to refer to a shop where union standards as to work conditions, hours of labor, and rates of wages as herein stipulated prevail, and where, when hiring help, union men are preferred, it being recognized that, since there are differences in degrees of skill among those employed in the trade, employers shall have freedom of selection as between one union man and another, and shall not be confined to any list, nor bound to follow any prescribed order whatever. It is further understood that all existing agreements and obligations of the employer, including those to present employees, shall be respected; the manufacturers, however, declare their belief in the union, and that all who desire its benefits should share in its burdens."

Elements of the New Plan. — The relative security for this agreement was found in the very elaborate and satisfactory method of adjusting differences through the Board of Grievances and Board of Arbitration. This has been described in the chapter on Arbitration and does not call for further notice here. Within such a plan for settling possible difficulties, adjustments were amicably made. The plan first of all secured the adoption of union standards as to wages, hours of labor and sanitary conditions. To establish these standards the union must have a real life. This strong union came into touch with a strong organization of employers and adjustments were made as among friends rather than foes, involving mutual respect, good faith and confidence.

The plan further insured the existence of the union. Its members sat on the Boards of Grievances. As an organization, it was largely responsible for shop control. No one needed to fear the displeasure of the employer by joining the union. Other sources of annoyance also were cleared away. Existing agreements between employers and non-union employees were respected. As to choosing employees the manufacturer gave preference to union men of equal skill and the union must see to it that the membership was sufficiently large. If a non-union man was hired either because of his superior skill or because of a limited number of unionists available, it was to the interest of the new employee to join the union if he wished to protect his job against union men in the future. If he applied in good faith, the union must accept him to membership. The open membership to unions was one of the essential features of the entire plan. Should any employee refuse to join, the union could secure his removal from the shop as soon as a union man of equal skill presented himself. Should the employer be suspected of acting in bad faith in making discrimination in matter of skill, there arose a grievance which was put through the regular course of settlement where the charge would be cleared up.

Thus while the shops were not entirely closed to non-union men, the unionists had the preference and at the same time the employer had a practical degree of choice in matter of skill and fitness for work. Joining the union gave an advantage to the man and placed him in line to share the burdens as well as to reap the benefits of such organization.

In short, the employer obligated himself to employ union men as long as any applied; and he was free to choose from among them the ones best adapted to his needs. The union must be open; all qualified applicants must be admitted without discrimination.

This agreement was entered upon by the Manufacturers' Protective Association, with a membership of 123 firms and 15,000 employees. Later the membership of both firms and employees materially increased. Practically the entire cloak, suit, and skirt industry came under either the Protocol agreement or under shop contract agreements that were essentially the same.

Success of the New Plan. — That the plan worked satisfactorily is evidenced by its continuation for so long a time. Grievances have been numerous; yet the reports do not classify them in such a way as to make it possible to tell just what proportion arose over suspected discrimination against union employees.

During the first two and one-half years of the agreement there were 7,656 grievances settled. Of these 97% was adjusted in the first stage, while only twenty cases were carried up to the final hearings before the Board of Arbitration. This fact warrants the conclusion that complaints against the preferential union-shop clause of the Protocol, if there were any, were readily adjusted.

Further evidence of the adaptability of the preferential union shop was established in later agreements. By the spring of 1913 six protocols had been signed all in the general industry of women's clothing. They covered six separate branches of the industry, included both New York and Boston employers and involved 65,000 persons. In each of these agreements the preferential union shop was a feature.

Spirit of Parties to the Agreement. — Concerning the spirit in which this part of the agreement was entered upon, two or three brief extracts will explain. The general secretary-treasurer of the International Ladies' Garment Workers Union explained the plan: "In such a shop the non-union worker may obtain employment, but in a protocol shop they are laboring under a disadvantage, because while the employer may pay him the same scale of wages and work the same number of hours, his employment and his rights are limited, for he is the first to go down and the last to be taken up." The spirit of the employers appears, for example, in the statement from the Dress and Waist Bulletin, the organ of the manufacturers: "The attention of members is called to the fact that the theory of the preferential union shop, to which they are bound to adhere under the protocol, requires in general that in laying off workers manufacturers shall lay off non-union workers before laying off union workers, skill being equal." When it developed, as it did in some of the shops that the membership of the unions did not increase as it had been expected to do under the new plan, there appeared an editorial in the organ of the Manufacturers' Protective Association which read as follows: "Every reasonable effort should be made by members to induce their employees to join the union. This is only just and fair, not only because the association is morally obligated to do this, but also because it is a simple matter of justice for all the workers to contribute their share in the way of dues to the union toward meeting the greatly increased expenses involved in carrying out the protocol conditions in the shops. There need be no coercion and there should not be, but if the matter is presented properly to the workers who have not yet affiliated themselves with the union there is no doubt that they can be induced to join.

"A strong union will be a benefit to the manufacturers, and members of the association should make every effort to increase the membership in the union so that its officers may have complete control of the workers and be enabled to discipline them when necessary. With half the shop union and the other half non-union, it is easy to be seen that this is impossible and that friction is bound to result."

Later Discord. — An interesting difference developed in the operation of the first protocol and the later ones. In the cloak, suit, and skirt industry there was an increase in the membership of the unions. The association also increased its membership. The expected advantage to the union in the preference extended to union members was realized. In the dress and waist industry, as the study of the Federal Bureau of Labor Statistics shows, these results did not follow. The preferential union-shop clause in the protocol was in the same words, indeed copied from the earlier one. Yet the membership in the dress and waist unions decreased during the first year. This fact led to suspicion on the part of the union leaders, and they preferred charges against the employers on the ground that they were discriminating in favor of non-union labor. Their case before the arbitrators showed that in many of the shops, some of them belonging to officers of the association, less than one per cent of the labor was union. The association admitted the fact but denied the validity of the implications that were suggested. Their explanation placed the blame on the policies of the unions themselves, prejudicing the workers rather than attracting them. The finding of the board of arbitration technically freed the employers from these charges, though they were not entirely exonerated. It was recognized by the board as perfectly clear that the membership of the union was probably only one-half what it was six or eight months before. On the question of fixing the blame it seemed to the board that practically both parties had been at fault, and that it would be necessary for both parties to "exert themselves greatly to carry out the plan which was originally in their purpose."

Efforts towards Coöperation. — Following this it appears that serious and sincere efforts were made on both sides to carry into effect the principle of the preferential union shop. From the officials of both organizations appeals were sent out urging both employers and employees to observe faithfully the terms of the agreement. The employers' appeal was that the members of the association should regard the obligation to support the union in its effort to extend its membership. "Some of our members have failed to appreciate that the work of coöperation between the association and the union would fail if the union did not have the moral support and coöperation of the manufacturers, as guaranteed by the protocol. The first place at which this moral support and coöperation is established tangibly on the part of the manufacturers is in the observance of the principle of the preferential union shop." "The protocol has come to stay. So has the association, and so has the union." The obligations growing out of these changes the employers must recognize and observe. Apparently the employers were convinced of the advantages of this form of union shop. They appeared to be quite insistent upon its maintenance.

The representations of the union leaders revealed a different situation. Their communication and appeal concerned membership dues. The reasoning was clear enough. "Of course the union cannot live without its members' contributions. If the union is doing good work for the workers, they should support this good work. . . . In the case of the member of the union, suspension means the loss of the preference which the protocol guarantees to the union workers. Since the employer is responsible for the guaranteeing of this preference, the suspended member of the union loses rights guaranteed under the protocol." "Some workers are under the impression that because they work in a protocol shop they are freed from the duty of paying their dues to the union. This contention of our members is very erroneous, because the protocol provides definitely that all workers who enjoy the benefits of the union and of the protocol must share its burdens. . . . Any worker who enjoys the benefits of the union and the protocol and does not contribute his or her share of the expenses of maintaining the union is a shirker and is unworthy of any respect or consideration. The obligation of paying dues to the union is not only a constitutional one, but is a moral one as well."

The situation as revealed here is very significant. If the laborers seek to reap the benefits of organization without sharing in its obligations, the unions do not have the membership lists from which the employer must choose. This necessitates the employment of non-unionists. The fewer members there are the greater the chances of permanency in non-union employment. If the union membership shrinks to small proportions then there is even less inducement for paying membership dues. From the point of view of the individual laborer this may seem safe reasoning. Wherever the unions find that the tendency revealed in this case is becoming general it is altogether probable that the security of any agreement like the preferential union shop will be seriously undermined. Stronger pressure will be brought to bear to bring the workmen into the unions. So long as this tendency to decrease in membership is apparent, the preferential union shop, as an industrial institution, cannot be regarded as secure. Either the employers, to save what they seem to regard as a satisfactory arrangement, will voluntarily aid in restoring the prestige of the union or the unions themselves will be driven to a more aggressive attitude and renew the demand for the closed shop.

The Agreement Abandoned. — For nearly five years this protocol providing for the preferential union shop in the ladies' garment trade in New York City was in force. During this period it was widely regarded as the nearest approach to an ideal settlement that had been reached in the garment trade, and one of the best in the wider industrial field. In the early spring of 1915, rumblings of trouble were heard. These developed seriously. In May the outbreak came. Working relations were broken off and the protocol was abandoned. Much effort was expended on each side to establish its own innocence and the guilt of the other side. The growing dissatisfaction on both sides and the earnest efforts that were made have been shown in the previous pages. It seems probable that causes deeper than those which either side assigns were responsible for the final outcome. Realizing, as all parties did, the necessity for reëstablishing working relations before the situation developed the seriousness of a passionate fight, steps were made at mediation. It was finally agreed that the Mayor of the city should appoint a board of six members to investigate and propose a settlement. As a result, a compromise was reached and a new agreement signed in August. The details of the plan are not necessary to the understanding of the point under discussion. The preferential union shop was not a part of the new agreement. The employers were left free to select and discharge their workers at their own discretion, with the further understanding that the workers were in no way to be discriminated against because of any of their union activities.

So far as the closed shop is concerned, it is no part of this new agreement. Indeed, the preferential union shop is no longer one of the elements. As the closed shop was in the first place refused, so now the preferential union shop has been abandoned. It is the end of the story for the present. Other principles were embodied in this agreement, but they will be discussed in the chapter on Trade Agreements.

CHAPTER XVIII

THE TRADE AGREEMENT

No list of important activities of unionism would be complete without reference to trade agreements. They embody a policy and reveal a purpose that extends below the surface and reaches down to the fundamentals of unionism itself. Variously known as collective bargains, labor contracts, or joint, industrial or collective agreements, as well as trade agreements, they embody the very best of the trade or industrial union spirit.

Definition. — If definitions help to understand what they are, the two following may be selected: "The collective agreement in its purest form is the final statement of the terms of settlement arrived at as a result of the direct negotiations between employers and employees — the direct result of collective bargaining between those desiring to purchase and those desiring to sell labor power." "By trade agreement," says Hon. Seth Low, "I mean an agreement entered into by the representatives of the employers in a given trade with the representatives of the employees in the same trade by which agreement the hours of labor, the rates of pay, and all the various other elements that enter into the relationships between employer and employee are agreed upon for a fixed period of time."

Relation to Other Bargaining Activities. — Narrowly construed these agreements have for their purpose the prevention of strikes and lockouts. They are akin to conciliation, mediation and arbitration in that they tend to industrial peace. Unlike mediation and arbitration they do not contemplate the use of outside agencies, except as a special resort in case the provisions of the agreement itself fail to prevent an outbreak. More like conciliation, the trade agreement represents an attempt to maintain working relations through mutual adjustments. If a distinction exists, and, as pointed out in the chapter on Arbitration it seems wise to recognize one, the distinction is that conciliation is a plan to be called upon for special occasions and to meet particular needs. The trade agreement is broader than this. It seeks to eliminate possible points of dispute. While a comprehensive trade agreement will provide methods of settling differences, this is secondary in importance. Primarily it assumes that normally there will be no need for them. It arranges working relations instead of fighting relations. Only when the working relations are disturbed does the agreement aid in preventing the substitution of fighting relations.

True Spirit of an Agreement. — In order that a trade agreement may be truly representative of a mutual desire for working harmony, the parties must be in position to enter upon the agreement voluntarily. A union that is strong enough to establish a closed shop and has fixed shop rules and conditions suitable alone to its own wishes should not be said to have made a trade agreement. On the other hand, an employer who hires employees individually and then arbitrarily posts shop rules and adjusts wages and hours of labor which the employees may accept or leave the shop should not be spoken of as having a trade agreement. The real trade agreement is in the nature of a contract to which both parties without unreasonable coercion voluntarily bind themselves. It may further be noted that such an agreement may be in writing or simply oral. The latter form is so vague, indefinite and especially so difficult of interpretation in case of dispute that it is better to consider it as a quasi-agreement, one in process of development from a crude form of collective bargaining to a real trade agreement. Agreements may exist, of course, between an employer and his unorganized employees. When such is the case, it is lacking in the essential quality of stability, there being no organization or group of officers to accept responsibility and no feeling of either solidarity or responsibility among the workmen. It is better to regard such an agreement, also, even though it may be in writing, as only a partially developed form.

Form and Content of Agreement. — Trade agreements are not standardized as to either form or content. Generally speaking they deal with the points peculiar to the industry, the location and the nature of the organization. (1) They set a time at which the agreement goes into effect and a time for its expiration. Three years is a very common period. Some continue for as long as five years. Others are annual. (2) They provide for conciliation or arbitration in case of differences of interpretation or in case conditions arise that were not contemplated at the time the agreement was made. The details of organizing the arbitration are definitely specified. (3) They fix in detail the conditions and provisions of the labor contract: rates of wages, hours of labor, overtime work, holidays, shop rules, rules of apprenticeship or regulations for hiring more labor, functions and rights of foremen, regulation of output, new machinery, rights of employment and discharge, and other points that enter into the working contract. So far as is practicable the tendency appears to be in the direction of standardization. Only so far as trades differ is there much difference between agreements except as to the order of arrangement of the material.

Number of Agreements. — It is quite impossible to tell how many trade agreements have been made and how many are in effect at any given time. No record that is at all satisfactory has been made. The Massachusetts Bureau has compiled some figures to show the number of agreements that were in effect in that state at the end of the year 1911. Of 1,226 locals that replied to the inquiry, 530 reported signed agreements with one or more of their employers, and forty-two declared that they had verbally accepted agreements. It appears that these agreements existed generally among the larger unions. The membership of the 1,226 locals was 185,414 and in the 530 locals that had agreements there was a membership of 105,478. Forty-three per cent of the unions reporting had signed agreements and these contained fifty-seven per cent of the membership. Of this group 259 unions, or twenty-one per cent, with a membership of 42,398, or twenty-three per cent, had signed agreements with all of the firms in their jurisdiction.

In the list of trades in which these agreements are found are some of the largest employers of labor as well as some of the most progressive. Nearly all railroads have contract agreements with the railroad brotherhoods. These are among the most respected agreements to be found anywhere in the industrial world. Coal operators in a large area of the mining regions have working agreements with the five hundred thousand United Mine Workers. The method of formulating these agreements has been worked out with unusual thoroughness. Districts are marked off and from these representatives are chosen to the convention. It is to all intents a representative legislative body with two branches. Each "house" represents its interests and from conference and deliberation an agreement is developed that has the force of a binding contract on both parties represented. These agreements adjust details of wages and other conditions to the natural differences that obtain in the several coal fields, and within each section the natural inequalities are evened up so as to bring about a fairer kind of competition among operators and fairer working conditions for the laborer. In many sections of the country the building trades have brought out of the chaos of former conditions a sort of order through the trade agreement. Upwards of fifty employers' associations have this understanding with the many thousand of their employees. These agreements are not so stable as those just referred to. Yet progress is being made in the face of serious difficulties peculiar to the trade. Many street railway systems have satisfactory agreements with unions of their employees. Here again they are somewhat unstable. In the boot and shoe industry the organized workers are particularly proud of their achievements in this line. The Stove Founders National Defence Association early made contracts with the Iron Molders Union. In 1891 an agreement was made that has been renewed annually since that date. During the fall of 1915 several agreements were made that were of more than usual importance. Three of these were (1) in the Chicago street railway surface lines, (2) the Chicago carpenters, and (3) the longshoremen of New York and vicinity. Their importance lies in the fact that they involve unusually large numbers of employees; they brought serious disputes to an amicable settlement; and they have been extended to employees who have not previously used the trade agreement.

Importance of Trade Agreements. — The foregoing has dealt with the more obvious importance of trade agreements. It appears that they are not to be disregarded as trivial. Yet they are often underestimated even from this point of view. They lack the sensational elements of the strike, the lockout or the boycott. Ten thousand men on strike is an event that will find its news place in large headlines. A settlement of such a strike by mediation or arbitration will also be worthy of prominent notice, usually to the undue glorification of the mediators or arbitrators. But a trade agreement by which ten thousand men and their employers continue peacefully to operate the industry seldom receives a passing notice even by a line in the news sheets. The general public has been very appreciative of the fact that an Anthracite Coal Commission brought to an end a great strike. It has been quite unmindful of the much more important fact that operators and miners have, by means of agreements drawn up and signed by their delegated represent-atives, prevented strikes in the organized bituminous fields for many years. This popular underestimate is clearly a false one. John Mitchell does not exaggerate when he says that "the hope of future peace in the industrial world lies in the trade agree-ment."

It is a hopeful sign that these agreements are increasing in number. Though figures of any one year may be misleading, it is beyond doubt that the custom of establishing working rela-tions in this way is slowly gaining ground. It is better not to have a rapid gain. Too rapid an increase would probably be undesirable, though constant agitation and urging is very much to be desired. Only as employers and employees both become fully impressed with the advantages of this method of coöpera-tion will there be a healthy growth. Mutual confidence is essen-tial. As unions become more firmly established, as they pass beyond the first period of danger attendant on all new organiza-tions and begin to realize the responsibility of their newly acquired power, they will be in better position to handle this new device. In many instances it has been true that the unions have not been able to measure up to this responsibility. At present there are undoubtedly unions that could not enter upon this line of bargaining because they would not be equal to its demands. To force a trade agreement policy upon such or-ganizations would not alone be detrimental to their own development. It would react very unfavorably upon other unions and upon the policy generally.

Evidence of Growing Spirit of Coöperation. — Trade agree-ments should be regarded as much more than devices for avoid-ing strikes and lockouts. They accomplish more than the mere suppression of outbreaks, covering over a condition potentially dangerous and preventing open hostility. They must be re-garded as an index of more positive meaning. They reveal a growing willingness on the part of each side to recognize the claims of the other. They indicate something of friendliness, of more cordial coöperation in the carrying on of industry. They mean the recognition by each side of the value as well as the necessity of collective bargaining. Collective bargaining reduced to definite and permanent terms, "put down in black and white," is an advanced step of real significance. Trade agreements begin by admitting the principle of collective bargaining. They recognize the existence of *a* union and often the existence of *the* union. They recognize the fact that the employer has an interest. Even employers' associations enter into these agreements through their designated officials just as do the union workmen. When each comes to sign the agreement, it is realized then, if not before, that sides formerly regarded as irreconcilably hostile can find a standing ground of mutual interest. The trade-union agreement represents the fundamental thing for which unionism, both trade and industrial, stands. If to many leaders the trade agreement means all that has just been stated, to others it means even more.

Notable Instances. — Of special seriousness is a strike in a daily newspaper plant. Realizing this, the American Newspaper Publishers' Association and the International Typographical Union of the United States and Canada have maintained a trade agreement that is notable. After years of fighting in which both sides sustained losses a compromise was effected in 1900 that was at the time regarded as somewhat of an experiment. It was to continue in force for one year and provided for arbitration of disputes that might arise within that time. The results were on the whole so advantageous that, with some modifications of the details, the agreement has been renewed first for a one year period, then for five years at a time. The agreement is now in its third five-year period and will continue until April 30, 1917, thus making seventeen years of continuous operation of a trade agreement in this industry. By the provisions of this agreement the wages, hours of labor and general working conditions are adjusted. By no means the least important part of the agreement is the provision for arbitration of any disputed points that may arise under the agreement. Local boards and a national board of arbitration are provided for. The local boards are composed of two from each side, the local union and the Publishers' Association. If they do not reach an agreement the hearing is opened again with a fifth member chosen by the president of the International Union and the chairman of a special committee of the Publishers' Association. At the conclusion of this hearing, the original four members attempt to reach a decision. If they do not succeed then the chairman casts the deciding vote. An appeal may be made to the national arbitration board. This board is unique in that it has an even number of members one-half from each side, though of a personnel that is not directly connected with the case at issue. The idea is that if the case has any justice in it, it will be possible to make it appear to enough members of both sides to win a majority vote. While complications are very easily possible, the fact that this form represents an evolution of twelve years' experience is evidence that it has decided advantages.

An agreement was entered into on the first of January, 1913, between the Newspaper Publishers' Association of New York City and Typographical Union No. 6 that was described in the New York State Labor Bulletin as "very unusual if not entirely unique." The agreement provided for arbitration of cases of discharge of union men by foremen. The plan was adopted as a substitute for one that had been in force about three years and which experience had shown to be too complex and to involve too great delay in settlement. The publishers took the initiative in bringing about the adoption of the new plan. Under the new agreement the provisions for employment and discharge were fully specified. "When a member is discharged for any of the foregoing reasons, and such action of the foreman is contested by the union on behalf of the member affected, the contention shall be referred to a conference committee of three representatives of the employers and three representatives of the union." A decision reached by this conference committee was to be final, to be accepted by both parties. "If an agreement cannot be reached the conference committee shall select a seventh member, and the decision of the committee as thus made up shall be final." In case the conferees failed to agree on the seventh person, a supreme court judge was to make the appointment.

Without delay the joint arbitration committee was organized and immediately took up its first case. A compositor had been discharged by a foreman for "incompetency," being accused of taking too much time in setting up a piece of work. The complaint was that the foreman had been "unduly prejudiced" against the journeyman. After a four-hour hearing the arbitrators decided unanimously in favor of the discharged man and ordered his return. For five months no other case was presented to the board. The opinion was expressed in the printing trade of New York City that "this is owing to the fact that foremen are exercising more than ordinary caution in the matter of dismissals, realizing the necessity under the new rule of showing good and sufficient reasons for the removal of workmen." Should this plan prove on longer trial to be mutually satisfactory there is reason to hope for its further extension, not only in the printing trade but in other industries which have developed stable union organization.

Employers' Attitude. — Especially noteworthy among the evidence of increasing popularity of trade agreements is the changing attitude of employers. Not all of them by any means favor this policy. Such could not be expected in an industry where unionism is yet undeveloped and irresponsible, or where employers themselves still cling to the idea that there must be no "outside interference" with their business. In many lines of industry, as has already been shown, trade agreements represent the normal method of establishing collective bargaining. Among many employers there is an awakened sense of community of interest. This expresses itself in open advocacy of the definite contract agreement. They appreciate that such a policy leads to stability in the industry. Many now operating under the trade agreement openly declare that they have no desire to return to the conditions that existed prior to the adoption of their agreements. One employer, representing this class, declares that he urges his men both to join the union and to attend meetings regularly. On one occasion a shop committee came to him for a conference. He asked the men if they had any authority. Upon their reply in the negative he told them to go back and get authority from their union, so that he could talk with them. "I want to tell you," he says, "that there are some mighty good scrappers in these committees, and they tell you some things that you would never learn otherwise." A reason frequently urged for retaining agreements is that they insure the delivery of a contract without strike interruption. The agreements economize effort in employing men, the unions do not try to interfere with the business. The employer can run his own business just the same. Hours of labor and wage rates are both "perfectly arbitrable." Such are some of the expressions of practical opinion from employers who have had experience.

Again, somewhat more philosophically, an employer formulates the principles on which he would establish trade agreements, even though, based on them, they should last but a year. First: Unions are a natural result of economic conditions and are here to stay, for a time at least, and longer than anyone can predict — possibly until the tendency toward other forms of control is also met. Second: Employers' associations cannot destroy unions. Third: No progress has been made toward the ultimate solution of the problem, by any purely "fighting associations." Citizens' alliances and employers' associations have afforded effective relief and have corrected many abuses, but they have not disposed of the union, or the question of relations between employer and employee. Fourth: Fair agreements, based upon accurate data, honest relations, varying conditions, and upon arbitration (with all its present limitations) where necessary, suggest far more rational solutions than strikes and lockouts, intimidation and injunction, with their attendant cost, hardship and engendered hatred.

Educational Influence. — Speaking from a much broader point of view, Mr. John Graham Brooks says: "If anywhere in the future the wage system is to be modified in the direction of more coöperative and democratic methods, the joint agreement in some form has to be strengthened and extended. For the kind of education we most need, politically and industrially, I do not know a more disciplining agency now working in the United States than the joint agreement as it may be seen, for example, in our soft coal districts and among the longshoremen and cigarmakers and stove makers." To this may be added the opinion of Mr. John Mitchell: "It must not be supposed that the trade agreement will prevent all strikes. It will undoubtedly minimize these industrial conflicts, by obviating misunderstandings, by showing each side the position of the other, by creating a more friendly feeling between employers and employees and finally by making strikes and lockouts, when they do occur, so wide-spread, general and expensive, that their recurrence will be avoided. The fact that failure to reach an agreement would result either in a great strike or a general lockout impels each side to respect the reasonable demands of the other. If it were not for that possibility, the more radical and uncompromising elements could not be induced to forego their claims. With each new agreement, however, both sides become more conservative and more willing to sacrifice a part of their demands, and with each passing year, the industries in which trade agreements prevail become established on a firmer and more permanent foundation of peace."

Estimate of Its Value. — On the whole the evidence seems conclusive that where the trade agreement is developed on conservative lines and entered into in good faith by both parties, it acts decisively as a steadying influence. It has been shown as a matter of fact that where well-adjusted trade agreements are in force and are respected alike by both parties the mutual confidence inspired leads to the elimination of many of the objectionable practices centering around the restriction of membership or of output on the part of the workmen and the speeding up processes and nerve exhausting paces insisted upon by the employer. Interesting evidence is stated by the recent reports of the Massachusetts Bureau: "It would appear from a study of the prevalence of collective agreements and from the numerous awards which have been made by boards of arbitration in this state (Massachusetts) that the industrial agreement as an instrument for securing industrial harmony is being accepted with increasing favor by both employers and employees."

NEW YORK GARMENT TRADES: THE PROTOCOL

The passing of the agreement in the garment industry of New York City must be characterized as of more than ordinary importance. This "protocol" provided for the preferential union shop. The breaking of the agreement and the strike of the summer of 1915 led to the appointment of a council of six by the Mayor of the city. After some weeks of careful investigation of the entire situation an agreement was drawn up and was accepted without change by the contending parties.

The New Agreement. — This agreement marks in a sense a

return to principles less advanced from the union point of view than those on which the preferential union shop was based. In framing its statements the council has been conspicuously successful in reducing to practical working terms the theoretical considerations that have been slowly gaining ground in the public consciousness. It is not the ideal of either side, nor does it go as far as the advanced leaders of public thought would like to go. That is admitted in the report. It is not an ideal. It is, rather, in the opinion of the council, all of the ideal that can be secured at present through the voluntary agreement of all parties.

In making the report the council records "on behalf of the general public their appreciation of the peaceful and progressive relations which have existed in the cloak-making industry during the past five years, a state of things due not only to the enlightened self-interest of the employers and wage earners, but also to the large social ideals which have animated both sides. If this fair prospect has for the moment been clouded, and these friendly relations have suffered a temporary interruption, it is the aim and the hope of this council to pave the way for their resumption, not only to prevent ground previously gained from being lost, but to bring about advance in new directions." Tribute is paid by the council to the "very notable achievement" attained in the adoption and operation of the "protocol." Its strong points should, in the opinion of the council, be preserved, and it should be altered only in those particulars wherein it has been found to be defective. In its endeavor to accomplish this the council lays down a "fundamental rule" that must be regarded as a distinct advance in the general field of industrial adjustment. It is quoted at length together with the application made to each party in accordance with it.

The Council's "Fundamental Rule." — "In the endeavor to work out the plan of a new compact of this sort the council has laid down the following fundamental rule:

"That the principle of industrial efficiency and that of respect for the essential human rights of the worker should always be applied jointly, priority being assigned to neither. Industrial efficiency may not be sacrificed to the interests of the workers; for how can it be to their interest to destroy the business on which they depend for a living, nor may efficiency be declared paramount to the human rights of the workers; for how in the long run can the industrial efficiency of a country be maintained if the human values of its workers are diminished or destroyed. The delicate adjustment required to reconcile the two principles named must be made. Peace and progress depend upon complete loyalty in the effort to reconcile them.

"We, therefore, find:

"I. Under the present competitive system the principle of industrial efficiency requires that the employer shall be free and unhampered in the performance of the administrative functions which belong to him, and this must be taken to include:

"(a) That he is entirely free to select his employees at his discretion.

"(b) That he is free to discharge the incompetent, the insubordinate, the inefficient, those unsuited to the shop or those unfaithful to their obligations.

"(c) That he is free in good faith to reorganize his shop whenever, in his judgment, the conditions of business should make it necessary for him to do so.

"(d) That he is free to assign work requiring a superior or special kind of skill to those employees who possess the requisite skill.

"(e) That while it is the dictate of common sense, as well as common humanity, in the slack season to distribute work as far as possible equally among wage earners of the same level and character of skill, this practice cannot be held to imply the right to a permanent tenure of employment, either in a given shop or even in the industry as a whole. A clear distinction must be drawn between an ideal aim and a present right.

"The constant fluctuations — the alternate expansions and contractions to which the cloak-making industry is so peculiarly subject, and its highly competitive character, enforce this distinction. But an ideal aim is not therefore to be stigmatized as utopian, nor does it exclude substantial approximations to it in the near future. Such approximations are within the scope of achievement, by means of earnest efforts to regularize employment and by such increase of wages as will secure an average adequate for the maintenance of a decent standard of living throughout the year. The attempt, however, to impose the ideal of a permanent tenure of employment upon the cloak-making industry in its present transitional stage is impracticable, calculated to produce needless irritation and injurious to all concerned.

"II. In accordance with the rule above laid down that the principle of efficiency and that of respect for the human rights of the workers must be held jointly and inseparably, we lay down —

"(a) That the workers have an inalienable right to associate and organize themselves for the purpose of maintaining the highest feasible standard as to wages, hours, and conditions, and of still further raising the standards already reached.

"(b) That no employee shall be discharged or discriminated against on the ground that he is participating directly or indirectly in union activities.

"(c) That the employees shall be duly safeguarded against oppressive exercise by the employer of his functions in connection with discharge and in all other dealings with the workers. It is to be carefully noted that the phrase 'oppressive exercise of functions' need not imply a reflection on the character and intentions of the high-minded employer.

"An action may be oppressive in fact, even though inspired by the most benevolent purpose. This has been amply demonstrated by experience. No human being is wise enough to be able to trust his sole judgment in decisions that affect the welfare of others; he needs to be protected, and if he is truly wise will welcome protection against the errors to which he is liable in common with his kind, as well as against the inspirations of passion or selfishness.

"For this reason a tribunal of some kind is necessary, in case either of the parties to this covenant believes itself to be unjustly aggrieved. And because the construction of such a tribunal is a delicate and difficult task, demanding the greatest care, lest on one hand the movements of industry be clogged by excessive litigation, and lest on the other hand the door of redress be closed against even the most real and justified complaint, therefore,

"III. In accordance with these general principles the council propose that an agreement be entered into by the Cloak, Suit and Skirt Manufacturers' Protective Association, and the International Ladies' Garment Workers Union and the Joint Board of

Cloak and Skirt Makers' Unions embodying these principles and providing the following:

"(a) Every complaint from either organization to the other shall be in writing, and shall specify the facts which, in the opinion of the complaining organization, constitute the alleged grievance, and warrant its presentation by one organization to the other. Such complaints shall be investigated in the first instance by the representatives of the two associations, chosen for the purpose, it being impressed upon them that they use and exhaust every legitimate effort to bring about an adjustment in an informal manner. In case, however, an adjustment by them be not reached, the matters in dispute shall be referred for final decision to a

"(b) Trial board of three, consisting of one employer, one worker, and one impartial person, the latter to be selected by both organizations, to serve at joint expense and to be a standing member in all cases brought before the board. The remaining two members shall be selected as follows:

"The association and the union shall each make up a list of ten persons, to be approved by the other. From these two lists, as each case arises, each party shall select one person."

Many of the leading provisions of the former agreement were embodied without change. These pertained to the shop conditions, the use of machines, the subcontracting, the charges for material, the home work, and the many other details that did so much toward clearing up the earlier situation of many of its most perplexing problems. In this is included the very important provision for the joint board of sanitary control.

The Union Shop. — With reference to the union shop, it is provided that "each member of the manufacturers is to maintain a union shop, a 'union shop' being understood to refer to a shop where union standards as to working conditions, hours of labor, and rates of wages as herein stipulated prevail, and where, when hiring help, union men are preferred, it being recognized that, since there are differences in degrees of skill among those employed in the trade, employers shall have freedom of selection as between one union man and another, and shall not be confined to any list, nor bound to follow any prescribed order whatever." All existing agreements with present employees are to be observed and the manufacturers "declare their belief in the union, and that all who desire its benefits should share in its burdens."

Responding to the requests made by the Mayor and others the council states its willingness to remain organized for a longer period for the purpose of investigating more thoroughly "the fundamental problems of regularization, standards of wages, and enforcement of standards throughout the industry, of trade education, and a more thorough organization of the industry, and on the basis of such investigation it shall submit a constructive policy to both organizations."

"Finally, since peace in industry, as in families and among States, is the offspring of good will, and since no peace can be sound or enduring that is not based on this indispensable prerequisite, it is agreed that the leaders on both sides shall exert their utmost endeavors to create a spirit of mutual good will among the members of their respective organizations, such good will taking the specific form of a disposition to recognize the inherent difficulties which each side has to meet — a spirit of large patience under strain, and withal, a belief in the better elements which exist in human nature, be it among employers or wage earners, and the faith that an appeal to these elements will always produce beneficent results. These recommendations, when accepted by both parties, shall constitute the agreement between them."

Estimate of Importance of New Agreement. — An analysis of the agreement reveals a meaning that may be regarded as of either much or little importance. Evidently the conditions of employment and the security of union men will be the crucial test. The specific guarantee of the preferential union shop that assured the union man a preference has been abandoned. In its place appears the form of statement that has from the beginning caused so much of the trouble. The employer is to be entirely free to select his employees at his discretion; to discharge the incompetent, the insubordinate, the inefficient, those unsuited to the shop or those unfaithful to their obligations. On the other hand, the employee is not to be discharged or discriminated against because he may be participating in union activities, and he is to be duly safeguarded against an oppressive exercise of the employers' functions of discharging workmen.

That the second part of the agreement cannot be fully adhered to without a limitation on the entire freedom of the employer to hire and discharge is very evident. The effort is made to reconcile these two "freedoms" in the statement which asserts the equal importance of the principle of efficiency on the one hand and that of respect for the human rights of workers on the other. These two principles are to be held "jointly and inseparably."

Whether this can be done remains to be seen. The study of the experiences discussed in the chapter on The Closed Shop does not offer much encouragement. Efficiency as manifested in "scientific management," according to the study made for the Commission on Industrial Relations, does not appear to give enough attention, in practice, to the human rights of labor.

While the declared purpose of the council in framing the terms of agreement is to be practical, to observe the clear distinction between an ideal aim and a present right, it does not point out in what way these two principles, theoretically joint and inseparable, can be kept so in application. Two ways are proposed. The one is by the formation of the trial board before whom grievances may be brought. This involves the wholesome element of publicity and may do much in holding in check the more selfish instincts of both parties. The other is an appeal to the moral obligation of both. Mutual good will is to be the atmosphere of the agreement; such good will as will take "the specific form of a disposition to recognize the inherent difficulties which each side has to meet"; a "spirit of large patience under strain"; a "belief in the better elements which exist in human nature"; and a "faith that an appeal to these elements will always produce beneficial results." These statements of moral attitude and the statement of the more specific points together constitute the agreement.

On the face of this new agreement it appears that the same old elements of discord are present. Whether or not they cause trouble will depend not so much upon the terms of the agreement as upon its spirit. It also appears that a distinct step forward has been made in the attempt to coördinate two principles, making them both equal and inseparable, in face of the recognized difficulty of doing so; and further in making the mutual moral obligations rather definitely stated a part of the agreement. This virtually constitutes the trial board as a moral as well as a legal tribunal. The educative value of this agreement cannot be doubted. What it will mean to the future of the garment industry remains to be revealed.

CHAPTER XIX

RESTRICTION OF MEMBERSHIP AND OUTPUT

There is much discussion and much difference of opinion over the question of restriction of membership and the limitation of output. On these two points the grounds on which intelligent judgment may be based are very unsatisfactory. Reliable information is difficult to secure, and the facts that may be known are not so easily explained or interpreted.

RESTRICTION OF MEMBERSHIP

To what extent membership in unions and the apprenticing of new men are regulated cannot be stated with accuracy. Every union has its conditions of membership, usually stated in its constitution. This is a matter that is relatively public. There are the initiation fees, the willingness to pay the regular dues and the assessments, the requirements of the constitution and by-laws, and the election ("being voted in"). In some cases these matters are left for determination largely to the locals. The tendency seems to be toward establishing uniformity among locals of the same union in all of these requirements. In some instances of the more skilled trades, the candidate must pass an examination. These examinations are not standardized. They are set by members of the locals and the examination is graded by the same members. Sometimes these examinations have a real value and at other times they appear little less than ludicrous. On one occasion a harpist was to be employed in the Metropolitan Opera House Orchestra. Before the agreement could be completed an examination must be given by the officers of the musicians' union preliminary to admission to membership in the local. The harp was taken on a dray to the office of the examiner "over on the east side," the examination was satis-

318

factorily passed and the whole matter adjusted, apparently without difficulty.

Obviously the degree of restriction established in the way of membership depends quite entirely upon the spirit in which these various regulations are administered. Even in the face of quite uniform standards, there is possibility of wide variation in the application. In times of adversity, when membership may be dropping off, it is quite possible to adjust the application of rules so as to induce men to join. If, on the other hand, the reverse conditions prevail, the tests may be made more rigid.

Of ninety-four national unions examined by Professor Adams it appeared that twenty had passed no provisions relating to admission to membership. Thirty-eight had provided merely that the applicant must be a competent workman. Eighteen required three years or more of service in the trade. Fifteen required two years or less of similar service. Membership of employers, foremen, or others who would have the power to discharge workmen was prohibited in fourteen unions, while in eleven others such membership was allowed under certain conditions. White persons only were admitted in seven unions. There were scattering instances of other limitations such as persons directly interested in the liquor business and discrimination on account of nationality or citizenship. Speaking in general of the results of the study Professor Adams was of the opinion that "the cases are rare in which a union deliberately refuses to receive a body of competent workmen and then boycotts them as 'scabs.'"

Apprentices. — As to the number of apprentices the situation is much the same. Here again rules made by locals vary and they are enforced with different degrees of strictness. The reasons for the situation are somewhat different, however. Tradition has preserved for us the word apprentice, while modern industry has greatly modified its meaning. In earlier days the working unit was the master, the journeyman and the apprentice. The relations were much more intimate than those of the modern employer and his workman. The purpose was largely educational. Master and journeyman were alike interested in seeing that the apprentice was well grounded in the trade. Changes were so moderate that they seldom interfered with the personal interests of any member of the trio. In present conditions the educational element is quite wholly lacking. The employer is after profits. He fits his labor supply, just as he fits the supply of any other element of the business, to the end of larger profits. Against this the laborer seeks to defend himself through his organization. Young men, quicker and more adaptable, soon acquire enough skill to take the places of their older instructors. Profits dictate that the substitution shall be made. To this inclination on the part of the employer the laborer replies with a refusal to furnish instruction as freely as the employer may wish. This situation is the historical successor to the older apprenticeship system in the days of domestic industry. Further, it may be added that the employer's objection to a restriction on immigration is based upon his desire for a good labor market. Unable to restrict the coming of the immigrants, efforts are made to set up the barriers at the door of the trade and resist the unrestricted admission of apprentices.

Some investigations have been made into the facts of this restriction. Professor Bemis has found that of forty-eight nationals with a combined membership of 500,000, there were 28, with a membership of 222,000, which made no restrictions as to number of apprentices. Ten more, with a membership of 197,000, left the question to the locals. These latter were practically all carpenters, printers, cigar makers, painters and decorators. In the Chicago local of cigar makers there were between 700 and 800 apprentices to a membership of 1,900. In the typographical local the rules would have permitted 250 apprentices and there were, in fact, 140. In another instance an investigation of 1,255 printing establishments outside of the large city dailies revealed the presence of 7,599 journeymen printers and 3,710 apprentices and helpers. Other instances support the same evidence. It appears that there is not the general restriction that is supposed in some quarters to exist. Concluding, Professor Bemis adds that "As final proof that the trade unions are losing interest to a great degree in the restriction of apprentices, reference may be made to the small number of strikes for this purpose."

As illustrating the two sides of the problem the situation in the carpenter trade may be referred to. The Brotherhood of Carpenters and Joiners claimed to admit anyone of sufficient skill and to encourage boys who wished to learn the trade. A local established the rule that one boy should be allowed as apprentice for each ten men. This was charged against them as an instance of unwarranted restriction and was eagerly circulated by the employers. Not so generally was it known that there were at the time in the same city 3,000 idle carpenters, all young, able-bodied and skilled. In the light of this fact, well known to the members of the union, the restriction does not appear to be so burdensome.

Reasons for Restriction. — There are quite generally two reasons advanced by those who do establish some limitation. First, it is the necessity for securing thorough training on the part of those who do learn the trade. Second, it is for the purpose of keeping up or raising the wages through a limitation of the supply of skilled labor.

Conclusions. — While it cannot be said that there is no longer cause for complaint on the part of employers, it does not appear that the situation is as serious as it is presented by some. It seems quite probable that even the rules that do exist are to no small degree survivals of an earlier practice. They have never been repealed. They are not enforced with very great vigor. Modern conditions have made the rules of very little practical importance. To the more capable among the leaders it has appeared that the whole policy is a short-sighted one. Trades are not so difficult to learn that beginners are dependent on unionists for their instruction. It is beginning to appear that it is of more importance to teach both the trade and the principles of unionism than to refuse to teach the trade and lose the opportunity to control the new member as a unionist. The union which adopts the policy of such restriction "while working with one hand for the complete organization of its industry, cultivates a new crop of non-unionists with the other." The questions inherent in the situation are much broader than the questions of unionism. They reach out into much wider fields. Industrial training, industrial education, the proper adjustment of employments and of unemployment, the distribution of immigrants, all are perplexing questions. The proper distribution of apprentices is but a phase of the much larger group of questions.

From the report of the Commission on Industrial Relations it is learned that there are a few unions that do adopt the practice of excluding qualified persons from membership through the device of high membership dues and initiation fees and other means. Such a policy, it is asserted, "is condemned by the more important unions and is prohibited by their rules."

RESTRICTION OF OUTPUT

Laborers' Motive. — The earlier economists who explained so glibly the wage-fund doctrine taught the laborers a lesson that they have not been slow to apply. If, as these economists claimed, there was a fund set apart for wages and this amount must be made to "go around," it was evident that a large number of workers meant a small wage. It was as evident as arithmetic itself, which declares that a fixed dividend and a large divisor mean a small quotient. The logic of such a position leads very naturally to the practice of restriction of apprentices and of output as well.

But while this theoretical discussion has beyond doubt had its effect on the mind of the laborer, it partakes most too much of theory to furnish a leading motive. The laborer's reasons for acting as he does are more practical. If there are twenty houses to paint, the jobs will last longer if five men are put on than if double the number are set to work. If there is an order for five hundred pairs of shoes, the job will last longer if the men take their time than if they rush the work. In this very concrete way it is easy for a workman whose outlook is no wider than the narrow bit of work that he does to insist on putting a limit to his efforts in order to make the job last longer. Wider considerations do not influence him. For him, it is quite simply personal. He has a family to provide for. When work is scarce the employer lays off men. He may be laid off at the end of the very job on which he is working. This attitude is not peculiar to organizations of labor. It is human nature. But when one is a member of a union, his next concern after his own personal and family interests is for those of his fellow unionists. He is willing to assist them. This willingness is the more hearty because of their inclination to assist him. This bond of union between the organized members of a trade is not a new thing. It is simply more intensified by the fact of association and the realization of interdependence.

The Facts of Restriction. — As to the facts of this case, it must be said that they are at best confusing. The constitutions of unions and the published by-laws of the locals do not make public what the policy is. Rules are established that are generally regarded as secret. Just what they are is consequently difficult for the public to know. If this fact is realized at the outset, it becomes a wholesome antidote to the many rumors and false reports that find their way into print. Employers who are particularly desirous of creating a public opinion favorable to themselves will often misstate or give a false inference to some things that happen in the shop. Energetic reporters, looking for the striking and the sensational, will send in as news statements that are either partly or wholly false. These statements impress the unionist as so obviously libelous of his local and his union associates that they are denied with a vehemence that often carries the defendant as far to the other side of the truth.

Sifted of these dangers, the facts seem to stand out that limitation of output is purposely practiced by laborers, in unions as well as out; that there are locals whose members have deliberately adopted rules providing for such restriction and imposing a penalty for their violation; that the extent of this limitation has often been exaggerated in public discussion. Rules have been found to be in force in some locals such as the following: "Any member guilty of excessive work or rushing on any job shall be reported, and shall be subject to a fine of five dollars." "Any member who does an unreasonable amount of work, or who acts as leader for his employer for the purpose of getting all the work possible out of the men working in the same shop or job with him shall be fined for the first offence ten dollars; for the second offence he shall be suspended or expelled." Any member introducing piece work where it does not now exist; or any member running two machines where one had been run before by one man became subject to expulsion. In many other instances it appears to be well established that laws and rules have been not only enacted but often enforced in order to accomplish restriction of output.

With reference to the introduction of machinery, one form of restriction, the situation is much the same. In this regard the hostility is traditional. It has passed quite beyond the machine-smashing stage, yet there still is antagonism. Stogie makers refusing to admit machine workers to their union; iron molders doing the same; coopers opposing the making of casks and barrels by machines; stone cutters and plumbers ordering the members to have nothing to do with certain mechanical improvements; flint glass workers proposing to the employers that a machine for blowing lamp chimneys be bought up and eliminated, the price of chimneys being advanced to cover the cost; plate printers insisting on keeping hand presses for years in the United States Bureau of Engraving and Printing; — such are a few of the many instances of such a policy.

Employers' Share of Responsibility. — Before passing judgment on such acts, another group of facts should be called to mind. Employers on occasion do not hesitate to restrict output. It is generally regarded in many quarters as a legitimate act to limit output in order to steady the market or to steady prices. This is the same as saying that the restriction is to prevent a fall in prices. Another form of restriction is more generally heard of and less easily justified. It is a restriction in order to increase profits. Monopoly profit may often be very materially increased by this plan. It is also true that employers sometimes resist the introduction of machinery or mechanical appliances. It is common knowledge that air brakes on freight cars are of undoubted advantage. Yet it was necessary to enact legislation requiring this equipment before it was used. It was a hard fight to get the legislation and for a time even then there was difficulty in enforcing the law. The same experience will be recalled in connection with automatic couplers. Child labor is continued, as is often stated, because without it machines would have to be installed to do the work at so small a cost. The buying up and suppressing of patents is a fact that does not any longer need proof. Such facts as these in regard to the employer should not be left out of account.

Evidently both laborers and employers have been guilty of these practices. That they are contrary to public policy is a fact that needs no arguing. That they are done in accordance with a short-sighted view of self-interest should be clearly evident.

But there is still more to the subject. If the employer is

known to adjust his output and his use of machinery for the purposes of larger profits, it may appear to the laborer that he may shape his course with regard to output and machines for the same object. The morals of the reasoning are not very sound. But nevertheless the laborer has adopted, more or less consciously, just this reasoning.

Conclusions. — From what has already been said it appears that certain conclusions may be pretty definitely made. It must be admitted that workmen, both union and non-union, do as a matter of fact restrict their output. Even granted that many popular estimates of its extent are exaggerated, there remains truth in the accusation. None the less the exaggeration must not be lost sight of. Further, it is doubtless true that some restriction is due to false economic reasoning, a remnant of the old wage-fund doctrine. Some is due also to the remnant of the tradition established in the machinery-wrecking days of the early factory period. Again some is due to the inspiration of the employers' example of restriction to gain his personal ends. With these several causes in mind it will be more accurate to say that restriction of output, so far as it is practiced, is the resultant of these several causes, a cumulative force that prompts laborers to act without any philosophical analysis of the reasons.

Labor's Reply to Employer's Policy. — The most important phase of the whole subject remains yet to be considered. Evidence seems clear that agreements or rules to regulate output are but the workman's reply to the modern tendency of speeding. Employers are, in the minds of the workmen, the embodiment of industrial methods. The demands for large output and low costs place the employer in a position where, willingly or unwillingly, he must push both machines and men. Machines may be geared up by simple and well-known mechanical devices. There is no back talk from them. Such speeding up must be extended to the men also. But they can reply. They object to being pushed to what they regard as a point of exhaustion or a pace that means early old age. When a rule of a union is brought to the attention of an employer, he is very apt to say that it is simply a device by which the union seeks to make it an offense for a man to do a good day's work. That is all it means to him. When a unionist is questioned about such a rule, he may claim that it is simply the union man's reply to the employer's practice of paying a few men extra wages to act as pace makers. There is much evidence that after the speeding up has been accomplished and a faster pace established, the higher wages that are at first offered as an inducement are not permanently higher. They fall to the lower level sooner or later and by degrees, perhaps, while the new standards of output are insisted upon. This is particularly aggravating to employees in the case of piece work. By extra energy and effort the number of pieces is increased and a large wage earned. This is followed by a lowering of the piece rate.

Jacob Riis has told us in The Making of an American of his experience in this matter. "In a planing-mill in which I had found employment I contracted with the boss to plane doors, sandpaper them, and plug knot-holes at fifteen cents a door. It was his own offer and I did the work well; better than it had been done before, so he said himself. But when he found at the end of the week that I had made fifteen dollars where my slow-coach predecessor had made only ten, he cut the price down to twelve cents. I objected, but in the end swallowed my anger, and by putting on extra steam and working overtime made sixteen dollars the next week. The boss examined the work very carefully, said it was good, paid my wages, and cut down the price to ten cents. He did not want his men to make over ten dollars a week, he said; it was not good for them."

It may be admitted that in some instances at least the laborer appears to have the better of the argument. In a rolling mill the union had established a limit of 5,750 pounds of a particular kind of plate as a fair day's work for a man. The president of the union admitted that some men were exceeding this limit and violating the union rules, making as much as 7,500 pounds in an eight-hour day. But such a man, he declared, "does not consider himself physically, morally, or any other way. He does not consider the evil effect he is having upon his trade. He has no regard for his children who may follow after him." It will appear that the charge of holding back ambitious and energetic men and preventing them from making the most of their abilities cannot be taken into account by itself. Modern industry is so shaped that the energetic men do not appear to reap the results of their abilities and men naturally slower and yet necessary to the industry as a whole are driven to the point of exhaustion and premature old age.

Before the Industrial Commission the situation was well described in the following words:

"There has always been a strong tendency among labor organizations to discourage exertion beyond a certain limit. The tendency does not always express itself in formal rules. On the contrary, it appears chiefly in the silent, or at least informal, pressure of working-class opinion. It is occasionally embodied in rules which distinctly forbid the accomplishment of more than a fixed amount of work in a given time; but such regulations are always felt by employers, and almost always by other persons who are not of the wage-working class, to be obviously unjust, short-sighted, and socially injurious. This adverse public opinion outside the unions themselves has doubtless had some influence in discouraging such applications of the principle. These rules have not by any means, however, absolutely disappeared." "That the tendency of workingmen is to restrict the output of their labor within more or less definite limits, which they have come to consider right and just, is undeniable."

A Two-Sided Issue. — It will be seen that there are clearly two sides to the issue. If speeding up is not to be checked in any other way, if men are to attend upon machinery instead of machinery upon men, it is evident that the laborers are very sure to take the matter into their own hands. They may not deal with it from the point of view of community welfare. Certainly they will not adjust it in such a way as to benefit the employer. They may not do what in the long run may be best for the industry. They make no professions, certainly none that recognize their obligation to be geared up along with the mechanical part of industry for the purpose of contributing what they look upon as an added portion to the employer's profits. In their own view they would say: we are not depriving the more energetic men from adding to their own reward; we are depriving the employer of a reward which he would derive from his more energetic men.

To one who would understand the relation of trade unionism to the perplexing questions, it is quite essential that the workingman's position be understood. The policy may be wise or it may be foolish. The laborer regards it as wise, because of the conditions that he faces. The reasons for his view, this chapter has aimed to set forth.

To one sitting in judgment upon the correctness of the laborer's attitude it is not sufficient to condemn it. In most instances it should be condemned. But the condemnation should be extended. The system out of which the practices have grown must be readjusted so as to eliminate the unfavorable elements that lead to the trouble. If this is ever done, then the practices of restriction may be unreservedly condemned; — if, indeed, there be any left to be condemned.

CHAPTER XX

TRADE-UNION BENEFITS

Of the various activities of unions, one that occupies a prominent place is the raising of funds for benefit purposes. Though this has not always been regarded as of any considerable importance to the fortunes of unionism, it has from early times been a part of union activity. In the last quarter of a century the importance of benefits has been given a new emphasis. The first burst of enthusiasm for union organization had both the advantage and the disadvantage of all fresh enthusiasm. It moved to action but did not have staying qualities. In the face of reverses the enthusiasm waned. The ties of universal brotherhood did not bind with permanency. There began to appear to the minds of many leaders a necessity for more substantial bonds. In the work of many local organizations was found mutual benefits of various kinds. These were based on payments in the nature of investments and established a claim on benefits when needed, and in accordance with the rules adopted. This idea appealed to the national leaders. It was taken up and championed by them as a desirable policy for the national associations. The form was already present and furnished the opportunity for further development. The outcome has been that within recent years strong benefit provisions have become highly essential to the making of strong unions. Members who are tied in their membership by bonds in the shape of weekly or monthly dues establishing a claim on the funds thus accumulated are the more certain to keep up a membership with prompt payment of all financial obligations.

Extent of Benefit Policy. — Practically all of the large national and international organizations now maintain benefit funds in one or more forms. The one most frequently provided is the death benefit. This was adopted by the largest number of unions in the years from 1880 to 1900, though many have adopted it since then. Disability benefits, permanent and temporary, though not so numerous as death benefits, were also adopted in by far the larger number of cases in the last two decades of the nineteenth century. Superannuation benefits do not occupy so large a place. Other forms of benefit found more occasionally are for death of member's wife, for death of dependent widowed mother of an unmarried member, for unemployment, for widows and orphans, for indigents, for travel, for tool insurance, for shipwreck, and even for tobacco while sick or in hospital (for sailors).

Details of Management. — In arranging details for the management of these funds, the greatest variety prevails. There are substantial reasons for the variety. In many instances the locals existed first as independent societies and were conducting one form or another of mutual insurance or benefit. When these locals were gathered up into the national or international, the various methods were not interfered with. Even in cases where the national has adopted a benefit or insurance plan, as has frequently been done, the new plan has been superimposed upon the local plan. This makes, in many instances, a double plan with divided administration. Thus, in the case of the Brotherhood of Carpenters and Joiners, sick benefits are paid solely by the locals, permanent disability and death benefits are paid by the national, and strike benefits are paid by the locals, the district council and the national combined.

Then the nature of the trade has much to do with the character of the plan. Well-established trades, requiring skill and furnishing a good degree of permanency, will be in position to develop substantial funds and to pay large benefits because of relatively large fees. Unskilled and irregular employment cannot succeed in building up permanent funds. Dangerous trades, due to frequent and unpreventable accident or to exposure and disease, have difficulties to face. The demands on such funds are heavy. If wages are low and the labor supply shifting it will be quite impossible to maintain a secure fund. If, on the other hand, the dangers be adequately realized and the trade a permanent and well-paid one, this may lead to a very strong fund because of the realization of the necessity and the ability to meet it. The Typographical Union is of this sort. These reasons will be sufficient to explain the variety of forms of administration of these funds.

Illustration: Typographical Union. — One of the best organized of these benefit plans is that maintained by the Typographical Union. In 1891 a defense or strike fund was established. That fund is still maintained and is administered by the
executive council. In case of strike a benefit of five dollars a
week to single members and seven dollars a week to married
members is paid, when the strike has been ordered in the regular
way. The nature of the demands on this fund has changed in
recent years. In the earlier times strikes were more frequent.
The extension of trade agreements and methods of settlement
of disputes have led to a reduction in the number and seriousness
of strikes. They are now reported as being "so few and small as
to be of little importance." The result is that the fund is now
used to defray all expenses incurred in the work of officers and
representatives engaged in settling disputes and adjusting or
negotiating agreements.

In 1892 was established a burial benefit of fifty dollars payable
on the death of a member in good standing. This was to be
supported by a tax of five cents a month from each member.
Later the tax was raised to seven and one-half cents and the
benefit to be paid was advanced to seventy-five dollars. Still
the leaders were dissatisfied. Proposals for changes led, in 1911,
to further increase. One-half of one per cent on all earnings of the
members was assessed. A payment was adopted beginning with
seventy-five dollars for membership of one year or less, and increasing by six grades to four hundred dollars for membership
of five years or over.

In 1905 began the discussion for a pension fund. This resulted
in the adoption of a plan in 1907, to go into effect the following
year. At first the provision was four dollars a week to members
sixty years of age of twenty years' good standing in membership
and unable to obtain sustaining employment. In 1910 was
added the provision for members seventy years of age with a
membership of ten years. Provision was also made for members
totally incapacitated for work if they had a twenty years'
membership. By later changes the amount has been increased
to five dollars. During the experience with this fund the assessment has increased from an average of thirty-seven cents per
member per month in 1909 to forty-three cents per member per
month in 1914. Up to May 31, 1914, applications to the num-

ber of 1,770 had been received, of which 1,691 were approved. Deaths have reduced the number of pensioners to 1,210. Of these eighty-seven are under sixty years of age. Seven are women.

One other feature of this organization must be mentioned. It is the Home for Union Printers, maintained by the Typographical Union at Colorado Springs. It was erected in 1892 at a cost of $70,000, was free from debt at its completion with a surplus of $13,000 as a credit fund. At a later date a hospital annex was added at a cost of $40,000. Other additions have been made since; library, laundry, boiler plant, superintendent's cottage, greenhouses, and barns. Together with the eighty acres of land the entire plant is valued at $1,000,000. In nineteen years the Typographical Union has expended in building and maintaining the Home something over $1,250,000.

This union has paid out for

Pensions	$ 947,094.00	in 14 years
Mortuary benefit (old)	653,045.00	in 20 years
Mortuary benefit (new)	522,540.75	in 2 years
Strike benefit	4,136,577.18	in 22 years
Total	$6,259,256.93	

Though no union has a more elaborately worked out and more substantial system of benefits than the Typographical Union, there are others whose systems are both thorough and reliable. The Cigar Makers Union has been from its beginning one of the pioneers in the field. Its sick and death benefits were established in 1881; death benefits for members' wives, in 1887; death benefits for widowed mothers of unmarried members, in 1891; permanent disability benefits for members, in 1902; unemployment benefits for members, in 1889.

The Order of Railway Conductors instituted their mutual benefit department in 1882, providing for death and permanent disability benefits and the privileges of a Home for Aged and Disabled Railroad Employees of America. This Home is maintained by the joint support of the railroad brotherhoods of engineers, firemen, conductors and trainmen.

Common Elements in Management. — There is no uniformity in the arrangement and management of benefit funds. Yet a general description may be given that will convey some idea of methods. The funds are raised as a part of the dues and assessments of members. In most cases a single sum is assessed as constituting the dues for the week or the month. Of this amount a designated portion goes to one fund; another portion to a second fund, and so on around. In such cases the funds for the several purposes are kept separate. In other instances there is but one fund into which all dues are paid and from which are taken the benefit payments provided for. The latter is coming to be the more usual method. These funds are usually in charge of the general officers, the president, the secretary-treasurer, or the executive board or council. Reports are submitted and audited at regular intervals.

There is no approach to uniformity in the kinds of benefits maintained by the several organizations or in the amounts paid. Generally there is an effort to scale them in accordance with some plan of progressive payments, dependent upon the length of membership, the age and the earning capacity.

Amount of Funds. — No accurate statement can be made as to the amounts paid out by these unions. An idea of the extensiveness of the funds handled may be formed from some typical figures. The International Association of Machinists, from 1898 to 1914, paid for death benefits a total of $593,464.00, and for strike benefits a total of $4,321,238.00. The Brotherhood of Carpenters and Joiners, during the years from 1883 to 1910, report having paid benefits to 20,442 cases amounting in all to $2,514,166.75. A further report from this union shows that during a period of thirty-four years in which the benefit provisions have been in existence there have been paid out from the insurance department $4,051,709.91 in death and disability funds. In the same time the locals from their funds paid out $2,600,000 in sick benefits. Strikes and lockouts cost $1,300,000 and organization work, $1,200,000. To other unions was donated the sum of $356,607.26. This makes a grand total of $9,508,317.17. The International Molders Union reports the amounts that have been expended from the date of establishment of the fund to the end of the year 1914.

Strike benefit....................	1859	$4,576,463.00
Death benefit....................	1880	936,946.25
Disability benefit................	1880	105,200.00
Sick benefit.....................	1896	2,522,373.00
Out-of-work benefit..............	1897	316,168.25
Total...................................		$8,457,150.50

Reports of the unions affiliated with the American Federation of Labor show the expenditures as reported through the executive council.

	1905	1913	1914
Death benefits.......$	742,421.23	$1,958,892.83	$2,157,241.27
Death benefits to widows...........	24,800.00	58,420.00	57,275.00
Sick benefits.........	582,874.13	816,336.41	1,031,098.13
Traveling expenses....	62,989.71	33,693.10	54,404.90
Insurance of tools....	5,180.41	2,875.24	3,278.07
Out-of-work.........	85,050.72	69,445.70	99,024.88
Total...........$	1,503,316.20	$2,939,663.28	$3,402,322.25

These statements do not include the unions not affiliated with the American Federation of Labor nor the locals that have funds separately administered. Any statement that would include the entire amount of all unions with all locals for all purposes would necessarily be but a guess. It is estimated on the basis of the latest information that during the year 1913 the organizations of the United States and Canada disbursed $15,000,000 in benefits to members. Of this amount $3,500,000 were used as strike benefits. The remainder was used for the other benefits that would come within the list. This estimate is not made to include sums granted for special cases, as these figures are not usually included in the official reports.

The significance of this branch of union activity is not to be measured in terms of insurance value alone. Yet as insurance value it cannot be overlooked. This gives rise to two standards by which the importance of the policy may be estimated.

Insurance Value: To Laborers. — As a means of insurance it has a value that is not to be underestimated. No one can doubt the importance of general insurance. In modern society this provision for the future has passed quite entirely from the hands of the individual. It has been both organized and socialized. The laborer with his relatively small income and large family, his rising standard of living and his more slowly rising wage increase, is not able to cope with the question by himself. In recognition of this, various means have been organized for his assistance. Commercial life insurance policies have been written for his special benefit, carrying small amounts and with small premiums due at frequent intervals. Because this business must be solicited often in a field where prejudice against it is strong and because it must yield a profit to its managers, this form of insurance, reasonable as it may be in price, is none the less expensive to the laborer. Besides, it is more generally life insurance only and does not cover other forms of benefit except at prohibitive prices.

Employers' Plans. — Large employers have in many cases established benefit funds for their employees. These include many of the railroads, the United States Steel Corporation, the International Harvester Company, and a large number in other industries. In some cases the employee contributes a small portion of his wage to the fund while the employer provides the rest. In other cases the employer sets aside the entire amount. A definite schedule of benefits against sickness, accident, or other disability is arranged. The company administers the fund, thus taking care of all clerical expense.

Response of Employees. — The laborers have not responded very heartily to these various efforts. They regard them as paternalistic. Further, they hold that such plans do not leave them free to change employment. The provisions naturally require a stated length of service with the company before the individual employee is entitled to become a beneficiary of the fund. The employee insists that his own interests require that he shall be free to change from one employer to another at will. In addition to this there is a deep-seated feeling in the minds of many that in some way the employer reimburses himself through a readjustment of wages for any outlay made in a benefit fund. This means suspicion, and whether justly founded or not, it at once undermines the mutual confidence necessary to such a plan.

State Insurance. — The progress in America has been slow along lines of state insurance. There is no policy or principle of state activity in accordance with which any definite program may be anticipated. Employers' liability in case of accidents has quite completely broken down. It never did extend to benefits or provisions other than accidents and obviously related injuries. As for state insurance along other lines what the future may hold has not yet been revealed. Once started, the accident provisions have made surprising progress in the form of compensation legislation. Industrial diseases are even now the subject of careful and extensive investigation and already proposals have appeared for legislation along this line.

Practical Difficulties. — The whole situation, however, is full of difficulties. The laborers are not standing by and allowing the more or less visionary reformers to have their own uninterrupted way. Compulsory sick insurance may suggest to the employer the establishment of health tests. As industrial disease often comes slowly, it may by these tests be detected in an early stage and the employee laid off before he can become a charge upon the industry. If it be unemployment and the establishment of state employment agencies, the laborers are alive to the cut in wages that may be made as a result of getting everybody employed. Such difficulties as these must be met or the proposals may be found to have the opposition of both employers and employees, and may come to be characterized as visionary or impractical.

Again, there are experiments that have not yet assumed proportions that would justify them in promising much. One of these is the savings bank plan of insurance as adopted in Massachusetts. In accordance with this plan a savings bank may write life insurance, the policies and provisions being protected by law. The particular advantage lies in the fact that they cannot go out to seek the business through field agents or advertising, and that much, if not all, of the clerical and administrative work can be charged against the running expense of the bank. This very materially reduces the expenses and makes possible low premiums. Though the first reports of this activity are promising, the plan is yet only in the experimental stage.

The above-named plans are the leading ones that exist for providing the laborer with insurance protection. In addition to these the unions have developed their own. In face of the competition, the union benefits have increased in size and have become more general. At the time of their beginning, speaking of them as representing a policy rather than as isolated instances, the other agencies that have been named did not exist. The idea was that of individual responsibility and each laborer was supposed to lay aside from his wages enough to provide for his own protection. After the other methods were developed, the unions have steadily clung to the idea that provision for themselves through mutual efforts was preferable. It seemed more in accordance with the American idea of independent action. It left the beneficiaries free to seek any field of labor within the trade. It left the management of both funds and policy entirely in the hands of their own officers, elected by themselves and responsible directly to them. The whole underlying principle has been one that has appealed strongly to the laborer's love of independence. It seems quite probable that these benefit funds will continue to be an important part of unionism. Though less frequently heard of because a less sensational part of union activity, they stand on their own merits and they accord with the ideas and ideals of American unionism.

Benefits as a Means to an End. — But their significance may be emphasized from another point of view. They have just been reviewed as an end in themselves. They may be regarded also as a means. American unionism has certain clearly defined objects in view. These objects can best be pursued consistently by strong organization. Every agency that binds members to the union by ties that remain strong in times when other bonds become weak is an agency to be cultivated. It becomes at once obvious that these various benefit funds are additional ties that bind the members to the union. After payments into the funds have been made over a long period, their investment value becomes more apparent. To break away from the union and to default in payment of dues will mean the loss of all payments made and the surrender of claims to the benefits. In this way, briefly stated, it must appear that the benefit funds of unions are important factors in strengthening unionism for the attainment of its larger purposes.

Newer Phases of the Movement. — Of the newer phases of policy, some of the points seem to be significant. There is a very distinct call from some of the more influential leaders for an increase in dues, and also for greater uniformity. That both fees and dues for all locals in a union should be uniform, is being insisted upon by many. Moreover, low as well as uniform initiation fees are urged. The low fee will lead to a greater willingness to join. Once in, it is the duty of the union to impress its advantages so clearly that somewhat higher dues will be paid. The higher dues should then be set and adjusted to the needs of the day and the creation of a reserve. It is urged as a warning that estimates of payments of the various benefits be conservative. It is better that the estimates be low and sure rather than more attractive but less reliable. It is easier to raise than to lower the payments and any excess of funds may go to the reserve.

At the conventions of the American Federation of Labor it has been proposed that the Federation itself establish an insurance department. This plan has been favorably reported by the committees to which it has at different sessions been referred. No steps have yet been taken to put such a plan in operation, however. Its general outline indicates that it contemplates the establishment of a fund under the control of the Federation officials. That it would greatly augment the influence of the Federation if it were a success goes without saying. It would probably be on the whole more economical. Overhead charges would be reduced through economies of management. This would represent a very considerable saving. Probably a greater portion of the fund could be kept in investment than is now the case with the several separate funds. Also it would appear that the risks to be covered would be in the aggregate less through the establishment of the larger group. One practical difficulty would of course be the adjustment of the rates to be paid by the different trades. Another, the arrangements that could be made for consolidating the several funds now existing, all carrying different benefit privileges. To secure mutual satisfaction on this point would require rare judgment and diplomacy.

Defects as well as Benefits. — While much may be said for the way in which benefit funds have been managed, it is nevertheless true that there are defects. The management has, in many cases, if not generally, been experimental. It has not been based upon actuarial experience. Indeed no such experience has been available in many cases. This deficiency and its attendant shortcoming has been counteracted by the variation of the rate or the dues payable. If funds were running low, the dues have been increased. This seems to have met with surprisingly little protest, probably because of the confidence placed in the managers. The funds, and indeed the whole plan, cannot come into such a position as to command general confidence until some more generally recognized insurance principles are adopted.

Another source of weakness is found in the fact that generally the benefit fund is not kept as a separate account. Indeed, it is urged that in all cases each union should have but one fund into which shall go all receipts and from which shall be taken all payments of benefits as well as other expenses. Such a policy does not seem to arouse confidence in the general plan of benefits. It admittedly keeps the benefit feature of unionism in a subordinate relation. It is at this point that a significant difference of opinion as well as of policy arises. As a fighting organization — and the militancy of unionism must not be lost from view — every particle of fighting strength must be at all times available. To separate a strike benefit from other benefits as a separate fund would place a limit on the militant strength of the union. This would tend to weaken unionism. On the other hand, if a strike once voted goes so far as to consume funds that have been accumulated for other benefit purposes the strikers might yield and return to work. It may be that the members would hold off longer before voting the strike. If the employer realizes this, he may refuse the longer to yield. Thus the steadying conservatism engendered by the hesitancy to enter upon a strike for fear of exhausting a fund may react to the gain of the employer and the disadvantage of the union. As to just how it does act in any particular case is difficult to tell. Clearly there are these tendencies in a direction that runs against the effectiveness of unionism as an aggressive bargaining machine and toward the conservatism of a mutual benefit association. Unionism halts between these tendencies. Which it will choose must be left for the unions to decide. It can hardly choose both.

Present indications seem to be that unionism rather than benefit protection will continue to be the choice. "An entirely false conception of the whole subject of trade union insurance is inevitable," writes John Mitchell, "unless one bears in mind that insurance is always subordinate to the trade policy of the unions. Trade unions are interested in protecting their members and paying them benefits in case of death, sickness, or disability, but are even more vitally interested in raising wages and improving conditions of employment."

PART IV
POLITICAL ACTIVITY

CHAPTER XXI

LEGISLATIVE METHODS

While it cannot be said that legislative activity is the main object of organized labor, it is one to which its leaders have given much attention. Though these unions no longer "go into politics" as so many of them did in the earlier years of their experience, they do not eschew that activity entirely. The organization of political parties, so long the dream of many labor leaders, has been abandoned for the present at least, and the parties already existing are chosen as the media through which their political desires are sought to be realized. Legislatures have seemed to be the special branch through which this might be done. Labor legislation has occupied and still continues to occupy a large place in the attention of leaders of the labor movement.

In a former chapter it has been shown how in an earlier day organizations were formed in the states for the purpose of exerting an influence on legislation. The unions had special programs that they wished to see enacted into law. There began to develop methods for accomplishing this. As time passed these methods were more fully elaborated. At the present there exists a specialized department that has for its particular function the securing of laws favorable to the cause of organized labor. It is the purpose of this chapter to describe the leading features of this work.

It will not be possible to describe the details of method as adopted by all of the numerous associations. Nor is such a course necessary. Many labor organizations have existed for a time or for a particular purpose no record of whose proceedings has been preserved. Some of these have undoubtedly been very influential along the line of their special interest. Many others have continued their existence and are still active. Among these are the several state organizations, now generally allied with the American Federation of Labor. These work for legislation in their respective states. The Federation itself is the strongest labor representative at Washington and it takes as one of its most serious duties the shaping of labor's legislative interests at the national capital. These allied organizations form a very strong influence and their effects upon legislation are beyond doubt. For the legislative departments of the city governments there are the city centrals. These are also very generally allied with the American Federation of Labor. They greatly strengthen the entire network of the organization. Then there are the unaffiliated unions. These too have their legislative departments.

Among all of these organizations there is a general similarity in methods of work, though of course varying somewhat in detail. The major portion of the material upon which this chapter is based is taken from the reports of one or two organizations as typical of methods generally adopted. This is done in the confidence that material so used will give a fairly accurate picture of the general influence that is being exerted for the purpose of securing the passage of laws in which laborers are directly interested.

The consideration of legislative methods may be conveniently divided into three parts: (1) the working of the annual conventions in session, including preliminary work; (2) the efforts to seat and unseat legislators according to their "records"; (3) the work done during the sessions of the legislatures, mainly by legislative committees.

ANNUAL CONVENTIONS

Fixing Time of Meeting.— The annual convention marks the beginning of the work. First of all it should be noted that considerable importance is attached to the time of meeting. In some of the states January has been selected, when the legislatures are just beginning the sessions and are in condition to be most strongly impressed by any action that the convention may take. In other instances the late summer or early fall has seemed preferable. At that time the candidates for the legislative positions are seeking nomination and they can be made aware of the wishes of trade unions along legislative lines. Previous to 1902 the American Federation of Labor held its annual convention in December. This date was at the time regarded with favor as it came just after the President's message had been read and before Congress settled down to serious work. This situation was favorable both to greater newspaper space in reporting its proceedings to the public and to larger influence with Congressmen as the work of organization was still in progress. Experience has led to a change and November is now the month of meeting. This November date is regarded as having superior advantages. It comes after the fall elections, before the opening of Congress and while the President's message is in preparation. This affords opportunity to impress upon Congress the wishes of the Convention while legislative work is being shaped for serious discussion.

Representative Nature of Convention. — With the time for meeting thus chosen with care, the next step is taken in the convention itself. Here much serious work is done. As has been described in a former chapter, these conventions are delegate bodies. Any union or any local may instruct its delegates to present to the convention a proposed line of legislation and to urge its adoption. Sometimes bills already drafted are presented through these channels. In other cases the convention will be presented with the object to be secured and asked to have a measure drafted that will accomplish the purpose. In either case the subject becomes then a matter of business before the convention and must go through the usual stages of consideration. It is generally the practice, and in some of the older organizations it is necessary, to refer any such measure to the executive council for endorsement. Obviously, an approval by that body will greatly strengthen the measure when it is brought before the convention. The disapproval of the council, however, does not necessarily prevent its introduction as an independent measure. In the same way, a measure originating with a local union may be endorsed by the central union of which the local is a member and such endorsement will have influence; but the withholding of such approval does not prevent the introduction of the measure before the convention. In practice, any local that has a measure to introduce will seek the approval of both the central union and the executive committee.

As a matter of fact a large number of proposals come before

the convention in this way and the endorsement of the central bodies and the executive council usually insures for them a favorable consideration, if not a favorable vote. The large central bodies are more active in originating bills than are the smaller ones, while comparatively few measures are originated by local unions not united with centrals. Through these agencies and this coöperation the articulation of local unions, central bodies, state and national organizations has been growing more perfect as the need for coöperation and unity of effort has developed.

Convention Initiates Measures. — In this way the convention is seen in one of its rôles, a revising, adjusting and regulating body. In addition to this is a second activity, that of originating measures of its own initiative. These may be proposed by the executive council, the president in his annual message and report, by the other officers or organizers of the association in their reports, or they may develop unexpectedly in the course of the work of the convention. This last is the most unusual in the better organized conventions. In such a case it is probable that the matter would be referred to the council for consideration and report at the next session. In the newer or more radical organizations a measure might be put through with no further consideration than this.

The Convention's Work. — With such a stream of bills and resolutions coming from such a variety of sources and representing such a complexity of interests often conflicting in character, the work of adjustment is indeed no easy matter, and the sessions of the convention are often exciting. In general the work of the convention is outlined by the executive council in the form of a program or list of measures. Copies of such programs are previously sent to each of the unions for its consideration before the time of the convention, and delegates often come instructed by their unions on particular measures. At present the proceedings of the convention are made as public as possible, though this has not always been the practice. The convention during its session listens to the report of the president outlining the general situation and calling attention to such particular questions as may be of current importance. The report of the legislative committee is also presented, describing the work of the past session of the legislature, recounting the fate of bills and the attitude of members of committees, and making special recommendations. The convention is divided into the several standing committees provided for by the constitution, and such other additional committees as may be necessary. To these committees all matters are referred for consideration. This regulation applies to all measures, both those previously instituted by local unions and those inaugurated by the convention itself. An important rule is that each committee must report, either favorably or unfavorably, on every bill or resolution referred to it. Their reports are then either adopted or rejected by the convention. A large number of the resolutions fail of a favorable report from the committee. The number varies, and different estimates are made. One reliable authority fixes it at about thirty per cent. The general policy of the conventions is stated by one intimately connected with their workings to be "to take favorable action for legislation upon propositions concerning which there is entire agreement, and to avoid that on which there is division."

The Legislative Program. — No matter how many conflicting interests may appear in the convention, after the adjournment there stands a definite program for the coming session of the legislature. The purpose of the convention is accomplished up to this stage in a very thorough manner. Out of the extreme complexity in the beginning has come in the end a well-defined policy as the result of a well-organized system of selecting, rejecting and uniting. A legislative program has been formulated. It represents the wishes of the members in so far as those wishes are regarded as practical and within reach.

EFFORTS TO SEAT LEGISLATORS

This legislative program must now be written into law. A part of the work has already been anticipated through agencies already organized, and results are secured as far as possible. Experience soon taught that efforts to influence legislators already seated are not sufficient. If members can be nominated and elected who are in favor of labor in general, much is gained at the beginning. There are two ways of working to secure such results. One is by independent local action to nominate a candidate within a district, and, if possible, elect him. The other is to unite the voting force of the unions within a district and turn it in favor of that party candidate already nominated who will make the most satisfactory pledges. From preference many unions will choose the former, but conditions often give them balance of power where they have not strength enough to carry an independent nomination. Hence they more frequently accept the pledges, relying as best they may upon their redemption. The influences tending to prevent independent political action are very real and very strong. They have been strong enough to prevent the plan of independent nominations of labor candidates from being generally adopted. Attempts in many instances to elect "labor representatives" to legislatures have met with failure while in but few has success been the outcome. This result has led very generally to the effort to select districts where the labor vote is large and to request the leading political party in those districts to nominate as their candidates members in good standing in labor unions affiliated with the state organization who should voice the wishes of the laborers in the legislature. This policy has grown out of the fact that however enthusiastic a laboring man may be in the interests of labor, he is at the same time something more than a laborer, and that this something holds him by ties too strong to permit of independent local political action. Together with this tendency there developed out of experience a practical difficulty that evidently was not at first foreseen. There were men of influence in the legislature who had served well the interests of labor. They took notice of the nomination of independent candidates. They made it known in unmistakable terms to the members of legislative committees of the unions that they saw no point in continuing to advocate labor measures only to have labor candidates nominated against them at the next election. They might have added further that for the same reason they would be unable to secure support from any of their colleagues in the future. The present tendency is away from independent nominations, at least until they can be made more general than district nominations, and towards the use of organized balance of power, in order to turn the scale as far as possible in favor of one of the candidates already nominated. Every effort is now made by leaders of the labor movement to seat friends of labor from both parties and then rely on their assistance for the passage of bills. In these efforts they are supported in a greatly varying degree by the labor voter. In general, he is prevented by numerous other considerations from following blindly the candidate who is most outspoken in his loyalty to the cause of labor.

Pledging the Candidates. — One way of getting a candidate to commit himself is to submit to him in public a pledge. These pledges are drawn up by the executive council and sent out to every senate and assembly district. In various ways and with as great publicity as possible the leaders in these districts ask the candidates to pledge themselves. The pledges name the leading measures to be presented to the legislature at its coming session. The number of measures inserted in the pledge varies from year to year, but the intention is to include the few that are regarded as of greatest importance.

Its Value. — There is difference of opinion among labor leaders themselves as to the real value of this system of pledging candidates. It has been used rather widely and for a long time. Resolutions have been introduced in the sessions of some of the conventions favoring the abandonment of the entire plan. Some leaders insist that it accomplishes nothing at all. It is, however, the only centralized effort made. All others depend much upon the locality, and vary greatly in efficacy according to the degree of enthusiasm that exists locally for the labor movement.

LEGISLATIVE SESSIONS

In this way a program of labor bills is prepared for presentation, and efforts made to secure legislators who will favor it. The problem that now confronts the managers may be summed up as follows: Given a number of bills to be enacted into law and a legislature only a few of whose members can be relied upon as friends through thick and thin, how can the greatest possible number of these bills be passed with the fewest possible changes or amendments?

Legislative Committee. — The organization's chief reliance for the accomplishment of this end is the legislative committee. This committee may be made up of members of the executive council, or it may be a special committee elected by the convention at its annual session. In the case of the elected committee one member will be designated as chairman. It will be his duty to be present at the capital during the entire session of the legislature to watch the interests of the laborers in the bills before the session and to call in his associates when needed. Such an arrangement centralizes very effectively the influence of the organization and maintains close communication with all members.

Its Varied Work. — To describe definitely and accurately the work of such a committee is difficult owing to the scope of its powers, the variety of their uses and the complexity of the interests involved. It is quite impossible to estimate mathematically the result of the work. The only way to secure an adequate idea of the extreme patience, tact and watchfulness necessary to the accomplishment of any results at all is to follow the work of a committee through a session of the legislature in one of the larger industrial states. A fairly clear idea may be gained from a reading of the reports of the committee and the resolutions and discussions of the annual conventions. The core of the work consists in taking the bills, getting them introduced, attending the hearings before committees, and urging individuals to vote favorably when the matter comes to a vote before the house. Yet if this were all that a committee did, no results at all could be expected. When is a bill to be introduced? Shall it be introduced first in the lower or in the upper house, or in both simultaneously? This settled, which member shall be chosen to introduce the bill? Will the bill be given a hearing? Will it ever be reported from committee? If so, will it be amended? Will it come to a final vote? If the bill lives through all this, there are the same dangers awaiting it in the next house, and in addition arise the questions: Has it passed the first house in time? If amended, is there time for a reconsideration? If finally passed by both houses, will it be signed or vetoed? Multiply these dangers by the number of bills to be cared for, and the product gives only a part of the duties and responsibilities of a chairman of a legislative committee in one of the larger states. Reports show that more bills are introduced in the lower than in the upper house and proportionately more bills pass the former. The introduction of the bills is looked after with much care. For instance, in one case there were thirteen bills to be introduced. The legislative committee called a conference with the legislators who were "known to be affiliated with organized labor," recognizing that it "was very essential that the members of the legislature in our favor should coöperate with us." Seven members responded to the call and the thirteen bills were divided among them for introduction. The work of the legislative committee at the time of legislative hearings is of extreme importance, as it is at this point that failure awaits by far the larger number of bills. Even while the measures are before the governor, the committee is still at work, and conferences between the governor and the chairman and the president of the state federation are by no means unusual.

The duties already described make the work extremely complicated. But still other matters increase the complexity. In most earlier cases there was no labor committee on the list of committees of the legislature. Labor bills were then distributed among a number of committees for consideration. This would often result in several hearings being set for the same hour, as well as in increasing the number of committees to be watched. In such cases efforts were strongly bent in the direction of securing a labor committee as one of the standing committees of the body. In many legislatures this effort has been successful.

Obstacles in the Way of Success: Too Many Bills. — A serious handicap in the accomplishment of the work is the presentation of too many bills. The convention, through the necessity of various compromises, will endorse a long list of measures all of which are turned over to the care of the legislative committee. Experience soon began to teach its lesson at this point. Again and again in the reports of these legislative committees to the annual conventions warnings have been raised against this danger. "We have too many bills." "The greater the number urged the less our chances on any of them." "We believe that if determined action was taken, and only two or three bills presented at each session, more work would be accomplished."

However reasonable it may appear that the number of measures should be limited, in practice this proves very difficult to accomplish. The complaint is one of long standing. Yet the number of interests represented in all the different unions is so great and so varied that it seems quite impossible to hold the organizations together in the face of the opposition that would arise if a narrow limit were established in the number of bills chosen. The number of interests is so large and the importance of keeping them all in line is so great that in practice the list of measures placed in the hands of the legislative committees is still quite too long. The contrast will appear if two states are taken as examples. In one of these the state federation recently confined its campaign to eight specific measures: a constitutional convention; workmen's compensation; short firers' law; eight-hour law for women; anti-injunction law; building law; and a ventilation law for metal workers. This list seems reasonably short and one upon which the legislative committee could profitably concentrate its efforts. What was done by the numerous organizations who proposed measures that were not incorporated into the program is not a matter of record. If the legislative committee did not have some of them to contend with as independent lobbyists before the legislature adjourned, they escaped in very good fortune indeed.

In the other of these two cases the state convention drew up a legislative program. One of the leading labor papers of the state printed the list with the following interesting comment: "The list includes a wide range of social activities, and is an emphatic denial that labor unions are only interested in 'more money.'" Then followed a list of "the most important of the proposals." This partial list contained twenty-seven measures to be enacted into law. Evidently these were only some of the bills. There were the initiative and referendum, women's suffrage, home rule for cities, a free state university, forbidding the sale of prison-made goods in the open market, supervision of all employment agencies, representation of labor on all commissions having a membership of three or more, — these are some of the "most important of the proposals." All were to be dealt with in the single session of the state legislature. If experience can count for anything, it would not be difficult to guess the outcome of such a program.

Not only is the number of bills a detriment. Many of them prove to be poorly drafted. Much time is spent in correcting them, if indeed they are not thrown out entirely because of this fault. "I would further recommend," says one president in his annual report, "that all bills that we pass for the legislature be examined with care and all defects removed therefrom, so that the legislative committee will be enabled to present an almost perfect bill." "Sometimes," reports a committee, "bills come into the hands of your committee in such bad shape that it is necessary to have a lawyer revise them."

Too Many Committees. — And in addition to these drawbacks other obstacles arise. Especially in the earlier years of the development of these legislative methods there were several committees in the field, representing rival labor organizations. Prior to 1897 in New York State there were three separate legislative committees urging three separate programs. These resembled each other in only a few leading measures and differed in numerous essential points. Where the rivalry between the branches of the Knights of Labor and those of the American Federation of Labor has been keen, there have been maintained two separate committees. In such a case it not infrequently happens that two labor bills on the same subject will be introduced in the same session of the same legislature, one coming from each committee. This will necessitate delay before the legislature while the two committees either fight it out between themselves or come to a compromise draft of the bill. During the agitation against Pinkerton men in New York there were three separate bills urged by three separate organizations each claiming to represent the interests of organized labor in the state. Each committee worked hard to get its own bill reported in preference to the others. Finally the codes committee, to which the measures had been referred in the legislature, told the contending parties that if they would draft a bill agreeable to all concerned, it would be reported favorably. The year following this experience a State Printing bill came up for consideration and the three committees joined hands in pushing it.

As if to add to the confusion it will sometimes happen that local societies will bring their own measures forward as labor bills. It may be that they have attempted to secure an endorsement of the measure at the annual convention and failed, or it may be an instance of a local society not affiliated with a state federation. In any case such a measure will be urged as a labor bill. If such measure has not been endorsed by the state organization, the legislative committee will oppose it. This has at times led to great confusion and much uncertainty as to what are labor bills and what are not. In the reports of the New York

State Workingmen's Assembly occur complaints that indicate the frequency of this difficulty. The following is a typical statement from one of the reports: "There is no previous record of so large a number of bills being introduced or so many representatives of labor organizations being present. The Workingmen's Assembly, the state branch of the American Federation of Labor and the Knights of Labor, also several small societies, each had a full committee present. There was a deluge of labor bills. Not one real labor bill became a law. Members of the legislature who have watched and been friendly to labor legislation for years say there was too much of it, and they were right. To say that fifty labor measures were introduced is putting it mildly."

On another occasion a report states that "such diversity tends in a great measure to weaken our efforts, to defeat our plans and to prevent us from securing the legislation necessary for our protection and welfare. . . . Members of the legislature tell us that if we could only make up our minds as to what we want we might get something."

Organization Measures. — Wherever it has been possible to centralize authority the organization has endeavored to distinguish between its measures and those of others. It then announces that only its own bills are to be regarded as "labor measures" and that its own committee is in charge of all "official" measures. When this plan succeeds it destroys the influence behind a large number of local measures. The legislative committee quite generally adopts the policy of withholding its influence from any measure that has not received the endorsement or is not a part of the legislative program of the state organization.

One other source of confusion exists, one that is not so easily brought under control.

There is the introduction of bills dealing with labor interests by persons not considered to be "labor" men, and even by legislators themselves. Even though these may be excellent measures, the labor leaders usually refuse to recognize them. They undoubtedly consider this attitude necessary for the maintenance of efficient organization and supervision. Yet it cannot be said to be the full explanation. They take a very well-defined position in the matter. "More than half the labor bills introduced," they say, "are introduced for the purpose of giving the introducer political prestige in his district, or are introduced by scheming persons claiming to represent this or that labor organization, while the real object in view by the promoter is gain for himself." This is without doubt an unjustifiable accusation for any labor leader to make in such general terms, yet it shows the determination to keep the initiation of laws as much as possible in their own hands. It also shows an unwarrantable impatience with others who have very often only a desire to promote the good of all.

An instance of action on the part of the unions not affiliated with the American Federation of Labor is found in Indiana when, during the last session of the legislature, a coöperative board was formed by the agreement of eight representatives of the Brotherhood of Locomotive Engineers, Brotherhood of Locomotive Firemen and Enginemen, Order of Railroad Conductors, Brotherhood of Railroad Trainmen, and Order of Railroad Telegraphers. These men agreed to "support each other in every possible way." Three bills out of five were secured, the credit for which this group claims. One of the bills that was lost dealt with some requirements favorable to telegraph operators. It was opposed by a member of the legislature who was also a member of the Order of Railroad Conductors. Of this member the representative of the telegraphers reports to his union: "The interests of the telegraphers in a legislative way will probably have a better chance in the future if they see that Mr. W——— is kept in charge of his train on the . . . railroad instead of helping elect him as a representative."

Speaking of the results of the work in general the report concludes: "This was our first time to be represented at the General Assembly and our first effort to obtain favorable legislation, but it should be by no means our last. The representatives of the other brotherhoods have put many valuable laws on the statute books of the state of Indiana, due to their hard and persistent work during the sessions of the General Assembly. The telegraphers, due to their lack of representation, have practically no laws of a remedial character. What we are able to do in the future will be governed to a great extent by the amount of influence we can bring to bear in the political field, and each and every one of us should get into the game in our respective localities and see that our friends are rewarded and our enemies kept at home."

The Legislator's "Record." —· Reference has already been made to the plan of submitting pledges to candidates. After their election the idea is applied still further by keeping a careful record of all votes on labor bills. These results are embodied each year in the report of the legislative committee, and legislators are classified according to their records. Various classes have been made from time to time and in the several states. Some of these are "special mention"; "favorable mention"; "black list" and "dodgers." In other cases the two latter ones are "luke warm" and "black list." Other lists begin with "roll of honor." Legislators are assigned places in these lists according to the number of labor measures for which they vote. More recently the plans have been changed in some of the organizations. A list of names of all the legislators is printed and opposite each name is stated the number of bills supported, the number opposed and the number of absences at the time of voting. This is regarded as being a more reliable representation of the attitude of each one of the members. Those who have an unfavorable record, according to the classification adopted by the organization, are marked and the voters are supposed to "remember" them at the next election. The members of the legislative committee have learned from experience that such a list standing by itself is not to be taken as altogether conclusive. Even a good record is not always to be taken as favorable to the legislator. As they have stated in their reports the committee know of many cases where bills have been "held back through subterfuge or excuse until the last days of the session. Then the member, for the purpose of 'making a record,' will move the passage."

Close Touch with Locals. — The committee is always in correspondence with local organizations. This enables them at the critical point to draw in from local unions resolutions, letters or telegrams to members, and even special visits of delegations from some field where a doubtful vote may be turned or a hostile attitude modified.

Plans have been formulated from time to time for carrying this legislative organization still further. It has been proposed to organize local legislative committees or appoint local representatives in every district. This would enable the central agency at the capital to come in touch more quickly with the voters for the purpose of a demonstration. The local representative would be communicated with and it would be his duty to arouse those within his influence. It is supposed that a letter or a call from a member or a delegation of a constituency has far more weight with a legislator than pressure brought to bear from many other sources. Through the local committees advantage might be taken of this influence quickly and forcibly at those critical times when votes are needed and when other means of securing them have failed. This plan has not been easy to apply and it has not been extended to the lengths that it was at first hoped it would be.

Estimate of the System.— This is the outline of the system. In many points it is strong, in many it is weak. It is above all an intensely practical system. It aims to benefit labor and labor alone. It is suspicious of outside interference and jealous of suggestion. Its organization is becoming stronger as it is learning by experience. The demands of the future may be relied upon to modify its workings still further, and such modification will tend to eliminate the weak points and to strengthen those already strong. It may even now be regarded as a powerful influence in legislation. As to results, positive statements must be made with extreme caution. In general it may be said, beyond the possibility of contradiction, that the organization above described has been a potent factor in securing that body of laws known by the general name of labor legislation.

While it cannot be doubted that positive influence has been exerted, great difficulty arises in determining its exact extent. So numerous and interwoven are the various interests represented in the legislative halls that to single out any one of them and make a mathematical calculation of its force is impossible. To attribute the passage of any given law to the influence of any single organization, or to that of a group of allied organizations, is wholly unsafe. Even the opposition of directly conflicting interests may enlist in favor of a movement interests which were at first neutral.

Taking the laws that are denominated labor laws by the state departments of labor and tracing their development in the sessions of the legislatures, and at the same time making a parallel study of the proceedings of the conventions of the labor organizations, the reports of their officers and the legislative committees, it is believed that the study will show in a striking way, in nearly every case, both the activity of the labor organizations and their determined advocacy of the bills that have been enacted into law. The conclusion seems warranted that in securing the enactment of labor laws labor organizations have taken a very active interest and that, as compared with other organizations, they have exercised the greatest and in most cases the determining influence.

Recognition of the influence of labor leaders with the legislative bodies comes from unexpected sources and with no little authority. A leading New York daily has asked why labor is not represented in the legislative halls of the nation by its men of power and purpose. To this another New York daily replies. Having in mind the enactment of the Seamen's bill and the exceptions in favor of the farmer and the laborer made in the Clayton bill, it speaks directly to the point. "There is no need of such representation. Congress is a subordinate branch of the American Federation of Labor. . . . The men of 'power and purpose' among American laborites scorn to enter a body on which from the exterior they can impose their will. . . . The unsleeping watchmen of organized labor know how intrepid most Congressmen are when threatened with the 'labor vote.' The American laborites don't have to send men to Congress as their British brethren do to the House of Commons. From the galleries they watch the proceedings. They are mighty in committee rooms. They reason with the recalcitrant. They bulldoze the weak. They fight opponents in their Congress districts. There are no abler or more potent politicians than the labor leaders out of Congress. The labor representatives in it are usually small fry. . . . Why should rulers like Mr. Gompers and Mr. Furuseth go to Congress. They are a Supercongress."

CHAPTER XXII

LABOR LEGISLATION

With such a machine built up to secure legislation the question naturally arises: What results can it show? This question can be answered only in part; and this for two reasons. First: legislation is the result of a set of forces far too complex for such fine measurement. Other agencies and associations coöperate either purposefully or incidentally in the work of the lobby. The results cannot be separated to the definite credit of these various and separate factors. Labor organizations, for example, are quite uniformly in favor of child labor legislation. Yet the National Child Labor Committee is admittedly the leader in pushing this line of legislation, while the legislative committees of unions give very active support. In such a case it would obviously be equally unfair to give to either one of these organizations the entire credit or no credit for child labor legislation. Even this illustration takes no account of other groups that actively work in this particular line. Second: it is not easy to draw a clear line between labor legislation and other legislation. When a law is passed requiring the registration of tuberculosis cases it is difficult to classify. Some cases of this disease are clearly due to industrial causes, others are not. Yet the law makes no such distinction. Legislation requiring the licensing of chauffeurs or of operators of moving picture machines might be backed by a union of chauffeurs or of moving picture operatives, or it might be the result of a recommendation of public administrative officials made solely in the interests of public safety.

Difficult to Measure Results.—With such difficulties of analysis and classification in the way it is clearly impossible to state definitely the legislative results that are due to the labor-union lobby. Yet, speaking generally, there can be no doubt that the effort along this line has led to very positive results. The enthusiastic unionist is very firm in his claim that the large number of laws now in force for the benefit and protection of the human factor in industry is due solely to the persistency of union activity. The statement is undoubtedly an exaggeration of a truth. A study of the situation in its broader phases leads to the conclusion that the legislative activity of unionism is to be accorded a large part of the credit of having secured that body of law that we call labor legislation. Within the past few years, it must be admitted that other groups have played a very important rôle. The National Child Labor Committee with its state branches in many industrial states, the National Women's Trade Union League, the Consumers' League, the American Association for Labor Legislation; these are some of the important agencies in securing a large portion of the progressive industrial legislation of the past decade. They have usually worked in close coöperation with the legislative committees of the unions.

Early Phases of Legislation. — For reasons already stated, as well as because of limitation of space, it will be impossible in this chapter to do more than illustrate the results that have been won. Taking the earlier phases of this legislation, it must be noted that they antedate the labor movement as it is known to-day. Mechanic's lien laws, laws that reorganized the terms of militia service, and even the first ten-hour day legislation were the products of another movement. This era has been briefly referred to in a former chapter. Our factory legislation also was in its beginnings the product of other forces. English precedents coupled with some of our first serious investigations into factory conditions at home started a line of legislation that has been constantly augmented. Labor unions early in their own experience joined in with other agencies to push this group of laws. Recent movements to increase the number of inspectors have been strongly backed by the unions. These have met generally with success, often leading to the appointment of active trade-union men to some of the new positions created by the laws.

Bureaus of Labor. — One of the earliest movements seriously taken up by the legislative departments of the state organizations was the establishment of departments or bureaus of labor in the several states. This has been actively pushed until at present at least thirty-eight of the states, besides Hawaii, Porto Rico and the Philippines, have special legislation for this department of state administration. Seven other states have more limited activity in the same line, as factory or mine inspection. In several of these thirty-eight states there has been a reorganization in the form of an industrial commission that combines in one group the activities of the bureaus of labor and all other matters pertaining to industry in the state. These various departments of labor have been regarded by the unions as in some respects their own peculiar interest. Very frequently the heads of the departments have been chosen either from among the labor leaders themselves or upon their recommendation.

Immigration. — Immigration has been a subject in which unions are vitally interested. One phase of this is alien labor and laws regulating it. Not many kinds of alien labor can be regulated by law and so public works have been the center of attention. In nine states the employment of aliens on public works has been either prohibited or closely regulated. These laws have received the special attention of union legislative committees.

Varied Subjects of Legislation. — In mediation and arbitration there are numerous laws. Many states have state boards that are the result of legislation especially urged by union labor. There has been legislation along this line in thirty-four states. Hiring armed guards has been dealt with in ten states. Blacklisting of employees by employers has been subject to legislative action in twenty-six states. Laws against coercion of employees in trading are found in twenty states; regulating or forbidding company stores, eleven states. In twelve states laws declare that labor agreements are not conspiracies. In eleven a statement of cause of discharge is a legal requirement. The eight-hour day has been secured in some one of its phases in thirty states. Concerning employment offices provision has been made either for establishment of public or the regulating of private agencies in thirty-three states. Regulation of hours of labor appears to be frequent: in mines and smelters, fifteen states; railways, twenty-eight states; street railways, ten states; on public works, twenty-seven states. Concerning payment of wages in scrip thirty states have legislated; and in regulation of time and mode of wage payment, thirty-one states. There are laws for the protection of employees as members of labor organizations in nineteen states; laws requiring sufficient crews on trains in twenty-one states; laws regulating the construction of caboose cars on railroads in eighteen states. In nine states there are laws regulating rates of wages on public works.

In addition to these lines there are many special trades in which laws requiring examination, licensing or other regulation have been secured. Barbers have secured provision for examination and registration in fifteen states. In twenty-two states the licensing or other regulation of chauffeurs is provided for. Similar regulation is provided for horse-shoers in four states, plumbers in twenty-one states, steam firemen and engineers in ten states.

These are some of the lines along which union leaders have secured laws presumably in favor of workingmen. In practically all of these instances the laws are in a peculiar sense labor laws. They have been secured for the express purpose of benefiting the laborer in some way and giving him a point of advantage or removing a handicap in his bargaining power.

That this line of legislation is of increasing volume as well as importance will be made clear by a very brief comparison. Social legislation is very distinctly the order of the day. Reforms are numerous and each seeks legislative aid in accomplishing its immediate purpose. Labor legislation is very properly a part of social legislation.

Extent of Labor Legislation. — The United States Bureau of Labor Statistics has published on several occasions a compilation of the labor laws of the United States. The first of these was published for the year 1890 and contained 507 pages of law text. For the year 1896 a second compilation was issued, that time containing 1,178 pages. The latest issue is in two volumes and has over 2,000 pages of law text. The increase will appear still greater when it is considered that in each successive issue the line of distinction has been more strictly drawn, eliminating some material previously included.

Reports of actual results occasionally appear, though they are not in such form as to make comparisons reliable from year to year. For the year 1913 a report compiled by the American Federationist shows a total of 287 labor laws secured in that legislative year in forty states and the federal Congress. California led the list in point of number of laws, showing twenty statutes. Massachusetts enacted fourteen; New York, Ohio and Pennsylvania twelve each; Connecticut and Michigan ten each. Arizona and Georgia were the lowest in the numerical order, each enacting one such statute. These enactments included laws on workmen's compensation, employers' liability, health and sanitation, safety devices, convict labor, loan agents (or sharks), mining, eight-hour day, hours for women, mothers' (or widows') pensions, minimum wage laws for women, child labor, semi-monthly payment of wages, private employment bureaus, trades disputes, mediation and conciliation, state bureaus of labor, anti-injunction, and direct legislation. This report for a single year is typical alike in the number of laws in recent years and the variety of subjects dealt with.

Such a representation is but an approximately accurate showing of what labor's legislative campaigns have done even in securing legislation. On the negative side the list does not suggest at all what has been done. Many bills are introduced the effects of which the unionists regard as against their interests. Such measures are fought with all the vigor and effectiveness that the system can command. In many instances their opposition is successful. No count, even an approximate one, can be made of these measures. From the trade-union point of view it is quite as essential that such measures be defeated as it is that some others be passed. There is much, therefore, in the way of negative results that must be taken account of in any estimate of this legislative system.

Recent Tendencies of Unions. — In recent months there has appeared a tendency to check somewhat this legislative activity. For a time it seemed that unions had decided to attempt to write their every wish upon the statute books of the states as the shortest and surest way to the desired end. But experience is teaching its lesson and it is becoming evident that the lesson is being well learned. It has been found that the real vitality of a law lies quite as much in its administration as in its enactment. The enactment has proved to be comparatively easy. It has become evident that a factory inspection law may be quite effectively vetoed by having a limited number of inspectors. Again, if the powers of these inspectors are inadequate their effectiveness is seriously impaired. An inspection law, then, must be supplemented by legislation providing for sufficient numbers of inspectors armed with adequate powers. Then comes the personnel. If that be faulty, the entire plan so carefully and laboriously worked out comes to naught. It is being suggested that, after all, if the workingmen will organize and present, each group for its own shop, the demands for these improvements, they can be secured without legislation.

Experience has taught also that standards set by a law may easily be taken by an employer as a maximum while they are intended by the laborer as a minimum. This of course leads to difficulty. If after a bill has been finally fought through to a place on the statute books it proves to be an argument in the mouth of the employer for not going beyond its requirements, it develops into a boomerang. The policy of unionism is to continue demands one after another for the improvement of labor. A law setting up certain standards, as for example sanitary conditions in factories, is for the unionist a step in a forward movement. If it is not so, then the aggressive leader will naturally turn his back on the law as an aid and go in all the more energetically for collective bargaining.

Again, experience has shown that the employer can exert an influence also. In matters of shaping legislation the union leader has learned that to the employer lobbying is not a game with which he is entirely unfamiliar. The recent investigation of the "insidious lobby" to which President Wilson called the attention of Congress led to some very interesting if not surprising revelations. The knowledge that the employer can use his ability in the legislative field has undoubtedly checked somewhat the number of lines of work engaged in by the legislative representatives of organized labor.

Once more experience may be referred to as a teacher. Behind the legislature stands the court with its power to set aside laws as being out of accord with constitutional principles. Many a bill has been presented by trade-union conventions, urged upon the legislature, fought through in the face of the most stubborn resistance until finally the signature of a governor has made it a law. The expense in both time and money has been heavy. At the end an appeal is taken to the court and the whole of the work is undone in a court decision. To the laborer whose interest seems so intimately wrapped up in the matter, the court appears as an obstacle to the attainment of his ends. Collective bargaining, if employers can be made to accept the terms, will have no such tribunal of appeal.

Is the Policy Changing? — Such experiences as these are having a direct effect on the political policies of unionism. The advisability of their extended use is being more seriously questioned. This changing attitude is beginning to appear more conspicuously in the extension of maximum or minimum standards. At first the legislation establishing legal minimum wages for women was actively supported by union leaders. The same is true of maximum hours of labor. More recently the situation has begun to appear in a new light. To secure conditions of labor in this way may result in weakening the feeling of dependence upon the union. Should such laws be extended so as to include men in mines, men in extra-hazardous trades and men in less dangerous industries; should the principle of police power be extended to cover public welfare in terms of the workers' welfare then workers would become quite entirely dependent upon legislatures and there would be felt no need for organization into unions and collective bargaining through union representatives. This prospect is by no means an inviting one. To prevent its development leaders are already beginning to speak out plainly against an extension of legislative activity.

By those who speak for this newer policy it is pointed out that "there is a broad and very significant difference between a minimum wage set by law and a minimum set by a trade union." A rate set by law is usually rigid, the conclusions of politicians in the forming of which employees have no voice, since they are usually adopted in trades that are largely if not entirely unorganized. In this sense the employees are treated as wards of the state. Minimum wage rates when established by trade unions are flexible and are the result of "free action on the part of free men and free women." "It is hoped" that laborers "will never permit state legislatures or state commissions in combination with employers the privilege of setting the wages of any male adults in the United States. That prerogative must remain at all hazards in the hands of the workers themselves as free men through their own organizations."

Will it be Abandoned? — It should not be inferred that this development indicates the abandonment of this line of work.

It is being pushed with vigor.   On the occasion of the revision of the constitution of New York state the officials of the State Federation of Labor called a conference in labor's interests. There were present officers of the American Federation of Labor, representatives of many local unions in the state and officers from twenty-five international unions.   A program of demands was drafted and a hearing held at which these demands were urged upon the convention for adoption, a strong argument being that the resolutions represented the wish of 700,000 members of organized labor.   As the Constitutional Convention did not acquiesce in the wishes of these labor leaders, practically the entire influence of the spokesmen of unionism in the state was raised against the adoption of the proposed amendments. The labor press of the state strongly urged that the labor vote of the state be cast as a "no" vote.   What influence this may have had in the overwhelming negative vote at the election it would be hazardous to say.   It seems very probable that it was one of the causes that brought about the result.

The instance of the La Follette bill for seamen is fresh in mind and illustrates well the strength of that union backed by the influence of the American Federation of Labor and the ability of Senator La Follette.   Everyone will recall the long legislative fight of the American Federation of Labor for the amendment of the Anti-trust law.   The session of 1915 finally enacted as a statutory declaration that "the labor of a human being is not a commodity or article of commerce."   The fight for statutory restriction of the use of the injunction is another item to be placed to the credit of this active organization.   The state federations of labor also continue to adopt their legislative programs.   These are regularly presented by the legislative committees for enactment into law.   There seems to be no cessation in this activity.

It appears from all the evidence at hand that the legislative activity of unions will continue.   It may run along somewhat restricted lines as experience directs.   It will be perfected into a still stronger agency and will continue to be a powerful weapon in the hands of labor leaders to be used at such time, in such manner and for such measures as may be dictated by a policy that is above all sternly practical.

CHAPTER XXIII

POLITICAL LABOR PARTY

The question of political party organization has been ever present with trade unionism. Whether or not a labor party will ever take a place among our political parties is a practical question, even if unanswerable.

The Lesson of History. — History throws some light upon the problem, but a light of varying color. From one angle of observation it appears that union movements have had their sad experience and have learned to let political organization alone. On the other hand, it may be made to appear that as the experiments in politics represent one phase of development, so too the later movement away from party activity is again but another phase of development in a later period. As conditions again change doubtless policies will be altered to suit the needs of the changing conditions. It appears from these somewhat conflicting views that prediction is hazardous.

Certain it is that experience must teach its lesson. Labor parties in the past have not been successful. The workingmen's parties of the late twenties and early thirties proved to be the death of the labor movement of that era. Since that time the experiment has been repeated with very much the same results. It seems characteristic of these early movements that, not knowing the reasons for their lack of influence, the leaders sought to eliminate the weakness through party organization. Politics seemed so inviting in its prospects, it is not to be wondered at that the laborer so recently enfranchised should look to the ballot. Its helpfulness seemed beyond estimate or expression. Its dangers had not yet appeared. Yet from the vantage ground of experience it can be seen that one of the most serious pitfalls of the organization movement of the past was that of political activity. Politics proved a deceptive attraction. Even as late as 1872 high hopes centered in the naming for the first time of a labor candidate for President of the United States. But political managers of the established parties proved too shrewd to be caught. It was easy for them to turn the movement to their own account.

Yet it does not follow that these experiences will be sufficient to deter the unions from further attempts. Labor unions may again be made the tools of party managers. It must be remembered also that labor unions out of politics are by no means free from the same danger. On the large platform of national affairs there is the effort of the Socialist Party to "capture" the American Federation of Labor and also some of the powerful nationals. At each of the conventions of the Federation for several years past one of the most exciting debates has been over the resolution introduced by the Socialists to commit the convention in some form or other to the Socialist Party. Similar efforts are made in the conventions of many trade unions. In the state federations and the city centrals the situation is even more exciting at times. Though the American Federation has not been carried by any of these resolutions, some of the state federations, — as Wisconsin, Michigan, Iowa and Minnesota, — have, at different times, voted in favor of a socialistic program of collective ownership and operation of productive enterprises. Many city centrals have voted in favor of such a program. Among these are New York, Cleveland, St. Louis, Milwaukee, Columbus, O., Erie, Wilkesbarre, Haverhill, Brockton, Terre Haute and others representing no particular size or locality. These votes have been passed at different times and do not mean necessarily a permanent adoption of such principles. It means that there is a predominance of delegates who feel safe or warranted at the time in such a vote. Many of the national unions have officially endorsed the socialist program. In 1907 there were found no less than sixteen such unions with a membership of 330,800. This is not to be taken as meaning that the entire membership was socialist. There was presumably in every case a minority of voters opposed to the resolution. Nor does it mean that this number of unions is either constant or increasing. The vote of one year may be rescinded the next. The situation means that there is in trade-unionism a strong following which holds to the principle that "the trade-union movement is the economic wing and the Socialist Party the political wing of the labor movement."

The other side of the relation is seen by a few facts that are typical. During the socialist régime in Milwaukee, five of the twelve socialists in the city council were trade unionists; also four of the five socialist supervisors and four of the six socialist members of the legislature. Evidence from other localities shows a large proportion of trade unionists among socialist candidates for office. It is further claimed that many more socialist candidates are unionist in sympathy, but from localities where there is no organization in their trade.

Local Politics. — Local politicians are constantly on the watch for opportunities to control city centrals. Discussions at all their meetings is closely followed and anyone suspected of having a political axe to grind is immediately set upon most vigorously by opposing interests. Indeed the surest defense in these centrals against being captured by any one of the parties is the clever watchfulness of members of other parties. What one cannot do because of the shrewdness of others, others cannot do for the same reason. These meetings sometimes resolve themselves into the most spirited of debates in which personalities are freely indulged in and accusations and counter-accusations pass into such excitement that an inexperienced observer would expect to see the meeting break up in a fight. Only a strong presiding officer can hope to prevent such an outcome at times.

Attitude of American Federation. — The American Federation of Labor has faced squarely the issue of political action. Its position is not one of drifting. The proposal first assumed definite form as a national question in 1893. From the first the plan was rejected. At the 1897 convention the Federation adopted a resolution as follows:

"Resolved, That the American Federation of Labor most firmly and unequivocally favors the independent use of the ballot by the trade unionists and workmen, united regardless of party, that we may elect men from our own ranks to make new laws and administer them along the lines laid down in the legislative demands of the American Federation of Labor, and at the same time secure an impartial judiciary that will not govern us by arbitrary injunctions of the courts, nor act as the pliant tools of corporate wealth.

"Resolved, That as our efforts are centered against all forms of industrial slavery and economic wrong, we must also direct our utmost energies to remove all forms of political servitude and party slavery, to the end that the working people may act as a unit at the polls at every election."

Essentially the same policy was indicated in the action of the last meeting. In resolutions adopted by formal vote it was urged that all state branches give attention to the legislative records of legislators as such records are issued and distributed, "to the end that workers generally may learn from reliable and authoritative sources who are the 'friends' of labor," and further that city and state bodies as well as locals be impressed with the necessity of electing their "friends" to city, state and national legislative bodies. In every possible case, it was urged, preference should be given to such friends as carry paid-up union cards.

Political Activity: Party Organization. — Though so strongly opposed to political party organization, the Federation by no means aims to keep clear of politics. This has been made plain in former chapters. Political activity without party organization is the straight and narrow way into which leaders have sought to direct all trade unionists. Political questions may be discussed freely but party questions are strictly taboo. The Constitution itself is made to regulate this in the provision declaring that "party politics, whether they be Democratic, Republican, Socialistic, Populistic, Prohibition, or any other, shall have no place in the Conventions of the American Federation of Labor." From the first, as it so fully appears, the Federation has urged its members to free themselves from party ties and to vote "for the good of the order;" to "keep politics out of the union and the union out of politics." Three specific recommendations made by the Executive Council in 1906 are still alive: (1) "Defeat all who have been hostile or indifferent to the demands of labor." (2) "If both parties ignore the demands of labor, a straight labor candidate should be nominated." (3) "The men who have shown themselves to be friendly to labor should be supported and no candidate nominated against them."

So far as present indications may be relied upon, there is no immediate prospect of a political party of laborers. The efforts are now being concentrated along other lines. The methods already described seem to offer to the minds of most of the leaders the more definite promise of results. Elections are regarded as of great importance because laborers may often carry a balance of power. As is urged by some of the more discerning, a representative can generally be elected only by having a majority of the vote. Even in case of a three-cornered contest a plurality vote must be cast by the laborers before a candidate of their own nomination can be elected. On the other hand, a minority, sometimes a small one, may organize a balance of power. It can then insist upon a suitable candidate or withhold the vote. In pursuit of this policy results have already begun to appear. In the Sixtieth Congress there were six men with union cards. At the next Congressional election this was increased to ten. In the Sixty-second Congress there were fifteen, and in the election of 1912 for the Sixty-third Congress the number elected was seventeen. This policy was begun in a formal and active way in 1906 when the president of the American Federation of Labor openly opposed in their own home districts Congressman Littlefield and Speaker Cannon. In his last report before the Federation convention, the president lays emphasis on the fact that "the Labor Group in Congress, consisting of seventeen union-card men, was of material assistance in outlining and carrying into effect a campaign to secure favorable action by Congress upon Labor's demands." The policy of a formal endorsement was put to its most ambitious application in the presidential election of 1908 when the officers of the Federation openly endorsed the Democratic candidate. These officers had presented their "demands" to each of the parties at its nominating convention. The action of the Democrats in embodying in their platform some of the policies which the Federation leaders were calling for was the cause of the endorsement. The result revealed the limitations of this movement. To Professor Hoxie the incident makes clear that "there is in America to-day no 'labor vote.' The evidence seems to show that no formidable proportion of the workers can be relied upon even to support working-class as against middle-class policies and leaders." Again, when President Roosevelt took the "open-shop" position in the government printing office in the Miller case, the order was sent out from headquarters at the next election instructing voters to vote for Parker.

Coupled with the many resolutions which indicate the present deliberate purpose of the American Federation of Labor is the opinion of leaders whose advice has always carried much weight. Warnings are sounded from these sources against the error of committing labor to any one political party, either to one of those already in existence or one formed by and from workingmen themselves. Writing in his book, Organized Labor, Mr. Mitchell says: "There is no doubt in my mind that the purposes of workingmen can better be attained by the formation of a solid group of men united in their political aspirations and their political demands, but not committed to the policy of forming a third party, than in any other way." To secure this solidification Mr. Mitchell urges upon all labor a closer alliance with the American Federation, the state federations and the city centrals as the basis of such organization. Only through these agencies should any trade seek to secure legislation.

Sentiment Favoring Party Action. — This view is not unanimously held, however. Among the more radical unions there appears at intervals the expression of an opinion favorable to more definite and positive political action. These views may be prophetic; they are not yet dominant. At the convention of the United Mine Workers in January, 1914, it was resolved that the time had arrived, "owing to the present economic conditions and the machinations of the interests in many places for the laboring people to come together in a political labor party." The resolution was left indefinite as to plan or details as no party was designated and no preparations for a new party were embodied in the resolution.

Other Forces at Work. — From other considerations it appears to some that a labor party may be expected before very many years. Two forces are emphasized as probable causes of such a development. The first of these is the success of associations of employers in curbing the activities of unions along collective bargaining lines and also in their efforts to check the enactment of labor legislation. There is no doubt that these associations in recent years have given labor leaders much anxious thought. Open shops have been established, strike funds have been accumulated in amounts that appear almost fabulous to some unions, and subtle substitutes for the blacklist have been developed in a very practical way. Parallel with this development the second force has appeared in the line of decisions made by the courts. In these views and the decisions resting upon them the labor leaders see an increasing difficulty placed in the way of what they regard as fair methods of bargaining collectively. For these obstacles they hold the courts responsible. Both of these lines of recent development have been matters of serious concern to trade unionists. They have led to a determination on the part of leaders to overcome the opposition found in them. In what way this can best be done appears not to be generally agreed upon as yet. There is reason to believe that this phase of the situation may result in a more definite political activity. Professor Carlton, speaking of the effects of employers' associations and the decisions of courts, comes to a definite conclusion, declaring that "a labor party is certain to appear soon after the average union man is thoroughly convinced that the old line business unionism has met obstacles which it cannot surmount." Undoubtedly there is ground for such a conclusion. The uncertainty lies in trying to determine where the limit of activity of business unionism will lie and when it will appear that the present unionism is helpless because of its form of organization. There are stages of development that lie between the present and this fundamental change that will in all probability be passed through. These stages have great possibilities without incurring any radical departure from business unionism as a form distinguished from political unionism.

One of these stages has already been described at length. That labor unions can shape legislation is a well-known fact. The mass of labor legislation on our statute books testifies to its truth. Even opponents admit it. "There are many evidences," writes one who represents the manufacturer's point of view in speaking of the legislation of 1913, "that organized labor achieves nearly all of its larger purposes in Washington. Not only do the better known of class labor measures pass without difficulty, though time is sometimes required for the work. Less conspicuous though equally significant things seem to be even easier of accomplishment." It seems certain that there are possibilities of perfection in this method of work that are yet undeveloped.

As a next stage lies the energetic advocacy of some of the

current progressive political movements. The initiative, the referendum, the recall and the direct primary all appeal to the unionist as potentially strong aids in securing labor legislation. The appeal doubtless lies in giving through these means a greater effectiveness to numbers and in checking very materially those methods of control which are so commonly associated with the party convention and party caucus control of legislative and administrative officers. Again with reference to the courts they appear strongly in favor of the judicial recall, the popular election of judges and the establishment of short judicial terms. All these various changes appeal to the laborer as very strongly in his interest in securing the legislation he desires and in holding in check legislative proposals to which he is hostile. That further advocacy of these measures will develop would seem evident from the fact that others champion the same reforms though not entirely for the same reasons. There is possible a union of forces, and this would not be so easily possible in the case of a separate party organization.

Three Obstacles to New Labor Party: Tradition. — Behind all this lie somewhat obscure yet very real difficulties. There are three obstacles that appear in the way of a new labor party. The first is an obstacle that confronts any such movement. Tradition has led us to speak of our two-party system and our third-party movements. The three or four such party organizations now existing are all referred to as "third parties." Evidently Americans have adjusted themselves quite generally to the idea that there are two parties and several "third parties." A new labor party would have to be, for a while at least, a "third party" and once that characterization was fastened to it, it would be difficult for it to become anything else. It is not to be overlooked in any practical reckoning.

Complex Modern Party Machinery. — Secondly, there is the machinery and complexity of the modern political party. This takes both time and money to build up. Experience and peculiar abilities of leadership are not only requisite; they are rare. The funds necessary to the legitimate work of a modern political party would be quite beyond the reach of the labor unions, burdened as they necessarily are by their present needs.

Old Party Loyalty. — Lastly, it must be remembered that to draw a voter to a new party it is necessary to draw him from an old party. Party affiliation is a factor to be reckoned with. Party leaders have acquired great skill in making their appeals. There is always the special form of appeal to workingmen. It is too well known to need more than passing reference. Yet its effectiveness cannot be overlooked. Laborers have interests other than those that arise within the narrow limits of the shop. Outside this sphere they do not all think alike. It is a task of time and of no small degree of difficulty to form from laborers a group of voters who will all think alike politically, and who will all place political interest subordinate to the interests of their labor.

Present Tendency. — More recent developments in the split of unionism into the trade and the industrial wings are significant. Industrialism has but little of party politics connected with it. Revolutionary industrialism has none. Socialism, on the other hand, is a recognized party movement, but it is not a unionist movement. Not alone is it broader than unionism; it is more inclusive than the labor movement itself. It stands for the improvement of society directly, though dealing with labor primarily. The union movement is not so broad. (The distinction will be suggested though not fully expressed in these statements.) Because of this distinction and because the socialist party comes in from the outside to claim labor's vote, it must meet with opposition. It appears in this light as a competitor with the other political parties. Trade unionism and industrial unionism occupy the middle ground. Revolutionary industrialism goes to the extreme against all political action. Socialism points to the other extreme; to political action for social revolution, but through agencies not primarily "unionist" in nature. Trade unionism has for the present taken its positive stand on middle ground between these two extremes, and it shows no significant signs of weakening in this attitude.

Taking into account all the various elements in the situation it appears extremely doubtful that a political labor party will appear within the next quarter century, even if it be admitted that there are elements that tend at present in that direction.

CHAPTER XXIV

LEGISLATION VERSUS COLLECTIVE BARGAINING

To understand the attitude of trade-union leaders toward political questions involves more than has yet been presented in these pages. It has been shown that they have a highly developed system for securing legislation; that by its means they have placed upon statute books a large number of labor laws; that there are always present among them some who are strongly in favor of more definite political action through a political party of laboring men. At this last point there appears a radical difference of opinion. The positive stand that the majority has taken against such action, successfully maintained thus far, can continue to hold its following only by securing the desired results in some other way. This is now being done through the adoption of a policy that at first sight may appear to be a direct and unaccountable reversal of former programs. It is the position that advises against so much legislation and in favor of more unionist activity; against aiming to secure ends by means of laws and in favor of accomplishing them through direct negotiation and agreement with employers. The explanation of this involves a long story. Though live with interest and very significant in all of its details, it is too long to be related in full in these pages. It can only be indicated in outline. It is the story of another phase of labor legislation, the side that does not always appear in statutes now in force among the laws of the states.

Lessons of Early Legislative Experience. — An early hope of the American laborer was a shorter day. Slowly through the middle of the last century the hours were reduced from the length which custom had established under the domestic system to the more regular, uniform and somewhat shorter hours adapted to the factory system. This movement was not rapid enough for the more impatient among leaders. Political action was popular and its aid was sought. Hours of labor became the subject of legislative enactment. In New York as early as 1867 a law had been enacted declaring that "eight hours of labor, between the rising and setting of the sun, shall be deemed and held to be a legal day's work, in all cases of labor and service by the day, where there is no contract or agreement to the contrary." The statute further provided, however, that no person was to be "prevented by anything herein contained from working as many hours overtime, or extra work, as he or she may see fit, the compensation to be agreed upon between the employer and employee." The law was applicable to mechanics generally as distinguished from agricultural labor and service "by the year, month or week." In 1870 it was further provided that the eight-hour provision should apply to all workmen employed by the state or any municipal corporation or any contractor doing public work. Such a statute is the expression of a wish for an eight-hour day. It goes no further. Of course it is evident on the face of it that the weak point in the law was the provision by which an agreement between employer and employee was sufficient to set aside the requirement of the statute. It is equally obvious that if the law had not contained such a provision it would have been held unconstitutional by the courts. The principles here involved, both legal and industrial, find early expression. The clash between them thus early resulted in favor of the law rather than of industry. This experience has been repeated many times. Statutes intended to adjust wage relations by law have been disappointing to those who thought the way would be so simple.

Another illustration of the same principle is found in the experience of the miners of Pennsylvania. In 1875 a law was passed to regulate the weighing of coal as a basis of wage payments. It provided that every operator should weigh the coal in the car as it came from the mine instead of waiting until it had been freed from slate or other impurities. This should be done in all mines where payment was by weight instead of by the day. But the act was not to apply in case a contract was made with the miners to do otherwise than was provided in the act. The investigation made by the Anthracite Coal Strike Commission, as stated in its report, shows that the law had never been of any significance as a factor in fixing the wage bargain. No charge of violating the law could be made to rest against the coal operators, because of the provision allowing the operators to agree by contract with miners to do otherwise than the law required. Such contract had been assumed by the operators to be a part of the terms of employment. The court had not been called upon to consider the statute, but there can be no doubt that, had the law been passed in 1875 without this special contract provision, it would not have been upheld.

Results of Early Lessons. — Such laws as these the laborers soon learned from experience were of no real value to them. To allow freedom of contract to agree otherwise meant quite uniformly that a different agreement would be made. The employer's superior bargaining advantage led to the practical annulment of this kind of legislation. All possible benefits of the laws were lost to the workers and the situation remained as it was at the outset, one of bargain, pure and simple.

Change in Policy. — The realization of such a situation led to a change of policy. This opened a new era and led to a new line of legislation. The question of wage payment was taken to the legislatures for regulation. In mines, lumber camps and other remote places employers had adopted the expedient of the company store as a convenient means of securing supplies for laborers. As trade with these stores could be carried on by accounts instead of cash, the companies soon found that pay orders, or scrip, could be substituted for money. Doubtless the introduction of the company store and scrip payments met a real need of these communities in the earlier days. Transportation and communication were difficult and expensive. The camps, or groups of workmen, even when housed with their families, were very much isolated. The inducements for individual enterprise were not great. And yet the situation was essentially monopolistic. Competition with the company stores was not welcome. Prices and terms for using scrip payments were regulated solely by the company. Abuses were charged against which the workmen declared their inability to protect themselves. As the centers of these industries became more easily accessible the potential competition was checked by more arbitrary rules made by the companies. Payments were made only in scrip and the scrip was good only at the company stores, as it was not redeemed at par if presented through any other channel. The workmen could get money only by discounting the scrip. Employment could be secured only upon agreement to accept these conditions of scrip payment and willingness to trade at the company stores. Against these disadvantageous conditions the only hope seemed to be from the legislature. Campaigns were organized and laws secured in several of the states regulating or prohibiting the company store and the use of scrip in wage payments.

In 1880 such a law was taken to court in Maryland and was declared to be valid. In 1886 a law for a similar purpose in Pennsylvania was declared void. Three years later the West Virginia court overthrew a law in that state. During the next decade Illinois, Missouri and Kansas had passed this legislation and in each case it was held by the courts to be unconstitutional. In 1901 the United States Supreme Court upheld a decision supporting a law which the Supreme Court of Tennessee had declared valid. Since that time there has been legislation in a number of states dealing with scrip payment of wages and company stores. As the laws now stand, the employees are fairly well protected. In cases where scrip may be used, its use is guarded by requirements for redemption at par within short time limits and for interest payments if not redeemed at an early date. Company stores, where allowed, are generally subject to penalties for charging unfair prices.

Results of the Change: Two Theories Developed. — The effects of these experiences have not been forgotten by the unionists. The legislation to which courts have given their sanction has been held by them to rest upon the inequality of bargaining power and the need for protection to the laborer. Running through the opinions is the idea that the laborers are lacking in strength and need the assistance of the government. This patronizing attitude the union man does not like. On the other hand, where courts have held the laws unconstitutional, the reasoning has been less satisfactory. The laborers were regarded by the courts as citizens in the full meaning of the term, independent to choose or reject working conditions. A statute that forbade scrip payment was regarded by the courts as an infringement not only on the freedom of contract of the employer but upon that of the employee as well. Each party to a wage agreement must be left free to bargain for wages and conditions of payment. The kind of interference proposed by the laws was not warranted by any public necessity and consequently was an unjustifiable infringement on the laborer's right to contract.

If leaders have disliked the former line of reasoning they have disapproved still more the latter. The objections to the former were general, if not theoretical. To the latter the objections are practical and specific. Conditions left the freedom of contract quite entirely with the employer. The laborer was free to accept the conditions or "seek work elsewhere," which generally meant go without work.

Further Application of the Principle. — This principle was applied in other lines of legislation also and with results that were essentially the same. Either the laws were upheld by a reasoning that placed the laborer in an undesirable position of dependence or they were declared void on the grounds that they interfered with freedom of contract and with the liberty of the workman.

Joining the results of these two stages of development, it has appeared that if statutes are framed with a provision that by agreement their provisions may be set aside, they amount to nothing. If such a provision is not included, then the laborer becomes in some sense a ward of the state or he is deprived of the advantage of the law in the interest of his freedom of contract.

Efforts to regulate hours of labor in dangerous trades, in mines and smelters, on railroads and on public work have all had varied results in different court jurisdictions. Again, special trades have appealed to law-making bodies for protection. Barbers wanted Sunday closing and a shorter day. These were secured by law and were brought to court for the constitutionality test. The courts of New York, Georgia, California, Illinois and the United States Supreme Court were scenes of trial in which important principles were discussed. In California and Illinois freedom of contract was asserted to be unwarrantably violated. The barber should not be restricted from entering into an agreement to work on Sunday if he chose to do so. In New York and in the United States Supreme Court the laws were upheld as a valid exercise of legislative police power. The one day rest in seven is a rule that, in the opinion of these courts, is recognized throughout the whole civilized world as necessary to physical and moral welfare.

The application of this rule to the trade in question is but a recognition on the part of the legislature of its need. Here again is essentially the same two conflicting principles forcing the unionists to the disagreeable necessity of choosing between them when neither is acceptable.

Further than this stage, the developments of legislation have been carried in the direction of restriction of hours of labor for women and the establishment of a legal minimum wage. Laws that regulate the hours of labor for women, after the defeat in Illinois in 1895, have now been very generally accepted. The principle of such regulation may be said to be legally established, Illinois in 1910 having reversed its former decision. It rests upon the fact that women are of necessity handicapped in the struggle that goes with wage bargaining and that laws are necessary to equalize bargaining power so that workdays may be kept within the limits that physical welfare and the health of coming generations have established. Minimum wage legislation has been enacted but recently, and the courts have not yet finally passed upon it. If it is overthrown it will probably be upon the ground that public necessity does not call for so radical an interference with freedom of contract. If supported it will probably be as a social necessity, both for better bargaining conditions on wages and better health conditions made possible by a minimum living standard.

Experience brings Reaction. — Such an outline review of legislation as a means of protection for bargaining over labor conditions will be sufficient to suggest how trade unionists feel toward an unlimited program of legislation. They are beginning to draw rather sharp lines of limitation. More recently some very outspoken statements have been heard against placing so much reliance in legislation. It is now found expressed in the issue: legislation *versus* unionism; or, legislative dependence *versus* strength in bargaining power. This distinction is becoming more clearly marked. As a result leaders who formerly urged strongly in favor of going to the legislature to "demand" their rights now raise their voices against such a policy. Laws wiped out and court opinions unfavorable have brought about a reaction. The keynote of the newer policy is that unionism must do for itself through its own strength in bargaining what it wishes to have done toward a satisfactory wage agreement.

Unionism must strengthen itself not politically but economically. Wage bargaining must be backed by stronger and more general organization. When this is accomplished there will be no one to declare the agreement unconstitutional. The employer must meet labor's terms because labor is economically strong enough to compel him. He will live up to the agreements for the same reason. The result of this change of attitude is a renewed energy in the campaign for organization, for by this means will it be possible to act independently of legislatures. Unionism should not have any of its economic activities "chained to the police power of the state," declares the president of the Cigar Makers Union. Comparing eight hours by law and eight hours by unionism, he shows what his organization has accomplished. Through the efforts of the union an eight-hour day was established as early as 1886. If the attempt had been made to secure this through legislation, failure would almost certainly have been the result. With this shorter day has come lower death rate and less disease, greater earning capacity and more happiness. All this, it is asserted, has been accomplished "without being bound, gagged, and delivered to the state."

When the proposition of a legal minimum wage is advanced these leaders openly and positively reject it. Laws made for this purpose lead to commissions to adjust wage scales. On these commissions the laborers are not fairly represented. Even when a union man is appointed on a commission, he represents the state. This is true also of employers. They are both state representatives. "If the workers on wage boards are appointed by the state, or for that matter if the employers are appointed in the same way, then neither the workers or the employers in the trade are represented on the board. . . . The board represents the state." The inference is that the conclusions reached must be political rather than industrial. This chain of consequences is followed one link further and it is asserted that even the unions themselves, subject to state-adjusted wages, must become state unions. "We have in fact a practical assurance in all minimum wage statutes that the wages boards are the forerunners of state-made unions." The wage adopted is usually, if not always, a compromise. It is made for them and not by them. This the unionists do not want. They propose to strengthen their organization and assert their own demands, and if a compromise is necessary it will be one of their own making. More than this, a union minimum wage is but temporary. It must be ever pushed upward. Legal standards become relatively more permanent. For this reason again they are objectionable.

When unskilled workers "organize and demand increases they secure higher rates than wages boards have yet attained. When a union in the course of bargaining agrees to a minimum wage it is usually the maximum or near it that is paid in the trade. It is the business of trade unions in fact never to *agree* to the actual minimum which prevails in a trade which is un-organized or partly unorganized, even if in defeat it ultimately accepts it."

Even in cases of legal minimum wages for women, there are those who urge that the policy is a wrong one. Its justification, based on the fact that women are difficult to organize, does not appear to be valid. If difficult to organize, then greater efforts at organization should be made. If weak, even when brought together into unions, then the strong unions should lend the hand of support. The state should not be arbiter even in this line of wage fixing.

Securing wage scales in this manner, it is insisted by union labor's representatives, meets the opposition of unionism be-cause it is not in accord with union methods. "The method of the true union is to bargain," they declare. "The function of all labor unions, trade, industrial, radical or conservative, is to act as a driving force in the economic world in the interests of labor, and to determine the cost and direction of labor. . . . No bargainer ever entered the field of bargaining with the announcement to all possible buyers what the lowest price is at which he will sell."

Growing Sentiment for Union Bargaining. — This attitude is more and more emphasized. The latest utterance at this time is that of the Executive Council of the American Federation in its report to the convention of 1915. Here again protest is raised against the philanthropic character of many of the efforts to improve the industrial condition of women. They insist that their industrial problems are in no wise different from those of men. "Industrial welfare cannot be worked out on a sex basis." The welfare of wage earners in industrial work must be "based upon fundamental principles which conserve human welfare and protect and develop all. These principles in nowise differ as between men and women." In order that these principles may be worked out and applied, the women, as the men, do not need "charity," "uplift work," "social clubs and social centers." They need organization that will enable them, as the men, to maintain a wage scale that will make possible a proper standard of living.

Following the same line of discussion, the report states that "the trade-union movement has opposed the regulation of working conditions, hours of work and wages for men in private industry by law or by political agents. Where equality between men and women is established, the endorsement of this principle for women becomes also a very serious menace to the liberty of the men wage earners. Any legislation that bestows upon political agents the right to control industrial relations in private industries becomes a serious menace and infringement upon the rights of free workers." Any theory that would bestow "upon the state the right to control and regulate industrial relations" would establish "a sort of political paternalism that might secure sole advantages for the wage earners, but would deprive them of their real freedom." "Since men and women now work on equality in industry, it is becoming daily more apparent that the paternalistic policy cannot be adopted in the case of women without danger to men."

Limits to the Reaction. — Such statements should not be interpreted as meaning that unionism, trade unionism more particularly, is about to abandon its policy of shaping legislation so far as possible to its own ends. There is a relative importance as between the two methods, the one political and the other industrial, and the greater emphasis is being placed more prominently on the latter. Speaking somewhat along this same line the president of the American Federation of Labor has said editorially: "The problems to be solved and the forces that will be effective are economic — hence the wisdom of the policy that the A. F. of L. has steadfastly pursued. There have been many other advisers, some sincere, others actuated by ulterior purposes, who have advised their wage-earners to put their faith in the ballot and to 'go to Congress.' But politics is concerned with providing opportunities, maintaining the right to activities, establishing ways and means by which things can be done — politics does not enter directly and intimately into industrial relations. Politics is a secondary force in industrial affairs. . . . The center of power has shifted from politics and government to industry and commerce. . . .

"Of course labor will 'go to Congress,' but it will be for the purpose of securing the largest degree of freedom to exercise the necessary normal activities of the workers for economic betterment; for the constructive work which the government alone can enact; and to voice the new demand for Labor's complete disenthrallment from every form and fact of unfreedom and inequality before the law."

"The best law made," it is insisted, "is made by labor itself." In evidence of this it is pointed out that the building trades have an eight-hour "law," and they do not have to go before a court to ask its constitutionality. The best labor laws are made in the union, not in the legislature. "There are two methods for securing for workers wages and working conditions in accord with ideals of justice: one, to place upon the workers themselves initiative and responsibility for working out their own welfare; the other, to place initiative and responsibility in some outside agency either private or governmental. The first method is based upon democratic principles, the other upon paternalistic."

President Gompers insists that women must have the ballot as a matter of justice to them. They cannot without it assume equal rights with free men in the struggles of life. At the same time this political power is not the prime requisite. "Industrial freedom must be fought out on the industrial field. It will be achieved when wage-earning women hold in their own hands the right and the power to participate in determining the conditions under which they shall work and the wages they shall receive. They can delegate this power to no outside authority if they wish industrial freedom. Industrial freedom is not a sex problem; it is a human problem. The same principles apply to men and women alike." To secure such results organization is essential. Organization and self-assertion through organization is the gospel preached by this experienced labor leader. The movement must be "real and candid; it must not allow itself to be suffocated or devitalized by frivolities and

386 AN INTRODUCTION TO STUDY OF ORGANIZED LABOR

pink-tea imitations that have so long kept women from healthy, sane living." Further, in much the same strain, women workers are warned against those who profit by exploiting the labor of women and at the same time offer substitutes for the trade-union movement; as "welfare work, vocational associations, and other charitable or semi-charitable institutions," in the name of the "usable tradition of the economic dependence of women." The trade-union movement is the one great movement that "offers women the opportunity to secure freedom as well as industrial protection."

With this very positive note of independence which must be regarded as applicable to legislative protection as well, may be placed the action of the last convention of the National Women's Trade Union League. A very comprehensive legislative program was outlined in the report of the legislative committee. It included most of the details that go to make up the wage contract; the eight-hour law, one day rest in seven, elimination of night work, weekly payment of wages, and minimum wage commissions to establish wage boards for each industry, having an equal representation of employers and workers and representatives from the public. This last proposal was discussed at length. The final vote expressed the determination of the convention to include the minimum wage provision in the legislative program. There was but one dissenting vote. The Consumers' League is another organization that is greatly interested in legislation for women workers. The American Association for Labor Legislation, as its name implies, is doing much in pushing legislative programs.

Summary. — Whether or not the strong influence of organized labor will be thrown on the side of these efforts is not yet fully revealed by this changing attitude. The situation is such that it cannot much longer remain in doubt. Should all these organizations coöperate, the influence will be quite irresistible. An increasing amount of labor legislation may confidently be expected. Should labor direct its efforts only along lines that prepare the way for greater bargaining strength, such as anti-injunction laws, freedom from anti-trust laws, for example, the situation will be changed. It not only would cease to advocate many practical measures which it is now understood to support. It would cease to coöperate with such associations as those just named. Such an attitude would be quickly seized by the opponents of these measures and construed into arguments. Labor itself, it would be urged, does not want such laws. It is extremely doubtful if much legislation now regarded as very desirable as social legislation could be enacted in face of such opposition. The situation at present is interesting because of this uncertainty. Much depends upon the extent to which organized labor will go in the next few years in placing insistence upon union collective bargaining as a substitute for legislation.

PART V

TRANSITIONAL STAGES

CHAPTER XXV

TRADE-UNION JURISDICTION

A source of friction well known to union men and their employers and little heard of outside of industrial circles is disagreement over jurisdiction. What is known as the jurisdictional dispute has in modern times come to be a serious cause of trouble. Not only does it lead to strikes, particularly sympathetic strikes, but it causes rivalry, antagonism and open fighting between locals and even between nationals that results in great confusion among employers who are willing to concede a large measure of collective bargaining.

Jurisdictional control may be of at least two kinds. One has to do with geographical limits; the other with trade or craft activity. Of the two, the latter is by far the more complex and troublesome.

Territorial Jurisdictional Disputes. — Territorial jurisdictional disputes come naturally from the growth of unions and the absorption of locals into nationals. As this concentration of organization has progressed, disputes of this nature have grown steadily of less importance. The presence of organizers in the field as national officers makes it still more rare for disputes to arise between locals of the same trade. These organizers form the locals and bring them into the union. Naturally the locals look to the nationals as their creators, the source of their authority. The national constitution fixes jurisdictional responsibility and control and in questions of interpretation the national officials are judges. Trouble of this kind is avoided by the nationals through regulations noted in a former chapter. The consent of existing locals must be secured when new ones are proposed where there is a prospect that trouble may arise. It is a general rule that locals applying for membership in the nationals will have their territory very clearly defined.

Early Locals. — Much trouble developed in the earlier period because locals sprang up in remote regions and through expansion extended their claims of territorial jurisdiction until they came into conflict. The Granite Cutters, for example, originally planned to limit their control to New England. Locals of granite cutters appeared, however, in neighboring states and asked for charters. Canadian locals also became applicants. Rather than see two or more independent nationals with doubtful permanency of territorial boundaries, it was decided to depart from the original plans. The applying locals were admitted to membership, and the union became an international.

An incident is recorded that has its amusing side though all the elements of serious trouble were present. A railroad was building a tunnel which began in the jurisdiction of one local and ended in that of another. One set of workmen belonging to one of the locals completed the work. The officers of the local whose jurisdiction had been invaded presented to the intruding local a demand for initiation fees and dues from the intruders. This was a quarter of a century ago and throws an interesting light upon the conditions of the day.

Growth of Nationals. — Though much of the possible friction has been removed by the growth of the more powerful nationals and the affiliation of so many of them into a national federation, sources of friction still remain. Some workmen are opposed to yielding control to a central authority. These may form an independent society. Its existence can hardly escape the vigilant observation of the officials of the national union of the trade. If the independents persist in standing out against all inducements to join the national movement, it is quite likely that means will be found for forming a rival local of members that are not opposed to nationalism. Thus two local bodies will dispute for jurisdiction in that locality, to the serious embarrassment of even kindly disposed employers as well as the confusion of the public mind. In some cases the discipline of the national may be too rigorous. Either suspension or secession may be the result. In other cases ambitious local leaders may build up a following and, failing to secure the recognition that they think they merit, may head a secession movement. Almost inevitably the national will seek to repair its loss by building up another local and affiliating it. This again will give rise to controversy over territorial jurisdiction.

It does not always happen that an independent movement

or a secession movement will be restricted to local territory. There are rivals for national territorial jurisdiction as well. These result from an inability of either to summon enough strength to bring the other to terms. There have been two associations of carpenters; the Amalgamated Society of Carpenters and Joiners having a membership of about 10,000 with headquarters in New York, and the United Brotherhood of Carpenters and Joiners of America with over 200,000 members and national offices in Indianapolis. The last named belongs to the American Federation of Labor, the charter of the former having been revoked in 1912. Electrical workers have two organizations. Each one is known as the International Brotherhood of Electrical Workers. Each has central offices in Springfield, Illinois. The membership of these two is about the same, though only one belongs to the American Federation. Such instances as these show the possibility of trouble over national territorial jurisdiction. The preponderating influence of the American Federation of Labor and its policy to issue charters to but one of two or more applicants that may be in territorial rivalry make this type of jurisdictional dispute less likely to arise.

Trade Jurisdictional Disputes. — The question of jurisdiction over trade or craft is far more important as it causes much more trouble and is far more difficult of adjustment. On the surface it would seem a very simple thing. Carpenters may rightly exercise jurisdiction over all carpenter work, and a union man belonging to a mason's union cannot dispute the claim with him. So a boot and shoe maker insists upon a difference between his work and that of garment making. The jurisdictions are clear and each recognizes the claims of the other. Rival unions may exist, to be sure, each claiming the right to represent unionism in garment making or in shoe making. A struggle of this nature is of course one of jurisdictional control but not the kind of strife that is causing most trouble in modern industry.

Changing Trade Lines. — Division and subdivision of labor, extensive use of machinery, changing methods of work, substitution of materials; all these exercise a constant influence upon conventional craft lines. Eighteenth century "trades" were broad and inclusive with clear cut dividing lines. Those of the twentieth century are so narrowed by the changes of modern industry as to be hardly recognizable by comparison. In the eighteenth-century sense of the word there are but few "trades" now. To maintain jurisdiction in the midst of these changes has caused great confusion and great embarrassment to the progress of the trade-union movement.

Confusion and Complexity. — Though simple to see so far as facts are concerned, the situation is not easy to comprehend. A solution seems baffling at present. If a roof is to be put on a building, the material will lie in different jurisdictions. If shingle, it belongs to the carpenters, presumably. Slate or tile would bring in the International Slate and Tile Roofers Union of America. A composition material would give rise to jurisdiction claims on the part of the Brotherhood of Composition Roofers. Laths in the past have been put on by carpenters. But for metal lath there is the Brotherhood of Metal Workers. But all lathing work is claimed by the Wood Wire and Metal Lathers International Union. With the extension of electric transportation, car drivers have become motormen. Steam railroads have established electric power and use their engineers on the electric engines. This opens a way for trouble between the Association of Street and Electric Railway Employees and the Brotherhood of Locomotive Engineers. When imitation marble or marbleithic tile is to be set there are the claims of the Plasterers International Association, the International Association of Marble Workers and the Ceramic, Mosaic and Encaustic Tile Layers and Helpers International Union. Metal doors and metal casings, known as "metal trim" is being used in fire-proof construction. Both carpenters and sheet metal workers claim this work as being within their respective jurisdictions. Pneumatic tubes, such as speaking tubes, delivery tubes and such, are coming into more general use. This kind of work has led to trouble between plumbers and gas fitters. The introduction of the linotype raised an issue between the printer and the machinist. An operator of a linotype under union rules could not repair the machine he operated. It was not clear whether selling meat in a meat market was work that belonged to the jurisdiction of the Brotherhood of Butcher Workmen of America or to that of the Retail Clerks International Protective Association.

These random illustrations show the complexity of jurisdictional disputes. When there is the work of employing many trades on one job the situation becomes a hopeless tangle. This has been woven into a brief description by Dr. Whitney that is well worth quoting in full. A large modern fire-proof building is to be erected.

"The work of excavation, requiring mainly unskilled labor, is claimed by the Hod Carriers and Building Laborers Union, and, except where the excavation is so deep that a hoisting engine or other machine is needed to bring up the dirt, it may be regarded as conceded to this union. If the foundation walls are built of stone, they will be claimed by the stonemasons, who are a part of the Bricklayers and Masons Union, since the jurisdiction claimed by this union covers the setting of all stone. If the foundation had been of brick, the work would have been controlled by the same national union. If the foundation had been of concrete, the Cement Workers would have laid claim to the work, while the Bricklayers and Masons Union would also have been likely to demand control of it, on the ground that the concrete was being used as substitute for brick or stone.

"The framework of the building, being of structural steel and iron, will be conceded to the Bridge and Structural Iron Workers Union. For the outside walls, if granite is used, the stone must be cut by the Granite Cutters, who have exclusive jurisdiction over the cutting of that material. If a sandstone or any stone softer than granite is used, the Journeymen Stone Cutters Association will control the cutting, though this may be contested in some cases by the stonemasons, who claim that very often it is necessary, or at least expedient, for them to cut stone in connection with setting it. On the other hand, the Stone Cutters may claim the placing of the stone in the wall on the score that the setting of stone is a branch of the stone cutter's art, but generally stone setting is yielded to the masons.

"The roof, if made of composition, slag, or other roofing material such as asphalt and gravel, will be built under the control of the Composition Roofers, who have jurisdiction over the placing of this roofing material; if the roof is of slate or tile, it is conceded to the Slate and Tile Roofers. The floors are likely to be of reinforced concrete. In that case the Carpenters will claim the building of all molds and forms; the mixing and the handling of the concrete will be demanded by both the Cement Workers and the Hod Carriers, while the Bricklayers will contend that such work ought to be done under the direction of a bricklayer foreman. Finally, the metal sheathing which forms the basis for the concrete is claimed both by the Lathers and by the Sheet Metal Workers. If the floors are made of wood, they will be conceded to the Carpenters as their work. The lathing of the building will be done by the Wood, Wire and Metal Lathers, though on one side this work approaches closely the trade line of the carpenter, and on the other that of the sheet metal worker.

"The painting and the decorating of the building will be claimed by the Painters, although the putting up of picture molding is demanded by the Carpenters on the ground that the material is wood and is attached by the use of carpenters' tools. The placing of the hollow metal doors and sash throughout the building will be considered by the Carpenters as belonging to their trade because this work requires the use of their tools and their skill and because the use of sheet metal is displacing what was formerly carpenters' work, while the Sheet Metal Workers regard this as part of their trade, inasmuch as they manufacture this material and do nothing but handle sheet metal, so that they have the skill necessary to erect it. Plumbing, heating and lighting are trades not very difficult to distinguish, but if a vacuum cleaning system, a sprinkler system, or some other extension of one of these older trades is to be installed, difficulties arise. The Steam Fitters maintain that custom ought to be the guide, that is, that it should be ascertained which trade group was originally regarded as the most competent to do the work, as evidenced by the choice of the builder. The Plumbers would also claim this work on the ground that they have men in their organization who practice these trades, and that the whole pipe-fitting industry ought to be united under their jurisdiction, but this complication arises out of the existence of dual associations, and is not due to uncertain trade lines.

"The construction of the elevators will be claimed in its entirety by the Elevator Constructors, but this demand will be opposed for different parts of the work by the Electrical Workers, the Sheet Metal Workers, the Machinists, the Structural Iron Workers, and the Carpenters, each of these unions claiming such part of the work as it regards as lying within its trade. The Elevator Constructors maintain that the whole work is so closely connected that it cannot be conveniently or properly performed in parts by different trades. The plastering of the building will be conceded to the Plasterers, since the work of applying plastic material to walls is pretty well defined. However, if certain forms of decorative plaster, which are made up in factories and cast in sections all ready to be nailed to the wall, are used, the Plasterers will still insist on the control of the work because the use of this material is displacing the older form of plaster, and the Carpenters will demand it on the ground that to nail these blocks to the wall is essentially their work since it is performed with their tools. The interior marble work for stairs, mantels, fireplaces and columns will be done under the jurisdiction of the Marble Workers, who have control of the cutting and setting of interior marble work, whereas if the same material were used on the outside of the building the Stone Cutters and the Masons would have control. The erection of the scaffolding used in various stages of the construction of the building will be claimed by the Hod Carriers and Building Laborers on the ground that it requires little skill and is therefore to be classed as laborers' work; by the Carpenters, because carpenters' tools are used; and, when scaffolding is to be used by the Marble Workers, by the Marble Workers Helpers on the ground that the erection of the scaffolding is closely associated with the placing of the marble."

Supplementing this statement with another made from the point of view of the troublesome strike arising over jurisdictional disputes, it has been insisted that "unless the related trades bargain jointly with employers and make joint agreements, the policy of waging sympathetic strikes increases the number involved in each conflict without reducing the number of such conflicts. For example, the carpenters engaged in the construction of a building declare a strike for higher wages, and the members of every other trade on the building quit work in sympathy. When this trouble has been adjusted, the plumbers discover that the employer has violated his agreement with them; and all trades again go on strike. Next, the elevator constructors and the hoisting engineers quarrel as to which of them shall run the completed elevator. The other trades take sides and all building operations are suspended until the dispute can be settled. Then the business agent of the plasterers' union finds that his trade has a grievance and orders every one to leave the building. This is not a very exaggerated picture of conditions in the building industry as they existed in Chicago just before 1900 or in New York during the spring and summer of 1902. Building operations were seriously demoralized. The time for the ultimate completion of a building was a matter of gamble with all odds in favor of delay. Building contractors, landlords, and the general public joined in a chorus of protest against the arbitrary methods of the unions."

Attempts to Solve Difficulties. — How to prevent conflict when these disputes over jurisdiction arise has thus far remained an unanswered question. Many attempts at solution have been made but none have met with very marked success. The plan of having the workman join two or more unions has been tried. This may help the individual laborer out of his embarrassment but it does not remove the cause of the difficulty. While the bricklayers and stone masons were organized in separate locals, in one instance a workman joined both locals. The bricklayers struck a job and the workman secured work on a stonemason job. His work called for drilling some holes for gas pipes through fire-proof arches. This was a bricklayer's job and consequently he was fined by his bricklayers' local for violating their rule against doing work on a struck job. An appeal to the national convention of bricklayers led to a revision of rules and a better adjustment between the trades.

Efforts are made by the nationals to make more and more clear the specific jurisdiction of their authority. In the constitution is stated as fully as possible the limits of the particular trade. Then every local applying for a charter must state what work it will control. If the local be a mixed local each member must register in one branch. In the Marble Workers Union, for example, a member must register himself as a cutter, polisher, machine hand, helper, quarryman or any other of the subdivisions. The carpenters as early as 1886 defined their jurisdiction. "Those persons are eligible to membership who are competent carpenters and joiners, engaged at wood work; and also any stair builder, millwright, planing mill bench hand or any cabinet maker engaged at carpenter work or any

carpenter running wood working machinery shall be eligible."
More recently these statements have been made much more
elaborate. The Electrical Workers declare that "each charter
must state the class of work and the geographical jurisdiction
covered by the charter and a record of each charter and its
jurisdiction must be kept with the International Order." The
Granite Cutters somewhat dictatorially assert their jurisdiction: "It is hereby declared and set forth," declares the Constitution, "that the Granite Cutters International Association
of America claims the right of jurisdiction over cutting, carving,
dressing, sawing and setting all granite and hard stone on which
granite cutters tools are used;" also all machine work for the
same; and further "declare and set forth that no other trade,
craft or calling has any right or jurisdiction over" these named
activities. The Typographical Union claims that its "jurisdiction shall include all branches of the printing and kindred
trades, other than those over which jurisdiction has been conceded by agreement." The Bricklayers, Masons and Plasterers
have an elaborate definition of what shall constitute bricklaying
masonry, stone masonry, artificial stone masonry and plastering. Of these the jurisdiction over artificial stone masonry
seems the most arbitrarily asserted. "The cutting, setting
and pointing of cement blocks or artificial stone, and all cement
that is used for backing up external walls, the building of party
walls, columns, girders, beams, floors, stairs, arches and plaster
block partitions, where substituted for brick."

By this means a national may control its locals. But this
is not the most serious phase. When nationals claim jurisdiction against each other, there is no controlling authority to
act as peacemaker. Recent trade-union history has some sad
stories in its pages because of these struggles between nationals.

The core workers organized a separate national union. Being
too weak to maintain a separate existence, they were forced
to amalgamate with the International Molders Union. Then
work in brass became more important. The molding of brass
was work for brass workers. It was also molding work. The
International Molders Union claimed jurisdiction. So also did
the Metal Polishers, Buffers, Platers, Brass and Silver Workers
Union of North America. A lively contention has been waged
between these nationals for more than a dozen years with no

permanent settlement other than voluntary "agreements" between "sovereign" officials. The Molders are also under the shadow of an amalgamation of all metal trades. The editor of the Molders trade journal in opposing this movement makes two points. Amalgamate, he says, means "to unite, to interweave, to intermingle, to make one and the same of what had formerly been separate bodies." To amalgamate would mean virtually that the Molders Union would pass out of existence as a separate body and its affairs would be managed by machinists, pattern-makers, blacksmiths, boilermakers and other metal trade workers while the molders would become responsible for all these other trades as well. As an example of what would happen, the editor then refers to the fate of the core workers. Until 1903 they had a separate national affiliated with the American Federation. They amalgamated with the Molders. This brought an end to their union with all its laws, policies, and its separate funds. They were governed by laws and policies as determined by the majority of molders.

In 1898 the Steam and Hot Water Fitters Union applied to the American Federation for a charter. The application was opposed by the Plumbers Union. The Federation granted a provisional charter providing that the Plumbers should keep their present members who were steam or hot water fitters and that they might admit to their membership others in towns that were too small for both unions to maintain locals. The plumbers continued their opposition. In 1911 the Federation extended the jurisdiction of the plumbers over all steam and hot water fitting work and the following year it refused to seat representatives of the Steam and Hot Water Fitters Union, extending the jurisdiction of the plumbers over all pipe trades. The result has been the formation of the United Association of Journeymen Plumbers, Gas Fitters, Steam Fitters and Steam Fitters Helpers of the United States and Canada, affiliated with the American Federation of Labor, and the separate existence of the International Association of Steam, Hot Water and Power Pipe Fitters and Helpers of America.

Tendency toward Amalgamation. — In such struggles as these there has resulted an amalgamation of the unions into a common organization with a single constitution. Details of laws and rules have been worked out in each instance to meet the particular case. Even the names of some of the associations suggest much of strife and adjustment on the basis of a working agreement. The Amalgamated Bluestone Cutters, Flaggers, Curb and Bridge Setters of America; International Brotherhood of Boiler Makers, Iron Ship Builders and Helpers of America; International Brick, Tile, and Terra Cotta Workers Alliance; Bricklayers, Masons and Plasterers International Union; International Union of Carriage, Wagon and Automobile Workers; Brotherhood of Painters, Decorators, and Paper Hangers of America; International Union of Pavers, Rammermen, Flag Layers, Bridge and Stone Curb Setters; International Union of Shingle Weavers, Sawmill Workers and Woodsmen; Hotel and Restaurant Employers International Alliance and Bartenders International League of America — such associations as these reveal one method of solving the difficulty. Nearly all of them are smaller unions with enough interests in common to lead to some kind of amalgamation. When one union is more powerful than its jurisdictional rival the result tells a different tale. The Typographical Union has won against the Association of Machinists in the contest for jurisdiction over machine tenders in printing establishments. Both Brewery Workers and Mine Workers have won over the Engineers. At the convention of the American Federation of Labor in 1914 there were many contests still unsettled. The Association of Longshoremen and the Seamans Union were at odds over the jurisdiction of men employed in marine warehouses. A long controversy between the United Brotherhood of Carpenters and Joiners and the Amalgamated Society of Carpenters and Joiners was announced as having been ended. Trouble was reported as still unsettled between the International Brotherhood of Steam Shovel and Dredgemen, the Associated Union of Steam Shovelmen, and the International Union of Steam and Operating Engineers. The Cigar Makers International Union and the National Stogie Makers League were at odds. Other controversies were those between the Brewery Workers and the Coopers International Union; the International Printing Pressmen and the International Plate Printers Union over new processes and new presses; Stove Mounters and Sheet Metal Workers; Machinists and Elevator Constructors; Blacksmiths and Bridge and Structural Iron Workers; Plasterers and Carpenters; Lithographers, Printing Pressmen and Photo-Engravers; Lithographers and Lithographic Pressfeeders; Hod Carriers and Cement Workers; Upholsterers and Carpet Mechanics; Blacksmiths and Tunnel and Subway Constructors; Tunnel and Subway Constructors and Compressed Air Workers; Electrical Workers and Theatrical Stage Employees; Flint Glass Workers and Machinists; Teamsters, Brewers, Bakers and Laundry Workers (over drivers of wagons); Electrical Workers and Engineers; Carriage and Wagon Workers, Blacksmiths, Upholsterers, Machinists and Metal Polishers.

Such a list of jurisdictional difficulties is more significant than entertaining. Reading between the lines it reveals a situation that means much, for good or for ill, to the labor movement. If the unions are unable to adapt their organization and activities to industrial changes, they will have given into the hands of their enemies a powerful weapon. To keep pace with all the readjustments that are now made in the name of science and efficiency requires a degree of adaptability and flexibility on the part of trade unions that they do not appear to possess.

Settlement through American Federation. — The natural way to deal with the inter-union differences would appear to be through the American Federation of Labor. But many of the unions do not belong to the Federation. In other instances refusal to apply for a charter on the part of a trade union has been followed by the deliberate formation of a rival in the trade, one that will hold a Federation charter. This may extend the influence of the Federation but the gain is not a net gain until it is offset against the existence of a new jurisdictional struggle, the results of which concern employers as well as union men. Even where the struggle is between unions that are affiliated with the Federation the situation has not been handled with uniform success. Though forced to recognize the existence of these disputes, it has done so reluctantly. A study of the Federation's relation to some of the more important struggles has led to the conclusion that its policy has been marked by "great vacillation." "It is difficult to see," says Blum, "how their mediation has been of great moment though it is probable that the conferences and conciliatory efforts had a certain moral influence in bringing about an adjustment." Again this same writer adds, "There has been no logical ending" to so many of the disputes. "The good offices of the American Federation of Labor have been of no avail, . . . the controversy, not decided by anybody or on any principle, is won by the stronger union." From his study of the building trades controversy Whitney concludes that the American Federation of Labor fails as an arbitration agency. His study, he declares, "will convince anyone that it is not without cause that the unions are unwilling to rely for a decision as to their jurisdiction claims upon the justice and impartiality of either the American Federation of Labor or the Building Trades Department." Even the outspoken friends of the American Federation admit its weakness in this regard. "The American Federation of Labor," writes Mr. John Mitchell in his Organized Labor, "has accomplished a great deal toward preventing the outbreak of jurisdictional disputes and toward settling them where they have already occurred. In this matter the American Federation of Labor should be greatly strengthened."

Without attempting to sit in too rigid judgment upon the effectiveness of the American Federation in dealing with cases of jurisdictional controversies, a moment's thought as to its own organization will be helpful in explaining. This organization is essentially a *federation*. As has been described in a former chapter, it is made up of self-governing national unions. Its existence depends upon the support of such unions. This limits very much the authority of the Federation, forcing it in behalf of its own continued existence to adopt the course dictated by "practical expediency." The more powerful national unions do not yield gracefully to a decision in favor of a weaker rival. Their voting strength, their financial support, their tacitly recognized community of interest with other larger nationals all tend to make them at times quite independent of the Federation's authority. The Federation's Executive Committee to which its troubles are usually referred is made up largely of leaders chosen from among the strong nationals. Discipline, exercised upon a national by the Federation, may prove to be a boomerang. The Federation is, by its very nature, compelled to be "practical" in securing its ends. The American Federation of Labor fails as an arbitration agency in such disputes, as Whitney points out, "for the reason that its very existence is too intimately dependent upon the members and the contributions of the affiliated unions for it to be absolutely impartial in passing upon disputes in which the size and strength of the contending unions is very dissimilar."

Lack of Principle in Disputes. — The main reason for failure and confusion, on the part not only of the Federation of Labor but of the unions as well is the entire lack of any general principle or universal basis of settlement. The situation is confused not a little by the evolution of industry as well as by personal rivalries and mutual distrust. Several "bases of settlement" have been proposed and some of them have been invoked in connection with successful adjustments. It would be bold to assert that they were the causes of settlement. Sometimes the material used is urged in support of a contention; as when the metal workers claim jurisdiction over metal doors and metal trim, or iron workers over shipbuilding. Sometimes the nature of the operation involved is urged; as lathing, whether wood, metal or wire; plastering, whether spreading soft plaster or nailing blocks of ready-made plaster in place. Again the tools used make a basis for distinction; as stone cutting, granite cutting and marble cutting tools, or carpenters' tools instead of masons', when plaster blocks are put in place. The character of the establishment in which the work is done appears to some as conclusive; as machinists on linotypes in a printing shop, or coopers in a brewery, or wood workers in a piano factory. Other claims equally partisan have been put forward as decisive, and these only add to the confusion. In fact none of them is rational. Trade jealousy or self-defense, as the case may be, dictates the establishment of a jurisdictional claim. Once established, the claim must be supported by "argument." The argument is then made to fit the side. Little heed is paid to consistency. Carpenters, who claim plaster work because carpenters' hammers and nails are used to fasten the blocks in place, claim shipbuilding work though the tools have to be quite different. Plumbing, gas fitting and steam fitting, each had its separate reason why its particular union should exercise jurisdiction over all three.

The importance to the industrial world generally of a settlement of these disputes is not so great as it is to the interests of unionism. While there are differences, the employer may take advantage of them. They sometimes lead to strikes. The public very naturally looks upon them as phases of factional strife which concern one union as against another or one group of leaders in rivalry with another. In a sense they are right.

Unionism's Problem. — It is a problem for unionism itself to settle. Outsiders as arbitrators cannot settle anything. Not much, if indeed anything more than a temporary adjustment, was settled when Judge Gaynor decided that metal trim and doors should lie within the jurisdiction of carpenters. A committee of architects in Chicago said that in case of the construction of the Northwestern Depot the imitation marble should be set by the marble workers and not by the plasterers. The Hon. Seth Low decided that the installing of thermostats, regulating the heating apparatus, belonged to plumbers and not to the steam fitters.

So long as the differences exist, the employer will seek to take advantage of them. Different wage scales may exist and the cheaper workmen may be fully competent to do the work. The employer can hire them and still claim that his shop is "union." If one group strikes, the employer may hire union substitutes and in that case one union "scabs" on another. In one case a contractor employed pointers to point up the walls after the bricklayers had done their work. The pointers were organized. The bricklayers claimed jurisdiction over pointing, struck the job to compel the discharge of the pointers, won the strike, compelled the employer to pay the higher bricklayer's wage for the pointing work, and established their case in court as a "lawful" strike.

Its Ability to Solve it. — So far as jurisdictional disputes are due to industrial evolution, they cannot be prevented. Unionism must find a way of adjusting them. The trade-union form of organization does not promise to do this very effectively. Precedent and tradition take a strong hold even on unions of laborers. Traditional trade lines and precedents in division of work have been rather firmly established. The unions do not easily readjust themselves. Conservatism is further strengthened by the accumulation of large strike funds, of various forms of benefit funds which cannot be readily and equitably readjusted to rapidly changing trade conditions. The least that the strictly trade unions can do, if they are to adhere to the trade principle of organization, is to develop some more effective forms of federation or coöperation than has yet appeared. The American Federation of Labor is itself a step in this direction. The five departments into which it has associated many of its affiliated unions is a further step toward the same end. More remains to be done. So far as the disputes arise primarily from changing trade lines that accompany evolutionary changes in industry, the only salvation in sight within the hypothesis of *trade* unionism is an automatic part of the internal organism that shall work quickly and continuously for inter-trade peace and harmony. Further discussion of this phase would lead to changes in the structure of unionism, a topic dealt with a little later.

So far as jurisdictional disputes arise from factional strife and internal rivalry, the remedy is easier to discover if not simpler to apply. Here the one necessary element is leadership and education. The rank and file have a large responsibility to their own movement. They do not appear fully to recognize this. Short-sighted demands that run counter to the course of industry, even though vigorously insisted upon by the majority of a trade, can lead only to trouble. Failure lies ahead of such groups of workers. One trade prospering at another's expense cannot be justified on any rational grounds. The man in the ranks must see this.

Greater than the responsibility of the men who follow is that of the leaders. This is not the place to discuss trade union's need for developing the right kind of leadership. It is clear, however, that many of the disputes over jurisdiction are due to factional strife and personal ambition. Rival unions are generally due to the existence of personal rivalries. Failure to demark clearly between overlapping or changing trades is also too frequently due to jealousies between leaders, each able to persuade an unintelligent following that his is the just cause. To hear the reasons urged, the reflections cast, the personalities and recriminations expressed in some of these discussions is quite sufficient to reveal selfishness as the cause of all the *trouble*, if not of all the *disagreement*.

When unionism can relieve itself of this last named group of causes, the way will be open to adopt some machinery for settling those difficulties that are inherent in industry. With good leadership and intelligent following the way may be open to adopt Mr. John Mitchell's advice when he says that "the various organizations claiming the same work should be compelled to submit the question in dispute to the arbitration of technically equipped special committees appointed by the American Federation of Labor. The respective claims of the parties to the dispute should then be passed upon and the award should be absolutely final. The national unions should support the Federation in its decisions, and all organizations which refuse to abide thereby should be punished according to the judgment of the Federation. It is important that any decisions arrived at should be national and not merely local in their scope, and that they should be strictly enforced."

CHAPTER XXVI

INDUSTRIAL UNIONISM

In an earlier chapter the two different principles of organization were pointed out: the one, the principle of common interests of all laborers; and the other, that of trade or craft interest. On the former was built up the Knights of Labor. On the latter rest the American Federation of Labor and the group of national and international trade unions. The Knights of Labor has an interest now that is historical only. The American Federation of Labor with its affiliated trade unions represents the life and spirit of the American labor movement of to-day. But there is coming into prominence a third form of union, the *industrial* union, and this demands attention.

Basis of Industrial Unionism. — As the name implies, its basis of membership is the common labor interest of an industry. The industrial union is the union of the workmen of an industry. Whether this be a principle or not is a question of no great practical importance. It may be styled a new principle of organization, or it may be classed as a compromise between the broad common-interest-of-all-labor principle on the one hand and the much narrower trade-or-craft-limitation principle on the other. Whether the one or the other, so far as principle of organization is concerned, the industrial union is commanding close attention mainly for reasons purely practical.

With so influential a champion of the strict trade-union principle as the American Federation of Labor in the field, industrial unionism has encountered strong opposition. Yet its determined advocates have persisted in the fight until the issue has become an open one. Two strong national unions represent conspicuously the new type. Others appear to be approaching it in changes that are being made, while in still other industries there is turmoil that hardly presents any promise of being cleared up except by reorganization on some industrial basis rather than trade basis.

Types of Industrial Unionism. — The United Mine Workers of America is one of the strongest types and champions of industrial unionism. It includes within its membership all workers in and around the mine. There are no subdivisions along trade lines, no affiliations or alliances of trade groups into the larger unions. All workmen without regard to skill, kind of work or age belong to the local and the locals form the sub-districts, the districts and the international. That there is a subdivision of labor in mining becomes evident when one encounters a list of the various activities. Engineer, fireman, machinist, ashman, trapper, barnman, oiler, teamster, blacksmith, carpenter, gateman, inspector, loader, culm driver, washery man, slate picker, braker boy, mule driver, electrician, track layer, timber man, day laborer: these are some of the scores of different occupations in and around a coal mine. The various operations furnish to the membership of the United Mine Workers representatives of twenty different nations speaking as many different languages and dialects. The struggle with the engineers for control of that specific trade within the mines has been referred to in the discussion of jurisdictional disputes. Other controversies have arisen, the present outcome being that the miners' organization exercises unquestioned jurisdiction over all the various divisions of mining labor. This has not been accomplished without opposition, but the nature of the mining industry favored this form of organization and to-day there seems none to question not only the fact but the advisability of industrial unionism in mines. The same is true of the Western Federation of Miners. Its avowed object is "to unite the various persons working in and around the mines, mills and smelters into one central body," and this it does very effectively.

Similarly the brewers have extended their jurisdiction until the unit of organization has become the industry. After some vigorous fighting over jurisdictional control, engineers and firemen, carpenters and blacksmiths, coopers, teamsters and painters, in short all who are employed both in and around breweries, come into the membership of the locals of the United Brewery Workmen. The field of the union is the entire industry and all workmen are members of the same locals.

Mixed Types. — Of the industries in which confusion exists and for which some form of industrial unionism seems the only practical solution there are several. One that represents an advanced stage of industrialization is the International Longshoremens Association. This has directly affiliated local unions of unloaders of vessels and ships, grain elevator employees, general cargo dock laborers, lumber inspectors, tallymen and handlers, and others. It is also a federation of the following international unions: Licensed Tugmens Protective Association, Tug Firemen and Linemens Association, International Dredge Workers Protective Association, International Rock Drillers Association, and the General Fishermens Association. The desire is to make one big industrial union of all these.

The printing industry is being more nearly dominated by the Typographical Union. In earlier years the tendency in this industry was the other way. The first membership was of type setters and pressmen. Then press work became divided as a separate trade. Bookbinding was another division. Other branches were set apart one after another. Yet all were in the one union. One by one separate unions came into existence along the lines of the separate trades. More recently, however, the Typographical Union has been reaching out. They have had jurisdictional troubles with other unions. They have won their case against the Machinists. They have as allied locals some of the German-American printers, also some of the mailers, newspaper writers, and type founders. They are having misunderstandings with other trades, as the bookbinders, pressmen and others. The size and strength of this organization give them great advantage over other trade unions in the same industry. Because of these the leaders are able to adopt either waiting or fighting tactics as the case seems to warrant. A dispute with the International Brotherhood of Bookbinders over jurisdiction arose, due to the fact that the Typographical Union also admits bookbinders to its membership. "These men and women," says the president of the latter organization in his annual report of 1915, "are entitled to and will of course continue to receive our full protection in their employment and in their membership in this union. When the other parties to this controversy are ready to adjust it on an equitable basis the officers of the International Typographical Union will not keep them waiting." The present policy in this trade is the building up of an alliance between the several independent and semi-independent unions. The Allied Printing Trades is formed by the alliance of the International Printing Press and Assistants Union, the International Brotherhood of Bookbinders, the International Stereotypers and Electrotypers Union, and the International Photo-Engravers Union. This may or may not prove to be a step toward a real industrial union in the printing trade. The dominating Typographical Union is in a position to guide developments at present and they are endeavoring in every way to build up the strength of the Allied Councils.

The meat packing industry affords another fertile field for the development of industrial unionism. In this industry there have been more than fifty different unions organized among workers in the Chicago packing houses alone. These were arranged in groups of some ten or fifteen different national trade unions affiliated with the American Federation of Labor. The subdivision of labor has been extended to such great lengths in this industry that nothing worthy the name of a trade remains. A few highly skilled operations supplemented by activities of relatively unskilled workingmen and women constitute the meat packing trade. If such a group of laborers is to establish effective bargaining power, the experience of the miners appears to many to be the example for them to follow.

Still another industry full of confusion is that of garment making. Lines of division that were formerly fairly clear have in recent times lost their effectiveness. The Journeymen Tailors did the custom made work. The ready-made clothing industry has been the field for the United Garment Workers, itself a combination of several separate operations or trades. Then came ready-made garments for women. As these have led to regular industrial organizations, they have been followed by the laborers with their unions. Cloaks, suits and skirts; tailor made garments; dresses and waists; misses and children's wear; wrappers and kimonos; and white goods or underwear; each in turn has its separate organization of workers. These have consolidated in the International Ladies Garment Workers Union. The history of efforts to adjust difficulties and make a strong union in this industry is a long and complicated one. Some reference has been made to it in another chapter. It has given the "Protocol," the Sanitary Board, the Preferential Union Shop. A recent effort to industrialize the trade has for the present come to naught. Some seceding locals of the United Garment Workers joined forces with the Journeymen Tailors Union and the latter changed its name to the Tailors Industrial Union, claiming within its jurisdiction all the needle and garment trades. Though this movement did not succeed, it still appears that there are elements present in the garment industry that invite further efforts along the line of industrial unionism.

In other fields the case for the industrial unions does not seem quite so clear. In the building trades there have been jurisdictional disputes without number. Trade lines cross and recross in great confusion. Boards of delegates and building trades councils in the larger cities have sought to unite the forces and suppress the internal strife. Success has not been such as to encourage hope for the future. An inherent difficulty lies in the fact that trades engaged in building are also engaged in other activities not logically or practically classified within the building field. Engineers who run hoisting engines also run pumping engines for mines as well as engines for numerous industrial plants. Carpenters make not only buildings but furniture, pianos and organs, carriages and wagons.

From these various illustrations it will appear that industrial unionism does not find an equally fertile field in all lines of industry. Unequal adaptation has fostered irregular development. That such will continue to be the case seems inevitable.

Reasons Favorable to Industrial Unionism. — The reasons urged in favor of this newer form of unionism are both practical and theoretical. While the latter do not carry so great a weight of influence, they are often urged. They have a favorable effect in some quarters. Industries that are made up of many trades with but a small number in each make it quite impossible to form strong trade locals. If formed, their interests attach more directly to the trade fellows who work elsewhere than to fellow workmen in the same plant. This creates divided rather than united interests among employees. Particularly is this true when the industry is isolated as is the case in mining. The laborers are remote from large centers where unionism is more active, and the chances for association with larger numbers in the same organization are few.

Force of Practical Reasons. — But it is the practical side that appeals most strongly. Collective bargaining with an employer is more effectively carried on through industrial unionism. In a miners' controversy the union feels much more strongly intrenched if it can control the engineers who operate the pumps. Though they usually continue them at work, there is always the possibility that they can be called out. This affects the employer very directly, for by stopping the pumps the mines are flooded and much property is destroyed beyond recovery. The brewers insist that it is critical that they control the delivery as well as the preparation of their product. So they insist that teamsters as well as all others join their industrial union.

An advocate of industrial unionism in the textile industry cites some real experience. There was a recent strike among union "cop-packers." Yet the operative spinners remained at work "producing cops for blackleg cop-packers." So also "trade union carters carried them to the station, trade union railway men to their destination, to be woven into cloth by trade union weavers, and finished by trade union bleachers and dyers. Thus it was not the employers, but we . . . fellow trade unionists in the same industry . . . who smashed the cop-packers' strike."

In the textile strikes of Lawrence, Little Falls, and other centers, the trade union, the United Textile Workers of America, was severely criticized for having neglected to include in its membership the unskilled workers of the mills. This organization has combined to some degree the different lines of work, thus departing to that extent from the strict trade union. It has limited its membership, however, to the relatively skilled workers. When the trouble broke out it was quite helpless before the leaders who brought this neglected element together in their aggressive organization. From the more practical point of view, the industrial unionists have a powerful argument when they urge that the workmen are much more effective in dealing with an employer when all the working force is combined under one organization and one leadership. The force of the argument is apparent.

Attitude of American Federation. — The attitude of the American Federation of Labor toward industrial unionism is not easy to state. Its acts and its declarations do not look in exactly the same direction. Founded as it was on the principle of trade unionism and successful to a degree surpassing any previous effort, it is inevitable that the form of organization that seems to have determined its survival against its former great rival, the Knights of Labor, should be held as sacred. This principle the Federation has reiterated again and again. Industrial unionism, it urges, savors of the breaking down of trade autonomy. It looks again in the direction of the Knights. This is enough to condemn it. But when some particular application of the issue comes up for adjustment, the practical takes precedence over the theoretical. Both organizations of miners have developed a high degree of industrial unionism while residing under the roof of the Federation. The brewers have not suffered any serious reverses in their policy of industrialism, though members of the Federation in good standing. The Typographical Union is pushing its claims in the face of complaints made to the Federation by its rivals. In 1901 the engineers working in mines were seeking to retain their trade relations against the opposition of the miners. The Federation decreed that the engineers working in mines should join the Miners Union. The case was made to appear as an exception rather than a policy, however. Reference in the report was made to the "magnificent growth of the American Federation of Labor," this being "conceded by all students of Economic thought to be the result of organization on trade lines." It was declared that "as a general proposition, the interest of the workers will be best conserved by adhering as closely to that doctrine as the recent great changes in the method of production and employment make practicable." This last statement paves the way to the exception. It is then admitted that "owing to the isolation of some few industries from thickly populated centers, where the overwhelming number follow one branch thereof, and owing to the fact that in some industries comparatively few workmen are engaged over whom separate organizations claim jurisdiction, we believe that the jurisdiction in such industries by the paramount organization would yield the best results to the workers therein; at least till the development of organization of each branch has reached a stage wherein these may be placed without material injury to all parties in interest in affiliation with their national trade unions." The Coal Hoisting Engineers refused to accept this decision of the Federation in favor of the United Mine Workers. Upon this the Federation expelled them from its membership.

Again in 1903, the convention of the Federation had the question to consider. Again the trade principle was strongly pronounced. President Gompers asserted that the movement toward industrial unionism "is perversive of the history of the labor movement, runs counter to the best conceptions of the toilers' interests now, and is sure to lead to the confusion which precedes dissolution and disruption." In 1904 a committee of which Mr. Gompers and Mr. John Mitchell were both members again reasserted the principle but again admitted the practicability of making exceptions to meet special needs.

The Federation does not, however, yield to every attempt to industrialize an organization. Evidence of this appears in the recent issue between the tailors and the garment makers to which reference has already been made. Certain locals had withdrawn from the United Garment Workers of America. The Journeymen Tailors Union had by referendum vote decided to change its name to Tailors Industrial Union. They also changed their membership requirements so as to include all needle and garment trades. They made an alliance with the seceders above mentioned, who claimed to be the real United Garment Workers organization. This gave the right to use the union label of that organization. As the constitution of the American Federation forbids any affiliated organization to change its title or extend its jurisdiction without first receiving the approval of the Federation, the Federation immediately became concerned. At the 1914 convention the Tailors were instructed to rescind the action as to name and jurisdiction and return to their former status. The membership of the Journeymen Tailors was about 12,000 while that of the United Garment Workers was about 60,000, with about 70,000 more in the other trades included in the International Ladies Garment Workers Union. The Federation was actively supported by the United Garment Workers Union whose officials strongly opposed the effort to usurp its jurisdiction by a few "would-be leaders" from among seceders, and further roundly denounced such a "dastardly attempt to disrupt and destroy a *bona fide* labor union which has been of such great benefit to the workers in the men's clothing industry." Through the energetic measures of the Federation by its Executive Council this attempt at industrial unionism in the needle trades has been frustrated. That the outcome was one of purely practical considerations is clear from the fact that the numbers on the one side were largely preponderant and that the initial move was made by an organization in a trade the relative importance of which is waning. Though refusing to sanction the arrangements made, the Executive Council did report it as their belief that some form of closer alliance ought to be brought about among the various branches of this trade.

Industrial unionism is usually brought before the annual convention of the Federation in such a way as to force a test vote in an endeavor to commit the Federation to the policy. At the 1914 convention two resolutions were introduced. One was presented by the National Brotherhood of Operative Potters and was as follows:

"Whereas, The various National and International Unions affiliated with the American Federation of Labor have complete autonomy over their respective crafts; and

"Whereas, Under this system of organization there has been no end to the number of disputes over the question of jurisdictional rights; and

"Whereas, All such disputes could be prevented by having the workers of all crafts in an industry, under the jurisdiction of one organization; therefore, be it

"Resolved, That the American Federation of Labor go on record in favor of organization by industry, and take whatever steps may be necessary to bring about such change."

Another set of resolutions was presented by the delegate representing the Illinois Federation of Labor. It had been adopted by the State Federation and was introduced at the latter's instructions. It was in the following form:

"Whereas, The lines are being closely drawn between capital and labor; the capitalists of the country have organized the National Manufacturers' Association and other large employers' organizations, very compact, cohesive bodies, having for their purpose the destruction of the trades union movement, and, realizing that in unity there is strength; therefore, be it

"Resolved, That, in order to combat these compact and powerful organizations of employers of labor, this convention endorses and adopts the plan of organization by industries instead of by crafts, which often divides the forces of labor, and that the officers of the State Federation be instructed to use every effort to influence and mold sentiment along these lines; and be it further

"Resolved, That the delegate from the Illinois Federation of Labor to the A. F. of L. be instructed to use his vote and influence for the industrial form of organization."

Neither of these resolutions was adopted. They served a purpose, however, in affording the industrialists in the convention an opportunity to agitate the question.

Illustration of Agitation: Metal Trades. — A matter of interest during the summer of 1915 was the discussion of an amalgamation project in the metal trades. It appears to have been started by the Machinists Union in 1914 when the officers and business agents of that organization met informally and discussed the advisability of such a change. The conference drafted a resolution in the following form and presented it for consideration:

"Whereas, The introduction of modern machinery and methods of doing work are rapidly bringing a number of the metal crafts so closely together that it is practically impossible to define the line of demarkation in relation to the jurisdiction of said crafts; and

"Whereas, We believe that it is not only possible, but entirely feasible, to bring about the amalgamation of a number of said organizations; and

"Whereas, We believe that said amalgamation can be perfected by establishing a district or divisional form of organization working under one general constitution and one set of general officers, and by granting to each district or division the right of self-government to the fullest possible extent, subordinate to the constitution of the Grand Lodge; therefore, be it

"Resolved, That this conference go on record as recommending that the International President and G. E. B. (General Executive Board) immediately proceed to take a referendum vote on this resolution and get in touch with the general officers of the following organizations, with this object in view: Machinists, Boilermakers, Blacksmiths, Brass Workers and Metal

Polishers, Sheet Metal Workers, Iron Workers, Electricians, Plumbers and Steam Fitters, Elevator Constructors and the Machinists now members of the Carpenters and Joiners; and be it further

"Resolved, That in the event any one or more of the organizations being agreeable to said plan of amalgamation, the executive officers shall proceed to work out such plan of amalgamation with the favorable organizations at the earliest possible date, and that the above mentioned organizations be requested to publish the report of this committee and this resolution in their monthly journals."

These resolutions were ratified by a referendum vote of the Machinists Union and sent to the officials of the other metal trades. It has not met with general enthusiasm though the different trades are still considering it. The Boilermakers Union through its Executive Board adopted strong resolutions against amalgamation. Several reasons were stated. "First, Past experiences have taught us that such an organization cannot be made a success. Second, We believe that our present forms of organization will meet all the requirements of the workers, namely: The metal trades department of the A. F. of L., the railway department of the A. F. of L., and the system federation, when perfected. . . . We believe that all true trade unionists should lend their undivided support to the present form of organization rather than to encourage new and untried forms and thereby retard our progress."

Discussion by Molders. — The Molders Union, though not included in the list named in the Machinists' resolutions, became involved in the discussion. A Molders' local secured the second to its motion by the requisite nine locals and forced a referendum upon the members of that union. Here again the officers were opposed to the amalgamation and judging from the various letters contributed to the discussion there was a division of opinion in the membership. In the discussions there appeared the usual line of argument on each side. One side represented by "A Member for Forty Years" writes that "The molders of this country can point with pardonable pride to their acheivements. Since 1859 our old banner has never touched the ground. We have fought the good fight, lost and won our battle, but have never been discredited. We have built up an organization that extends to all parts of the molding industry, from the Gulf of Mexico to the northern end of civilization." Another appeals to the practical difficulties of such an amalgamation. "The more skilled a group of workmen become, a greater number of purely craft questions arise which only men of their craft are competent to decide. The molder would be no more competent to pass upon a question of what caused a poor weld than the blacksmith would be to point out the cause of the warping or cracking of a casting. The electrical worker would be no more competent to determine who was to blame if a boiler leaked than a boilermaker would be in endeavoring to place the responsibility for a faulty insulation. The disputes which arise between employers and mechanics over technical trade matters are far more numerous than all others put together."

On the other hand, it was urged that many of the unions are already amalgamations and that the proposed larger one is but another step in the same direction. The core makers have been absorbed by the molders. The Molders Union includes machinery molders, stove molders, brass molders, bench molders as well as core makers, and each of these is becoming more and more a separate craft or trade. With such an amalgamation as proposed there would be no longer any "fear of union pattern makers making patterns for the molders who take our places when on strike or of union machinists finishing the castings made by struck shops." Some go even further and urge that foundry laborers should be taken in as members. "How often," it is argued, "the helpers and laborers in the foundry have been used to break the strikes of the molders, while if they had been amalgamated with the I. M. U. they would have been out with the molders fighting in the union's cause." The vote cast on this referendum was 1,946 in favor of amalgamation and 10,758 against, showing a majority of 8,812 opposed to the proposed plan of amalgamation.

The Cigar Makers. — The Cigar Makers International Union at its last convention was called upon to consider resolutions favoring industrial unionism. The result was a pronounced defeat for the industrial advocates. A strong set of resolutions was adopted setting forth in elaborate form the position of this union. The American trade-union movement, it was declared, is one of constant growth, development and expansion. The American Federation of Labor has been the most beneficial organization, furthering in every practical way the "unity, solidarity and fraternity of the organized workers" and stimulating "closer coöperation, federation, and amalgamation of existing trade unions." The policy was endorsed of forming central bodies, state federations, and industrial departments for federation and coöperation. Further, the resolutions declared that "there is still much to do," but they "repudiate the insinuation which is implied by the term Industrial Unionism as it is employed in antagonism to Trade Unionism." "The advocates of so-called Industrial Unionism imply in their slogan that the trade unions are rigid and do not advance, develop or expand, whereas the whole history of the trade-union movement in the past thirty years has demonstrated beyond contradiction that there is not a day which passes in the trade-union movement in America but which witnesses the highest and loftiest spirit of sacrifice in order to coöperate with our fellow workers for their interest and common uplift." Finally the delegates of the organization to future conventions of the American Federation of Labor were instructed "to continue to do all in their power to have the work of more thoroughly organizing the unorganized workers pursued to its fullest extent; to urge upon the organized workers a more thorough coöperation; to advocate amalgamation of organizations of kindred trades and callings to a more thorough federation of all organized labor."

This attitude is made more clear in its practical phase by the announcement of an amalgamation of the National Stogie Makers League and this same Cigar Makers International Union. This was effected through the agency of the Executive Council of the American Federation of Labor. Terms were agreed to by the joint conference by which the members of the Stogie Makers League were to be admitted to the Cigar Makers Union without the payment of an initiation fee, provided the local unions of stogie makers place their funds in the general funds of the International Union. Those who favor industrial unionism will claim that this is a distinct step toward that goal, while the trade-union advocates will explain it as nothing more than a closer union or even an amalgamation purely in the interests of the trade. Whichever it may be, the change is clearly a step in the direction of fewer unions and more clearly defined jurisdiction within an industry. Stogies, cheroots, tobies and cigars all come now within the control of the Cigar Makers Union. The National Stogie Makers League on the date fixed "automatically disbands and ceases to exist as such." The laws of the Cigar Makers Union govern "all local unions and members, regardless of the branch of industry of which they are made up or in which they are employed." "All properties and funds of the National Stogie Makers League (not otherwise determined by the agreement) shall be forwarded to the headquarters of the Cigar Makers International Union."

Will Industrial Unionism Become General? — It appears that industrial unionism has received a new impetus. Whether or not it is to become general is a matter of prophecy rather than description. It has been shown that a few unions are now organized on the basis of industrialism. In other instances there are distinct tendencies in that direction. It should not be taken to mean, however, that the future will see a general movement in the ranks of all unionism toward the industrial basis of organization. There is too great variety in the interests and the activities of the various trade unions to justify one in expecting this. For some time to come the trade autonomists will in most of the unions hold their own. The appeal to the past is still made with moving effect. "It is all well and good," runs one of the appeals, "for some of the young fellows who have come into this organization with conditions that were never dreamed of years ago, but which thousands of us old codgers have been fighting all our lives to obtain, and it comes with poor grace for others to propose giving away that which they never sacrificed for, but which we fought so hard to obtain, and I am quite satisfied that the old members of our organization, and there are thousands yet in the fold, who will never under any circumstances permit that which our sires and we have fought for to be given away by those who cannot realize the sacrifices we made. We were out on the firing line and fighting ofttimes without the wherewithal to keep our stomach and backbone apart before (this young group) was ever dreamed of, and what we fought and won and have we will not let those who came in and inherited give away." Such sentiment is of course natural and the frequency of its expression in various forms indicates clearly that there are conservatives as well as progressives within the ranks of organized labor. The old struggle with the Knights of Labor, the skill and diplomacy that have been necessary in building up an American Federation of Labor made up of affiliated and autonomous national trade unions have left a deep and lasting impression in the minds of the older men among the leaders. Trade autonomy, to them, is synonymous with the very existence and perpetuity of the labor-union movement.

Position of Trade Union Advocates. — Endorsing the position that the trade autonomist takes are some very real facts of industry. The various organizations have divergent as well as common interests. Skilled crafts and unskilled workmen have rivalries, competitions and other differing interests. The unskilled workman may be looking for promotion. The skilled does not want his position open to such competition. Skilled workers may aim to secure increases of wages even at the expense of their less skilled associates in the industry. Or the unskilled may be plotting for independent wage increases. Union dues cannot be paid with equal ease by both classes. Benefit funds of various sorts can be adjusted to different ages and different risks only with the most complex arrangements. Strikes in sympathy are not cordially entered upon. There are undoubtedly aristocrats among laborers, and human nature asserts itself here in very much the usual way. Self-interest first and altruism second takes the form of trade or craft first and labor second.

Position of Industrial Union Advocates. — The industrial unionists are aggressive and urge their cause with great practical force. Experience to them is a thorough teacher. They point to union firemen working for non-union locomotive engineers and union engineers teaching strike-breaking locomotive firemen to fire locomotives. In the strike of meat packers in the summer of 1904 the engineers and firemen remained at work keeping the refrigerating plant "alive" to preserve the abundant stock of meat on hand. They were asked to leave the job, but by the time they had referred the request to their own union officials and had finally secured permission to strike, the employers had provided for others to take their places. The strike was lost and the Amalgamated Meat Cutters and Butcher Workmen have always insisted that the failure was due to the lack of coöperation on the part of the engineers and firemen. In the more detailed account of the events connected with the meat packing industry, the point has been still more forcibly made by the industrialists.

"The meat wagon drivers of Chicago were organized in 1902. They made demands for better pay and shorter hours. Unchecked by any outside influence they walked out on strike. They had the support of all other workers in the packing houses. They won. But before they resumed work the big packing firms insisted that they enter into a contract. They did. In that contract the teamsters agreed not to engage in any sympathetic strike with other employees in the plants or stockyards. Not only this, but the drivers also decided to split their union into three. They then had the Bone and Shaving Teamsters, the Packing House Teamsters, and the Meat Delivery Drivers.

"Encouraged by the victory of the teamsters, the other workers in the packing houses then started to organize. But they were carefully advised not to organize into one body, or at the best into one National Trades Union. They had to be divided up, so that the employers could exterminate them all whenever opportunity presented itself.

"Now observe how the dividing-up process worked. The teamsters were members of the International Union of Teamsters. The engineers were connected with the International Union of Steam Engineers. The firemen, oilers, ash-wheelers were organized in the Brotherhood of Stationary Firemen. Carpenters employed in the stock yards permanently had to join the Brotherhood of Carpenters and Joiners. The pipe and steam fitters were members of another national union. The sausage makers, the packers, the canning department workers, the beef butchers, the cattle butchers, the hog butchers, the bone shavers, etc., each craft group had a separate union. Each union had different rules, all of them not permitting any infringements on them by others. Many of the unions had contracts with the employers. These contracts expired at different dates. Most of the contracts contained the clause of no support to others when engaged in a controversy with the stock yard companies."

It is needless to point out further illustrations of this situation. There can be no doubt that the industrial unionists make a strong point in showing this. It is not alone lack of coöperation. It is the use of one trade union to defeat the ends of another.

Not only would strikes be more effective, claim the industrialists, but boycotts could be pushed with greater vigor. When the typesetters were pushing a boycott of a paper and urging readers not to buy, the pressmen would agree with them instead of placing their endorsement on a product that other workmen were condemning as non-union. So with the support of the union label. And still further, it is urged that the questions of promotion would be more easily adjusted: — firemen to engineers, trainmen to conductors, hod carriers to masons, blacksmiths helpers and others; all these now afford opportunities for discord where harmony should prevail.

The membership of the American Federation of Labor contains a strong minority of those in favor of industrial unionism. This minority is active, vigilant and seems to be growing in numbers. More, rather than less, will be heard of industrial unionism.

Conclusions. — It does not appear that it will be the prevailing type, however. The solution is being slowly worked out in an experimental way and changes are constantly occurring. Already there is coming into currency the new phrase "amalgamation of related trades." This means compromise so far as it represents the struggle between the trade and the industrial unionist. It means also better adjustment and more effective working relations in cases where the common interests dominate over the rivalries. Amalgamation is used with varying shades of meaning. The industrialist uses it as representing essentially the idea for which he stands. The trade autonomists, on the contrary, freely talk about amalgamation while vigorously denouncing industrialism. In this field of constant change it is not so much the name as it is the fact that is of greatest importance. A closer union upon some practical working basis of trade workers who now find themselves at a disadvantage in collective bargaining because of rivalries is quite sure to go forward. To apply only so radical a remedy as is necessary to effect a cure is on the whole a wise policy. Hence exist city centrals, state federations, trade councils, and trade departments, as means of bringing about coöperation. In some lines these succeed and so they are sufficient. In other lines they are not enough. Therefore something else must be done. Amalgamation is more radical but it becomes necessary. Where this in turn proves ineffective, still stronger measures are inevitably suggested. As necessity seems to require it, they will be adopted. This will mean no sudden or universal shifting from trade to industrial unionism. There will be irregular changes, and these will come in each line separately as expediency seems to demand.

CHAPTER XXVII

REVOLUTIONARY INDUSTRIAL UNIONISM

The arrangement of the present chapter following the two previous ones may suggest that this one is to treat of industrial unionism carried a step farther. It is, in fact, that, but it is more. The step farther leads into new fields of very different fertility yielding a product that is quite strange. Revolutionary industrial unionism is the name of a movement; the Industrial Workers of the World, the name of an organization; and Syndicalism, of a philosophy. All three of these one finds strangely compounded into a mixture which if not entirely new, has some new features and many strange ones.

To the casual observer it may have appeared that ten years ago there suddenly sprang into existence a new thing made out of whole cloth and never before dreamed of by man. The Industrial Workers of the World was a surprise to many in 1905, its first appearance, and has been a continuous surprise to some ever since. As a matter of fact this new organization has its place in the development of events and this development constitutes a chain with related links extending both forward and back. It will be convenient to speak of the organization first, the philosophy next, and then the movement.

The Organization. — It has been shown in a former chapter that there are many phases or varieties of industrial unionism. Many experiments have been made and many adjustments tried for the purpose of finding its best form. Some have felt that there must be a form that could be generalized and adapted to all industry. This effort has led to some interesting experiments.

New Line-up of Forces. — There was in the last years of the nineteenth century an important change in the line-up of industrial forces. A new struggle was opening. While the initial events in the career of the Industrial Workers of the World appeared to many as the first outbreak of this new situation, it cannot be properly understood as the disconnected appearance of a new movement. The feeling on which it was based was manifest in introductory events.

Beginnings. — The strength of the Knights of Labor was passing. Its successful rival, the American Federation of Labor, was steadily increasing its influence. This may be interpreted as the passing of the *labor* union and the rise of the *trade* union. Yet it was not so simple as that. There were groups of active union men who could find no place in the trade-union scheme. They were not the kind to disband because of this. Industrial unionism presented the way out and they seized upon it. The brewery workers in 1887 changed their name from the Brewers Union to the National Union of United Brewery Workmen and insisted upon including in the membership all who worked in the breweries, regardless of special trades. Thus it became a pure industrial union.

In 1893 was formed the Western Federation of Miners, an organization that has taken a prominent place in labor activities in the west. Its membership was made up from among the hardy pioneers largely of native American stock, possessed of a high degree of independence and aggressiveness. They embodied a new spirit of unionism combining the industrial form of organization with strong socialist tendencies and a determination to take a part in politics.

As a party the Socialists had been making eager efforts to dominate both the Knights of Labor and the American Federation of Labor. Failing in this, the leaders of the Socialist Labor Party, in 1895, brought into existence a labor organization that would be socialist in spirit. This was named the Socialist Trade and Labor Alliance and it did, in fact, work in close coöperation with the Socialist Labor Party.

Other events, too, were exercising a very real influence. The Homestead strike of 1892, the Cœur D'Alene strike in 1893 and the Pullman strike in 1894 left deep impressions. Court activity in freely granting injunctions to employers who were seeking to resist strikes and break boycotts, legislation of a restricted character and cases against unions successfully prosecuted at court; these are some of the developments that shaped the temper of the more aggressive labor leaders and incited them to more vigorous measures.

Coming together in larger groups the leaders in 1898 formed the Western Labor Union, from among the large numbers of unskilled laborers. This new organization was dominated by the spirit of the Western Federation of Miners, a "new type" of unionism. Its aggressiveness led it to look to the east and see an opportunity there. The outcome of this was again another organization, this time the American Labor Union, formed in 1902, based on the spirit of the western unions and looking eastward for a greater membership.

This was the situation in 1905. It will be clear that certain elements of the labor movement had been left out in the cold by the passing Knights of Labor and that they could not affiliate with the rising Federation of Labor. These elements had but few interests in common, as later developments have proved, yet one fact impressed them all, industrialists, socialists, anti-politicalists and anarchists alike; namely, they were not making effective progress in their common warfare against capitalism.

Conferences and Manifesto. — Informal and secret conferences of leaders soon resulted in a determination that something effective must be done. A more formal conference, in January, 1905, became known as the Industrial Union Congress. Following a call issued broadcast to unionism a convention was assembled in the early summer of the same year and the Industrial Workers of the World came into existence.

The January conference was of importance primarily in that it finally determined upon the need for a new organization, laid out the lines along which it should be formed and fixed a time for a meeting to organize the new association. It was all summed up in a manifesto issued and signed by twenty-seven persons. Though somewhat lengthy it did not announce much that was new. It was broad enough to receive the endorsement of several shades of belief. On the negative side, its first declaration was the increasingly familiar one of denunciation of the current capitalist system. Human skill is being displaced by machines and the power of the capitalist is being steadily strengthened by the increase in control over such machines. As an immediate result "trade division among laborers and competition among capitalists are alike disappearing." "New machines, ever replacing less productive ones, wipe out whole trades and plunge new bodies of workers into the ever-growing army of tradeless, hopeless unemployed." Such conditions are being encouraged by capitalists who favor every effort to subdivide the trades while combining themselves into more effective associations. "The employers' line of battle and methods of warfare correspond to the solidarity of the mechanical and industrial concentration, while laborers still form their fighting organizations on lines of long-gone trade divisions." "This worn-out and corrupt system offers no promise of improvement and adaptation. There is no silver lining to the clouds of darkness and despair settling down upon the world of labor." Such a situation, it is asserted, renders industrial solidarity impossible. "Union men scab against union men; hatred of worker for worker is engendered, and the workers are delivered helpless and disintegrated into the hands of the capitalists." The unions set up barriers by way of initiation fees, union cards and union labels which stand in the way of general coöperation. These "hinder the growth of class consciousness of the workers, foster the idea of harmony of interests between employing exploiter and employed slave." Turning from the criticisms of things as they are, it is declared that "universal economic evils afflicting the working class can be eradicated only by a universal working class movement. . . . A movement to fulfill these conditions must consist of one great industrial union embracing all industries, providing for craft autonomy locally, industrial autonomy internationally and wage-class unity generally. It must be founded on the class struggle, and its general administration must be conducted in harmony with the recognition of the irrepressible conflict between the capitalist class and the working class." Then follow the main features of a proposed organization which should be formed to carry forward the principles.

Elements Represented. — At the appointed time those who responded to the appeal came together. The group consisted of two hundred delegates from thirty-four local, state, district and national organizations and representing more than forty distinct occupations or trades. The memberships of the represented associations totaled a little less than 150,000, though delegates fully authorized to enroll their constituents in the new proposed organization represented only slightly over 50,000. The Western Federation of Miners, with a membership of 27,000, was represented by 5 delegates; the American Labor Union, with 16,750, sent 29 delegates; the United Metal Workers, 3,000 strong, sent 2; the United Brotherhood of Railway Employees, 2,087 in number, was represented by 19 delegates; and the Socialist Trade and Labor Alliance, with 1,450 members, had 14 delegates. This gives for the "Big Five" a total of 50,287 members and 69 delegates. As the voting strength was assigned on the basis of members represented, it will appear that the Western Federation of Miners held the controlling vote, though only 5 delegates sat in the conference.

An Organization Formed. — The preamble to the constitution of the new Industrial Workers of the World was a mildly expressed summary of the Manifesto issued by the January conference. It contained one clause that proved to be ambiguous and that figured prominently in the succeeding conventions. This clause declared that between the working class and the employing class "a struggle must go on until all the toilers come together on the political as well as on the industrial field, and take and hold that which they produce by their labor, through an economic organization of the working class, without affiliation with any political party." It will be noticed that reference is here made to the necessity of political as well as industrial action, though there must be no affiliation with existing parties.

The constitution contained the structure of the new union and provisions for its administration. Large powers rested in the convention. The General President, the General Secretary, Treasurer and a General Executive Board were provided for; these having wide powers. The organization itself was to be divided into thirteen international industrial divisions, subdivided into industrial unions of "closely kindred industries." Provision was made for a "Universal Label" for the organization. All membership books, official buttons, labels and badges were to be of uniform design. There was to be free interchange of cards between subordinate organizations, and any paid-up membership card was to be accepted as initiation without fee in any other recognized union.

Spirit and Personalities of Movement. — Any description of the emergence of the Industrial Workers of the World from the confusion of this period would be inadequate if it confined itself alone to preambles, constitutions and formal declarations of conferences and conventions. Both the strength and the spirit of the Industrial Workers rested on the personalities of its group of leaders. The five men who dominated the January conference were William D. Haywood, Eugene V. Debs, William E. Trautmann, Daniel DeLeon and A. M. Simons. Soon Vincent St. John joined the group. Of these men all were members of the Socialist Party except two. Daniel DeLeon was a leader of the Socialist Labor Party and William E. Trautmann represented the anti-political element. These were all men of seasoned experience, born leaders with an idealism that has furnished them the "vision" and a practical turn born of close associations with the turbulent and often unsuccessful movements of the day.

Developing Discord. — Begun under apparently favorable auspices and aggressive leadership, with a claimed membership of 100,000 at the end of the first year, with active organizers in the field and a lively weekly paper, the new organization which had promised so well was soon on the rocks of discord. At the second convention, factional strife led to an effort to depose the president; to his resistance to the movement and to his final withdrawal from the organization together with the Western Federation of Miners. The arrest of Haywood in 1906 left a position of leadership difficult to fill. A second dissension broke out in 1908, this time over political policies. The political element in the leadership insisted that the Industrial Workers be committed formally to political action. This was opposed by the anti-political element. But the political unionists were divided and in rivalry. The Socialist Party and the Socialist Labor Party were both bidding for the support of the laborers' votes. DeLeon and Simons became distrustful each of the other. The victory was won by the anti-political wing and in 1908 the Industrial Workers was put on a non-political basis, the preamble was changed accordingly and a more distinctively revolutionary spirit characterized the movement.

With reference to political action the preamble now declared that "a struggle must go on until the workers of the world organize as a class, take possession of the earth and the machinery of production and abolish the wage system." The earlier reference to the weaknesses of trade unionism and its misleading of the workers "into the belief that the working class have interests in common with their employers" gave way to a more positive declaration. "Instead of the conservative motto, 'A fair day's wages for a fair day's work,' we must inscribe on our banner the revolutionary watchword, 'Abolition of the wage system.' It is the historic mission of the working class to do away with capitalism. The army of production must be organized, not only for the every-day struggle with capitalists, but also to carry on production when capitalism shall have been overthrown. By organizing industrially we are forming the structure of the new society within the shell of the old."

A "Purified" Movement. — When these radical changes were made and the group stood definitely committed to its more radical program, most of the organizations withdrew leaving a determined group of revolutionary leaders to carry forward the new movement. The fact seems to be that most of these unions had never been very formidable. "Several of the organizations," says Brissenden, "which finally merged into the Industrial Workers of the World had little behind them but leaders." The Socialist Trade and Labor Alliance, the United Metal Workers and the American Labor Union were "really more shadow than substance."

Significance of the "Purification." — Before following the fortunes of the Industrial Workers a step further, the significance of the political struggle should be pointed out. Those who have more carefully analyzed the elements present at the inception of the movement find three quite distinct groups. One regarded the organization as the "economic backbone of the political socialist movement." Another regarded economic organization as of prime importance with the political movement subordinate. A third group were more or less open anarchists. This last group though few in number, was outspoken and denounced any form of political activity. In the end the last group has quite fully dominated. Mr. Haywood, no longer a member of the Socialist Party, has come into aggressive leadership with Mr. Trautmann, a revolutionary industrialist actively seconding the former's efforts.

The matter came to a climax when the convention refused to seat a representative from the Socialist Labor Party. The faction withdrew and called a convention at Detroit. This faction has continued the name and professes to be the original organization. The result is that there are two separate organizations both under the name Industrial Workers of the World. The smaller one is known as the Detroit Branch and is the Socialist Labor wing of the movement. The other is known as the Chicago Branch and represents the more radical anti-political or direct actionist group. It is called by some the anarchist group. Each organization still maintains its headquarters, one at Detroit and the other at Chicago, and each has its staff of officers, its paper and its program. The organization most generally referred to when the name is used is the Chicago Branch.

The first four years of life had left the Industrial Workers but a shadow of its former self. The Brewery Workers, though retaining their industrial unionism had been readmitted into the American Federation of Labor. The Western Federation of Miners was tending in the same direction and has since been granted a Federation charter. In short, as Levine sums it up, "The enthusiasm which the I. W. W. at first awakened had been steadily subsiding during the first two years of its existence. The revolutionary elements in the labor and socialist movements now regarded it with disappointment and distrust. The I. W. W. had shrunk to a mere handful of leaders, revolutionary in spirit and ideals and persevering in action, with a small, scattered and shifting following and an unsatisfactory administrative machinery."

The New Following. — Such a situation inspired rather than baffled these leaders. They would find a following. Indeed there was one at hand that would respond readily to their urgings. The unskilled and unorganized laborers had not been receiving much attention from leaders of ability and force. To these the captains of the Industrial Workers turned for recruits. They formulated a revolutionary propaganda appealing in its force and adaptable in its content and went to work with renewed vigor.

Though the Industrial Workers of the World was formed in 1905 it did not come into real existence as it is known to-day until three years of struggle against outside opposition and factional strife within had coördinated its component parts. Trade union hopes had been crushed. Individual leadership had been established between rival groups. Most important of all the question of political action had been settled. It was not until these things had been accomplished that the Industrial Workers of the World was in position to enter seriously upon the career that it has pursued in the past seven years.

Two sets of events made the new organization. The success of the McKees Rocks Strike in 1909, a strike of unskilled steel workers brought to an end in six weeks showed the fighting spirit of the new movement. The "free speech" fight in Spokane taught its lesson also. In that city ordinances were passed forbidding street corner speaking. These were enforced by arrests. The call went out to all Industrial Workers to come to Spokane, speak on the corners, fill the jails and bankrupt the city. For three months the fight was waged, about five hundred men and women were put in jail, several were killed and others beaten by the police, while those in jail persisted in adopting the hunger strike. Finally it was realized that the city was spending some $20,000 and making no progress. In the end a compromise was reached. The Industrial Workers were allowed to speak unmolested. They have had that liberty ever since. This showed what this form of direct action could do. The year 1909 was the year of the second birth of the Industrial Workers of the World. Following immediately upon these events came the strikes at Lawrence, Paterson, Little Falls, Philadelphia, Lowell, Akron, and other places in the east. These performances were all staged in such a way as to startle the entire eastern section of the country and in many quarters they awakened a state of mind almost akin to a panic. The Industrial Workers of the World had taken on a new lease of life.

The Philosophy of the Movement: Syndicalism. — Turning to the philosophy of the movement, the situation becomes confused. To say it is the philospohy of syndicalism is to state but a part truth, and even then the term itself is vague. Syndicalism is of French origin in its more definite formulation. It has been in part engrafted upon American revolutionary industrialism, as it furnishes ideals and forms of expression that are easily adapted to the American situation. It will not be possible here to attempt even to outline the elements of French Syndicalism as a philosophy worked out by Sorel and others. Its American adaptation is all that is necessary to notice. More than that, the need for such description becomes still less when it is realized that French syndicalism was used in America as a buttress rather than a foundation for the activities of the Industrial Workers of the World. The independence of the worker from everything but himself is the key note; from the state, from the politician, from the employer, from the capitalist. Not independence as understood in a mild way, but domination over or extinction is the only real independence. Syndicalism does not recognize the employer's right to live "any more than a physician recognizes the right of typhoid bacilli to thrive at the expense of the patient, the patient merely keeping alive."

John Spargo has formulated what may be taken as a convenient brief summary of American syndicalism. "Syndicalism is a form of labor unionism which aims at the abolition of the capitalist system based upon the exploitation of the workers, and its replacement by a new social order free from class domination and exploitation. Its distinctive principle as a practical movement is that these ends are to be attained by the direct action of the unions, without parliamentary action or the intervention of the State. The distinctive feature of its ideal is that in the new social order the political state will not exist, the only form of government being the administration of industry directly by the workers themselves." Summing up, he formulates five principles upon which all syndicalists are agreed.

"(1) Capitalism is to be destroyed and with it must be overthrown the political state.

"(2) These ends can only be accomplished by the working class itself.

"(3) They are not to be obtained through political action, but as a result of the direct action of the workers, that is, as direct results of economic conflict and not indirectly by means of legislation.

"(4) Society is to be reconstructed by the workers and economic exploitation and mastery will be abolished.

"(5) In the new Society the unions of the workers will own and manage all industries, regulate consumption and administer the general social interests. There will be no other form of government."

The American followers prefer to be known as industrialists rather than syndicalists. Syndicalism means in France primarily "unionism." In this country some groups of anarchists call themselves Syndicalist Circles. To the group here considered it seems to avoid confusion by making clear the distinction between trade unionism on the one hand and anarchism on the other. In fact the Industrial Workers of the World have not remained a pure syndicalist organization. The Syndicalist League of North America follows European syndicalism more closely. This League and the Industrial Workers are openly critical each of the other. The fact remains that in the popular mind the Industrial Workers and syndicalism are closely associated. The indefiniteness of the latter seems quite consonant with the vagueness and mysteriousness of the Industrial Workers. Syndicalism will doubtless remain an important word in the vocabulary of those who speak much of revolutionary unionism, even though it continues to express itself in "metaphysical quiddities and literary rhapsodies."

With the appearance of the Industrial Workers of the World have come other expressions that are accompanied with sinister significance. The general strike, direct action, sabotage: each of these has a hard sound to an ear accustomed to listen to such expressions as strike, boycott, trade agreement, mediation, labor legislation. To define these ominous terms clearly is quite impossible. They have no clear definition. The leaders who use them so freely are not primarily philosophers or scientists. They are men of action, opportunists, quick to seize any situation and by skillful use of words turn it to their advantage. They meet an immediate situation and seek to dominate it. This they often do by cloaking the description in generalities and rhetorical appeal. The terms in such wide use can be described, then, in only a more general way. Accurate definition seems impossible.

The General Strike. — The general strike of course is no invention of their own. For long years dreamers have pictured a cessation of labor so far reaching and varied that all industries would be closed and society as a whole be completely at the mercy of one of its groups. The Industrial Workers have seized upon this idea and used it very effectively by very reason of its vagueness. Efforts at general strikes though always failures are explained in such a way as to show that with slightly different management they would have succeeded. The realization of the enormous power that would lie in the hands of the men who could successfully launch a general strike appeals with a new force on every new occasion where men are deeply stirred by emotional appeal. In a more definite way, general strikes are sometimes talked of as general throughout an industry. This brings the idea more nearly within the limits of the hopes of industrial unionists who plan to control industries instead of trades through their unions. Again, general strikes refer to community-wide cessation of labor. All the workers of a city, an industrial district, a group of mills or factories may be the unit that is set as the community. Then there is the general national strike. Even this is talked of as a possibility after the Industrial Workers of the World shall have extended their following widely enough. There is then a vague and pleasing indefiniteness about the general strike, and from this very fact arises its potency of appeal to the rank and file of the unskilled workers.

Direct Action. — Direct action is another expression that carries vagueness if not terror. In a sense it is a very reasonable term and reveals clearly the attitude of its users. The methods by which employers or capitalists control industry and its workers are regarded as *indirect*. They use machinery and sub-division of labor, trade unions and trade agreements, law-making bodies, law-enforcing officers, judges in the courts, armed guards, policemen, sheriffs' posses, militiamen. All these are said to be used at will by the power of capital to hold the worker in submission. Such are the claims made again and again and in multiple form by these industrialists. There are no indirect ways left by which helpless workers can check the growing power of their "masters." Direct action is the alternative. As so many of the indirect means suggested in the list just named are related with either trade-union organization or government, they denounce both. Political action is hopeless. The old unionism offers no chance. Consequently anti-political revolutionary industrial organization must be used. This is the idea behind direct action. Though it is not synonymous with the strike, it includes its liberal use. When used it is not the strike of the trade-union brand. Two requirements are essential to the direct action strike. It must be called at a critical time. This means by implication that in order to make it possible at the right time the laborers must not be hampered by any agreements or contracts. The very uncertainty created in the employer's mind is in itself an asset upon which they count when he feels that he has no agreement with his men. Again the strike must close down the entire plant. No groups to remain in and help strike breakers to defeat the strikers. No sense of responsibility for property loss. The industry must be crippled. It will not do to stop at causing the employer merely a little annoyance. This again means no trade divisions in the industry with separate agreements expiring at various times. In this sense the action in securing the objects desired goes straight to the point of forcing the employer in spite of his recourse to indirect action as a means of protection. The employers say they will not recognize the unions or have any dealings with them. "Very well," say the Industrial Workers of the World, "we too refuse to recognize employers. We quit work without consulting them. We go back to work without notice. In all ways they shall be ignored." "If capitalism is 'organized corruption' why should labor, the 'all-creative,' recognize it?"

CHAPTER XXVIII

REVOLUTIONARY INDUSTRIAL UNIONISM
(Continued)

Sabotage. — Closely associated with the terms described in the closing pages of the last chapter is the newer term sabotage. In this word lies the greatest indefiniteness of meaning. Even its origin seems to be somewhat in dispute. A good introduction to the idea is given by John Spargo in his book, Syndicalism, Industrial Unionism and Socialism, where he relates some personal experiences connected with what he asserts to be the first use of both the word and the idea. The story is given here in condensed form.

An Account of Origin of Name. — In 1895 there was in England a revival of interest in industrial unionism. Spargo with others were actively engaged in advocating the One Big Union idea. An aggressive industrial union was formed known as the International Federation of Ship, Dock, and Riverside Workers. Strikes were called by this union and were lost again and again. The whole organization was in danger of going to pieces. The men were sick of unsuccessful strikes. Political action was suggested, but discarded as of no practical promise. Experiences of other unions in parliamentary tactics offered no inducement. Moreover, most of the men in these occupations had no vote. At this juncture, with such a cheerless outlook, another policy was proposed: "Strike by stealth while keeping on the pay roll." When a workman "takes every advantage to slacken his efforts and to waste his time he is said by the English to be 'soldiering.'" But the English expression was too plain and matter of fact. A Scotch colloquialism was chosen in its place, the more "picturesque expression" *ca' canny* which means "go slow" or "be careful not to do too much." Workers were urged to adopt this *ca' canny* policy to "regard the employer and his agents as their natural enemies and to regard it as their duty to their class to strike the employers' pocketbooks, their real souls, in every possible way." As an example was repeated the story of the Chinese coolies who being refused an increase in wages cut off a piece from the end of their shovels saying, "small pay, small work." Regard for the safety of human life was insisted upon as the only limit to the destruction of the employer's machinery and other property. "Of course," says Spargo, "the idea was very easily extended. From the slowing up of the human worker to the slowing up of the iron worker, the machine, was an easy transition. A little dust in the bearings, especially emery dust, would do much. Soap in boilers would retard the development of steam. Judiciously planned 'accidents' might easily create confusion for which no one could be blamed. A few 'mistakes' in handling cargoes might easily cost the employers far more than a small increase of wages would." "Keep this up," it was urged, "and in a little while the employers will be on their knees to the union, begging us to restore our efficiency as workers." This was what the English came to know as the extreme application of *ca' canny*.

Continuing the account Spargo informs us that a group of delegates from France made a report on these conditions in England before their own French organization, the General Confederation of Labor (*Confédération Générale du Travail*). They could find no French word for *ca' canny*. Yet they were much in sympathy with its spirit and desired to recommend it to the Federation. There is a French expression *Travailler à coups de sabots*, meaning to work as one wearing wooden shoes, often applied to laggards or slow-moving people. From this was coined the word *sabotage*. The new word was used in the report. Sabotage stood to the French for the practices to which the English had given the name *ca' canny*. But the French were not content to let the word stand as representing a practice. It must be backed by a philosophy. In French hands, then, the idea has been much more elaborately developed. Thus in vogue in Europe, the Americans have borrowed the term as descriptive of the spirit of the Industrial Workers of the World.

Its Meaning. — The English experience helps very much to understand the content of this evasive term sabotage. In addition, a further idea of its meaning may be gathered from the words of two or three others who have attempted to describe it. "Sabotage as it prevails to-day," says one, "means interfering with the machinery of production without going on strike. It means to strike but stay on the pay roll. It means that instead of leaving the machine the workers will stay at the machine and turn out poor work, slow down their work and in every other way that may be practicable interfere with the profits of the boss, and interfere to such an extent that the boss will have to come around and ask 'What is wrong; what can I do to satisfy you people?'" Another definition runs somewhat the same. "Any conscious and willful act on the part of one or more workers intended to slacken and reduce the output of production in the industrial field, or to restrict trade and reduce the profits in the commercial field, in order to secure from their employers better conditions or to enforce those promised or maintain those already prevailing, when no other way of redress is open; any skillful operation on the machinery of production intended not to destroy it or permanently render it defective but only to temporarily disable it and to put it out of running condition in order to make impossible the work of scabs and thus to secure the complete and real stoppage of work during a strike."

As a final description a somewhat longer extract may be used. It but suggests some of the many ways that ingenuity and cunning will devise when the situation seems to the workers desperate enough to warrant it.

"Strikes may gain certain advantages for the workers, but sabotage well conducted is sure to bring about the employer's discomfiture. According to direct actionists, sabotage should be as far as possible beneficial to the ultimate consumer who, in the majority of cases, is a workingman. Workers in the wine and packing industries who refuse to 'wet' wines or who throw away harmful chemicals destined to preserve ephemeral liquids or embalm doubtful meat, cooks who waste so much margarine that this substitute for butter becomes as expensive as the original article, store clerks who refuse to sell a worthless 'just as good article,' insist on giving full weight, substitute truthful labels for those used on 'sale days,' painters who apply the specified coating of paint, etc., are engaged in beneficial sabotage.

"Another kind of sabotage aims at ruining the retailer's trade: bakers may produce bread and cakes unfit for consumption or containing foreign substances; clerks may refuse to show certain goods or call the customer's attention to their defects.

"Individual sabotage may assume a more aggressive form. Sebastien Faure and Pouget delivered recently on the subject of technical instruction as revolution's handmaid an address from which we quote the following extracts:

"The electrical industry is one of the most important industries, as an interruption in the current means a lack of light and power in factories; it also means a reduction in the means of transportation and a stoppage of the telegraph and telephone systems.

"How can the power be cut off? By curtailing in the mine the output of the coal necessary for feeding the machinery or stopping the coal cars on their way to the electrical plants. If the fuel reaches its destination what is simpler than to set the pockets on fire and have the coal burn in the yards instead of the furnaces? It is child's play to put out of work the elevators and other automatic devices which carry coal to the fireroom.

"To put boilers out of order use explosives or silicates or a plain glass bottle which thrown on the glowing coals hinders the combustion and clogs up the smoke exhausts. You can also use acids to corrode boiler tubes; acid fumes will ruin cylinders and piston rods. A small quantity of some corrosive substance, a handful of emery will be the end of oil cups. When it comes to dynamos or transformers, short circuits and inversions of poles can be easily managed. Underground cables can be destroyed by fire, water, plyers or explosives, etc., etc."

Evidently there are two sides to this from the unionist point of view, though but one from the revolutionist's standpoint. This is seen in a discussion of the policy of sabotage as argued by the members of the Commercial Telegraphers Union, where two different views appear. One runs as follows: "Sabotage can only be worked on a small scale where the individual is in a position to do his work upon his own initiative in a way that no one else is in on his plans. This requires independence of thought and action as well as one chief ingredient—nerve. I do not think there are enough commercial telegraphers with

nerve to make the plan worth while." To this comes the reply:
"Sabotage would fail to bring permanent results, because it
is not the weapon of courageous and progressive men. It is
on a par with the eavesdropper and stool pigeon of the telegraph
companies. A coward's tool to be used in the dark and cannot
stand the light of day. Suppose the Western Union did run into
an epidemic of 'bulled' and 'lost' messages. Wherein would
that help us organize, and that is what we are trying to do."

Deeper Meaning of Sabotage. — It yet remains to emphasize one point in regard to this strange weapon upon which the
members of this branch of unionism count so much. Its use
means the reaching of the verge of despair. Strikes and boycotts
cannot be effectively pushed by these groups of unskilled and
irregularly employed men. Their organizations, when built up
on the lines of the older unionism, do not stay together. They
lack coherence. In the political field they cannot make themselves felt. Their voting strength is greatly scattered by the
transitory nature of much of their work and they have no candidates of their own to push. The methods used by the substantial skilled unions have no effectiveness when adopted by
these workers. There seems no way but to terrorize the employer. Sabotage serves this purpose. Its main strength lies
in the furtiveness of its use. Individuals can use it singly as
well as collectively. Its vagueness causes the employer very
uneasy moments when he sees its results appear in his plant.
It means a kind of disorganization before the spread of which
he is helpless. Further it means that a reckless desperation
has seized his workmen and he knows not where it may lead
or at what point it will break out next. "Whenever a nation
loses hope of a peaceful solution of a problem, that moment all
the elements of war are present. Whenever a class or a portion
of a class loses hope in its policies, loses confidence in its policies,
all the elements of war are there and the idea of direct action
grows and a change takes place." So significant is this phase
of the movement that there are those who declare that "the
heart and the soul and the blood of the syndicalist movement is
sabotage."

The Industrial Workers of the World is the remnant of an
industrial unionist movement that at first sought to work
largely by bringing into its membership the aggressive wing of

the socialists and the more active of trade unionists. These all were to be industrialized. After a brief time these relatively less radical elements dropped out and the leaders remaining were determined to speak in such a way that they would attract a following and command attention. That following has been brought together from the unskilled workers and the large numbers of men and women whose work is most irregular. Textile workers, steel mill workers, lumber jacks, miners, farm and fruit laborers, railway construction gangs, all are more or less migratory groups with no prospect of anything more promising open to them. Discontent is a common factor among them. By the right kind of appeal these elements have been brought under the banner of the Industrial Workers of the World and there they remain only so long as the brilliant promises and fiery rhetoric of the leaders can hold them. They seek trouble, for trouble is their only hope of holding together. Strikes must be called, just for practice if for nothing else. Small strikes keep the members in training for the larger battles that are waged at advantageous times. In these industrial outbreaks they are uncompromising. "There is but one bargain the I. W. W. will make with the employing class," writes their Secretary, "complete surrender of all control of industry to the organized workers." All the "fortifications behind which the enemy has entrenched himself," land, mills, mines and factories, must be seized. "What is of benefit to the employers must, self-evidently, be detrimental to the employees." For the accomplishment of these ends the means used are judged by a single standard, effectiveness. "As a revolutionary organization," declares the Secretary, "the Industrial Workers of the World aims to use any and all tactics that will get the results sought with the least expenditure of time and energy. The tactics used are determined solely by the power of the organization to make good in their use. The question of 'right' and 'wrong' does not concern us."

An American Movement. — The Industrial Workers of the World represents a combination of English practices, French terms, French philosophizings and American conditions. Syndicalism, direct action, sabotage have a strong French flavor. Some of the leaders have visited France and know the General Confederation of Labor. Yet the organization is after all

American. It is the product of independent American leaders, American industrial conditions and American thought. There have been three parallel developments; in England, in France and in America. Each has been independent of the others, yet each has been influenced in some particulars by the others. The American movement is embodied in the Chicago Branch of the Industrial Workers of the World. It cannot be comprehended by seeking alone to understand French syndicalist philosophy, for that is too philosophical. French direct action and American direct action are not the same. The difference is that one is *American* and the other is *French*. It should be clearly understood that the Industrial Workers of the World represents a new American unionism.

Constitution of the Industrial Workers. — While it may be said that the structure of the Industrial Workers of the World is not so important as its spirit, yet there is a more definite organization than is popularly supposed. According to the constitution as modified in 1914 the Industrial Workers of the World consists of actual wage workers brought together in National Industrial Departments, National Industrial Unions, Local Industrial Unions, Local Recruiting Unions, Industrial Councils, and individual members. In localities where there are not enough to form a Local Industrial Union the Recruiting Union is organized temporarily, and even individuals are brought in where there is no Recruiting Union. The Local Industrial Union corresponds to the local of other national organizations, with the characteristic exception that it is composed of the wage workers "welded together in trade or shop branches or as the particular requirements of said industry may render necessary." The Branch then becomes the connecting link between the individual and the central authority. National Industrial Unions are formed by five or more Local Industrial Unions in any one industry having a joint membership of three thousand or more. An Industrial Department is made up of National Industrial Unions of "closely kindred industries appropriate for representation in the departmental administration." It may consist of two or more National Industrial Unions aggregating a membership of not less than 10,000. Industrial Councils for the purpose of establishing general solidarity in a given district may be organized composed of delegates from not less than five

Local Industrial or Local Recruiting Unions. Industrial District Councils hear all appeals on charges from members of local unions within their jurisdiction and their decision is subject to appeal only to the General Executive Board or to the convention. The Departments have general supervision over the affairs of the National Industrial Unions composing the same, "provided that all matters concerning the entire membership of the I. W. W. shall be settled by the referendum." Six Departments are provided for: Agriculture, Land, Fisheries, and Water Products; Mining; Transportation and Communication; Manufacturing and General Production; Construction; Public Service.

The general officers of the organization are the General Secretary-Treasurer, General Organizer and General Executive Board, the last named to be composed of the two general officers and one member of each Industrial Department. A provisional Executive Board is provided for until the departments are organized. It is composed of the two general officers and five additional members. The two named officers have voice but no vote in the General Executive Board. The officers are nominated by the convention and elected by referendum vote. The provisional members of the Executive Board are elected by the convention. Outspoken as the leaders are against the trade agreement, the constitution provides for such agreements subject to positively stated restrictions. Each agreement, before it shall be considered valid must be submitted to and approved by the General Executive Board. Agreements so made must not specify any length of time for its continuance; must not agree to give notice before making any demand affecting wages, hours or shop conditions; must not commit the workers to work only for certain employers or members of employers' associations; and must not agree to regulate the selling price of the product that they are employed to make.

The annual convention is the legislative body of the Industrial Workers of the World. Any change in the organic law, if adopted by the convention, must be submitted to the members by referendum vote. The membership of the convention is carefully provided for. Each subdivision of the general organization is allotted its number of representatives based upon membership. The general officers are members-at-large with one vote each. They do not carry the vote of any local organization. The legal membership is based upon dues paid for the last six months of the fiscal year. A local cannot be represented in the convention unless chartered three months before the time of meeting.

A universal label is provided for. It can never pass from the control of the organization and is to be used on a commodity as evidence that the work is done only by Industrial Workers. The finances are to be provided by charter fees, initiation fees and dues. The general membership can be made up only from "actual wage workers," but no member shall be an officer in "a pure and simple trade union." Provisions are elaborately made for the use of the referendum in all matters that may arise with reference to the policies of the organization. Each officer, in taking office takes a pledge in which among other statements usually found he pledges that he understands and believes in the two sentences: "The working class and the employing class have nothing in common;" and "Labor is entitled to all it produces."

This is the structure. Though worked out in detail, as the above statements will indicate, it has thus far been relatively unimportant. The authority of the officers is large, *de facto* if not *de jure*. Their effective leadership and their ability as the mouthpiece of the movement establishes this authority more effectively than any printed constitution could do. It is the spirit rather than the form of the organization that is important. Revolutionary industrial unionism is its essence. The socialization of industrial life with the industry as the unit; direct action the means, using any weapon that promises success; anarchistic rather than socialistic toward all the present forms of the state and toward all political action.

Effect of Movement on Employers and Unionists. — The trade union leaders as well as the employers have been obliged to heed this latest form of activity. Employers seemed at first completely terrorized. They have not yet fully recovered. Complacent trade unionists have been given a rude shock. Even socialists have felt the influence of the direct actionist policies. A running fight has been kept up between the Industrial Workers and the American Federation since the first. The vigorous and effective attacks upon the trade-union idea made by the industrialists struck home. The Textile Workers had unionized the more skilled of the workers but had neglected or deliberately decided not to include the unskilled. At Lawrence, Little Falls and Paterson these unskilled were massed and turned against both employers and trade unionists. The employers were threatened with a force they could not measure or understand. The trade unionists were met with a group of leaders who would have nothing to do with arbitration, trade agreements or union rules. Very much the same thing happened in other places. In one industry after another where the skilled trades have created what is called an organized labor aristocracy, the leaders of the Industrial Workers have been able to make a successful appeal by awakening the smouldering fires of discontent and hopelessness into the flames of revolutionary and anarchistic industrialism.

The trade unionists have been insistent that they could give no heed to the new methods. Their speakers and editorial writers have been loud in their denunciation of these "lawless" elements. At the same time their organizers have gone to work, more quietly but with renewed energy, to push the lines of organization further out among the unskilled. Choosing the lesser evil, employers have turned to trade-union leaders to secure assistance, making agreements on almost any terms with the national trade organizations in the hope that by the alliance the more turbulent element might be brought under control. Such arrangements can at best be but temporary expedients. No permanent agreements can be made with the Industrial Workers while their policy is animated by its present spirit. A rather far reaching readjustment seems just ahead. Trade unionism is facing a crisis. Its leaders for the most part seem very conservative. Yet industrial unionism is even now making its way in the American Federation though that wing has not yet become revolutionary. What the readjustment will be is for the future to reveal, not for any present day writer to relate.

Attitude of American Federation. — The American Federation denounces the general strike. Seeking to emphasize this position its president urges that "justice and fairness, particularly in the interest of the workers, forbid a general strike." Trade agreements are too important to be jeopardized in this way. "If agreements with employers are broken," he argues, "it is reasonable to suppose that they will not readily enter into new agreements." On the other hand, the Industrial Workers spurn agreements for the very reason that they do stand in the way of the strike. They stand in no fear that employers may refuse to enter into agreements with them. It is rather they who peremptorily refuse any such agreements. While conservative trade unionism is laying greater emphasis on the maxim "the power of the strike is in its restraint, not in its profusion;" revolutionary unionism holds that "the cure for lost strikes is more strikes; strikes more frequent, more aggressive and on a larger scale."

Its aim to include all workers in one single organization appears to the Federation leaders as a "nerve so colossal that it is positively ridiculous. Of course the two and a half million workingmen in the trade-union movement are entirely oblivious that they are included." Time will put this new movement down, they declare, "as the most vapid and ridiculous in the annals of those who presume to speak in the name of labor, and the participants in the gathering as the most stupendous impossibles the world has yet seen."

At the same time the Industrial Workers were characterizing their formidable opponent as the "American Separation of Labor," developing "crafty unionism." It is "neither American, nor a federation, nor of labor." It is "divided into 116 warring factions;" it "discriminates against workingmen because of their race and poverty:" it allows members "to join the militia and shoot down other men in time of strike;" it "creates three types very obnoxious to the industrial unionist: the aristocrat of labor, the union scab and the labor lieutenant."

The Ideal: One Big Union. — The ideal of One Big Union has from the beginning been kept to the front. Unions among the trades have not taken the places that were reserved for them and that they were expected to take. This has confined the following to the tradeless laborer, a development not deliberately planned but one that has been made the best of. There was to be room for all. This situation is aptly described as a "vast and nearly empty structure with groups of the lower grades of workers in some of the basic industries in their proper place in the scheme, but with all the rest a hollow shell."

Yet the ideal is clung to with great tenacity. "We are going down into the gutter," says a leader, "to get at the mass of the workers and bring them up to a decent plane of living. I do not care a snap of my finger whether or not the skilled workers join this industrial movement at the present time. When we get the unorganized and the unskilled laborer into this organization the skilled worker will of necessity come here for his own protection. Strange as it may seem to you, the skilled worker to-day is exploiting the laborer beneath him, the unskilled man, just as much as the capitalist is."

The call is for "one great organization — big enough to take in the black man, the white man; big enough to take in all nationalities — an organization that will be strong enough to obliterate state boundaries, to obliterate national boundaries, and one that will become the great industrial force of the working class of the world." "There are two economic classes (labor and capital) whose interests are diametrically opposed, and between the two classes the struggle must and will go on. In that struggle there is no compromise nor arbitration nor anything that can solve or settle it; either labor has to come into its own or go down." "We, the I. W. W., stand on our two feet, the class struggle and industrial unionism, and coolly say we want the whole earth."

Impressions: Historical View. — These various close-range glimpses give different impressions according to the angle from which the view is taken. But when viewed in its historical setting the Industrial Workers of the World appears as a natural product of evolution. Class rivalry has always been an important factor in social readjustments. In the earlier centuries royalty and feudal barons yielded to the merchant class. The American Revolution itself in 1776 was a middle-class revolution. Then came the extension of the suffrage in the political and the struggle for the legalization of the trade unions in the industrial fields. These marked distinct stages. They cannot strictly be termed revolutionary changes yet their effects were far reaching. The struggle of the artisans and skilled craftsmen has scarcely subsided when the unskilled appear with their demands. For a time satisfied because of their right to the ballot and hopeful of attaining their ends through its means, this element has been relatively contented. But they are now despairing of these hopes. Trade unionism does not appeal to them. They have no trades around which to form unions.

Socialism as an independent action is not meeting their needs. Even socialism is becoming conservative. Representatives, even when put in office, do not appear to make progress in the desired direction. Anti-political, revolutionary, direct industrial action appears to be the only remaining recourse.

The Future? — In other words, one class after another has secured a voice in the general management of industrial, political and social affairs. The movement has reached down to the unskilled and here the foment is working. Added to it are the mutterings of the unemployed, the rumblings of which have been distinctly heard of late. The leaders of the Industrial Workers of the World have been far-sighted enough to incorporate this element and it affords a following the strength of which is by no means uncertain though difficult to measure quantitatively. Viewed in this way the Industrial Workers of the World did not come as a surprise. It came as a natural step in our social, political and industrial development. Already since its inception some leaders have proven too mildly radical. They are out. Others have gone to the other extreme and, like William D. Haywood, have been voted out of the socialist and other parties. The lines of cleavage have been drawn. They may be drawn again. There are now two organizations of Industrial Workers of the World, one of which still adheres to the advocacy of a form of political action. The Chicago branch represents the extreme of discontent and radicalism. That is the situation at present. It may be that, following precedents established by other radical groups, these leaders may acquire some power and come to recognize some responsibility. If such be the case, they should, according to past experience, become more conservative, or at least less radical. In doing so, they will carry with them a portion of their following but leave behind another portion. This new segregation will give rise to a new organization, new leaders and new followers with a new name but still voicing the ultra-radical and impossible demands of the new day. Its appearance will startle many and shock some. In the mean time the Industrial Workers of the World will take its place with the trade unions — themselves once looked upon as the anarchistic element of industrial workers — and the political socialists — still regarded by many as the revolutionary element in political life. As both of these organizations, the unions and the socialists, have acquired a social respectability, so the Industrial Workers may, by changes due to the same forces, become "respectable." In that case it may be that we shall see the Industrial Workers directing their attacks upon the later and newer leaders whom they may in turn characterize as men of "colossal nerve"; a group of "most stupendous impossibles" who are seeking to undermine the foundations and defeat the glorious purposes of the Industrial Workers of the World. Though dependent upon imagination to picture the details of such a development, its main features are by no means outside of the realm of the possible. More than ever before is it true, however, that the development of such a situation is, at the present, fairly well within social control. How important and how radically disturbing this future "remnant" will be depends largely if not entirely upon policies now being formulated and applied.

PART VI
CONCLUSION

CHAPTER XXIX

UNIONISM

Without the presentation of any more material or the discussion of other policies and activities, the question must now be raised: *What is American unionism?* To such a question several answers may be given. It is an historical product. It is a part of our national industrial activity. It is a form of organization, or more properly, it is composed of a variety of forms of organization. It is a means of competing with employers. It is a fighting machine by which its members seek to add to their share of the community's wealth at the expense of other groups in the community. It is an organization that seeks to improve its own situation directly and others indirectly. It is one of the associated movements by which standards of living are to be raised and means furnished for supporting these rising standards; one of the general social uplift agencies. It may be viewed as an evolution. It may be looked upon as a structure. It may be understood as a function. It may be regarded as a means to the accomplishment of an end, in which the spirit of unionism becomes the element of primary importance.

The preceding chapters have sought to throw some light upon each of these phases of unionism separately. It is only by taking them all together that they can be made to reveal its true spirit. Even then the spirit is elusive. The spirit of any movement is much more difficult to catch and reduce to a printed page than is its form. In the case of unionism the difficulty is aggravated by the confusions and the dangers of misrepresentation that exist at every point.

The Ideal. — The spirit of unionism finds expression in a variety of forms. This variety is often so great and the contrasts so striking that errors arise from a failure to include the wider scope within the field of vision. There is, for example, a favorite form of statement that often becomes very inclusive. "Half conscious though it be," says one of the idealistic admirers, "the labor movement is a force pushing toward the attainment of the purpose of humanity; in other words, the end of the growth of mankind, — namely the full and harmonious development in each individual of all human faculties — the faculties of working, perceiving, knowing, loving; the development, in short, of whatever capabilities of good there may be in man." "The labor movement," continues the statement, "in its broadest terms is the effort of men to live the lives of men. It is a systematic, organized struggle of the masses to obtain primarily more leisure and larger economic resources; but that is not by any means all, because the end and purpose of all is a richer existence for the toilers, and that with respect to mind, soul and body."

Such statements may be duplicated again and again from union literature. Preambles, declarations and resolutions are filled with expressions of an exalted idealism toward which unions are struggling.

The Practical. — On the other hand, much may be heard and read that is far from idealistic. The hatred for the non-union man, the denunciation of the employer, the destructive tendencies manifested in times of strike or boycott, all these appear even side by side with actions and statements that seem in no possible way reconcilable. Yet wage scales, trade agreements, shorter hours; strikes, closed shops, picketing, intimidation; all are a part of the same whole into which enter such expressions as larger living and loftier outlook.

Their Combination. — Unionism has ideals. Unionism has also been obliged to struggle even for an existence. It has found itself in the midst of stern realities and under the sharp necessity for being very practical. In more recent times the question of continued existence has not been so acute. Yet the danger of extermination has not entirely passed. Leaders are constantly under the influence of the effects of the struggle for existence. In times of comparative quiet the ideals find expression. Sometimes these lead to pretty clear and definite action. At other times there is indefinite groping; a vague reaching out into a dark future. In times of stress and rivalry these ideals give way to prompt and positive action, a program that appears to be very frankly opportunist. As relations shift in the strain of industrial strife different phases of policy appear, always suggested by immediate needs and often misunderstood by the uninitiated. For these reasons interpretation of any one phase must be undertaken with caution and must be kept within strict limits.

Results of the Combination. — The fight for existence coupled with the emphasis upon larger idealism has not infrequently led to serious misunderstanding. False impressions are created in the minds of many, both inside and outside the unions. The trial of the officers of the Western Federation of Miners for the murder of Governor Steunenberg of Idaho or of the dynamite plotters of the Structural Iron Workers caused much commotion in all labor circles. Leaders saw in the prosecution of the cases a necessity for united action. Unions have become strong enough to attract the serious attention of employers and even to lead them to combine in their opposition. Such acts as those to which reference has just been made the employers could not be expected to allow to pass unnoticed. Unionists looked upon the prosecution as a plan by which the employers were going to renew their efforts to overthrow unionism itself. If through the trial of union officials unionism was to be attacked then unionism must defend itself through the defense of these same officials. In that way must the movement be supported. In accordance with that attitude large sums were raised by assessment of members over the entire country in order to carry on the fight in the form of a court trial. Thrown in this way on the defensive, they fought with a zeal born of desperation, perhaps, rather than of judgment. There could be no doubt of devotion to the cause of unionism in such a time of peril.

Again, it may be shown that the accumulation of large sums of money to accomplish the purpose of federating "the manufacturers of the country to effectively fight industrial oppression" has been met by the defense funds of the unions. If this new force was to be directed to the practical result of eliminating from all shops union leaders in particular and union men in general in the name of the freedom of the laborer, then the unionist must reply with his closed-shop policy and his insistence that all workers who wanted employment should come into the unions. When employers used espionage in detecting plans and thwarting the union's purposes, their officers have often replied in kind and resorted to blackmail and other unjustifiable methods. Whatever the methods used by opponents, they must be met by counter attacks with similar methods. Whatever was attacked must be defended. Shrewdness on the part of unionism's opponents has naturally dictated that attacks be leveled at the most vulnerable points. The loyalty of the unionists has prompted the defense at this point, not because of its inherent worth or essential value to the movement but because defeat at this point would seem to weaken the whole defense.

The mistakes in judgment at these points must of course be open to criticism. In so far as the methods adopted have been contrary to public security or welfare, they must be condemned. But condemnation of these matters should not stop short at unionism. Where they are provoked by actions on the part of employers that are equally unjustifiable when judged by the same standards, then the employers' association must not be allowed to escape. If indeed there is to be any difference at all in condemnation, the heavier burden must be made to rest upon employers and not upon workmen. Employers have the responsibility as well as the advantage of superior ability, superior opportunity and superior position.

Idealism Plus Opportunism. — Unionism examined in this way will be much easier of comprehension. The idealism on the one hand and the practical opportunism on the other are not irreconcilable. The opportunism of the union movement grows out of the obstacles that are to be met and overcome. The idealism arises from purposes well conceived and ambitions that are both progressive and lofty.

Union activities center around collective bargaining. Collective bargaining opens the way for industrial liberty. Industrial liberty is essential to all liberty. Liberty is necessary to the realization of fullness of life. Such are the stages in the analysis of unionism. Though they are not all apparent in the every-day unionism that one sees and hears so much of, none the less they form an undivided chain no link of which is intelligible if taken apart from the others.

Collective Bargaining Essential to Unionism. — Much has been gained in recent years in the contention of organized laborers that the only fair bargaining is collective on the part of employees. For it they have won much support. Yet they insist upon its importance beyond this point. In an earlier day when even the formation of a society to discuss wages was illegal conspiracy, that method of bargaining had no sanction except among the workmen themselves. It has been established more recently that associations of laborers for the purpose of maintaining wages or other favorable conditions of labor are not only not illegal, they are positively beneficial. This is very generally accepted. But the unions go further. It is not enough to say that unions *may* be formed and bargaining *may* be carried on through them. Unions *must* be formed and bargaining *must* be collective. The employer openly objects to this. The community is not ready to accept it. Yet unionism insists upon it. Here lies a difference and a source of misunderstanding. Unionists are not content with stopping at the right to associate and being stopped in the policy of enforcing collective bargaining on all laborers. The community generally insists that the right to associate marks the limit of the rights, either legal or moral, of the unions. The situation appears to the general community as one in which the individual worker must be protected against this coercion that unions would impose upon them. Employers have been quick to seize the advantage. It must be insisted, however, that whatever the employer may say about the necessity of preserving to every man and woman the liberty of bargaining individually cannot be taken seriously. It is couched in such familiar words that at first it seems convincing. Yet the self-interest in the plea is so apparent that it cannot conceal itself for long. The employer's side of the issue must be stated in other terms more frank and more sincere if it is to carry weight. Even judges in expressing official opinions on this situation have penetrated the disguise when legal rights were involved. "It is a notable fact in this connection," says one judge in writing the opinion of the court, "that the alleged constitutional right of the laborer to contract his labor at any price which seems to him desirable is not in this or any other reported case a claim urged by the laborer, but the earnest contention in his behalf is made by the contractors who are reaping the benefits" of a situation where the law has not previously protected the individual and unorganized workman. In another case it is written: "It may not be improper to suggest in this connection that although the prosecution in this case was against the employer of labor, who apparently under the statute is the only one liable, his defence is not so much that his right to contract has been infringed upon, but that the act works a peculiar hardship to his employees, whose right to labor as long as they please is alleged to be thereby violated. The argument would certainly come with better grace and greater cogency from the latter class."

The real situation must be clearly seen. The employer finds that he can make a better bargain by closing with each individual separately. The laborer who regards his class interest sees as clearly that by bargaining collectively he can meet the employer on terms more nearly equal. The non-union man thus becomes a factor of importance. The employer is directly concerned in keeping him out of the union. It is natural that he should be. It is to his business interests though he seeks to conceal the fact behind an assumed concern in the individual rights of the laborer. The unionist is just as vitally concerned in bringing him into the union, primarily, too, for the good of the union laborers. Their bargaining both for themselves and for other laborers will be more favorable.

The Closed Shop and Collective Bargaining. — Collective bargaining has other practical phases. When necessary the closed shop becomes one of the demands of unionism. Its relation to collective bargaining, however, should be clearly understood. The subject has been dealt with in a separate chapter. At the risk of unnecessary repetition it may be referred to again. It cannot be made too important. Evidence gathered from a wide variety of sources makes it quite plain that individual bargaining resolves itself sooner or later into a statement by the employer of what he will pay. This the laborer may accept or not, as he pleases. A leading railroad in a part of its educational advertising says: "The company has always recognized the right of any man to labor upon whatever terms he and his employer may agree, whether he belongs to a labor organization or not." But in fact a railroad employs men generally in gangs, especially the more unskilled labor. Boards of directors and executive committees decree what wage scales shall be. They are final. The laborer may accept them or look for work elsewhere. When one of the brotherhoods of employees speaks, however, there is then something like real bargaining even though it does not speak for its own members alone. Another large employer of labor registers it as his opinion that an employer should set the wages and conditions of labor just as he sets the price of his goods. If he sets wages too low, he will get no labor, just as he will make no sales if he sets prices too high. As to the individual laborer, his bargaining consists in deciding whether or not to take the job on the conditions set by the employer. It is the same as in the case of a purchaser in a store; if the price suits him, he buys; if not, he is not forced to make any purchases. Many employers hold this same philosophy. Individual bargaining has an outcome that is all too evident. The laborer of unionist tendencies will have nothing of it if he can help himself. He will also prevent other laborers from submitting to it if he can.

The Non-Unionist. — Again the non-unionist comes in for his share of consideration. It is shown by much evidence that the open shop easily becomes the anti-union shop. But even if union men are not discriminated against, still the open shop remains to the union man a denial of the right to bargain collectively. When non-union men come in, the union scale is broken, union standards fall and the purposes of unionism are defeated. The non-union man has received by far more attention than he really deserves. He is not very well understood by many who talk about him. Employers have eulogized him, seeing in him the salvation of all good qualities of Americanism. Usually he is greeted with open arms and large pay by an employer who wishes to break a strike. After the strike is over, even if won by the employer, these valuable men are allowed to drift on and their places are filled by the older men who one by one find their way back to their old jobs. President Emeritus Eliot has made himself very well known to labor leaders through his insistent championship of the non-union man, the strike breaker. This champion sees in labor more than many a laborer has been able to see. "The only limit that a man should desire to put on labor is the amount his bodily health and strength will permit. I don't want my labor limited to any less, that much is joy; and I voice a profound contempt for the man who wishes to do less than he can. . . . Money doesn't pay the laborer; besides this there is the joy of taking part in the great machine of men and women working together to produce as much as possible." Could such a condition be realized in the doing of all the work, labor troubles, as well as most other troubles, would probably cease. Many an employer appears to his employees to be quite willing that money should not pay the laborer; he seems very agreeable to the proposition that the "joy of taking part in the great machine of men and women working together to produce as much as possible" should be the reward. Those who come nearest to being a part of this great machine of men and women seem least willing to take their pay in joy. Because of the influential advocacy of strike breakers by President Emeritus Eliot, they have come to be known among union men as "Eliot's Heroes."

Though speaking on the more general subject of strikes and the use of violence to enforce them, the Anthracite Coal Strike Commission has set forth the side of the non-union man very clearly. The right to organize and to strike is admitted. Further, the beneficence of labor unions is acknowledged, in that though somewhat slowly and intermittently they have made real progress in improving relations between employer and employed. The strike to enforce demands, "whether wise or unwise in inception and purpose, is an exercise of no more than the legal rights that belong collectively to its members." Considering the man who does not wish to strike or the man who prefers not to join a union, the Commission has the following to say:

"The right to remain at work where others have ceased to work, or to engage anew in work which others have abandoned, is part of the personal liberty of a citizen that can never be surrendered, and every infringement thereof merits and should receive the stern denouncement of the law. All government implies restraint, and it is not less but more necessary in self-governed communities than in others to compel restraint of the passions of men which make for disorder and lawlessness. Our language is the language of a free people and fails to furnish any form of speech by which the right of a citizen to work when he pleases, for whom he pleases, and on what terms he pleases, can be successfully denied. The common sense of our people, as well as the common law, forbids that this right should be assailed with impunity. It is vain to say that the man who remains at work while others cease to work, or takes the place of one who has abandoned his work, helps to defeat the aspirations of men who seek to obtain better recompense for their labor and better conditions of life. Approval of the object of a strike or persuasion that its purpose is high and noble cannot sanction an attempt to destroy the right of others to a different opinion in this respect, or to interfere with their conduct in choosing to work upon what terms and at what time and for whom it may please them so to do.

"The right thus to work cannot be made to depend upon the approval or the disapproval of the personal character and conduct of those who claim to exercise this right. If this were otherwise, then those who remain at work might, if they were in the majority, have both the right and the power to prevent others who choose to cease to work from so doing.

"This all seems too plain for argument. Common sense and common law alike denounce the conduct of those who interfere with this fundamental right of the citizen. The assertion of the right seems trite and commonplace, but that land is blessed where the maxims of liberty are commonplaces."

Against such an estimate may be placed another, attributed to Dr. Rainsford and going the rounds of the labor press. "The scab is on a lower moral level than the union man. This may be an unpleasant doctrine, but it is only the truth, and both scab and labor unionist know and admit it. The scab has set himself against the recognized armies of his class and has become a traitor to his cause. I am not saying that that cause as advocated is necessarily good and just; whether it be either or neither does not make any difference. He has been forced to obey the crudest of all instincts — that of self-preservation — and to do this he has sinned against a higher, later, more complex, more advanced social instinct — viz., the instinct of class preservation, of class consciousness. To fill his belly he has betrayed his cause, and to betray it is to sin the unforgivable sin." Again there is the curt reply that emphasizes the differences between the moral and the legal rights of the case. "The trade union policy concedes the legal right of the strike breaker to earn his diploma of Doctor of Heroics, the latest addition to the degrees conferred by the head of Harvard University, but it emphatically denies his moral right so to do." The opposition is argued again in another and more practical way. The fight of unions to control the labor supply is the same as that of the

employer to control capital. Directors and executive committees, as is well known, represent minorities of stockholders.
They claim to know best the interests of all and insist that they
act accordingly. Even in fields other than business it is often
the active, organized minority that controls; that is, in fact,
expected to control. The claims urged by unions that they
represent labor appear from this point of view not so far fetched.
Labor leaders have the backing of an organized movement; union
labor is the nucleus of the aggressive spirit of labor as a whole.

The Non-Unionist and Liberty. — Liberty to the laborer has
a quite different meaning than to other classes. It is much more
concrete. Historical experiences still linger in memory. English history has been carefully studied. Equality of liberty the
laborers do not care to intrust too fully to the employing class.
The middle-class standards and ideals of a half century and a
little more ago were very narrow. Couched in general terms,
it was clear by the way in which they were applied that their
blessings were intended only for the middle class. The Webbs,
in their History of Trade Unionism, have made this clear so
far as the English middle classes were concerned. "The flagrant
injustice of the old Master and Servant Acts seemed justifiable
even to a middle-class Parliament." In accordance with these
laws when an employer broke a contract for service, whatever
the circumstances, he could be sued for damages. If the workman broke his contract for service and absented himself from
his work he was liable for a criminal offense, the penalty being
imprisonment for three months. A master sued by a servant
could testify in his own defense; a servant when tried could not.
Often the only evidence brought against the servant was that
of the employer. On an information or oath a single justice of
the peace could issue a warrant for arrest of a workman. The
trial could be held at the private house of the justice. The only
penalty was imprisonment, there being no alternative fine. The
decision of the one justice was final, there being no appeal. The
justices of the peace were generally themselves employers of
labor. The right to strike had been established but the agreement to do anything in prosecution of the strike was a conspiracy. All this in nineteenth-century England where liberty
was very much talked about.

American workmen know of these experiences. It gives warning to them to look behind the words when they hear employers talking so glibly about liberty of action and freedom of contract. The kind of bargaining that they experience when the unions are broken down and when the non-union man is used as a type of American manhood is a kind of bargaining, they insist, that does not lead to freedom. A statement that leaders are fond of quoting runs as follows: "Liberty does not consist in a theoretical right, but in the possibility of exercising it. The power to be free, in a régime which puts the workingman's life at the mercy of supply and demand; which exposes himself, his wife and his children to the hardships of a competition that knows no moderation; which sets no limit to his exploitation except the interests of those who employ him, — the power to be free in such conditions, when the need of subsistence is so pressing as to permit of no waiting, no choice, no hesitation, does not exist and consequently the laborer is not free." To this is added the statement attributed to Horace Greeley. "To talk of the freedom of labor, the policy of leaving it to make its own bargains, when the fact is that a man who has a family to support and a house hired for the year is told: 'If you will work thirteen hours per day or as many as we think fit, you can stay; if not, you can have your walking papers; and well you know that no one else hereabout will have you;' — is it not most egregious flummery?" Stated still again, this time more in the form that has much of the ring of a challenge, the President of the American Federation of Labor declares: "As between the employer's concepts of liberty for workers and the demands of the workers for the liberty they find necessary to enable them to live like men, the nation must choose."

Faults of Unionism Exaggerated. — Looking to the other side of unionism, there are two important matters to consider. Unionism cannot be regarded as having, as a movement, attained perfection. Far from it, as a matter of fact. But one important consideration is that its shortcomings are very much exaggerated. The general reading public learn from the daily press but little of what unions are doing in ordinary times. Their virtues are not cried from the housetops. But when there is an outbreak and the fighting spirit of the laborers is aroused by the cool consciousness of superior advantage displayed by the employer, the events are shouted at the reading public in first page head lines of startling size and color. Journalism thrives on the sensational and seizes upon any opportunity to exploit any event whether a labor controversy or any other event of the community life. Assault and battery, destruction of property, interference with car or train running; one act of any of these receives more space and attention than all the work of a year of all the unions of a community in their own mutual aid and fraternal activities. It is pointed out that men do not live up all the time to the ideals of the church, the state, the commercial world, or fraternal orders. Yet the public does not hold such exceptions as characterizing the purposes of these societies or institutions. Irrational as it seems, a large portion of the public judges labor unions by acts that are in fact exceptional rather than ordinary. Thus it comes about through unsatisfactory journalism and an unfortunate habit of public thought that labor unions are often in disfavor because of faults that they do not possess and traits that do not characterize them. If the truth could be generally known, the standing of unionism would be greatly improved.

Unionism Not Without Faults. — But even if this were so, there would still be a basis for criticism. Unions do many things that should not be done; many things, in fact, that defeat their own higher purposes. They are not as regardful of contracts as they should be. In time of strike they have not as strict a regard as they should have for the rights either of other laborers, of property owners or of employers. They often adopt policies that are heartless and oppressive. Revenge not infrequently figures prominently in guiding their actions. They restrict output, reach out for a monopoly of the labor supply, seek to establish arbitrary control over the supply of labor, and over the machinery and the materials that shall be used. Individual leaders raise themselves to authority by demagogic appeals and then find that they can retain their leadership only by reckless acts as they won it by reckless words. Locals sometimes acquire a reputation for irresponsible action and remain powerful enough to resist the discipline that the national officers may seek to enforce. Or, for reasons, the national officials may wink at the irresponsibility of the local. In this way a whole national may be characterized by the actions of one or two obstreperous locals. Opportunities for self-advancement may stimulate leaders to acquire power in order that they may sell out for the price that seems always ready to be offered. Corruption, bribery, blackmail, lawlessness in more forms than a few appear and from them the unions cannot escape responsibility. No one can safely condone them. No union can afford to overlook them, much less secretly harbor them. They must be frankly admitted to exist. The leaders themselves must not deny them. It is detrimental to all unionism for them to attempt denial. The burden of shouldering these responsibilities is heavy. It handicaps the better class of leaders very seriously. To deny the faults of unions is well-nigh suicidal to the cause. To admit them frankly would, on the other hand, disarm much criticism. It would clear the atmosphere of much of the haze that now obscures clear vision and make possible a much clearer view of the ideal of unionism as contrasted with the practices of some, or even many, of the unions.

Nature of Opposition to Unionism: Individualism. — As the activity of unions is shaped largely by the opposition they encounter, it will be profitable to notice more in detail this opposition. First there is the individualist who interprets all human relations in the light of his particular philosophy. To such an one the idea of subjecting one's self to the interests of a group whose improvement is made a mutual concern is quite incomprehensible, and the practice is wholly unjustifiable. Extreme individualism leaves no room for coöperation by which one surrenders an advantage of one kind for a gain much greater.

Perhaps unionism's severest individualist critic is President Emeritus Eliot. He has so often spoken out against the unions that his opposition is quite generally understood. To him "labor unionism is the most formidable danger of our future." It is a "moral danger as well as material." "The unions just rot a man's character and no one can escape their influence. The tendency is to work day after day with the deliberate purpose of doing as little labor as possible in the least number of working hours." This danger to the laborer is accompanied by another found in the fact that government officials are afraid to attempt to regulate them. "Politicians are becoming more and more afraid of organized labor, despite the fact that there are only about two million votes out of that class in a total of seventeen million voting strength of this country." All these evils appear to this critic to flow quite directly from the fact that the unions establish rules for the purpose of securing combined action and the force of numbers. When a member joins a union he seems to surrender his individual rights and this leads to the surrender of his manhood. The admirable independence of the strike breaker who asserts his right to work in whatever conditions he chooses regardless of the consequences upon the wage scales and the standards of living of the laborers as a class receives the unbounded admiration of this union critic. He seems in some peculiar way to be fighting the really important battle for labor. Such criticism as this involves a great deal. Its value cannot be determined apart from the value of individualism itself.

Individual Liberty and Unionism. — Individual liberty is a term that has always had a large place in American thought. Events show, however, that the two parts have not been well balanced. Liberty has been pushed by its active champions to an unwarranted extreme. In some instances it has stopped but little, if any, short of special privilege to intrude in an unlimited way into provinces belonging quite clearly to another. It is self-granted license rather than liberty. While thus expanding the term liberty, the word individual has not been given similar breadth. Theoretically it is the *ego* and the *alter*. In practice it depends very much upon who is the *ego* and who the *alter*. It has been used in the singular rather than in the plural sense. It has meant practically the individuals of a class or a group.

In Practice. — The wealthy class have interpreted it as their liberty to amass wealth whether by creative production or by mere accumulation at the expense of others. The politicians understand it as their liberty to carry elections, shape legislation and direct the administration of the laws according to their individual wishes, whether for the advantage or the detriment of others. In the courts it has meant, according to the high authority of a presidential message to Congress, that poor individuals were at such a disadvantage in our courts that it was difficult for them to secure justice against rich individuals. To employers it has meant individual liberty virtually to dictate wages and conditions of labor and an insistence upon the maintenance of the individual liberty of the employee to accept them. In short, individual liberty, a phrase put into circulation by the middle class to whom individualism meant in practice middle class individualism, has been kept rather well confined within its first limits. It has quite generally made a difference who is the individual, when the issue of individual liberty has been raised.

In Theory: Individualist Definition of Liberty. — Not only has the individualist's practice of liberty led to great inequality of liberty, his definition of the term has broken down. There is still good in the definition if that part of it could be enforced. The Declaration of the Rights of Man declared liberty to be the right of every man to do that which does not injure others. This statement was later cast by the individualist into a form more convenient for interpretation. "Every man may claim the fullest liberty to exercise his faculties compatible with the possession of like liberty by every other." This has amounted to the practice of every one extending his liberty by his own interpretation to a point where in his own judgment he would by going further intrude upon the liberty of another. Where the *other* would set up such a limit enters or not into the determination, according to what the influence of the other is. One politician may check the liberties of another. One employer may restrict another. The voter acting individually or the employee acting individually cannot set up serious limitations. Such a guide as this for determining the limits of liberty is about as serviceable as it would be in determining a line fence or an international boundary.

This issue was raised in still another form in an address two years ago by a former Chief Justice of the New York State Court of Appeals before the New York State Bar Association. In this address the former Justice asserted that the most serious question now before us is whether or not "individual liberty is still to obtain in America." The answer to the question, read from many typical signs of the times, is that "unless I am utterly mistaken, there is now a strong tendency in courts, in legislatures, and, worst of all, in the people themselves to disregard the most fundamental principles of personal rights." Somewhat mournfully, it may be imagined, the speaker declared that "judicial decisions are made, statutes are enacted, and doctrines are publicly advocated which, when I was young, would have shocked our people to the last degree." The crux of the address appears in the definition of liberty. "In those days," said the speaker, "liberty was deemed to be the right of the citizen to act and live as he thought best so long as his conduct did not invade a like right on the part of others. To-day, according to the notion of many, if not most people, liberty is the right of part of the people to compel the other part to do what the first part thinks the latter ought to do for its own benefit."

Such statements as these clearly raise more issues than one. As to one of these, there is the ideal consideration of the right of one class or group in the community to impose its will upon another class or group. Theoretically this is, of course, highly wrong. Practically, it is well known to all observers of conditions as they exist that it is quite unavoidable. The issue of more importance, however, is the more serious error involved in the statement. It compares an ideal of one day with the existing conditions of another day. The insistence that this is an error does not rest with unionists only nor does it characterize American trade unionism alone. The pertinent question is, did the conditions assumed in the definition quoted actually exist in earlier times? Is the situation described in the stated notion of to-day a new one representing a loss of desirable relations formerly realized? If these questions can be answered in the affirmative, the justice was right in his contention and he made a strong point. But the question must be answered in the negative. The more our knowledge of actual conditions is extended into the past the more clear it must become that such a description relates rather to an ideal than to the real life of the day. As a matter of fact, there can be no doubt that the latter part of the statement was more thoroughly applicable to late eighteenth and early nineteenth century conditions than to the present. There is no doubt that both politically and industrially it was even more true then than now that a part of the people "compelled" the other part. Limited suffrage; control by aristocratic families (New York State furnishes a conspicuous example of this); laws and decisions against even the right of trade associations to exist, much less to strike or insist upon collective bargaining; vague and free use of conspiracy charges—these are some of the elements that lead one to think that even admitting that part of the people "compel" the other part, the situation is not new "to-day" but that it extended back to the days of those who have gone before. True, there are differences in the degree of compulsion, as there are also (more important) differences in the part of the people that is compelling the other part. Perhaps the compellors of yesterday are the compelled of to-day. That, however, is not a fundamental difference. Clearly one cannot accept the definition of personal liberty as "the right of the citizen to act and live as he thinks best so long as his conduct does not invade a like right on the part of others." It may be an ideal to be sought but there is always the necessity for a common agreement on the very essential question, when does one's conduct invade the right of another? That cannot be left to either of the parties alone. The changing times must cause the line of limitation to be constantly though slowly shifting. No definite application of such a definition can be made that will be concrete enough for practical purposes.

Criticism of Definition. — In a destructive or negative way the criticism offered by Ritchie in his Natural Rights is pertinent. "Liberty in general," says this writer, "is too ambiguous a term to permit us to decide how far the right to liberty is a right which ought to be recognized by a well-regulated society. The principle that the liberty of every one should be limited only by the equal liberty of every one else has been shown to be incapable of any literal application as a fundamental principle of society." In a more facetious vein a humorist makes a serious contribution to this negative form of criticism. "The main problem of ethics," he says, "is to devise a form of liberty which will make a man who is subjected to it feel that he is free. When we consider the colored people of the south, for instance, it is clear that they have either liberty without freedom or freedom without liberty: both they have not. It is the same with woman's suffrage. The suffrage might emancipate our women, but it wouldn't give them freedom. It might give them freedom, but it wouldn't give them liberty. On the other hand, it might take away much of their liberty in the process of emancipation, in which event we could not give them back their liberty without hampering them in their freedom." To such a writer should be set the task of explaining the industrial liberty of the non-union laborer. In the opinion of T. H. Green, "by liberty we do not mean a freedom that can be enjoyed by one man, or one set of men, at the cost of a loss of freedom to others. . . . We mean by it a power which each man exercises through the help or security given him by his fellow men, and which he in turn helps to secure for them. When we measure the progress of a society by the growth of freedom, we measure it by the increasing development and exercise on the whole of those powers of contributing to social good with which we believe the members of society to be endowed." Still more forcefully is the constructive criticism expressed by Montesquieu in his definition: "Liberty consists in doing what we ought to will, and in not being constrained to do what we ought not to will." In a more practical way President Wilson has given us the illustration of the parts of a complicated machine. Each part must have its perfect adjustment and alignment, and liberty for the parts consists in their proper assembling and adjustment. Applying the figure, he says, "I feel confident that if Jefferson had lived in our day he would see what we see, that the individual is caught in a great confused mix-up of all sorts of complicated circumstances, and that to let him alone is to leave him helpless as against the obstacles with which he has to contend."

Certainly there is no lack of authority in urging that the individualist's idea of liberty be modified. The modification should not be undertaken, however, as a superficial matter. It involves fundamentals. Yet it is clear that unionism is not based upon an individualist philosophy. The worst that can be said of it justly is that its foundation rests on a class conscious movement. The best is that it is essentially a socializing movement.

Liberty, Justice and Unionism. — Unionism has ceased to place so much emphasis upon the word liberty. It now talks more of justice. But if liberty is difficult to understand justice is even more so. The kind of justice that follows upon the form of individual liberty that characterized the nineteenth century is not the kind of justice that the laborer is demanding. He insists that his share of the good things of life shall come to him as a recognized direct return for his efforts. There must be no philanthropic elements entering in. There can be no privileges extended by the good will of the employer of which he is graciously allowed to take advantage. There is a somewhat blind groping for the expression of an idea that describes relations that are to be somewhat new, for a set of terms that will distinguish between conditions as they have been under the dominance of the employer, and as they are to exist when shaped by the purposes of unionism.

CHAPTER XXX

UNIONISM (Continued)

Influence of Employers on Unionism. — Another point of importance in shaping the course of unionism is the organization to which employers are resorting. This fact has been of marked influence in later years. Notice has been taken in former pages of the growth of these associations. They have been in many cases peculiarly united and aggressive in their opposition to trade unions. In other cases they appear to be formed in recognition of the need for a more systematic collective bargaining. In the latter instances the effects are in the main wholesome, as they lead to greater mutual respect and to the establishment of better working relations. Of those fighting associations of the other type the same cannot be said. Their professions are loud in defense of the workingman's individual liberty to bargain by himself for his wages. On this point they are admirable individualists. But their consistency cannot pass unchallenged. Of course they do not bargain individually themselves. Their association is a collective bargaining medium. To be sure their individualism permits to them the privilege of joining such an association for such a purpose. Moreover, as a matter of fact, it does not restrain them from coercing (not illegally coercing; just plain coercing) other employers to join in with the purposes of the association. Then these individualist employers, having forced the formation of such an employers' association, deny the right of laborers to form a union and bargain through its agency. Such a course is regarded by them as a violation of the laborer's individual right, even though his entrance into the union is undertaken by the laborer with enthusiasm. Such a situation gives as a result the case of a representative, speaking for the members of an employers' association, actually refusing to negotiate a wage rate with an officer of a union, but demanding that each separate workman shall be dealt with separately and that the union of workmen shall not interfere with the individual freedom of the weak laborer who can be forced by the combination of employers to work at a low wage. In a development like this one so common to current industrial life the whole situation appears in its real light. Middle-class privileges, established when opposition to middle class interests was weak, are still insisted upon under a fiction of industrial liberty, and opposition to these privileges by another class whose welfare is at stake is characterized by another fiction named class struggle. Under individual liberty the public is content. Under class struggle it is greatly perturbed.

The Unionism of Different Unions. — To all these various and conflicting forces it is true that the different trade and labor unions do not respond in the same way. Some cling very tenaciously to their ideals, disregarding the passing and more temporary phases of the struggle. Others follow a different course. Having embodied in their fundamental law the statement of ultimate aim and purposes, they become so deeply engrossed in the details of the more immediate and perplexing problems of current activity that they appear to forget the higher purposes of their existence. Between these two lines of action, as marking two extremes, the various unions may be lined up, some tending toward the one and others toward the other. So great are the differences that they become almost differences in kind rather than in degree. Yet there are common elements of purpose and ideal that join them in spite of the divergences.

So pronounced are the differences that to some it appears that there is no unionism in any real sense. Professor Hoxie as the result of his careful analysis concludes as a basic hypothesis: "There is no such thing as trade unionism in the sense either of an abstract unity, or of a concrete, organic and consistent whole which can be crowded within the confines of a narrow definition or judged sweepingly as good or bad, right or wrong, socially helpful or harmful. . . . There is unionism and unionism, but looking at matters concretely and realistically there is no single thing that can be taken as unionism *per se.*"

From the point of view from which Professor Hoxie makes his study, there may be reason for agreement. But it is not the point of view of this book. From what has been said, it should be appreciated that in a very real sense there is such a thing as trade unionism. It is endeavoring to express itself in circumstances that are very unfavorable if not indeed positively hostile to its expression. Historical traditions, both labor-class and middle-class traditions; popular misunderstandings; conservatism, political and industrial; inexperience; relative incompetence, both of members and of leaders; the unusual importance of immediate material needs: these are some of the adverse influences, not to mention errors of judgment and open and flagrant dishonesty. In view of all these, it is no great marvel that unionism exists as a somewhat vague and in part unformed thing struggling for continued existence first and expression next.

Causes of Differences. — The differences within unionism are easily accounted for. They center about degree of skill and the nature of the trade; the method of its pursuit, as hand or machine, highly subdivided or otherwise, difficult or easy to learn; the nature of the industry; the location, in populous centers or isolated; character of the management; presence of foreigners in the industry, of women, of children, of negroes; the personality of leaders, their intellectual ability, their moral character, their force of will power; possible factional strife growing out of differences of opinion over proposed policies. Methods among unions will vary because of each of these differences. If unionism were primarily methods or means and not purposes and ideals, there would indeed be many forms of unionism just as there are many forms of unions. These unions are not all joined into one single and thoroughgoing organization. Even the relatively loose affiliation of the American Federation of Labor does not include within its membership all unions or even all of the larger and more powerful ones.

Rival unions exist in the same trade, each struggling for jurisdictional control over the entire trade. Jurisdictional strife between unions of different trades over the control of new processes and materials is frequent. In the midst of all the confusion and even internal strife there is still a purpose and an ideal for which all are striving. That ideal is not entirely one that is to be realized solely and only by union members. It is to be realized by them first and then extended to all labor. It is to be admitted that much selfishness appears and but little altruism. That is easily explained. When their immediate causes have been removed these unfavorable traits will disappear from their prominent place in the foreground. Though somewhat long, for one who calls for the ideal of unionism in a word, it cannot be any more clearly and comprehensively expressed than in the statement made by John Mitchell: "The average workingman has in his mind the desire to receive for his labor a definite reward; a reward which increases from year to year, from decade to decade, as the wealth of the nation increases. He believes that he should receive in wages for his labor an amount sufficient to enable him and his family to live healthy and normal lives; he desires to live in a house having sufficient rooms for comfort and privacy and equipped with modern conveniences; he desires books, and pictures, and music, those refinements which develop his higher nature; he desires education for his children; he desires to provide against sickness, accident and old age, to enjoy leisure time with his family, and to have healthful and sane recreation. There was a time, even less than one hundred years ago, when the demand for these things would have been ridiculous and their attainment impossible; but in the present century, through the application of machinery and the concentration of energy, the production of wealth is so abundant — is so far beyond the reasonable needs of man, especially in this country — that the workingman is warranted in desiring and in demanding a definite and, from time to time, as industrial conditions justify, a larger share of the wealth produced."

Deeper Meaning of Unionism. — Such living conditions as constitute the ideal are subject to constant change. They follow the increase in social wealth and claim an increasing proportion. As has been many times emphasized, the real significance of the movement of organized labor will not be clearly understood so long as it is regarded primarily as a bargaining combination only, merely demanding larger wages and shorter hours of labor. The movement of unionism is to get away from the dominating idea that labor is a commodity to be bought and sold as are raw materials, machinery and finished products, subject to "demand and supply." The standard of living must be an essential element. These standards are not to be fixed by legislative enactments. They are to be arrived at through mutual discussion and where necessary by mutual compromise. As a norm or standard of judgment is to be "the human needs of a family living in a civilized country." Admittedly this is not a very exact standard. It is not only vague; it is constantly varying. Yet it may at any time be stated with reasonable exactness and be approached with reasonable nearness. It is the voluntary association for discussion of these questions that is regarded as the essence of industrial freedom. Where employers seek to use those who will not become parties to the collective bargaining through union membership, the members insist upon crowding them out of the work. Where employers refuse to consider any standards other than those of bargain and sale in the market, the unionists become insistent upon thwarting such plans by methods that regard ends rather than means.

Here is the situation, then, in its essential elements. A larger life and a larger share in its material benefits; less human waste in labor and more leisure time for improvement; these benefits to be secured by organized activity as a "right" and not as a "philanthropy"; first gained by organized labor and then to be extended to all labor as they become more secure and as labor organizes more extensively; these benefits to become the basis of a real industrial democracy supplementing a regenerated political democracy. This will be freedom. The contrast with the present and the immediate past is indeed alluring. By the side of the present the desired seems a millennium, a Utopia worth travelling toward, if never quite to be reached.

Aside from the more general benefits that will come from the realization of progress toward such an ideal, there should be two immediate ones that are very important in themselves. The first would be the more general recognition of the value of collective bargaining as a means of reaching a fair wage scale. The significance of this has been many times emphasized. The second would be the realization that the pay roll is not the best and should not be the first point of economy when it is necessary to cut expenses. On this point there are hopeful indications. President Gompers, on being asked what would be the effect of the outlook for hard times on wages, replied: "I do not think wages ought to be reduced. . . . I have advised our unions to resist all attempts at such reduction. I advise them to strike against any cut in wages and I think the employers should see that such cuts will increase the bad times rather than lessen them." A large employer of labor, having more than the ordinary insight, also said: "The present-day employer, if he has been observant, has not failed to learn from what trade-unionism has taught that the old remedy of the incompetent superintendent to correct results of bad methods, ignorant shop practice and wastefulness by reductions in productive pay roll was vicious and ineffective; that labor's wages were the last thing to be touched; that dividends, officers' salaries and the expense account were the proper places for ordinary retrenchment."

The Employers' Responsibility. — When the employers of the country can approach the whole question with a sincerity and frankness that will inspire confidence, much will be gained. That there has not been, in many of their dealings, anything to indicate to the workers that they were honestly working for a mutual benefit, the past can confidently be called on to witness. The Industrial Relations Commission, whose final report has called forth a variety of comment, both favorable and unfavorable, speaks with authority on this point. Three commissioners were appointed especially to represent the interests of employers. These three made a special minority report signed only by themselves. In this minority report are two paragraphs that may be quoted in full.

"Despite the fact that we have been appointed to represent, on this Commission, the employers of the nation, we are free to admit that the investigations made by the Commission, and the testimony brought forth at our public hearings, have made it plain that employers, some of them, have been guilty of much wrong-doing, and have caused the workers to have their fullest share of grievances against many employers. There has been an abundance of testimony," the report continues, "submitted to prove to our satisfaction that some employers have resorted to questionable methods to prevent their workers from organizing in their own self-interest; that they have attempted to defeat democracy by more or less successfully controlling courts and legislatures; that some of them have exploited women and children and unorganized workers; that some have resorted to all sorts of methods to prevent the enactment of remedial industrial legislation; that some have employed gunmen in strikes who were disreputable characters and who assaulted innocent people and committed other crimes most reprehensible in character; that some have paid lower wages than competitive conditions warranted, worked their people long hours, and under unsanitary and dangerous conditions; that some have exploited prison labor at the expense of free labor; that some have been contract-breakers with labor; that some have at times attempted, through the authorities, to suppress free speech and the right of peaceful assembly; and that some have deliberately, for selfish ends, bribed representatives of labor. All these things, we find, tend to produce industrial unrest, with all its consequent and far-reaching ills. There is, therefore, no gainsaying the fact that labor has had many grievances, and that it is thoroughly justified in organizing and in spreading organization in order better to protect itself against exploitation and oppression.

"On the other hand, in justice to employers generally, it must be said that there has been much evidence to show that there is an awakening among the enlightened employers of the nation who have taken a deeper personal interest in the welfare of their workers than ever before in industrial history; that such enlightened employers are growing in number and are more and more realizing that if for no other reason, it is in their own self-interest to seek the welfare of their workers and earnestly to strive to better their conditions."

The Union's Responsibility. — Against the activities of unions the three members of the Commission on Industrial Relations representing the employers in their minority report make ten specific charges: (1) sympathetic strikes; (2) jurisdictional disputes; (3) labor union politics; (4) contract breaking; (5) restriction of output; (6) prohibition of the use of non-union made tools and materials; (7) closed shop; (8) contests for supremacy between rival unions; (9) acts of violence against non-union workers and the properties of employers; (10) apprenticeship rules. Most of these have been discussed somewhat at length in preceding chapters. Evidence shows that the charges are not without foundation. They may be compared with profit with the statement quoted at length showing the questionable methods used by "some" employers. These ten charges rest also against "some" unions. This portion of the report further charges much "poverty, suffering, wretchedness, misery, discontent and crime" to these unjustifiable policies of unionism. These policies or practices, the commissioners think, could with safety be omitted, one and all, for "when labor is effectively organized, it has two most powerful weapons at its command that the employer, as a rule, dreads and fears because of the great damage these weapons can inflict on him, namely, the strike and the primary boycott, both of which are within the moral and legal rights of the worker to use." These two weapons are held to be sufficient to secure reasonably fair conditions of collective bargaining. They are not the limits of union activity, however, and because this is true, this part of the report holds employers and employees alike responsible. "The result of our investigation and inquiries forces upon us the fact that unionists also cannot come into court with clean hands; that this is not a case where the saints are all on one side and the sinners all on the other. We find saints and sinners, many of them, on both sides."

Such charges against unionism are serious. No real progress can be made so long as they rest even as generally as they do against some of the unions. They are not to be condoned. So far as their effects are harmful and so far as the acts do not in themselves conform to recognized public standards of morals, they cannot be regarded as in accordance with a justifiable policy or as a means that will lead ultimately to what unionism is reaching out after. Nothing is to be said that can be interpreted as a justification.

The Responsibilities Measured. — The practices must, however, be viewed seriously and from more than one angle. The employer very naturally condemns them, largely because they do not conform to his method of fighting. They do not strike where he is best prepared to receive the blow. They do not follow his lead in selecting their methods of working. While the comparison cannot be followed out at this point, it will readily appear to the reader who will follow through the list of the ten charges that each one of them can be paralleled by methods equally unjustifiable which have been used again and again by employers; if not in relations with their workmen, then in relations with either competitors or consumers. But more than that is to be said. Much attention has been given in these pages to the emphasis of the union man's point of view. Historical development counts much. Immediate situations have to be dealt with practically. The union man's angle of vision is determined by his daily life and experiences. Education has taught him to think, but his schooling coming to a close in early boyhood, he is left to think about things very near at hand. The horizon is limited, but the light is very clear within these narrow limits. He sees sharply but not broadly. Professor Hoxie's remark is very expressive: "However invalid the laborer's ideas and actions may be from the employer's standpoint, they are apparently the inevitable outcome of the peculiar circumstances of his life and work, and that, considering his own immediate interests merely, they are not foolish, but on the contrary quite reasonable." His discussion leads to further conclusions that are expressed in the following words: "(1) that men circumstanced differently as to both inheritance and present environment are bound to reach quite different conclusions as to rights, morality, and sound economic policy; (2) that employers and laborers are so differently circumstanced that they are likely to differ radically on these points, and are likely to be altogether incapable of mutual understanding in regard to them; (3) that these differences do not necessarily indicate any lack of morality or intelligence on the part of either class; and, finally, (4) that on account of the peculiar circumstances of the laborer's life and work there is growing up a distinctive trade-union viewpoint which must be reckoned with, as a matter of fact in connection with all practical labor problems."

Responsibility of Leadership. — For some of the elements in this complex situation in which unionism is found the labor leader must be held accountable. A psychological study of this type would indeed be interesting. Much depends upon his abilities and his moral fibre. At his best the real labor leader is as self-sacrificing and devoted a person as could be found in any walk in life. His opportunities are large. His responsibilities are great. His temptations are numerous and insinuating. Many have in the past lived up to the exacting demands of the position and have discharged the duties devolving upon them with honor and distinction. There are many to-day who are doing the same. On the other hand, some have fallen prey to selfishness, to the traps set for them by crafty enemies, or have lacked the strength of will to stand by the cause. There are also some to-day who are in the same position. As usual, it is the case of failure that attracts the most general attention, while also it is true that success in unionism is not always regarded as success of the approved type. In this matter of leadership the situation is not altogether peculiar. Other causes have been under the necessity of evolving leaders. It has often taken time. Unionism is but a half century old; not in ideal but in organized pursuit of the ideal. Fifty years is not a long time to evolve a satisfactory type of leadership in sufficient numbers to lead three millions and more of workers. The requirements of the type are complex and exacting. Especially short is the time when the difficulties are taken into account. It is quite singularly a case of *natural* leadership uncultivated by the arts of special preparation. There are no fitting schools for the training of this kind of leader. Experience is the teacher and the union itself is the school. Learning by doing is here applied with a rigidity that sometimes approaches to cruelty. These labor leaders must lead, yet they must keep within sight of the followers. The whole organization is intensely democratic. Consequently the demagogue always has his chance. He is constantly dogging the heels of the more far-sighted leader and causing him to modify his plans and adjust his appeals in such a way as to make sure of his following. The labor leader has the task of working for the ideals of his union in two directions. Without, he must meet the non-union man, an unfriendly or hostile public and the opposition of the employer. Within, he must cultivate his following, lead the members out to a larger vision and watch the machinations of his rivals, more or less unscrupulous in their efforts to replace him. The wonder is not that men fall under the strain of this leadership. It is rather that American unionism can boast the number of clear-visioned men who are devoting themselves, heart and soul, to the cause of their fellow workmen with such able and unselfish service.

Unionism and Social Progress. — Unionism, as embodying an ideal, when related to the broader community activity appears in yet another phase. From this point of view it again appears to occupy a large place. "For many years," says Jane Addams, "I have been impressed with the noble purposes of trades unions, and the desirability of the ends which they seek." As an ideal the community may be said for many years to have cherished the hope of realizing those conditions of living that unionism has set for its goal. Dominated so largely by the individualism of the day and consenting to the middle-class interpretation of such ideals, the community has been content with a kind of modified *laissez faire* practice, leaving to the individuals to get or to fail to get, as favored by ability or opportunity, that which as an ideal it has hoped that all would have. Realizing for itself a large measure of success, this class has become more indifferent to the attainment of the other class. Looking at this situation in much the same way Miss Addams has expressed it in the following way: "Two propositions are really amazing: first, that we have turned over to those men who work with their hands the fulfillment of certain obligations which we must acknowledge belong to all of us, such as protecting little children from premature labor and obtaining shorter hours for the overworked; and, second, that while the trade unions more than any other body have secured orderly legislation for the defense of the feeblest, they are persistently misunderstood and harshly criticized by many people who are themselves working for the same ends. Scenes of disorder and violence are enacted because trade unions are not equipped to accomplish what they are undertaking. The state alone could accomplish it without disorder. The public shirks its duty and thus holds a grievance toward the men who undertake the performance of that duty. It blames the union men for the disaster which arises from the fact that the movement is a partial one."

From yet another point of view unions serve a very practical purpose. It is of course well known that the introduction of machinery will throw men out of work; men with perhaps a skilled trade and too far advanced in years to learn a new one. Consideration for increased output and decreased cost dictates that the men be put out and the machines be put in. Consideration for the human element would call for less haste and more planning for the welfare of the men who are put out. This is but one of the many instances of industrial readjustment that is continually going on. The advantages of this are large in many ways; but they are costly in human wreckage. The very rapidity of the changes gives no time for a readjustment of the human factor. It has almost been forgotten in the hey day of rejoicing at records of production broken and wealth increased. Serious attention was given to this phase of the situation only after the unfortunates began to speak for themselves. When unions with the strength born of their organization step in and compel more consideration for the losses as well as the gains coming from mechanical, industrial and commercial improvement, much unnecessary human suffering may be prevented. This, though perhaps retarding the changes and interfering with profits, results in a positive social gain. The rule of reason is applicable to all social changes. They may be so rapid as to be unreasonable. To insist that man shall still be master of and not mastered by his machinery is reasonable.

Unionism not Transient. — Unionism is here to stay. So long as our industrial organization remains on its non-socialist foundation and wealth continues to be distributed among the factors of production on the basis of competitive forces unionism cannot be eliminated. There must also remain a fundamental opposition between employer and employee. The interests are divergent, if not opposite. Wages, interest and profit lie in the hands of the employer, as the enterpriser, as an undivided sum and there are laborers, capitalists and employers to be satisfied. Bargaining is the instrument by which the division is made. It cannot be eliminated. It is the explanation of all that the employer does, whether of a selfish or an unselfish character. So it prompts all that the laborers do, whether the deeds meet with moral approbation or not. Reconciliation between "capital and labor" is a dream that often visualizes itself to the idealist. It is but a dream. Fundamentally, bargaining must continue. It may be accompanied by methods that should be denounced. It may become so one-sided as to lose its real character and become arbitrary dictation by one side to the other. It should by all means be regulated. All commercial bargaining is regulated. Wage bargaining must also be subject to regulation.

As developments now indicate, the equality will be preserved by strong organization on both sides. Such strength should inspire respect and that again should become a very substantial guarantee of industrial peace. As the rivalry will not pass with the continuance of strikeless industry, the existence of unions will continue to be of great importance. With their increasing importance will come their more careful study and their better understanding. Such study must become more deliberate, more scientific and less passionate. "Trade unionism and industrial warfare," declares Professor Hoxie, " are matters of fact. They are so in the same sense that institutions, animal and plant species, and physical conditions are matters of fact. As such they are the outcome of sufficient causation, and the problems connected with them, like all other problems of a scientific nature, are to be solved, if at all, not through passion and sentiment and guessing, but through a study of the causes which produce them. In short, if we are to solve the problems raised by trade-unionism, we must proceed in a scientific spirit. We must put aside passion and prejudice, and look at these industrial troubles as matters of fact. Calmly and dispassionately we must search for their underlying causes."

Such an attitude of study may some day realize for us the picture sketched in the report of the Commission on Industrial Relations. "The ideal day in the industrial world will be reached when all labor disputes will be settled as a result of reason and not as a result of force. This ideal day can be hastened if the employers, on the one hand, will earnestly strive to place themselves in the position of the worker and look at the conditions not only through the eye of the employer but through the eye of the worker; and if the worker will strive to place himself in the position of the employer and look at the conditions not only through the eye of the worker but through the eye of the employer."

The Future : Unskilled Labor. — It has been a difficult task to discuss unionism as it appears. Not only does it have a different appearance from each angle of vision. It is constantly changing in ideal, in purposes, in form of organization and in methods. Just now a far-reaching change is being made. Trade unionism is giving way to labor unionism, in the sense that the unskilled are coming in much larger numbers into the movement. The more aristocratic trade union with its membership of highly skilled artisans is losing its influence in the wider field. Many of these have altered the conditions of membership, taking in the less skilled of the same general line of work and also the "helpers" and the "hands." This policy has somewhat restored the lost prestige. In the general field a three hundred per cent gain in membership among the unskilled workers against a fifty per cent gain among the skilled shows clearly the tendencies. Such a condition rapidly developing indicates the nature of future changes in unionism. It is very true that "the key to the new unionism is the new importance of unskilled labor." The tendencies in the direction of industrial unionism, of political activity and socialism, and of revolutionary industrial unionism have been somewhat fully discussed in former chapters. These present large elements of the unknown.

Opportunism Versus Idealism. — Whether or not the American Federation of Labor will succeed in maintaining all of the distinctive differences between itself and the Knights of Labor is not quite certain. Tendencies toward the spirit of the Knights is manifest in the industrial form of organization. Though at present the Federation has quite completely routed its early rival, this must not be taken as final. There is a broader view than simply the present or past relation of these two bodies. Various phases of organization have been emphasized in the past at different times. There was an element of idealism in the Knights that strongly appeals to many of the laboring class even to-day. It may be doubted if the Federation places sufficient emphasis upon this. The more self-centered attitude of the skilled trade unions has of necessity emphasized the practical. It may have been over-emphasized. The ideal and practical are difficult to combine effectively. If in the past the Federation has placed strong emphasis upon the latter, the results appear to justify the course. It appears that there is a present danger of over-emphasis. Such a course will give cause for a revival of the spirit of the Knights of Labor, either through that organization or through another. Experience would indicate that the change will come through a modification of the American Federation itself.

Turbulent Elements. — One source of danger lies very near the surface in the newer unionism. The unskilled are more turbulent in nature, and less inclined to secure their demands by degrees. Their intensely democratic spirit opens the way to influence for the more reckless aspirants to leadership. Unless the lines of control can be kept in the hands of those who have experience and see steadily the importance of law and order, there is a possibility, if not a probability, that there will be a renewal of turbulence and irresponsible activity wherever the newer elements dominate. The balance against such a development lies in the real ability and practical qualities of leadership possessed by the men in office and in other positions of trust to-day. It also appears in the extent to which the advantages of collective bargain and trade agreement have been made clear to a large group of employers. Wherever the more turbulent elements in the unions appear, the employers throw their influence with the conservative union leaders. This situation has strong possibilities for steadiness and restraint upon all union activity.

Unionism Must Find Itself. — Unionism will not reach a position in which it can command the general approval that it desires until it has secured a strong control over itself. Turbulence will have to be controlled from within the organization, if it is to be satisfactorily controlled. The investigations into the lawlessness of the anthracite coal strike led the commission to embody in its report a very clear statement of the situation, not only as it existed then but as it will always tend to exist under present conditions.

"As has been said, the idle and vicious, who are in no way connected with the purpose or object of the strike, often unite with the less orderly of the strikers themselves in creating the deplorable scenes of violence and terror which have all too often characterized the otherwise laudable efforts of organized labor to improve its conditions. Surely this tendency to disorder and violation of law imposes upon the organization which begins and conducts a movement of such importance a grave responsibility. It has, by its voluntary act, created dangers and should, therefore, be vigilant in averting them. It has, by the concerted action of many, aroused passions which, uncontrolled, threaten the public peace; it, therefore, owes society the duty of exerting its power to check and confine these passions within the bounds of reason and of law. Such organizations should be the powerful coadjutors of government in maintaining the peace and upholding the law. Only so can they deserve and attain the respect due to good citizenship, and only so can they accomplish the beneficent ends which for the most part they were created to attain."

These lessons unions must learn. Agitation and even strikes are justifiable both legally and morally. Disorder, violence, lawlessness in any form has no justification either in law or in morals. So long as laborers feel that there is injustice they must join the movement that unionism embodies. There is the moral responsibility resting upon them. The movement cannot be carried on effectively without the organization that such combination implies, and organized agitation is the only effective form of agitation in these days. "People talk about agitators, but the only real agitator," it is said, "is injustice: and the only way is to correct the injustice and withdraw the agitation." This spirit reveals one side. The other is found in the equally impressive statement that "a labor or other organization, whose purpose can only be accomplished by the violation of law and order of society, has no right to exist."

The sooner the trade-unionism of to-day finds itself, becomes its own master, the sooner it will be in position to reap the benefits of its existence. It will then need fewer friends to champion it before the community. It will have fewer enemies to oppose its legitimate purposes. The future of unionism lies in its own hands.

INDEX

Printed in the United States of America.